COM+ Programming

A Practical Guide Using
Visual C++ and ATL

ISBN 0-13-088674-2

90000

9 780130 886743

Hewlett-Packard® Professional Books

OPERATING SYSTEMS

Fernandez	Configuring CDE: The Common Desktop Environment
Lund	Integrating UNIX® and PC Network Operating Systems
Madell	Disk and File Management Tasks on HP-UX
Poniatowski	HP-UX 11.x System Administration Handbook and Toolkit
Poniatowski	HP-UX 11.x System Administration "How To" Book, Second Edition
Poniatowski	HP-UX System Administration Handbook and Toolkit
Poniatowski	Learning the HP-UX Operating System
Poniatowski	UNIX® User's Handbook
Rehman	HP Certified, HP-UX System Administration
Sauers, Weygant	HP-UX Tuning and Performance
Stone, Symons	UNIX® Fault Management
Weygant	Clusters for High Availability: A Primer of HP-UX Solutions

ONLINE/INTERNET

Amor	The E-business (R)evolution
Greenberg, Lakeland	A Methodology for Developing and Deploying Internet and Intranet Solutions
Greenberg, Lakeland	Building Professional Web Sites with the Right Tools
Ketkar	Working with Netscape Server on HP-UX
Klein	Building Enhanced HTML Help with DHTML and CSS

NETWORKING/COMMUNICATIONS

Blommers	OpenView Network Node Manager: Designing and Implementing an Enterprise Solution
Blommers	Practical Planning for Network Growth
Lee	The ISDN Consultant
Lucke	Designing and Implementing Computer Workgroups

ENTERPRISE

Blommers	Architecting Enterprise Solutions with UNIX® Networking
Cook	Building Enterprise Information Architectures
Pipkin	Halting the Hacker: A Practical Guide to Computer Security
Pipkin	Information Security: Protecting the Global Enterprise
Sperley	Enterprise Data Warehouse, Volume 1: Planning, Building, and Implementation
Thornburgh	Fibre Channel for Mass Storage
Thornburgh, Schoenborn	Storage Area Networks: Designing and Implementing a Mass Storage System

PROGRAMMING

Blinn	Portable Shell Programming
Caruso	Power Programming in HP OpenView
Chaudri, Loomis	Object Databases in Practice
Chew	The Java™/C++ Cross-Reference Handbook
Grady	Practical Software Metrics for Project Management and Process Improvement
Grady	Successful Software Process Improvement
Lewis	The Art & Science of Smalltalk
Lichtenbelt, Crane, Naqvi	Introduction to Volume Rendering
Mellquist	SNMP++
Mikkelsen, Pherigo	Practical Software Configuration Management
Norton, DiPasquale	Thread Time: The Multithreaded Programming Guide
Tapadiya	COM+ Programming: A Practical Guide Using Visual C++ and ATL
Wadleigh, Crawford	Software Optimization for High Performance Computing

IMAGE PROCESSING

Crane	A Simplified Approach to Image Processing
Day	The Color Scanning Handbook
Gann	Desktop Scanners: Image Quality

OTHER TITLES OF INTEREST

Kane	PA-RISC 2.0 Architecture
Markstein	IA-64 and Elementary Functions

COM+ Programming

A Practical Guide Using
Visual C++ and ATL

Pradeep Tapadiya

Prentice Hall PTR
Upper Saddle River, NJ 07458
www.phptr.com

Library of Congress Cataloging-in-Publication Data

Tapadiya, Pradeep K. (Pradeep Kumar), 1964–
    COM+ programming : a practical guide using Visual C++ and ATL / Pradeep Tapadiya.
        p. cm. -- (Hewlwtt-Packard professional books)
    Includes bibliographical references and index.
    ISBN 0-13-088674-2
    1. Computer software--Development. 2. Object-oriented programming (Computer
science) 3. Active template library. 4. C++ (Computer program language) I. Title. II. Series.

QA76.76.D47 T37 2000
005.2'768--dc21   00-063686

Editorial/Production Supervision: *MetroVoice Publishing Services*
Acquisitions Editor: *Jill Pisoni*
Editorial Assistant: *Justin Somma*
Marketing Manager: *Bryan Gambrel*
Cover Design: *Nina Scuderi*
Cover Design Direction: *Jerry Votta*
Manufacturing Manager: *Alexis R. Heydt*
Buyer: *Maura Zaldivar*

© 2001 Prentice Hall PTR
Prentice-Hall, Inc.
Upper Saddle River, NJ 07458

Prentice Hall books are widely used by corporations and government agencies for training,
marketing, and resale.

The publisher offers discounts on this book when ordered in bulk quantities.
For more information, contact Corporate Sales Department, phone: 800-382-3419;
fax: 201-236-7141; e-mail: corpsales@prenhall.com
Or write: Prentice Hall PTR
            Corporate Sales Department
            One Lake Street
            Upper Saddle River, NJ 07458

Printed in the United States of America
10   9   8   7   6   5   4   3   2   1

ISBN 0-13-088674-2

Prentice-Hall International (UK) Limited, **London**
Prentice-Hall of Australia Pty. Limited, **Sydney**
Prentice-Hall Canada Inc., **Toronto**
Prentice-Hall Hispanoamericana, S.A., **Mexico**
Prentice-Hall of India Private Limited, **New Delhi**
Prentice-Hall of Japan, Inc., **Tokyo**
Pearson Education Asia Pte. Ltd.
Editora Prentice-Hall do Brasil, Ltda., **Rio de Janeiro**

To my mom and dad

Contents

2   Designing Interfaces   55

Introduction

Ever since software development became an engineering discipline, software development teams everywhere in the world have faced similar development and deployment problems. Among other things, developers today are concerned about:

- Reusing code that has been tested and used in other applications
- Developing flexible applications that can be customized to the users needs, but not at the expense of overburdening the development team
- Addressing anomalies and add features after the application has been shipped, while avoiding a complete rewrite of the application
- Improving application development time by leveraging against software code developed by third party software vendors
- Developing distributed and non-distributed applications in a similar manner

All of these challenges and many more are addressed by a single technology: the Microsoft Component Object Model, better known as COM. COM is a framework for developing software components, small binary executables, that provide services to applications and other components.

The incredible explosion of the Internet has caused a revolution in the way information has to be made available to the users. In developing enterprise systems, the traditional client/server model has been replaced with a three-tier programming model, enhanced for Internet applications. Developing such enterprise systems is a time- and resource-consuming affair, as the system has to meet extra enterprise-level requirements such as scalability, robustness, security, transaction support, etc.

COM+ is an advanced run-time environment that provides services to meet many of the above-mentioned enterprise-level requirements. It is an integral part of the Windows 2000 Operating System. Developers can leverage the services provided by COM+, instead of building the services themselves.

This book focuses on understanding the COM+ architecture from a developer's perspective and building COM+ applications using Microsoft Visual C++ and the Active Template Library (ATL).

COM+ is not a radical departure from COM—it is just the next stage in the evolution of the COM programming model. As a matter of fact, it is very difficult to determine where COM ends and where COM+ begins. In order to understand the COM+ architecture and the services provided by COM+, it is necessary to understand the fundamental component model at the heart of COM+. To this end, the book is divided in two parts. The first part builds the foundation that is COM and the second part explains the services provided by COM+ version 1.0.

About This Book

The purpose of writing this book is twofold. To help you:

1. Understand the COM/COM+ architecture, and
2. Explore the services provided by COM+ 1.0.

In order to achieve the stated goals, I have presented the material from a developer's perspective. I have illustrated the key concepts by writing some simple applications using Microsoft Visual C++ 6.0, Platform SDK (January 2000), and ATL 3.0. This book provides enough C++ code and tools to enable the readers to be more productive and to carry out further research.

As we progress through unfolding the COM+ architecture and services, I first present one or more software-engineering problems at hand, and then discuss the solution that COM+ has to offer. Whenever applicable, code snippets are provided to illustrate and explain the concepts.

In an attempt to focus on COM+ 1.0 architecture and services, I have refrained from including material that is not of any practical importance. Consequently, I do not discuss the origin and history of COM, or even Microsoft Transaction Server (MTS), a precursor to COM+ 1.0. However, whenever possible, I have touched upon the new services that are being planned for the future release of COM+ (COM+ 1.x).

Throughout the book, I have identified important points and tips for effective COM+ programming. The pad and pencil icon marks the important notes:

The light bulb icon flags the tip:

Choice of Language

COM+ is a specification. As such, it is language independent. However, most COM-based components are currently written in C++. This book uses C++ for almost all the server-side code. Client-side usage is shown in C++, VB, or in any other language that is appropriate for the given situation.

Prerequisites

The most important prerequisite for this book is your willingness to learn.

The book is written for intermediate to advanced developers. It is assumed that the readers have a working knowledge of the following:

- Windows 2000 Operating System
- C++ programming language
- VB programming language
- C++ templates. In particular, familiarity with C++ Standard Template Library (STL) is helpful
- Developing programs using Win32 API
- Windows 2000 security model

Strictly speaking, many of these assumptions can be relaxed. For example, knowledge of Win32 API or C++ templates is helpful but not mandatory. As we go through developing sample code, I am confident readers will automatically pick up the missing information.

Sample Code

All the examples provided in the book are concise and complete. For brevity, I sometimes show only the relevant code snippet in the book. However, complete source code is available on the companion CD. All the examples and tools have been compiled under Visual C++ 6.0 SP3 and Platform SDK (January 2000), and have been tested with the release version of Windows 2000 OS.

References

This book frequently refers to other books, Microsoft's Knowledge Base articles, articles from various journals, and from Microsoft's Developers Network (MSDN) Library. All the references for a particular chapter are listed at the end of the chapter. Each reference is indexed by a keyword that uses a combination of author's last name and year the reference was published. For example, Don Box's book *Essential COM*, which was published in 1998, is indexed as [Box-98]. In the book, each time I have to refer to an article, I use the keyword index of the reference.

Chapter Organization

The book is divided into two parts. The first part, *The Foundation*, consists of three chapters. It explains the fundamentals of Component Object Model and shows how to design and develop COM-based applications. Each chapter builds on the knowledge from the previous chapter.

The second part, *The Extension*, focuses on COM+ architecture and services provided by COM+ 1.0. Each chapter focuses on a specific aspect of COM+. These chapters are largely independent of each other. Chapter 5, however, explains the COM+ programming model, and should be read before looking into any other COM+ chapter.

Companion CD

The companion CD contains the following:

1. The source code for the C++ utility classes and tools developed in the book.
2. The entire source code for all the examples arranged by chapters.

More information about the contents of the CD can be found in the read-me file on the CD.

Acknowledgments

First of all, I'd like to thank Dr. Karim Valimohamed, a consulting engineer, who assisted me tremendously with the research, code, and review of the early drafts of the book.

Of the people who have helped me over the past eighteen months (this is how long it took me to write the book), I'd especially like to thank Shaju Mathew and Deepak Gajare, my colleagues at Hewlett-Packard, who, along with Karim, carried out research and offered me valuable suggestions on presenting my thoughts and ideas. A round of gratitude is also due for my teammates at Hewlett-Packard, in particular Doug Albright, Jeannine Klein, Paul Li, and Anup Pant, for reviewing my manuscript and offering me constructive criticism.

Of course, writing this book would not have been possible without the support of my earlier supervisors—Doug McBride and Laurence Sweeney. I owe thanks to these two souls for their confidence in me and for their constant encouragement.

I'd like to thank the editorial team at Prentice Hall PTR and Hewlett-Packard Press—Jill Pisoni (Executive Editor), Anne Trowbridge (Production Editor), Jim Markham (Developmental Editor), Susan Wright (Editorial Director, HP Press), and Scott Suckling (MetroVoice Publishing Services).

Special thanks to Dr. Richard Thayer, Professor of Software Engineering at California State University, Sacramento, who helped me find students to carry out some of my research.

Finally, and most important of all, I'd like to thank my wife Vrushali and my 18-month old son Jay, both of whom patiently stood by me throughout the completion of the book.

The Foundation

The Component Model

Constant innovations in computing technology have made a whole host of powerful and sophisticated applications available to users. The sophistication of the applications may include such things as fancy user interfaces or updating a single database or, in a more complex case, different parts of an application communicating with each other across the network, even across different hardware and operating system platforms, and perhaps updating multiple databases. Such sophistication, however, has brought with it many problems for the developers and software vendors. Developing, maintaining, and revising such large and complex software is not only difficult, but is also time-consuming. As such, developers are constantly looking for methodologies to help them reduce the size of the project by reusing existing code or buying third party modules that can easily be integrated into their own. Moreover, the methodology should allow them to extend this reusable code without breaking the existing consumers of the code.

Over the years, a number of paradigms and programming methodologies have been offered to help developers and software vendors develop reusable and extensible code. One such paradigm, *object-oriented programming*, has been received favorably by the software community. Under this paradigm, certain sets of related features are grouped in a single unit called an object. This creates a layer of abstraction that simplifies many programming tasks and provides extensibility to the object.

As an object-oriented programming language, C++ has enjoyed a large community of followers. The language's support for object-oriented programming principles such as encapsulation (the hiding of an object's implementation details) and inheritance (the ability to reuse existing objects in the creation of new, more specialized objects) has resulted in an emergence of a marketplace for third party C++ class libraries.

Despite the object-orientation of C++, there are a fair number of obstacles in building reusable class libraries. Many of these obstacles stem from the way a C++ compiler implements some specific features of the language, making it difficult to link the class libraries across various compilers. In this chapter, we look at the technical issues in developing C++ classes as reusable components. Using the interaction between electronic components as a concrete example, I will present programming techniques that address each of the key technical issues. Ultimately, I will show that by following two programming paradigms, we could develop reusable and extensible software components. The two programming paradigms, dynamic linking and binary encapsulation, form the foundation of the Component Object Model (COM).

COMPONENT REUSABILITY

It's late in the afternoon on Friday. No meetings were scheduled today, so you've spent most of your time implementing a very creative algorithm that will be incorporated in the forthcoming release of the product. Everything is coming together very well and the project is on schedule for delivery—this is too good to be true. You earned your pay and then some, especially considering your brutal effort over the past month. This weekend is going to be a welcome relief. As you sit back with a blank stare at the screen, lost in thoughts about your plans for the weekend, the project manager walks into your office and asks, "Dave, can we add support for browsing a web page within our application?" You take a deep breath and look at the ceiling as you focus on the problem and start thinking. *We will need to do some low-level socket programming to connect to a web site. We will need to parse the HTML document and display user interface components such as buttons, edit boxes, etc. As if this is not enough, we will also need to deal with embedded scripts in the HTML document. How about dealing with firewalls and proxy servers? To top it off, keeping up with browsing technology is not easy. From HTML to DHTML to XML and XSL, there is no end to it.* So you reply, "This is a lot of work and certainly not something we will be good at. Given the amount of resources and the deadlines we have, I think we will be better off not implementing this feature." Your manager considers this to be an unsatisfactory solution and is disappointed with your response. You are exhausted and feel guilty about having to upset your manager, but then what choices do you have? After all, you are aware of the consequences of feature creep. Are there any alternatives?

You sit back at your desk and start thinking. *Companies such as Netscape (now owned by AOL) and Microsoft have already developed the technology for browsing the web. And they continue to maintain and upgrade it. Why can't I leverage their work in a way that is transparent to the user? Why can't we all live together happily?*

This very thought is what COM is built on (well, except for the last part, which requires a force more powerful than COM). The ability to reuse one or more software components so that all the components integrate seamlessly and don't break when any individual component is upgraded is where the component model began.

Reusability of components is not a new concept. Hardware equipment has supported this notion for a long time. For example, I recently put together a home entertainment system. I bought a Sony amplifier/receiver, a GE TV, Energy speakers, a Pioneer DVD player, and a JVC DSS receiver. I hooked various inputs and outputs of all these components together and turned the system on. Voila! My TV was showing a channel received through the DSS receiver and the speakers were playing sound using Dolby surround sound technology. Through the supplied remote, I could conveniently switch between the satellite channel and the DVD player.

My home system operates as a single unit despite various hardware components from different manufacturers, each of which had little idea what the other components really did or what kind of internal circuitry the other components used. How was this possible? Was this magic?

Magic or not, it worked for hardware. Could we make it work for software?

TRADITIONAL SOFTWARE REUSABILITY

The original problem of adding web-browsing functionality to an application can be addressed in the following two ways:

- Obtain the complete source code for web-browsing from a third-party software vendor, compile and link the source code, and create the application executable. This technique, however, is not that prevalent, as most software vendors do not wish to share their source code.
- Obtain precompiled code in the form of a statically linkable library. The vendor supplies two pieces of information, a C++ header file (`WebBrowser.h`, for example) that contains the web-browsing class definition, and a static link library (`WebBrowser.lib`). You include the header file in your application's source code, compile the source code, then link the code with the static library to create the application's executable.

In either case, the programming logic from the software vendor has been absorbed. The header files and the library files are no longer needed to run the application.

There are several problems associated with such traditional approaches to software reusability, including the following:

- Let's say the software vendor found a defect in its implementation after you have shipped your application. The vendor is very cooperative and provides you with an updated library and the corresponding C++ header file. However, there is no way for you to field-replace the web-browser implementation by itself. You are forced to recompile your source code with the new header file, relink your code with the new library, and ship the new application(s) to the user. Ever bought a TV-VCR combo unit? Each time something breaks down in the VCR, you have to take the TV along with it to the repair shop. Do you feel the pain?
- Assume that the web-browser library occupies 50MB worth of space in your application's executable image, and that your software suite consists of four applications, each application linked with this library. Now you end up taking a whopping 200MB of hard disk space on the end-user box for what is essentially the same piece of code. Worse yet, when the user runs all the applications simultaneously, the same piece of code gets loaded into memory four times.

In order to overcome these problems, we need to take a closer look at the roles of the linker and the OS loader. However, before we go further, let me define our sample reference that we will use in this chapter.

REFERENCE HARDWARE COMPONENTS

In order to relate the hardware component model to software, I will frequently refer to two hardware components—a TV and a VCR. Furthermore, I will simplify the example by considering only the video signal interaction between the two components.

In order to obtain the video signal from the VCR, the video-output jack of the VCR needs to be connected to the video-input jack of the TV, as shown in Figure 1.1.

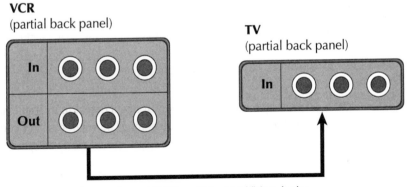

Figure 1.1   Connecting a VCR to a TV using Video Jacks.

Some advantages of keeping these two hardware components as separate units are obvious: a defect in VCR logic requires only the VCR to be field-replaced; the VCR can be upgraded without necessarily upgrading the TV; and any brand VCR will work with any brand TV, as long as they have standard jacks for video input/output.

I will now write a program to simulate the behavior of TV-VCR interconnection.

SIMULATION PROGRAM

In my simulation program, the VCR vendor has signed an agreement to provide a C++ class, CVcr, to the TV manufacturer. This class has a public method called GetSignalValue that, when invoked by the TV, will return the magnitude of the current video signal. The maximum value of the signal was decided to be 40.

```
// File vcr.h
class CVcr
{
public:
  CVcr(void);

  long GetSignalValue();

private:
  long m_lCurValue;
};
```

In my implementation of this class, I will return a value of five the first time this method is called. On each subsequent call, I will increment the value by ten. The implementation logic is shown in the following code:

```
// From vcr.cpp

CVcr:: CVcr ()
{
   m_lCurValue = 5;
}

long CVcr::GetSignalValue()
{
   long lReturnValue = m_lCurValue;
   m_lCurValue += 10;
   return lReturnValue;
}
```

As a VCR vendor, I present two files to the TV manufacturer:

- Header file vcr.h that contains the definition of class CVcr
- Library file vcr.lib that contains the programming logic in object code format.

My TV simulation application will obtain and display the signal values 10 times in a loop as shown here:

```
#include "VCR.h"
#include <iostream.h>

int main(int argc, char* argv[])
{
   int i;
   CVcr vcr;

   for(i=0; i<10; i++) {
      long val = vcr.GetSignalValue();
      cout << "Round: " << i << " - Value: " << val << endl;
   }

   return 0;
}
```

I will compile this program code and link it with library `vcr.lib` to create the final executable—`tv.exe`.

```
cl -c tv.cpp
link tv.obj vcr.lib
```

The VCR implementation is providing a service, and the TV code is consuming the services provided by the VCR. In general, the software component that provides a service is referred to as the *server* and the software component that consumes the services is referred to as the *client*.

Here is the output when I execute the simulation program:

```
Round: 0 - Value: 5
Round: 1 - Value: 15
Round: 2 - Value: 25
Round: 3 - Value: 35
Round: 4 - Value: 45
Round: 5 - Value: 55
Round: 6 - Value: 65
Round: 7 - Value: 75
Round: 8 - Value: 85
Round: 9 - Value: 95
```

Though the interaction between the TV and the VCR is working as expected, my implementation had a flaw in that the signal value should not exceed 40. Although a trivial solution is required to correct the implementation, it is too late. The client code has been shipped to thousands of customers and recalling the product is not an option.

Is there a way to field-replace the fix?

Let's peek under the hood and see how an application (more precisely, an application's executable) gets created by the linker and loaded by the operating system.

ROLE OF THE LINKER AND THE OS LOADER

When a program module is compiled, the compiler generates an object file that contains the machine language representation of the programming logic. However, the compiler cannot resolve any symbols that are external to the module. These symbols are still left as externals in the object file. For example, when the simulation program `tv.cpp` was compiled, the compiler did not have enough information to obtain the entry point for the procedure

CVcr::GetSignalValue. So it just marked this method as EXTRN, indicating that the symbol representing the method needs to be resolved later.

```
; define all the external symbols
EXTRN   ?GetSignalValue@CVcr@@QAEJXZ:NEAR     ; CVcr::GetSignalValue
; Other lines deleted for brevity
; assembly language code for line vcr.GetSignalValue
call   ?GetSignalValue@CVcr@@QAEJXZ
```

The original function GetSignalValue referenced in the source code has been represented by a different symbol within the compiled code. This is typical C++ compiler behavior. As the same function name can be defined multiple times either under different classes or with different argument types within the same class (referred to as function overloading), C++ compilers typically mangle the symbolic name of each entry point to uniquely identify a particular function. This technique is referred to as *name mangling*.

Once the object modules have been created, the linker combines all of the object modules and the libraries (a library is a collection of object modules) to create the final executable. It is the responsibility of the linker to resolve all the external symbols and replace them with appropriate procedure entry points. If any external symbol cannot be resolved, the linker will abort the process. In this case, either the final executable is never created or is partially created, depending on how the vendor of the linker chose to implement it.

In the case of the TV simulation program, had I not specified vcr.lib as an argument to the linker, the linker would have aborted the link process with the following error:

```
tv.obj : error LNK2001: unresolved external symbol
   "public: long __thiscall CVcr::GetSignalValue(void)"
   (?GetSignalValue@CVcr@@QAEJXZ)
```

When the executable (tv.exe) is run, the OS loader loads the executable image into memory and starts executing the code from the main entry point. The loader cannot load a partially created executable image.

Let's get back to the problem we are trying to solve. Our goal is to separate the programming implementation of the VCR from that of the TV so that we can field-replace just the VCR implementation in case of a defect. But we have a dilemma. The linker will not create the executable without resolving all the symbolic entry points. Even if it does, the loader will not load an incomplete image.

If only we could get away from linking the library statically. If only we could satisfy the linker by creating a fake entry point for each external symbol. If only the loader could resolve the external symbols before executing the image. If only we could…

Is there a way to use a library at run time?

DYNAMIC LINK LIBRARY

Fear not. Microsoft has provided a way of linking a library dynamically. Under Windows terminology, such a library is referred to as *Dynamic Link Library (DLL)*. A DLL is an executable file that gets loaded when an application that uses the DLL gets executed.

DLLs can reduce memory and disk space requirements by sharing a single copy of common code and resources among multiple applications. When more than one application uses the same DLL, the operating system is smart enough to share the DLL's read-only executable code among all the applications.

DLLs are compiled and linked independently of the applications that use them; they can be updated without requiring applications to be recompiled or relinked.

If several applications work together as a system and they all share such common DLLs, the entire system can be improved by replacing the common DLLs with enhanced versions. A bug fix in one such DLL indirectly fixes the bug in all applications that use it. Likewise, performance enhancements or new functionality in the DLL benefit all applications that use the DLL.

In order for us to use a DLL instead of a statically linked library, we have to:

- prevent the linker from complaining about unresolved external symbols, and
- provide enough information to the loader so that it can load the appropriate DLL dynamically and resolve the symbols to their corresponding locations in memory before executing the application

Using a special type of library file called the *import library* can satisfy both these requirements. This binary file does not contain any code; it contains all the references to the functions and other declarations to satisfy the linker and to help the loader resolve the symbols at run time.

When the application object modules are linked with the import library, the linker now has no reason to complain about unresolved external symbols. It will create the final executable. When this executable is run, the loader examines the image for all the DLLs that need to be loaded and tries to load them. The search path used by Windows to locate a DLL can be found in Visual C++ documentation [MSDN-00]. After loading each DLL, the loader resolves all the external symbols and patches the application image with the actual procedure entry points.

The loader will complain if:

- the DLL could not be located, or
- the procedure entry point for a particular symbol could not be located in the DLL.

In either case, the execution is aborted.

To facilitate locating a symbol in a DLL, the DLL has to *export* all the symbols that need to be exposed. One way to do this is to list all the symbols that need to be exported in a file called the *module definition file*. For the VCR code, we need to export two symbols—`CVcr::CVcr` and `CVcr::GetSignalValue`. Keep in mind that we need to use name-mangled versions of these symbols. Here's what the module definition file contains:

```
; File VCR.DEF

LIBRARY    VCR.DLL

EXPORTS
  ?GetSignalValue@CVcr@@QAEJXZ
  ??0CVcr@@QAE@XZ
```

Let's compile and link the VCR code to create a DLL.

```
cl -c vcr.cpp
link -dll -def:vcr.def vcr.obj
```

In the above commands, option `-dll` tells the linker to create a DLL file, and option `-def` tells the linker to use `vcr.def` module definition file (option `-def`). The linker generates two files of interest to us:

- The dynamic link library (`vcr.dll`), and
- An import library (`vcr.lib`) that exposes the two above-mentioned symbols.

Let's compile the TV code and link the object file with the import library to create the final application.

```
cl -c tv.cpp
link tv.obj vcr.lib
```

When we run this newly created application, the generated output is exactly the same as when it was a monolithic application. The only difference is that the new executable took a little longer to load, but nothing noticeable, as the loader had to resolve all the symbols during run time.

We have now broken our original executable into two components—`tv.exe` and `vcr.dll`. Both the components are required to execute the application. However, we now have the ability to field-replace the DLL, thus enabling an easy mechanism to fix a bug or upgrade to an enhanced version. Mission accomplished!

All that remains is to convince ourselves that field-replacing a DLL is foolproof.

FIXING A DEFECT

Our customers bought the TV (`tv.exe`) and the VCR (`vcr.dll`) and started using it. Meanwhile, the VCR vendor realizes that the logic of generating the signal values is not quite correct. The signal being generated from the VCR kept on increasing in magnitude with time, though the specifications indicated that the upper limit of the magnitude is 40. The fix is to reset the output after every four rounds (5, 15, 25, 35, 5, 15, 25, 35, 5, 15, and so on). To keep track of the current round, a private member variable needs to be added to the CVcr class. This is okay, as our C++ knowledge on encapsulation tells us that changing private member variables and methods of a C++ class does not require its users to modify their code. The new class definition is shown below:

```
class CVcr
{
public:
    CVcr(void);

    long GetSignalValue();

    vate:
      ng m_lCurValue;
        m_nCurCount;


         r ()

         e = 5;
```

```
  m_nCurCount = 0;
}

long CVcr::GetSignalValue()
{
  m_nCurCount++;
  if (5 == m_nCurCount ) {
    m_lCurValue = 5;
    m_nCurCount = 1;
  }

  long lReturnValue = m_lCurValue;
  m_lCurValue += 10;
  return lReturnValue;
}
```

Compile the code, create new vcr.dll (version 2.0), and distribute it to our customers.

Following is what customers see when they turn on the TV:

```
Round: 1 - Value: 5
Round: 3 - Value: 15
Round: 1 - Value: 5
Round: 3 - Value: 15
Round: 1 - Value: 5
. . .
```

What we expected to see was the output value cycling through 5, 15, 25, 35, 5, 15, and so on. Instead, what we witnessed was that the output value just toggled between 5 and 15. Moreover, the TV program was supposed to quit after 10 iterations. Instead, it went into an infinite loop.

In the hardware component scenario, being the electronic junkie that you are, you know that you have replaced the VCR many times. Each time, once you connect the video input/output jacks, the TV received video signals just fine. So what went wrong in our simulation program?

We will need to reexamine the hardware TV-VCR interconnection and see what we missed in our software simulation.

HARDWARE COMPONENT MODEL

The video output jack of the VCR sends out video signals according to a predefined "video" specification. The "video" service provided by the VCR is represented in Figure 1.2.

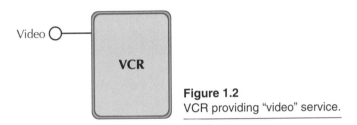

Figure 1.2
VCR providing "video" service.

The TV was designed for this "video" specification. Once you hook up the VCR to the TV on the "video" connection, all the TV has to do is start receiving "video" signals from the VCR. Any brand of VCR that adheres to the specification will be compatible with the TV.

By separating interface specifications from implementation, and guaranteeing that the specifications will not be altered, we have started to form the basis of the Component Model.

Can we apply this model to software? Let's get back to our simulation program.

SEPARATING INTERFACE FROM IMPLEMENTATION

Looking at our VCR code, at first glance it appears that the public member functions of our CVcr class definition form our "video" interface specification. By changing the private specifications, we still honor the basic rule of C++ encapsulation: Thou shall not change the public specifications of a C++ class. Then why did our TV simulation program break?

The reason is that, the encapsulation mechanism that C++ supports is semantic (in terms of public and private members) and not binary. To understand this distinction, let's examine how the compiler produced the object code for our TV program.

When the TV code was compiled, the compiler used two pieces of information from the CVcr class definition:

1. The interface specifications: To ensure that the TV program calls only the publicly available methods from the CVcr class and that the parameters being passed to these methods match the specifications.
2. The implementation details: The compiler needs to know the binary size of the class, that is, the amount of memory occupied by an instance of the class. This helps the compiler allocate appropriate memory when creating an instance of the class.

When we added the new variable to CVcr class, we changed its size. The first version of the class had a size of four bytes. The second version of the class had a size of eight bytes. As we didn't recompile our TV program with the second version of the class, the program continues to allocate just four bytes for the CVcr instance. However, the VCR code was recompiled with the second version, and therefore expects a CVcr instance to occupy eight bytes. When the VCR code writes to the memory location for the variable m_nCur-Count, it ends up stomping on a memory location that was being used by variable i in the TV program. That explains the unexpected behavior.

Our modifications to the VCR code would have worked correctly had we ensured binary encapsulation, i.e., had we modified only the implementation code without actually adding any member variables to the CVcr class.

Of course, I deliberately modified the VCR code such that the resulting behavior was an infinite loop. In general, whenever binary encapsulation gets broken, the behavior is completely unpredictable. The application may hang, crash right away, or the bug may stay dormant during the whole testing period and manifest itself when the customer uses it for the first time.

To ensure binary encapsulation, an obvious solution is to separate interface specifications from the implementation details. We can achieve this by breaking our original class into two classes—an interface class and an implementation class. The interface class should only define the methods that a client is allowed to call; it should not reveal any implementation details. The implementation class contains the entire implementation specifics. The idea here is that the binary layout of the interface class will not change as we add or remove member variables from the implementation class. The clients do not need to know any details from the implementation class. This effectively hides all the implementation details from the client.

Once we define the interface class and the implementation class, we need a way to traverse from the interface class to the implementation class. Defining an opaque pointer as a member variable in the interface class can do the trick. An opaque pointer requires just a forward declaration of the class it is pointing to, not the full definition of the class. Any method called on the interface class will just turn around and invoke an appropriate method through the opaque pointer. The logic is illustrated in the following code snippet:

```
// Video.h—Definition of interface IVideo

// Forward declaration of CVcr class
class CVcr;

class IVideo
{
public:
  IVideo();
  ~IVideo();
  long GetSignalValue();

private:
  CVcr* m_pActualVideo;
};

// Video.cpp—Implementation of interface IVideo
IVideo::IVideo()
{
  m_pActualVideo = new CVcr;
}

IVideo::~IVideo()
{
  delete m_pActualVideo;

}

long IVideo::GetSignalValue()
{
  return m_pActualVideo->GetSignalValue();
}

; File VCR.DEF
; Need to export
; IVideo::IVideo
; IVideo::~IVideo
; IVideo::GetSignalValue

LIBRARY    VCR.DLL

EXPORTS
  ?GetSignalValue@IVideo@@QAEJXZ
  ??0IVideo@@QAE@XZ
  ??1IVideo@@QAE@XZ
```

We are referring to our interface definition class as `IVideo`. By prefixing `I` to a class name, we are just setting up a convention to represent an interface class.

With the `IVideo`/`CVcr` mechanism in place, the TV program will create an instance of `IVideo` class and use it, as shown here:

```
#include "Video.h"
#include <iostream.h>

int main(int argc, char* argv[])
{
  int i;
  IVideo vcr;

  for(i=0; i<10; i++) {
    long val = vcr.GetSignalValue();
    cout << "Round: " << i << " - Value: " << val << endl;
  }

  return 0;
}
```

As long as we do not change the definition of `IVideo`, our TV program will continue to work with any upgraded version of `vcr.dll`. As a VCR vendor, we should not have any problems in guaranteeing the immutability for `IVideo` class, as we are not being held back from changing the implementation anytime later.

It seems like our original goal of field-replacing a component without any adverse affect on the overall system has been accomplished. By adding dynamic linking capability, we are able to field-replace a DLL. By separating interface from implementation and ensuring that the binary layout of the interface will never change, we have removed any adverse affect of field-replacing the DLL.

There are still a few weaknesses in the technique that was used to associate the interface with its implementation. These weaknesses are as follows:

• Compiler dependency: In order to use the interface class, all of the methods that the class exposes must be exported. If you recall, these methods need to be exported as name-mangled symbols. The problem is, the compiler vendors have not agreed upon a standard name-mangling scheme. Each compiler vendor implements its own name-mangling scheme. Lack of a name-mangling standard forces us to use the same compiler for each component.

- Performance penalty: The call to each method incurs the cost of two function calls: one call to the interface and one nested call to the implementation.
- Error prone: For a large class library with hundreds of methods, writing the forward call is not only tedious, but also susceptible to human errors.

Let's begin by focusing on the first problem, compiler dependency. In order to ensure that the interface class mechanism works across compiler boundaries, we need to limit the interface class definition to aspects of C++ language that are implemented uniformly across all C++ compilers. Let's identify such aspects of the C++ language.

COMMON ASPECTS OF C++ LANGUAGE

The following aspects of the C++ language can be assumed to be implemented uniformly across all compilers. Many of these aspects may require the use of conditionally compiled type definitions, pragmas, or other compiler directives.

- Run-time representation of basic data types is uniform: Basic data types such as `int`, `char`, `float`, `double`, etc., can be represented in the same way across all C++ compilers.
- Run-time representation of composite data type is uniform: Composite data types such as C-style `structs` can be represented in the same way across all C++ compilers. Sometimes compiler pragmas may have to be used to pack the `structs` in the same way.
- Argument passing order is uniform: All C++ compilers can be forced to pass function arguments for any specific function in exactly the same order (left to right, right to left).
- Argument passing convention is uniform: All C++ compilers can be forced to pass function arguments by value. In fact, this is the default behavior for all the compilers.
- Stack-maintenance responsibility is uniform: The responsibility of cleaning the stack, that is, popping the arguments from the stack, can be conditionally specified for the called function or the calling function.

- Case-translation convention: The linker can be forced to resolve symbolic references as case-sensitive or case-insensitive.
- No name mangling for C-Style functions: By declaring a C-Style function as `extern "C"`, the compiler's name-mangling mechanism for the specific function can be turned off.
- Implementation of virtual function is uniform: On any given platform, the machine language code generated when a virtual function is called is *equivalent* for all compilers. This is perhaps the most important assumption made so far and needs further discussion. The next section discusses this aspect in detail.

Many of these aspects can be controlled by just one compiler directive. For example, all WIN32 APIs are defined using the `WINAPI` preprocessor symbol. This symbol maps to `_stdcall` directive with the Microsoft compiler on the Intel platform. Table 1.1 summarizes the implication of this directive.

TABLE 1.1   Implementation of `_stdcall` Compiler Directive

Element	Implementation
Argument-passing order	Right to left
Argument-passing convention	By value, unless a pointer or reference type is passed
Stack-maintenance responsibility	Called function pops its own arguments from the stack
Case-translation convention	None

Let's look at how the compiler uses the definition of a class in generating machine language code. This will provide some insight on how to achieve compiler independence using virtual functions.

VIRTUAL METHODS IN C++ AND MEMORY LAYOUT

When we define a C++ class, we are actually informing the compiler to define the layout for a block of memory. The compiler takes into account the features of the host platform while defining the memory layout. The following code defines an interface class `IFoo` that has two member variables, namely, `m_nFirstValue` and `m_nSecondValue`.

```
class IFoo
{
public:
    int _stdcall GetFirstValue();
    int _stdcall GetSecondValue();

private:
    int m_nFirstValue;
    int m_nSecondValue;
};
```

Figure 1.3 shows the memory layout of this class. The host platform is an Intel machine running Windows 2000 OS.

Each instance of class IFoo should have enough memory allocated to hold this layout. A pointer to an instance of IFoo contains nothing but the starting address of this memory location.

The methods of the class, including the constructor and the destructor, did not contribute towards the memory layout. This is because these methods were not declared as virtual. Introduction of even one virtual method to the class changes the memory layout, as we will see later.

We will now examine various cases dealing with virtual methods and their implication on memory layout.

Let's revise our class definition to use virtual methods as shown below:

```
class IFoo
{
public:
    virtual int _stdcall GetX();
    virtual int _stdcall GetY();

private:
    int m_nFirstValue;
    int m_nSecondValue;
};
```

| m_nFirstValue |
| m_nSecondValue |

Figure 1.3   Layout of class IFoo.

Almost all production compilers implement the run-time behavior of virtual member functions using virtual function tables or vtbls. A vtbl is an array of pointers that point to the procedure entry address of each virtual function in a specific class. The memory layout of the class defines an additional entry that points to the vtbl for the class. This entry is called vptr. Figure 1.4 shows the memory layout and vtbl for the class after its methods have been changed to virtual.

Consider now, for example, the case when a client that holds a pointer to IFoo calls the method GetY as shown here:

```
void sub(IFoo* pFoo)
{
   pFoo->GetY();
}
```

In the case when the method being called is non-virtual, the compiler generates the following machine language instructions. I have added my comments for illustration.

```
mov   eax, DWORD PTR _pFoo$[ebp]
push eax                                ; push "this"
call ?GetY@IFoo@@QAGHXZ                 ; IFoo::GetY
```

When the method being called is virtual, the machine language instructions are:

```
mov   eax, DWORD PTR _pFoo$[ebp]
mov   ecx, DWORD PTR [eax]              ; load vptr in ecx
mov   edx, DWORD PTR _pFoo$[ebp]
push edx                                ; push "this"
call DWORD PTR [ecx+4]                  ; call the method whose
                                        ; address is stored in
                                        ; second entry of vtbl.
```

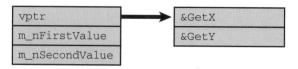

Figure 1.4   Layout of class IFoo containing virtual methods.

Each entry in `vtbl` is four bytes long on my host platform. The first entry is at location [ecx+0], the second at [ecx+4], and so on. The last machine language instruction shown above invokes a method that is stored as the second entry in our `vtbl`.

By calling a virtual method, we get away from the name-mangling issues, at the expense however, of a couple of more machine language instructions.

Also note the use of the `_stdcall` function directive. In general, each time a class method is called, the compiler has to make "`this`" pointer available to the method being called. Two common techniques to do this are (a) push "`this`" on stack and (b) make "`this`" available in a machine register. Compiler vendors choose their own technique. For example, the Microsoft Visual C++ compiler uses register ecx to accomplish this, that is, if no directives are specified. By using the `_stdcall` directive, we are directing the compiler to generate code that pushes "`this`" on stack.

Consider the case of overloaded virtual functions, as shown here:

```
class IFoo
{
public:
   virtual int _stdcall GetX();
   virtual int _stdcall GetY();
   virtual int _stdcall GetX(int y);

private:
   int m_nFirstValue;
   int m_nSecondValue;
};
```

In this case, the entries in `vtbl` are not guaranteed to be in order of declaration across all compilers. For example, the layout of the class as generated by the Microsoft's compiler is shown in Figure 1.5.

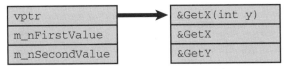

Figure 1.5   Layout of class `IFoo` with overloaded virtual functions.

As can be seen, the third virtual function declaration shows up as the first entry in the vtbl. The implication of this will be explained in the next section.

Consider the case where one interface is derived from another, as shown here:

```
class IFoo
{
public:
   virtual int _stdcall GetX();
   virtual int _stdcall GetY();

private:
   int m_nFirstValue;
   int m_nSecondValue;
};

class IBar : public IFoo
{
public:
   virtual int _stdcall GetZ();
};
```

The memory layout and the vtbl layout for class IBar are depicted in Figure 1.6.

If you compare the vtbl layout of class IBar with that of class IFoo (from Figure 1.4), you can see that the derived class' layout is just a binary extension of the base class' layout. Also note that the same vptr serves both the base and the derived classes. We can further generalize this as follows:

In a chain of derived classes, as long as each class is derived from exactly one class, the vtbl of the derived class is a superset of the base class. All the classes in the chain share the same vptr.

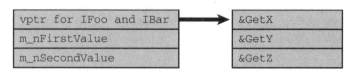

Figure 1.6   Layout of class IBar.

Finally, consider the case of multiple inheritances, that is, when a class is derived from more than one base class, as shown here:

```
class IFoo
{
public:
  virtual int _stdcall GetX();
  virtual int _stdcall GetY();

private:
  int m_nFirstValue;
  int m_nSecondValue;
};

class IBar
{
public:
  virtual int _stdcall GetZ();
};

class IFooBar: public IFoo , public IBar
{
public:
  virtual int _stdcall GetA();
};
```

The memory and the vtbl layout for class IFooBar is shown in Figure 1.7.

Figure 1.7 illustrates that in the case of multiple inheritance, several vptrs are created in the memory layout of the derived class.

Armed with the knowledge we have gained on vtbl implementation, let us see how we can come up with a scheme to obtain compiler independence.

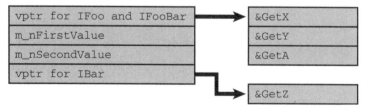

Figure 1.7   Layout of class IFooBar.

INTERFACE AS AN ABSTRACT BASE CLASS

If you recall, a major problem in achieving compiler independence was non-standard name-mangling schemes used by various compilers. However, as was seen in the earlier section, if a client calls a virtual method of a class, the generated machine language code for the client side does not refer to the method by its symbolic name. Instead, it uses the `vtbl` mechanism to invoke the method. Thus, if a client calls only the virtual methods, name mangling is no longer an issue.

Once we opt for using the virtual methods mechanism, three new issues arise.

If the interface class contains data members, the placement of `vptr` in the memory layout is chosen by the vendor. One vendor may wish to place it before the data members and the other after the data members. This problem can easily be avoided by not declaring any data members in the interface definition. This fits very well with our notion of hiding implementation details from the clients.

The second problem is related to multiple inheritance of an interface class. In this case, the memory layout of the class will contain more than one `vptr`, as we have seen earlier. However, there is no agreed-upon standard in the ordering of `vptr`s. We can overcome this problem by limiting the derivation to just one base class.

The third problem is related to the ordering of `vtbl` entries. The client-side compiler has to assume that the first entry in the `vtbl` is the address of the first virtual function declared in the interface class, the second entry is the address of the second virtual function declared, and so on. However, with overloaded virtual functions, this assumption is not valid across all compilers, as we witnessed earlier. Therefore, overloaded function declarations should not be allowed in the interface class.

Furthermore, by defining the virtual functions as pure, we can indicate that the interface class defines only the potential to call the methods, not their actual implementation.

In order to ensure that all compilers generate equivalent machine language code for client-side method invocation for an interface, the interface class definition should:

- contain only pure virtual methods
- not contain any overloaded virtual methods
- not contain any members variables

- derive from at most one base class where the base class also adheres to the same restrictions

By following these rules for defining interface classes, we can achieve our goal of compiler independence for interface class definition.

An interface class defined this way is called an *abstract base class*. The corresponding C++ implementation class must derive from the interface class and override each of the pure virtual methods with meaningful implementation. As we have seen earlier, the memory layout of such an implementation class is just a binary superset of the interface class.

The flexibility lost by restricting the interface definition to the abstract base class has not been much of a problem. Also, calling a virtual function results in just one more machine language instruction and is negligible compared to the number of instructions a typical function executes. However, the benefits obtained by defining an interface as abstract based class is well worth it.

The following code shows the definition of the IVideo class redefined as an abstract base class and the corresponding implementation of the CVcr class.

```
// Video.h - Definition of interface IVideo

class IVideo
{
public:
    virtual long _stdcall GetSignalValue() = 0;
};

// File vcr.h

#include "Video.h"

class CVcr : public IVideo
{
public:
    CVcr(void);

    long _stdcall GetSignalValue();

private:
    long m_lCurValue;
    int m_nCurCount;
};
```

Not only does this mechanism solve the compiler dependency problem, it also solves some other weaknesses with our old technique of using the opaque pointers. If you recall, the old technique had two weaknesses:

- Performance penalty: Each method call incurs the cost of two function calls—one call to the interface, and one nested call to the implementation.
- Error prone: For a large class library with hundreds of methods, writing the forward call is not only tedious, but also susceptible to human errors.

Deriving the implementation class from the abstract base class addresses both of these weaknesses.

We now have a new problem, however. The C++ compiler will not let you instantiate an abstract base class. Only concrete classes, such as the implementation class, can be instantiated. However, revealing the implementation class definition to the client would bypass the binary encapsulation of the interface class.

A reasonable technique for clients to instantiate a base class object is to export a global function from the DLL that will return a new instance of the base class. As long as this function is declared as extern "C", the client-side code will not run into any name-mangling problem.

```cpp
// Video.h
extern "C" IVideo* _stdcall CreateVcr();

// Vcr.cpp (implementation)
IVideo* _stdcall CreateVcr(void)
{
    return new CVcr;
}
```

With this "factory" mechanism in place to create the needed instance, our TV client code will look like the following:

```cpp
#include "Video.h"
#include <iostream.h>

int main(int argc, char* argv[])
{
    int i;
    IVideo* pVideo = CreateVcr();
```

```
for(i=0; i<10; i++) {
        long val = pVideo->GetSignalValue();
        cout << "Round: " << i << " - Value: " << val << endl;
}

delete pVideo;          // we are done with it

return 0;
}
```

This code will almost work, except for one subtle flaw—note that
"new" for pVideo occurs in the VCR executable, and "delete" occurs in
the TV executable. As a result, the destructor for class CVcr is never
invoked, and if the client uses a different C++ compiler than the server, the
result of memory deallocation in the client is unpredictable.

An obvious solution is to make the destructor virtual in the interface
class. Unfortunately, the position of the virtual destructor in the vtbl can
vary from compiler to compiler.

A workable solution is to add an explicit Delete method to the interface
class as another pure virtual function and let the derived class delete itself in
the implementation of this method. The code snippet shown here is the revised
definition of interface IVideo class and its implementation class, CVcr.

```
// Video.h - Definition of interface IVideo

class IVideo
{
public:
    virtual long _stdcall GetSignalValue() = 0;
    virtual void _stdcall Delete() = 0;
};

// File vcr.h

#include "Video.h"

class CVcr : public IVideo
{
public:
    CVcr(void);

    long _stdcall GetSignalValue();
    void _stdcall Delete();
```

```
private:
   long m_lCurValue;
   int m_nCurCount;
};

// File vcr.cpp
void CVcr::Delete()
{
   delete this;
}
```

With this mechanism in place, the revised client code looks like the following:

```
int main(int argc, char* argv[])
{
   int i;
   IVideo* pVideo = CreateVcr();

   for(i=0; i<10; i++) {
      long val = pVideo->GetSignalValue();
      cout << "Round: " << i << " - Value: " << val <<
endl;
   }

   pVideo->Delete();

   return 0;
}
```

In summary, by using an abstract base class for defining the interface, adding `Delete` functionality as part of the interface specification, and using a "factory" method to obtain the interface, we have finally achieved compiler independence.

Let's now consider how to achieve vendor independence, or, in other words, can we select a VCR from the vendor of our choice?

DYNAMIC SELECTION OF A COMPONENT

Let's look back at our hardware TV and VCR connection. Something seems very obvious—*any* brand of VCR will work with our TV as long as the VCR has a video-out jack that could send video signals according to the same predefined "video" specifications. The reason is very simple: the TV doesn't care about the VCR; it cares about the "video" specifications. As a matter of fact, you don't even need a VCR to provide these signals. You can instead use a DVD player, for example. As long as the DVD player has the video-out jack that outputs video signals according to the same predefined "video" specifications, the TV can display the output.

Where am I going with this? Let us reexamine our TV code. Though we claim that we support dynamic linking, we still always link with VCR.dll—a DLL provided by one specific vendor. Why can't we extend our model to use a DLL supplied by some other vendor? After all, we went through a great ordeal to separate interface from implementation. If another vendor supplies a better implementation for the same interface, doesn't it seem logical that we should be able to use the new implementation?

Logical indeed! However, if you recall, the OS loader automatically loads the DLL at the time of execution. We never get a chance to pick the DLL we wish to use. This is because we had linked our client program with an import library that had directives for the OS loader to load the specific DLL.

Obviously, we cannot use the import library mechanism if we wish to pick a vendor-specific DLL during run time.

Recall that the reason we had to use the import library was to resolve symbols that were external to the client program. If you look at our latest interface definition, the only symbol external to the program is the factory method `CreateVcr`. So, instead of letting the OS loader load the DLL and resolve this symbol for us, if we do it ourselves in the client code, we don't really need to link our program with the import library.

Help is on the way. Microsoft has provided a Win32 API called `Load-Library` that can be used to load a DLL dynamically. Another Win32 API called `GetProcAddress` can be used to resolve the procedure entry points. With these two APIs, I can write a client-side function, `CreateInstance`, that will:

- load the specified DLL
- resolve extern symbol `CreateVcr`
- invoke the method `CreateVcr` and return the interface pointer

The client code is shown here:

```
IVideo* CreateInstance(char* pszDll)
{
    // Define a pointer to the prototype of CreateVcr function
    typedef IVideo* (_stdcall *CREATEVCRPROC)(void);

    // Load the specified library
```

```
    HINSTANCE h = LoadLibrary(pszDll);

    // Obtain the procedure entry point for CreateVcr
    CREATEVCRPROC proc =
        reinterpret_cast<CREATEVCRPROC>(GetProcAddress(h,"CreateVcr"));

    // Execute "CreateVcr" indirectly
    return (*proc)();
}

int main(int argc, char* argv[])
{
    int i;
    IVideo* pVideo = CreateInstance("vcr.dll");

    for(i=0; i<10; i++) {
        long val = pVideo->GetSignalValue();
        cout << "Round: " << i << " - Value: " << val << endl;
    }

    pVideo->Delete();

    return 0;
}
```

Now the client code can specify the DLL that it would use during run time. A more innovative and comprehensive TV program would:

- ask the user to specify the specific VCR DLL to use
- deal gracefully if the requested VCR DLL is not found (instead of just shutting down, it can still show local broadcasts, for example)
- not load VCR DLL until the user requests to use it, thus conserving memory resources
- unload the loaded DLL once the user is done with it, thus recovering the allocated memory space

Not only have we achieved vendor independence, but we have also made the program more robust and less resource-consuming.

Let us see where we stand now. We have defined an interface so that it provides a binary encapsulation that is neither compiler-specific nor vendor-specific. A client is built based on this binary encapsulation. If the interface definition is changed and the client code is not recompiled with the new definition, the binary encapsulation gets broken. In this case, the behavior of the client is completely unpredictable, as we saw in an earlier example.

Even if just the semantics of the interface were changed without actually changing the interface, (for example, by returning a value greater than 40 in our case) the client would still break.

An interface, therefore, is a binary as well as semantic contract that should stay immutable.

But what if we find that the interface the client is using is not adequate, or we just wish to extend the functionality of the interface?

EXTENDING THE INTERFACE FUNCTIONALITY

As the needs of the clients evolve, the vendors at some point have to provide more functionality to the clients. In our scenario, let's say the VCR vendor decides to provide support for a newer set of specifications called "S-Video." This new signal provides better quality video pictures than the old one. Obviously, a newer model TV would be needed that could support this new signal. The VCR vendor, however, has a dilemma:

- If the vendor changes the current interface to provide an S-Video signal instead of a Video signal, all the existing TV clients would break, as they do not know how to handle the new signal type.
- If the vendor publicly states that she is moving towards the new S-Video signal and will not support the old signal anymore, then she will lose her existing customers and many new customers who do not have the newer model TV that can support the newer signal.

Ideally, the VCR vendor would like to support both the signal types. The TV manufacturer has a dilemma of its own:

- If the TV supports only S-Video, there are thousands of VCRs out there that still provide the old-style Video signal and thus will not work with the newer TV.
- If the manufacturer decides not to support S-Video, he is losing its market to its competitors.

Ideally, the manufacturer would like to probe the VCR to detect if it supports the S-Video signal. If the support was found, then it could use the new signal type. Otherwise, it would use the old signal type.

Let's extend our simulation program to deal with multiple interfaces and define a new interface for S-Video that supports a method to return the S-Video signal.

```
// SVideo.h - Definition of interface ISVideo

class ISVideo
{
public:
  virtual long _stdcall GetSVideoSignalValue() = 0;
  virtual void _stdcall Delete() = 0;
};
```

Note that, as established earlier, an interface always has to support the Delete method.

Using multiple inheritance, we can now add support for this new interface to our original implementation class, CVcr, as shown in the following class definition:

```
class CVcr : public IVideo, public ISVideo
{
  . . .
}
```

 It was our choice to support both the signals in our simulation program. It is up to the VCR manufacturer to support just the IVideo signal, just the ISVideo signal, or both signals.

Also note that the restriction of using multiple inheritance was placed on the interface definitions, not the implementation. The implementer is free to use multiple inheritance, as we did in our case.

We now need to add the semantics of "probing" for a signal type. Let's define a method, Probe, that takes a string input to specify the interface we are probing for. If the interface is found, the method will return the corresponding interface pointer. The client code snippet shown here illustrates the idea:

```
IVideo* pVideo = CreateInstance("vcr.dll");

ISVideo* pSVideo = pVideo->Probe("svideo");
if (pSVideo != NULL) {
  // use S-Video
}else {
  // use Video signal
}
```

The code requires that function CreateInstance return the IVideo interface. This would certainly not work with those VCRs that implement only the ISVideo interface.

If the prototype of `CreateInstance` is changed to return the `ISVideo` interface, then it would become incompatible with those VCRs implementing just the `IVideo` interface.

An easy way to solve this dilemma is to define a more general interface, `IGeneral`, that doesn't really do much except to provide the "probing" semantics for the other more meaningful interfaces such as `IVideo` and `ISVideo`. Each VCR would then implement this general interface and return a pointer to this interface when `CreateInstance` is called.

If all other interfaces are derived from this general interface, then every interface will automatically support the semantics of probing. Also, as all interfaces are required to support `Delete` semantics anyways, it makes a great deal of sense to move this method to the base class as well, as shown in the following code snippet:

```
class IGeneral
{
public:
   virtual IGeneral* _stdcall Probe(char* pszType) = 0;
   virtual void _stdcall Delete() = 0;
};

class IVideo : public IGeneral
{
   ...
};

class ISVideo : public IGeneral
{
   ...
};

extern "C" IGeneral* _stdcall CreateVCR();
```

Note that method `Probe` returns a pointer to the `IGeneral` interface instead of a specific pointer to the `IVideo` or `ISVideo` interfaces. A function can have only one return type; this is a syntactic limitation of C language (or any other language I can recall). The client code just has to reinterpret the type depending on the specified `pszType` parameter.

```cpp
// TV client code
int main(int argc, char* argv[])
{
  IGeneral* pVCR = CreateInstance("vcr.dll");

  // Use S-Video if available
  IGeneral* pGeneral = pVCR->Probe("svideo");
  if (NULL != pGeneral) {
    ISVideo* pSVideo = reinterpret_cast<ISVideo*>(pGeneral);
    UseSVideo(pSVideo);
    pSVideo->Delete();
    return 0;
  }

  // S-Video not available. Try old "video" type
  pGeneral = pVCR->Probe("video");
  if (NULL != pGeneral) {
    IVideo* pVideo = reinterpret_cast<IVideo*>(pGeneral);
    UseVideo(pVideo);
    pVideo->Delete();
    return 0;
  }

  // Neither S-Video nor Video
  cout << "This VCR does not have the signals this TV supports" <<
endl;
  pVCR->Delete();
  return 1;
}
```

Here is the revised definition of our implementation class, CVcr.

```cpp
class CVcr : public IVideo, public ISVideo
{
public:
  // IGeneral interface
  IGeneral* _stdcall Probe(char* pszType);
  void _stdcall Delete();

  // IVideo interface
  long _stdcall GetSignalValue();

  // ISVideo interface
  long _stdcall GetSVideoSignalValue();

private:
  // other member variables and methods not shown for brevity
};
```

Consider the implementation of CreateVCR code:

```
IGeneral* _stdcall CreateVCR(void)
{
  return static_cast<IVideo*>(new CVcr);
}
```

When returning the base interface IGeneral, the implementation statically casts CVcr instance to IVideo. This is because directly casting the
instance to IGeneral is ambiguous, as IVideo and ISVideo are both
derived from IGeneral. To help the compiler resolve the ambiguity, the
implementation has to pick either IVideo or ISVideo. It doesn't matter
which one.

Had the interface IGeneral been declared as a virtual base class for
both IVideo and ISVideo interfaces, the ambiguity would have disappeared. However, using virtual base classes introduces compiler dependen-
cies, as this C++ language feature has no standard implementation but many
proprietary implementations.

Now consider the implementation of the Probe method:

```
IGeneral* CVcr::Probe(char* pszType)
{
  IGereral* p = NULL;
  if (!stricmp(pszType, "general")) {
    p = static_cast<IVideo*>(this);
  }else
  if (!stricmp(pszType, "video")) {
    p = static_cast<IVideo*>(this);
  }else
  if (!stricmp(pszType, "svideo")) {
    p = static_cast<ISVideo*>(this);
  }

  return p;
}
```

Technically, our VCR implementation supports three interfaces, although there
are only two meaningful interfaces for TV users. The third interface,
IGeneral, does the magic of obtaining any of the other interfaces, or, by
extension, obtaining one interface from another interface.

The previous code appears to be a classic case of using the C++ language feature of run-time type information (RTTI). Why did we not use RTTI

instead of going through this extensive semantics of defining and using Probe? Because RTTI is yet another C++ language feature that is not compiler-independent.

Hang in there. We are almost done. The next problem has to do with lifetime management of the VCR object.

MANAGING THE LIFETIME OF AN OBJECT

If you recall our TV client code, the Delete method is being called at several different places. The client code has to remember that there was only one object created (using function CreateInstance) and thus only one Delete has to be called, even though the code is dealing with multiple interfaces from the object. For our simple TV client code, this is not a tremendous burden. In more complex applications, keeping track of the number of objects created and deleted is cumbersome, as well as prone to errors. For example, consider the case when you have multiple copies of interface pointers for the same object. You use one copy, and thinking that you are done with the object, decide to delete the object. Later on, when you try to use the other copy of the interface, it would result in accessing invalid memory location, resulting in unexpected program behavior.

There is also a semantic problem. The client should only deal with interfaces. The notion of actual object instance and its creation should be as invisible to the client as possible. From a client's point of view, it never creates an instance of the object; it always creates, or somehow obtains, an instance of the interface.

 This distinction between an object and an interface is very important. While dealing with an interface, the client knows that there is some object behind this interface. There are perhaps other interfaces that this object supports. However, the client never deals with the object directly. It obtains one interface from another interface, if need be.

Ideally, the client's logic should obtain an interface, use it, then delete it. This is illustrated in Figure 1.8.

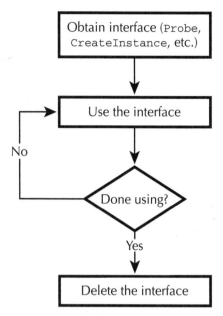

Figure 1.8 Client's use of an interface.

Based on this logic, the client code can be simplified to:

```
int main(int argc, char* argv[])
{
   IGeneral* pVCR = CreateInstance("vcr.dll");

   bool bRetVal = UseSVideoIfAvailable(pVCR);
   if (false == bRetVal) {
     bRetVal = UseVideoIfAvailable(pVCR);
   }

   if (false == bRetVal) {
     // Neither S-Video nor Video
     cout << "This VCR does not have the signals we support"
        << endl;
   }

   pVCR->Delete();     // Done with pVCR
   return 0;
}

bool UseSVideoIfAvailable(IGeneral* pVCR)
{
```

```
IGeneral* pGeneral = pVCR->Probe("svideo");
if (NULL == pGeneral) {
   return false;
}

ISVideo* pSVideo = reinterpret_cast<ISVideo*>(pGeneral);
UseSVideo(pSVideo);
pSVideo->Delete();
return true;
}
```

As seen, the lifetime management of the actual object has been pushed to the object implementation side. Now the implementation has to deal with the outstanding copies of interfaces for a given object. A simple solution is to maintain a reference count of the outstanding copies of interfaces, as shown here.

```
class CVcr : public IVideo, public ISVideo
{
public:
   . . .
public:
   // A helper function to increment the reference count
   void AddReference();
private:
   . . .
   long m_lRefCount;      // count of outstanding copies of interfaces
};
```

The reference count can be initialized to a value zero in the object construction, as follows:

```
CVcr:: CVcr()
{
   . . .
   m_lRefCount = 0;
}
```

Method `AddReference` increments the reference count. Method `Delete` decrements the reference count. If the reference count reaches zero, it implies there are no more outstanding references to the object. As the object is not needed anymore, it can be deleted, as shown below:

```
void CVcr::Delete()
{
   if ( (—m_lRefCount) == 0) {
      delete this;
   }
}
```

In this code, the statement "`delete this`" is the C++ equivalent of suicide. It is legal to do so, as long as no other calls are made on this instance that would involve using the memory layout of the instance.

Consider the locations where we need to increment the reference count. There are only two such entry points—during object creation and during a successful probe:

```
IGeneral* CreateVCR(void)
{
  CVcr* p = new CVcr;
  if (NULL == p)
    return p;
  p->AddReference();

  return static_cast<IVideo*>(p);
}

IGeneral* CVcr::Probe(char* pszType)
{
  IGeneral* p = NULL;
  if (!stricmp(pszType, "general")) {
    p = static_cast<IVideo*>(this);
  }else
  if (!stricmp(pszType, "video")) {
    p = static_cast<IVideo*>(this);
  }else
  if (!stricmp(pszType, "svideo")) {
    p = static_cast<ISVideo*>(this);
  }

  if (NULL != p) {
    AddReference();
  }

  return p;
}
```

With this mechanism in place, the TV client will be able to take the following steps in sequence:

1. Obtain the `IGeneral` interface pointer
2. Obtain the proper video interface pointer
3. Use the video interface
4. Delete the interface pointer
5. Delete the `IGeneral` interface pointer

The last call to `Delete` will cause the actual object to get deleted.

By using a simple reference counting mechanism, we reduced the complexity of dealing with multiple interfaces of an object.

There is just one more case of reference counting we haven't dealt with: the case when the client itself makes a copy of the interface, as in the following code snippet:

```
IGeneral* pVCR = CreateInstance("vcr.dll");
IGeneral* pVCRCopy = pVCR;
UseVCR(pVCR);
pVCR->Delete();
UseVCR(pVCRCopy);
pVCRCopy->Delete();
```

As far as the object code is concerned, there is only one outstanding reference. Thus, the first call to `Delete` will delete the object. This will result in a dangling pointer for the second copy, causing unexpected behavior (most likely a crash) when the client tries to use it.

The problem is that the object code never knew that the reference count had to be incremented.

We can easily solve this problem by pushing the responsibility to the client to inform the object that the reference count has to be incremented. All we need to do is make `AddReference` available to the client by defining it as part of the interface. As you might have guessed, the interface `IGeneral` is an ideal candidate to add this method to, as shown here:

```
class IGeneral
{
public:
  virtual IGeneral* _stdcall Probe(char* pszType) = 0;
  virtual void _stdcall AddReference() = 0;
  virtual void _stdcall Delete() = 0;
};
```

Note that `AddReference` is declared as a pure virtual method. This is in accordance with our rules of defining an interface.

With this mechanism in place, the client code should be revised as:

```
IGeneral* pVCR = CreateInstance("vcr.dll");
IGeneral* pVCRCopy = pVCR;
pVCRCopy->AddRererence();
UseVCR(pVCR);
pVCR->Delete();
UseVCR(pVCRCopy);
pVCRCopy->Delete();
```

The client's responsibility in dealing with interface lifetime can be summarized in the following way:

- If the client obtains an interface pointer from the server, it should call `Delete` when done using the interface.
- If the client makes a copy of the interface pointer, it should call `AddReference` on the copy. It can then call `Delete` when done using the copy. The client can call `AddReference` multiple times. However, for each `AddReference` call, there should be a corresponding `Delete` call.

At this stage, we should be reasonably comfortable in dealing with multiple interfaces or multiple copies of an interface pointer. However, the drawback of being an expert programmer is that our incessant obsession with efficiency and perfection demands that we consider methods to optimize the code we develop.

OPTIMIZATIONS

In the previous section we saw that in order to use an interface, the client had to obtain the `IGeneral` pointer first. Once this pointer was obtained, the client had to call the method `Probe` to get an appropriate video interface pointer, as shown here:

```
IGeneral* pGeneral = CreateInstance("vcr.dll");
ISVideo* pSVideo = (ISVideo*) pGeneral->Probe("svideo");
```

Clearly, the operations involve two round trips to the client. Each round trip implies a performance penalty. In our case, the performance degradation is not that significant as both the client and the server are running on the same machine and in the same process space. In the case where the server is running on a far away machine from the client or on a machine that is connected over a slow line, each round trip may take considerable time.

In some cases, round trips cannot be avoided and you have to live with it. But consider the case where the TV client knows that it will support only the S-Video signal. For such a case, it would make a great deal of sense to combine the above two operations into one and save one round trip, as illustrated below:

```
ISVideo* pSVideo = (ISVideo*) CreateInstance("vcr.dll", "svideo");
```

If you recall, function `CreateInstance` invokes server function `CreateVCR`. We will need to extend `CreateVCR` to take another parameter, a parameter similar to the one that method `Probe` takes. As a matter of fact, `CreateVCR` can just turn around and invoke `Probe` to get the appropriate interface pointer. The code is shown below:

```
IGeneral* _stdcall CreateVCR(char* pszType)
{
  CVcr* pVcr = new CVcr;
  IGeneral* pGeneral = pVcr->Probe(pszType);
  if (NULL == pGeneral) {
    delete pVcr;
  }

  return pGeneral;
}
```

This is the only coding change that is required on the server side. On the client side, we will need to change `CreateInstance` method to take the new parameter, `pszType`.

```
IGeneral* CreateInstance(char* pszDll, char* pszType)
{
  typedef IGeneral* (_stdcall *CREATEVCRPROC)(char* pszType);

  HINSTANCE h = LoadLibrary(pszDll);
  CREATEVCRPROC proc = reinterpret_cast<CREATEVCRPROC>
    (GetProcAddress(h, "CreateVCR"));
  return (*proc)(pszType);
}
```

With these two changes in place, not only did we improve the performance, we also simplified client-side logic:

```
int main(int argc, char* argv[])
{
  IGeneral* pGeneral = CreateInstance("vcr.dll", "svideo");
  if (NULL == pGeneral) {
    return 1;
  }

  UseSVideo(reinterpret_cast<ISVideo*>(pGeneral));
  pGeneral->Delete();
  return 0;
}
```

Moreover, the logic doesn't preclude the possibility that you really wish to obtain `IGeneral` interface and probe for a specific interface:

```
IGeneral* pGeneral= CreateInstance("vcr.dll", "general");
ISVideo* pSVideo = (ISVideo*) pGeneral->Probe("svideo");
```

Good job! Your TV-VCR system is now in place. You can turn the TV on, sit back, and enjoy the displayed video signals.

One day you come home, turn the TV on, and to your surprise, there is no display. What happened? You have no clue.

ERROR REPORTING

If you reexamine our VCR code, you will notice that although we handle failures gracefully, we haven't done a good job of unequivocally identifying the error conditions. For example, function `CreateVCR` returns NULL for two cases—when there is not enough memory to create the VCR instance and when the requested `pszType` interface is not found. How is the TV code supposed to know what the real problem is?

It is not really a coding problem. It is the way we designed the interface; it doesn't have any provision for returning error codes.

Let's do something about it.

Every interface method has a possibility of failing. A uniform mechanism for obtaining error status across all methods will simplify client-side code. However, an interface method can fail for a number of reasons, such as:

- The client ran out of memory while doing some memory allocations.
- The argument passed to the method had a value that is not acceptable by the server.
- In case of method `Probe`, the requested interface was not found.
- There could be some internal error in the server code that stops it from further processing.

Let's mandate that every interface method return an integer indicating the status. To distinguish this special integer value from other integers, let's define its type as VRESULT (for Video result).

```
typedef int VRESULT;
```

Let's define some possible error codes:

```
#define V_OUTOFMEMORY        1
#define V_NOINTERFACE        2
#define V_INTERNALERROR      3
```

If a method call doesn't fail, it should return an OK status:

```
#define V_OK                 0
```

In order to check for success or failures, let's define a couple of macros:

```
#define V_SUCCEEDED(P1)        ((P1) == V_OK)
#define V_FAILED(P1)           ((P1) != V_OK)
```

Now, let's rework our interface definitions.

Most current method definitions already return a value. This is the "logical" value that the client needs for its processing. If we change the method definitions to return the error status, we will need to obtain the logical return value as a parameter. For example, the old method prototype

```
virtual long _stdcall GetSignalValue() = 0;
```

would be modified to

```
virtual VRESULT _stdcall GetSignalValue(long* pRetVal) = 0;
```

The client usage will need to change accordingly:

```
// Old code
long val = pVideo->GetSignalValue();

// New Code
long val;
VRESULT vr = pVideo->GetSignalValue(&val);
if (V_FAILED(vr)) {
  ReportError(vr);
}
```

With the method definitions changed, the following is our new interface definition header file[1]:

```
class IGeneral
{
public:
  virtual VRESULT _stdcall Probe(char* pszType,
    IGeneral** ppRetVal) = 0;
  virtual void _stdcall AddReference() = 0;
  virtual void _stdcall Delete() = 0;
};

class IVideo : public IGeneral
{
public:
  virtual VRESULT _stdcall GetSignalValue(long* pRetVal) = 0;
};

class ISVideo : public IGeneral
{
public:
  virtual VRESULT _stdcall
    GetSVideoSignalValue(long* pRetVal) = 0;
};

extern "C" VRESULT _stdcall CreateVCR(char* pszType,
  IGeneral** ppRetVal);
```

Methods `AddReference` and `Delete` do not return `VRESULT`. These two methods deserve special treatment. They do not do any complex processing. They do not even take any parameters that possibly could be invalid. These two methods should never fail. If they do, you really have a bigger problem somewhere else in your logic.

---

[1] In case you are wondering why I chose "C" style pointer as a parameter type instead of C++ style reference, semantically, there is no difference between the two styles. I just picked one that COM interface definitions use, as we will see in the next chapter.

The VCR code needs to change according to the new method definition. The following code snippet shows the revised implementation:

```
VRESULT CVcr::Probe(char* pszType, IGeneral** ppRetVal)
{
  *ppRetVal = NULL;
  if (!stricmp(pszType, "general")) {
    *ppRetVal = static_cast<IVideo*>(this);
  }else
  if (!stricmp(pszType, "video")) {
    *ppRetVal = static_cast<IVideo*>(this);
  }else
  if (!stricmp(pszType, "svideo")) {
    *ppRetVal = static_cast<ISVideo*>(this);
  }

  if (NULL != (*ppRetVal)) {
    AddReference();
    return V_OK;
  }

  return V_NOINTERFACE;
}

VRESULT _stdcall CreateVCR(char* pszType, IGeneral** ppRetVal)
{
  *ppRetVal = NULL;

  CVcr* pVcr = new CVcr;
  if (NULL == pVcr) {
    return V_OUTOFMEMORY;
  }

  VRESULT vr = pVcr->Probe(pszType, ppRetVal);
  if (V_FAILED(vr)) {
    delete pVcr;
  }

  return vr;
}
```

Our TV code can now do a better job of error reporting:

```
void ReportError(VRESULT vr)
{
  char* pszError = NULL;
  switch(vr) {
```

```
  case V_OUTOFMEMORY:
    pszError = "Out of memory";
    break;
  case V_NOINTERFACE:
    pszError = "No such interface supported";
    break;
  case V_INTERNALERROR:
    pszError = "Internal error. Contact the VCR vendor";
    break;
  default:
    pszError = "Unknown error";
  }
  cout << pszError << endl;
}

int main(int argc, char* argv[])
{
  IGeneral* pGeneral = NULL;
  VRESULT vr = CreateInstance("vcr.dll", "svideo", &pGeneral);
  if (V_FAILED(vr)) {
    ReportError(vr);
    return 1;
  }

  UseSVideo(reinterpret_cast<ISVideo*>(pGeneral));
  pGeneral->Delete();
  return 0;
}

void UseSVideo(ISVideo* pSVideo)
{
  long val;
  VRESULT vr;
  for(int i=0; i<10; i++) {
    vr = pSVideo->GetSVideoSignalValue(&val);
    if (V_FAILED(vr)) {
      ReportError(vr);
      continue;
    }
    cout << "Round: " << i << " - Value: " << val << endl;
  }
}
```

A small coding style change is in order. In the main function above, a call to CreateInstance returns a value of type IGeneral*, even though we are requesting an svideo interface pointer. As we know that the pointer returned (pGeneral) is really a pointer to ISVideo, we just reinterpret pGeneral to ISVideo* later in the code. Instead, we might as well specify a return value argument of type ISVideo* as shown below. You will see this style of coding used quite extensively in the COM programming community.

```
int main(int argc, char* argv[])
{
  ISVideo* pSVideo = NULL;
  VRESULT vr = CreateInstance("vcr.dll", "svideo",
    reinterpret_cast<IGeneral**>(&pSVideo));
  if (V_FAILED(vr)) {
    ReportError(vr);
    return 1;
  }

  UseSVideo(pSVideo);
  pSVideo->Delete();
  return 0;
}
```

Let's summarize what we have achieved so far.

We took a monolithic application and broke it into two components with a desire to field-replace a buggy component or to reuse a third-party component. In the process we:

1. separated interface from implementation
2. added mechanism to dynamically load a component
3. defined a general interface that formed the base of all other interfaces
4. gave the server the responsibility of managing the lifetime of an object
5. gave the client the responsibility to cooperate with the server in managing the lifetime of the object
6. defined a simple reference counting mechanism in order to reduce the complexity of lifetime management
7. added some optimization on obtaining the initial interface pointer from the server
8. implemented an error-reporting mechanism

THE ESSENCE OF COM

Breaking a monolithic binary file into separate software components that are linked dynamically at execution time gives us the ability to:

- reuse a component from a third-party vendor
- field-replace a defective component

To assure that the communication among the software components does not break:

- the communication interface has to be separated from the implementation details.
- the interface class has to be defined based on certain rules such that it provides a binary encapsulation.
- the interacting applications have certain responsibilities in managing the lifetime of the object.

The whole architecture and supporting infrastructure for building and using component software in a robust manner is referred to as the Component Object Model or COM.

COM-based application development can be broken down into the following three steps:

1. Define the interface: A software vendor or a group of vendors collectively declare the services they intend to provide by defining one or more interfaces. An interface is a semantically related set of methods grouped together. It defines an immutable contract at the binary level between a vendor and its clients.

2. Implement the interface: A vendor that intends to provide the services of a specific interface implements the interface in its application. Such an application is called a COM server. Sometimes it is loosely referred to as a component.

3. Use the interface: The application that intends to use the service via the interface is referred to as a COM client.

The server program that implements the interface has certain responsibilities such as maintaining the reference count, returning meaningful errors, and providing thread safety. We will examine thread-related issues in a later chapter.

The client program that uses the interface has other responsibilities such as appropriately adding or releasing references on the object, and examining the return status from every method call.

The interface definition rules that we have examined in this chapter achieved C++ compiler independence. Our ultimate goal is to achieve programming language independence as well as network transparency. The operating system has to be extended to support these goals. The developers have to be provided with some standard documentation and Application Programming Interfaces (APIs) when developing COM-based applications. These APIs appear in the form of the COM Software Development Kit (SDK), sometimes referred to as the COM library.

The rules and responsibilities of the client, the server, and the OS infrastructure are all documented by Microsoft in *COM Specifications* [COM-95]. The *COM Specifications* contain the standard APIs supported by the COM library, the standard suite of interfaces supported or used by software written in a COM environment, along with the network protocols used by COM in support of distributed computing. These specifications are still in draft form, and thus are subject to change.

COM is the most widely used component software model in the world. It provides the richest set of integrated services, the widest choice of easy-to-use tools, and the largest set of available applications. In addition, it provides a viable market for reusable, off-the-shelf, client and server components. Table 1.2 summarizes some advantages of COM by means of some comparative examples.

TABLE 1.2   Advantages of Component Model

Advantage	Hardware	Software
Field-replacement	A problem in the VCR requires the VCR to be replaced, not the TV.	A buggy component can be field-replaced without rebuilding the application.
Choice of vendor	Choice of any brand of VCR as long as it supports "Video" or "S-Video" output.	Component from any vendor that matches the specifications can be used.
Rapid application development	A complete entertainment system can be put together rather quickly using various components.	An application can be snapped together from various components.

TABLE 1.2 (continued)

Advantage	Hardware	Software
Distributed computing	The VCR can be in the next room or in the next building.	A component can be located on a different machine.
Knowledge of component's internal workings not required	The technology used to build the VCR is irrelevant.	The C++ compiler used for the component is irrelevant. In fact, a component can be written in any programming language (as we will see in the next chapter).
Maximizing productivity	The TV vendor can focus on improving picture quality.	Application vendor can focus on what they do the best and the third party software vendors can focus on developing the best code.

In the chapters that will follow, we will take an in-depth look at the rules and responsibilities of developing COM servers and COM client applications. We will examine the APIs provided by the COM library and the role of the OS in facilitating the communication between various COM components.

SUMMARY

Traditionally, the reusability problem was solved by using software libraries, either written in-house or bought from a third-party software vendor. In this chapter, we saw that this solution had many problems. We went through a series of C++ programming techniques that could be used to solve the original problem as well as any new problem that arose in the process. Ultimately, we observed that by following two programming paradigms, we could develop reusable binary components that can evolve over time. The two programming paradigms, dynamic linking and binary encapsulation, form the foundation of the Component Object Model.

REFERENCES

[MSDN-00] "The Search Path Used by Windows to Locate a DLL," Visual C++ Documentation, Microsoft Development Network. *http://msdn.microsoft.com/ library/ devprods/vs6/visualc/vccore/_core_the_search_path_used_by_ windows_to_locate_a_dll.htm*

[COM-95] *The Component Object Model Specification*, Microsoft Corporation and Digital Equipment Corporation, 1995. *http://msdn.microsoft.com/library/specs/ S1D137.HTM*

Designing Interfaces

In the previous chapter we observed that in order to write a reusable component we need to separate the interface from details of implementation. We also learned that the first step in developing a COM component is defining the interfaces the component intends to expose.

The interfaces in the previous chapter were defined as C++ classes. This lets the vendor pick a C++ compiler of its choice and lets the client pick a vendor of its choice. However, in defining the architecture for COM, the COM committee had goals beyond C++ compiler independence and vendor independence. C++ language was not adequate to define an interface that would meet many of the goals. Therefore, COM specifies a language to define interfaces. This language is called the *Interface Definition Language* (IDL).

In this chapter we examine several goals that the COM committee wanted to achieve and their impact on the design of IDL. We then examine various keywords and data types defined in the language and show their usage from a programming perspective. The primary goal of this chapter is to make the developers feel comfortable defining fairly complex interfaces in IDL. A secondary goal is to help the developers write correct code in using the interfaces.

WHY A NEW LANGUAGE?

In the previous chapter we learned that separating interfaces from implementation provided a level of indirection that a) allowed the vendor to change the implementation class without requiring the client to recompile, and b) allowed the vendor to select a C++ compiler of his choice.

Given that most components are written and will continue to be written in C++, at first thought it doesn't make sense to use a new language for defining interfaces. Why must one go through the pain of mastering yet another language?

The reason is the inadequacy of C++ language for some of the goals that COM wanted to achieve. Let's examine these goals in detail and see why some of these goals cannot be achieved if C++ is used as a language for defining interfaces.

Programming Language Independence

Although C++ is an extremely useful programming language, there are other programming languages that are better suited to the task at hand. It doesn't make sense to restrict the developers to just C++. After all, we took extra steps to ensure that the client and the component do not know each other's implementation details. It seems logical that both of them should be able to use a programming language of their choice.

Logical indeed! The question, then, is: How can you define an interface that any programming language can understand? If interfaces are defined in C++, we are forcing the clients to work in C++.

One could possibly provide a tool to translate the C++ interface definition into every possible programming language. As the binary signature of the C++ interface definition is just a simple `vptr/vtbl` (see Chapter one), one could conceivably do the translation for a large class of languages.

A major problem with this technique is that C (and C++ as an extension) is fraught with ambiguities. Consider, for example, the following C declaration:

```
long* plValue;
```

Under C, this could refer to either a pointer to a single `long`, or the beginning of an array of `longs`.

Such an ambiguity, though very delightful to hardcore C developers, cannot be left unresolved if the declaration has to be mapped to other languages.

There is yet another ambiguity. The above declaration, when used as a method parameter, does not indicate if a value is being passed as input, or if the value is to be filled as output, or both.

Such ambiguities make it less ideal for mapping C++-style interface definitions to other languages.

Remote Transparency

Besides gaining programming language independence, it would be nice to facilitate the communication between client and servers, even when they do not share the same process space. At the same time, we should not overburden the software developers with the details of data handling between the two processes. Both the processes can run either on the same machine or, as a natural extension, on two different machines on the network. In order to achieve such interprocess or location *transparency*, one may have to provide extra information to COM infrastructure. An interface defined in C++ is not adequate enough to provide this additional information.

Given these goals for COM, the C++ language is not a good choice for defining interfaces. We need a different language, a language that does not have the inadequacies of C++.

INTERFACE DEFINITION LANGUAGE (IDL)

Based on the understanding from the previous section, we can refine our requirements for the new language as follows:

- to make C/C++ developers feel right at home
- to provide extra information to resolve any C language ambiguities
- to provide extra information that is needed to handle remote transparency

Note that the only reason we wish to use a new language is to *define* an interface. For this, we do not really need a *programming* language—we need a *declarative* language. To achieve this, COM looked to Open Software Foundation Distributed Computing Environment Remote Procedure Call (OSF DCE RPC) IDL. COM IDL simply added a few COM-specific extensions to DCE IDL to support COM-compatible data types and the object-oriented nature of COM such as inheritance, polymorphism, etc.

IDL inherited its syntax from the C/C++ languages. An IDL file primarily contains interface definitions using C++ syntax. In fact, the language supports basic C/C++ data types, `structures`, `enumerators`, and even `typedefs`, thus making it familiar to the large number of C, C++, and Java developers.

IDL Attributes

The "extra" information that could not directly be derived from C++-style definition, was provided by annotating it to the interface definition. These annotations are referred to as *attributes*. Attributes are applied to interfaces, each method in the interface, each method parameter, structure definitions, enumeration definitions, and many other definitions. Attributes precede a definition and are placed within brackets. More than one attribute is separated by commas. Again, this style of attribute specification was picked up from DCE IDL. The following example shows our C++ class definition of IVideo (from Chapter 1) transformed into IDL interface definition. For comparison, I have shown the original C++ class definition as well.

```
// C++ style definition

// IVideo interface
class IVideo : public IGeneral
{
public:
  // Obtain the signal value
  virtual VRESULT _stdcall GetSignalValue(long* pRetVal) = 0;
};

// Corresponding IDL style definition
[
  object,
  uuid(318B4AD0-06A7-11d3-9B58-0080C8E11F14),
  helpstring("IVideo Interface"),
  pointer_default(unique)
]
interface IVideo : IUnknown
{
  [helpstring("Obtain the signal value")]
  HRESULT GetSignalValue([out, retval] long* plRetVal);
};
```

Under IDL, an interface is defined using the keyword interface. An interface defined this way uses our familiar vtbl-based mechanism for invoking methods.

Just as a C++ class name is typically prefixed with a C, the convention that the COM programming community has adopted is to prefix the interface name with an I.

In the above example, note that:

- the interface definition `IVideo` has been annotated with attributes such as `object`, `uuid`, etc.
- the method definition `GetSignalValue` has been annotated with `helpstring` attribute
- the method parameter `plRetVal` has been annotated with attributes `out` and `retval`

How do these attributes help us solve our problems? Let's examine various issues that the COM task force considered when defining the language, and see how these attributes can come in handy for facilitating some of these goals.

IDL DESIGN GOALS

While developing the COM infrastructure, the COM committee had many goals. Some of these goals had a direct impact on the design of IDL.

Let's take a look at how these goals were addressed in the IDL.

Remote Transparency

One of the main goals of COM was to provide communication between the client and the server even when they were running as two different processes, either on the same machine (locally) or on two different machines on the network (remotely). A process, in the simplest term, is an executing application. It consists of a private virtual address space, code, data, and other operating system resources, such as files, pipes, etc. Two processes do not share their address spaces.[1] In order for one process to pass data to another process, it requires writing low-level communication code involving complex data-handling mechanism. The complexity increases when the processes are running on separate machines on a network. The complexity increases further if the two machines are running disparate operating systems. For example, one OS may treat integers as big-endian (the most significant byte stored first) and the other as little-endian. In this case, the low-level communications code will have to handle transformations between the two formats.

---

[1] Though there are ways to share a portion of memory between two processes, it is not relevant to this discussion.

While this complexity could be interesting architecturally, few developers want to program low-level communications code. COM alleviated this pain from the software developers. The developers can focus on writing the code instead of worrying whether the client and the server are in the same process (termed *in-process*) or in two different processes (termed *out-of-process*). The COM infrastructure took care of handling communication details in the most efficient manner.

Method Remoting

With a standard programming model, when the caller invokes a method, the caller and the callee are typically in the same process space. In this case, the parameters to the method are placed on the stack. The callee reads the parameters from the stack and writes a return value back to the stack before returning.

Under COM, however, the callee (the server) could be running in a different process space than the caller (the client), either on the same machine or on a remote machine. A valid memory location in the client's address space may not have any meaning in the server's address space. Therefore, the client and the server cannot just communicate directly using the stack.

The communication problem could be solved if some piece of the client code could a) read all the parameters from the stack, and b) write them to a flat memory buffer so they can be transmitted to the server. On the server side, some piece of the server would need to a) read this flattened parameter data, b) recreate the stack in the server address space such that it is a replication of the original stack set by the caller, c) invoke the actual call on the server side, d) pack the return values, and e) send it back to the client.

The process of serializing parameters from the stack into a flat memory buffer is called *marshaling*. The process of reading the flattened parameter data and recreating the stack is called *unmarshaling*.

Developers, however, would like to focus on using interface pointers, and would rather not deal with marshaling and unmarshaling. We need some mechanism that would make the marshaling process transparent to the developers. The solution offered by COM is to intercept every method call a client makes and transfer the control into the server's address space. For such *method remoting* to work, when the client requests an interface pointer, handing over the real interface pointer would not work. A logical choice that COM made was to provide a *proxy* interface pointer to the client. This proxy pointer supports all the methods of the *real* interface, except now it gives COM the ability to intercept every method call on the interface and marshal the data.

Note that the code implementing the proxy interface has to be *in-process* with the client. Otherwise, you will need a proxy to a proxy, and so on.

On the server side, COM provides a similar mechanism to unmarshal the data and pass the control to the actual server method. The code that does this is referred to as the *stub*. Just like the proxy, the stub has to be in-process with the server implementation.

Marshaling is a nontrivial task, as parameters can be arbitrarily complex—they can be pointers to arrays or pointers to structures. Structures can, in turn, contain arbitrary pointers and many other data structures. In order to successfully remote a method call with such complex parameters, the marshaling code has to traverse the entire pointer hierarchy of all parameters and retrieve all the data so that it can be reinstated in the server's address space. Clearly, writing marshaling code could easily defocus the developers from their main course of business.

Fortunately, COM provides a way to generate the marshaling logic based on the interface definition. Marshaling based on COM-generated logic is referred to as *standard* marshaling.

With standard marshaling, the method parameters are represented in a flat data buffer using a well-known data format called *network data representation* (NDR). The data format is specified by DCE RPC. It takes into account platform and architectural issues, and is very efficient in terms of performance.

By default, method remoting uses the COM Object RPC (ORPC) communication protocol.[2] The flow of method remoting is shown in Figure 2.1.

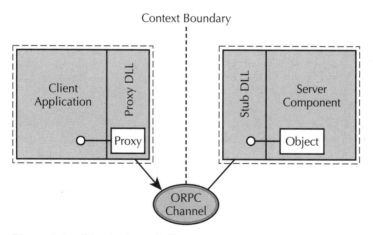

Figure 2.1   Standard marshaling.

---

[2] ORPC is layered over MS-RPC, a DCE derivative.

Figure 2.1 introduces a new term, *context*. As we will see in later chapters, marshaling is not just limited to process boundaries; marshaling is needed whenever an interface has to be *intercepted*. To clearly delineate when an interface needs interception, COM defined the term context. A context is a collection of objects that share run-time requirements. The run-time requirements that constitute a context will become clearer as we go through the next few chapters. Process boundary happens to be one such run-time requirement.

To generate the proxy/stub code that is needed for marshaling, each method parameter in an interface has to have at least one attribute that indicates if the parameter is being used for input, output, or both. This is done by attributes `[in]`, `[out]`, and `[in, out]`, respectively. The following example shows their use:

```
void Divide([in] long numerator, [in] long denominator,
    [out] long* quotient, [out] long* remainder);
```

The above function definition indicates that the function `Divide` takes two parameters as input, the *numerator* and the *denominator*, and fills two parameters, the *quotient* and the *remainder*, as return values to the caller.

Marshaling architecture is really outside the scope of this book. We will cover it on a need-to-know basis. Those interested can read Al Major's book, *COM IDL and Interface Design* [Maj-99]. For the current discussion, it is important to know that we may have to define many attributes, besides `[in]` and `[out]`, to assist the IDL compiler to generate efficient and, in some cases, necessary code.

Note that C++ does not provide any language constructs to specify the direction of method parameters.

Programming Language Independence

The software community always has a need to automate frequently-used functionalities of any application. Earlier versions of many commercial applications, such as Microsoft Excel and Microsoft Visual C++, had supported such automation by defining macro languages specific to each application. It was desired that a more general purpose, easy-to-use language be used for automation. The ease of use of BASIC language spawned many development environments such as Microsoft Visual Basic (VB) and Microsoft VBScript, a general purpose scripting language that is used by applications such as Microsoft Internet Explorer and Microsoft Windows Scripting Host (WSH). What was needed was an application that desires its functionality to be *automated* to somehow expose the functionality to other applications. This was a lofty goal, considering that the manipulator application could be based on a programming language different than the manipulatee application, and that the data types in one language need not necessarily map to a data type in another language.

COM addressed this cross-language issue and provided a way that makes it possible for one application to manipulate objects implemented in another application, irrespective of the programming language used, or to "expose" objects so they can be manipulated. This technology is referred to as *automation* (formally known as OLE automation).

An *automation client* is an application that can manipulate exposed objects belonging to another application. An automation client is also called an *automation controller*.

An *automation server*, sometimes referred to as an *automation component*, is an application that exposes programmable objects to other applications. The exposed objects are also called *automation objects*.

Based on COM support for automation, a slew of new technologies called Active (formerly called ActiveX) technologies were born. Some examples are Active documents, ActiveX controls, and ActiveX scripting.

Although, theoretically, it is possible to use a COM component in any programming language, the main languages of interest in the programming community have been Visual Basic (VB), Java, and ActiveX scripting languages such as VBScript and JScript.

Semantic Information

The binary form representation of the interface definition is sufficient to satisfy the development environment in terms of checking the syntax and producing appropriate machine language code to make a method call. However, quite often it is necessary to provide helpful hints to the developers on what the interface is about and when to use a specific method. Under C++ language, this is achieved by adding comments in the header file.

Though C++-style comments can be specified in an IDL file, IDL supports a formal attribute called helpstring that can be used to describe an interface, the methods in the interface, and many other constructs that we will cover later in this chapter. The following text fragment taken from a Microsoft-supplied IDL file for Web Event Browser ActiveX control shows the usage of the helpstring attribute:

```
[
    uuid(EAB22AC1-30C1-11CF-A7EB-0000C05BAE0B),
    helpstring("Web Browser interface"),
    . . .
]
interface IWebBrowser : IDispatch
{
    [
        id(100),
        helpstring("Navigates to the previous item in the history list."),
        helpcontext(0x0000)
    ]
    HRESULT GoBack();

    [
        id(101),
        helpstring("Navigates to the next item in the history list."),
        helpcontext(0x0000)
    ]
    HRESULT GoForward();

    [
        id(102),
        helpstring("Go home/start page.")
        helpcontext(0x0000)
    ]
    HRESULT GoHome();
    . . .
}
```

Note that IDL will honor C/C++-style comments. However, such comments get stripped out when the IDL compiler processes the IDL file, as we will see later.

Standardized Calling Conventions

In the previous chapter we discovered that in order to ensure a smooth interoperability between two C++ components, certain aspects of C++ language have to be treated uniformly. For your convenience, some of the important aspects are listed once again:

- Run-time representation of basic data types should be uniform
- Run-time representation of composite data type should be uniform
- Argument passing order should be uniform
- Argument passing convention should be uniform

- Stack-maintenance responsibility should be uniform
- Implementation of virtual functions should be uniform

These conditions hold true for the interface definitions as well. After all, an interface definition is nothing but a decorated C++ class. However, COM goes a step further. It specifies the precise standards to follow in defining and using the interfaces.

In view of COM's ability to interoperate between various architectures, platforms, and programming languages, some of these standards deserve special attention.

Return Value From a Function

Except in special circumstances, nearly every interface member method (and almost all COM API functions) returns a value of type HRESULT. HRESULT is a 32-bit integer. Its structure is shown in Figure 2.2.

The severity bit indicates the success or failure of the operation. The SDK header file defines the bit as SEVERITY_SUCCESS (value 0) and SEVERITY_ERROR (value 1). The SDK also defines two macros, SUCCEEDED and FAILED, to check the HRESULT for this bit. The following code shows their usage:

```
HRESULT hr = Some_COM_API();
If (SUCCEEDED(hr)) {
  DoSomething();
}
...
if (FAILED(hr)) {
  ReportFailure();
}
...
```

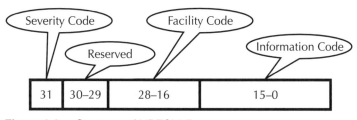

Figure 2.2   Structure of HRESULT.

There are many possible reasons for an interface method call or COM API calls to fail, even though the reasons are not evident sometimes. Therefore, always use SUCCEEDED or FAILED macros to check the return status of the interface method or COM API call.

As there are many possible success and error codes, the SDK follows a naming convention for different codes. Any code with an `E_` in it, either at the beginning or in the middle, implies that the function failed. Likewise, any name with an `S_` in it, either at the beginning or in the middle, implies the function succeeded. Some examples of error codes are `E_OUTOFMEMORY` and `CO_E_BAD_SERVER_NAME`. Some examples of success codes are `S_OK` and `CO_S_NOTALLINTERFACES`.

The reserved bits are reserved for the future and are not currently used.

The facility code indicates which COM technology the HRESULT corresponds to, and the information code describes the precise result within the facility. Table 2.1 shows some pre-defined facility codes.

TABLE 2.1   Facility Codes

Code	Facility
0x000	FACILITY_NULL
0x001	FACILITY_RPC
0x002	FACILITY_DISPATCH
0x003	FACILITY_STORAGE
0x004	FACILITY_ITF
0x005	Not defined
0x006	Not defined
0x007	FACILITY_WIN32
0x008	FACILITY_WINDOWS
0x009	FACILITY_SSPI
0x00A	FACILITY_CONTROL
0x00B	FACILITY_CERT
0x00C	FACILITY_INTERNET
0x00D	FACILITY_MEDIASERVER
0x00E	FACILITY_MSMQ
0x00F	FACILITY_SETUPAPI

Most facility codes have a self-explanatory name and are well documented in SDK. For our current discussion, `FACILITY_NULL` and `FACILITY_ITF` deserve special attention.

Any HRESULT that is universal and is not tied to a particular technology belongs to `FACILTY_NULL`. Table 2.2 shows some commonly seen HRESULTs from this facility.

TABLE 2.2   Some Common HRESULTs From `FACILITY_NULL`

HRESULT	Description
S_OK	Function succeeded
S_FALSE	Function succeeded but semantically returns a boolean FALSE
E_OUTOFMEMORY	Function failed to allocate enough memory
E_NOTIMPL	Function not implemented
E_INVALIDARG	One or more arguments are invalid
E_FAIL	Unspecified error

FACILITY_ITF is used to define interface-specific errors as well as user-defined errors. The SDK header files define interface-specific HRESULTs up to the information code value of `0x1FF`. However, a developer can use any information code value above `0x200` to compose a custom HRESULT. The SDK provides a macro called `MAKE_HRESULT` to accomplish this. Its usage is shown in the following code snippet:

```
const HRESULT MYDATA_E_QUERYERROR =
    MAKE_HRESULT(SEVERITY_ERROR, FACILITY_ITF, 0x200+1);
```

Note that the information code need only be unique within the context of a particular interface. Thus, one interface's custom HRESULTs may overlap with another.

Use `FACILITY_ITF` and `MAKE_HRESULT` to define your own HRESULT. Use a value above `0x200` for the information code.

Most valid HRESULTs have a text-based human readable description stored in the system message table. Win32 API `FormatMessage` can be used to obtain this description. The following code fragment shows how to obtain a description for a given HRESULT.

```
void DumpError(HRESULT hr)
{
  LPTSTR pszErrorDesc = NULL;

  DWORD dwCount = ::FormatMessage(
    FORMAT_MESSAGE_ALLOCATE_BUFFER |
      FORMAT_MESSAGE_FROM_SYSTEM,
    NULL,
    hr,
    MAKELANGID(LANG_NEUTRAL, SUBLANG_DEFAULT),
    reinterpret_cast<LPTSTR>(&pszErrorDesc),
    0,
    NULL);

  if (0 == dwCount) {
    cout << "Unknown HRESULT: " << hex << hr << endl;
    return;
  }

  cout << pszErrorDesc << endl;
  LocalFree(pszErrorDesc);
}
```

HRESULTs that use FACILITY_ITF and have the information code above 0x200 are user-defined HRESULTs and obiviously cannot be obtained from the system.

Visual C++ native support for COM defines a class, _com_error, that makes it easy to obtain the error description. Using this class function, DumpError, for example, can be redefined as follows:

```
void DumpError2(HRESULT hr)
{
  cout << _com_error(hr).ErrorMessage() << endl;
}
```

Visual C++ ships with a utility called ERRLOOK.EXE that can also be used to look up the description of an HRESULT.

To obtain the description for an HRESULT-type variable while debugging an application, specify `hr` as the display option in the watch window (as shown below) for a variable `hMyResult`.

```
hMyResult, hr
```

Stack Frame Setup

In order to produce a COM-compliant stack frame for any COM-related function call, the SDK defines a macro called STDMETHODCALLTYPE. Under Visual C++, this macro expands to _stdcall when targeting Win32 platforms. The implications of this compiler directive were explained in Chapter 1 (Table 1.1).

Almost all COM API functions and nearly every interface member method use this macro as their call type. The following code example shows its usage:

```
HRESULT STDAPICALLTYPE MyFictitousComFunction();
```

The SDK defines all the COM APIs as external C functions (keyword extern "C"). The SDK also defines a macro for extern "C" as EXTERN_C. In fact, EXTERN_C HRESULT STDAPICALLTYPE is so commonly used for COM functions that the SDK combines them under one macro—STDAPI.

```
#define STDAPI EXTERN_C HRESULT STDAPICALLTYPE
```

For Win32 compatibility, the SDK also defines another macro, WINOLEAPI, that maps to STDAPI.

```
#define WINOLEAPI STDAPI
```

The following is an example of a COM API called CoInitialize that uses WINOLEAPI.

```
WINOLEAPI CoInitialize(LPVOID pvReserved);
```

For COM functions whose return types are something other than HRESULT, the SDK defines another macro, STDAPI_(type), and its WINOLEAPI equivalent, WINOLEAPI_(type).

```
#define STDAPI_(type)      EXTERN_C type STDAPICALLTYPE
#define WINOLEAPI_(type)   STDAPI_(type)
```

As an example, the prototype for a frequently used COM API, `CoUnitialize`, is shown below:

```
WINOLEAPI_(void) CoUninitialize(void);
```

This basically expands to:

```
extern "C" void _stdcall CoUninitialize(void);
```

Interface methods are a little different than COM API functions in the sense that they are not EXTERN_C type and that they all need to be marked as virtual. To indicate a function as an interface method, the SDK defines a macro called STDMETHOD that takes the method name as the parameter, as shown in the following example:

```
STDMETHOD(MyXYZMethod)();
```

This statement expands to:

```
virtual HRESULT STDMETHODCALLTYPE MyXYZMethod();
```

Under Win32, this expands to:

```
virtual HRESULT _stdcall MyXYZMethod();
```

The declaration used in the implementation of this method is slightly different than that of the prototype, as C++ requires that the keyword virtual be dropped in the implementation.

```
// method implemented by a class CMyClass
HRESULT _stdcall CMyClass::MyXYZMethod()
{
    ...
}
```

For the developers' convenience, the SDK defines a macro called STDMETHODIMP that can be used in the implementation code, as shown below:

```
STDMETHODIMP CMyClass::MyXYZMethod()
{
    ...
}
```

What about defining those interface methods whose return types are something other than HRESULT? The SDK defines a variation of the STDMETHOD macro that takes the return type as an extra parameter:

```
#define STDMETHOD_(type, method) \
   virtual type STDMETHODCALLTYPE method
```

The following code shows its usage for an interface method, AddRef:

```
STDMETHOD_(ULONG, AddRef)();
```

Under Win32, this essentially expands to:

```
virtual ULONG _stdcall AddRef();
```

The developers can avail another macro, STDMETHODIMP_(type), for the implementation of the above method. The following code snippet illustrates its usage for implementing CMyClass::AddRef:

```
STDMETHODIMP_(ULONG) CMyClass::AddRef()
{
   ...
}
```

Table 2.3 summarizes the usage of these macros for declaring interface methods.

TABLE 2.3   Macros For Declaring Interface Methods

Return Type	Method Definition or Implementation	Usage
HRESULT	Definition	STDMETHOD
	Implementation	STDMETHODIMP
Other than HRESULT	Definition	STDMETHOD_(type)
	Implementation	STDMETHODIMP_(type)

Memory Management

Consider the following C++-based caller/callee scenario. The callee implements a method, GetList, that returns an array of numbers. The implementation allocates the appropriate amount of memory for this operation as shown below:

```
void CMyImpl::GetList(long** ppRetVal)
{
   *ppRetVal = new long[m_nSize];        // allocate memory as a long
                                         // array of size m_nSize
   // fill the array
   ...
   return;
}
```

Under this setup, when a caller invokes method GetList, it is the caller's responsibility to free the allocated memory.

```
long* aNumbers;
pImpl->GetList(&aNumbers);
// use aNumbers
...
delete [] aNumbers;        // deallocate memory allocated by the callee
```

The above technique of memory allocation (by the callee) and deallocation (by the caller) works fine under the standard programming model. However, this same technique under COM has a few problems:

- The semantics of new and delete are not standardized across various compilers and programming languages. Consequently, the results of memory deallocation in the client code are unpredictable.
- A more challenging problem arises when the client and the server are running as two different processes. Separate processes do not share their address space with each other. Consequently, the memory allocated using the operator new (or any of its variants such as malloc, LocalAlloc, etc.) does not get reflected in the client address space.

In order to make such memory allocation and deallocation work between the client and the server, there must be a standard mechanism accessible to both parties to deal with memory management, even across process/machine boundaries. This mechanism is COM's task memory allocation service. All the COM components are required to use this service whenever there is a need to exchange allocated memory between them.

The SDK provides two APIs, CoTaskMemAlloc and CoTaskMemFree, to allocate and free memory, respectively. The syntax for these functions is shown below:

```
// Prototype
WINOLEAPI_(LPVOID) CoTaskMemAlloc(ULONG cb);
WINOLEAPI_(VOID) CoTaskMemFree(void* pv);
```

Using these APIs, the previous code for caller/callee can be redefined as follows:

```
// Callee
void CMyImpl::GetList(long** ppRetVal)
{
   *ppRetVal = reinterpret_cast<long*>
      (CoTaskMemAlloc(nSize * sizeof(long)));
   // fill the array
   return;
}

// Caller
long* aNumbers;
pImpl->GetList(&aNumbers);
// use aNumbers
CoTaskMemFree(aNumbers);          // deallocate memory allocated by
                                  // the callee
```

APIs `CoTaskMemAlloc` and `CoTaskMemFree` go through the COM task memory allocator, a thread-safe implementation of memory allocator implemented by COM.

Identification

An interface class requires a human-readable name to identify it. This creates an interesting problem when two different interfaces (possibly from different vendors) share the same interface name. Consider the following scenario: two vendors decide to create a spell-checker component. Both vendors define their respective spell-checking interfaces. Both interface definitions will probably be similar in functionality, but in all likelihood the actual order of the method definitions and perhaps the method signatures will be somewhat different. However, both vendors will most likely use the same logical interface name, `ISpellCheck`.

If the client uses such a name-based mechanism to obtain an interface, it has the potential to accidentally connect to the wrong component, thereby obtaining the `vptr` to the wrong interface. This will inevitably result in an error or a crash, even though the component had no bugs and worked as designed.

Different vendors in different places develop components and interfaces at different times. There is no central authority that mediates issuing a unique interface name among all the vendors. Under such circumstances, how can one possibly guarantee a unique identification to each interface? COM's answer is GUID.

Globally Unique Identifiers (GUIDs)

A GUID (pronounced *goo-id*) is a 128-bit integer that is virtually guaranteed to be unique across space and time. This integer can be assigned to any element of COM that requires a unique identity. For each type of COM element, the GUID is referred to by a more appropriate term. Table 2.4 shows some elements of COM that require unique identification.

TABLE 2.4   COM Elements That Require GUIDs

Element	Referred to as
Interface	Interface ID (IID)
COM Class	Class ID (CLSID)
Category	Category ID (CATID)
Application	Application ID (APPID)
Data Format	Format ID (FMTID)

A GUID has the following data structure:

```
typedef struct _GUID {
   DWORD  Data1;
   WORD   Data2;
   WORD   Data3;
   BYTE   Data4[8];
} GUID;
```

All other forms of GUIDs are just a `typedef` representation of this structure, as shown below:

```
typedef GUID IID;
typedef GUID CLSID;
. . .
```

The SDK provides a macro called `DEFINE_GUID` to fill this structure with values. The following example defines the GUID for our interface, `Ivideo`:

```
DEFINE_GUID(IID_IVideo, 0x3e44bd0, 0xcdff, 0x11d2, 0xaf,
   0x6e, 0x0, 0x60, 0x8, 0x2, 0xfd, 0xbb);
```

This basically maps to:

```
extern "C" const GUID IID_IVideo =
   { 0x3e44bd0, 0xcdff, 0x11d2,
   { 0xaf, 0x6e, 0x0, 0x60, 0x8, 0x2, 0xfd, 0xbb } };
```

A GUID can also be represented as a string in a format dictated by the OSF DCE. The following example shows the string representation of our IVideo interface. Note that the curly braces and the hyphens are all part of the standard.

```
{03E44BD0-CDFF-11d2-AF6E-00600802FDBB}
```

The SDK provides an API called CoCreateGUID to generate a GUID. This API employs an algorithm that originated from OSF DCE. To guarantee uniqueness with a very high degree of certainty, the algorithm uses, among other things, the current date/time and globally unique network card identifier. If the network card is not present, the algorithm still synthesizes an identifier from a highly variable state of the machine.

Most development environments include an application called GUID-GEN.EXE that can be used to generate one or more GUIDs and paste them in the source code.

Compiled Type Information

Entering interface information in an ASCII file is very convenient. You can use your favorite text editor to edit the IDL file. However, developing code using an IDL file as a direct source is not practical. It requires that the IDL file be parsed. Unfortunately, parsing is subject to interpretation. Each language may interpret the information in a slightly different way, which may cause the client-server interaction to break down.

There is also a more fundamental issue. COM is supposed to be a binary standard for interoperatibility. The actual interface should really be defined in terms of binary memory layouts and method calls, and not as a text file.

It makes sense to provide the interface information in a binary form—a form that is free from any ambiguities or misinterpretations and one that is truly interoperable in the context of multiple architectures and OS platforms.

Under COM, such a binary form of the interface definition is called a *type library*. A type library is a binary file that contains tokenized interface information, obtained directly from the source IDL file, in an efficiently parsed form. It allows COM-aware environments to produce language mappings for the interfaces defined in the original IDL file. It is the equivalent of a C++ header file, but for all COM-aware environments.

Strictly speaking, a type library is not a true representation of a source IDL file. Some information is lost during translation. Perhaps the COM task force will define a better binary representation in the future. Currently, a type library is the only binary representation of a source IDL file.

Any interface information that needs to be saved into the type library needs to be defined in a section called `library` in the IDL file. As with interfaces, the library is uniquely identified by a GUID, though in this case, it is referred to as a Library ID or `LIBID`.

Component Identification

From the previous chapter we know that, under COM, clients deal only with interfaces. We also know that once a client has one interface pointer to an object, it could navigate through and get other appropriate interface pointers. Two questions arise:

1. How does the client uniquely identify a component in order to instantiate the object?
2. How does the client get the first interface pointer to the object?

The answer to the second question will be covered in chapter 3. Let's see how we can solve the first problem.

In order to help a COM client identify a component, an abstract term called *COM class* has been coined. A COM class, or `coclass`, is a named declaration that represents concrete instantiable type and the potential list of interfaces it exposes. Like interfaces, a COM class requires unique identification. Associating a GUID to the class does this, though in this case it is referred to as a Class ID, or `CLSID`.

PROCESSING IDL FILES

We have come to terms that interfaces will be defined in a language called IDL. The interface definitions and the associated information are saved in a text file, referred to as an IDL file. This file generally has an extension of *.idl*. The question now is: What can we do with the IDL file in terms of developing the program code?

Let's look at the issues we need to address:

- We need a mechanism to check the syntax of the newly defined interfaces.
- A vast majority of components are developed in C++ language. The C++ language compiler cannot interpret IDL text, at least for now. We need to translate the interfaces into C++ abstract base classes to help the C++ compiler understand the interface syntax.
- We need to generate the type library info, if need be.
- We need to extract the marshaling information from the interface definition and generate proxy/stub code.

The SDK provides an executable, called MIDL.EXE, to accomplish the above-mentioned tasks. This executable, referred to as the MIDL compiler, is the primary consumer of an IDL file.

Typically, MIDL is executed as follows:

```
Midl.exe -Oicf inputfile.idl
```

The optional flags for MIDL are documented in the SDK. Flag -Oicf causes MIDL to generate output that takes a considerably smaller memory footprint, resulting in better performance for Windows NT 4.0 and Windows 2000 OS.

Upon execution, the MIDL compiler will:

- perform a syntactic check on the input file, generating error messages and warnings, if necessary
- generate several output files. Figure 2.3 shows the generated output files for a sample IDL file, Video.idl

By default, the generated files, except for DllData.c, have names prefixed with the base filename of the IDL file. However, MIDL has command line switches to rename each type of output file.

Based on the functionality, the output files can be divided into three groups: C/C++ development files, type library files, and proxy-stub files.

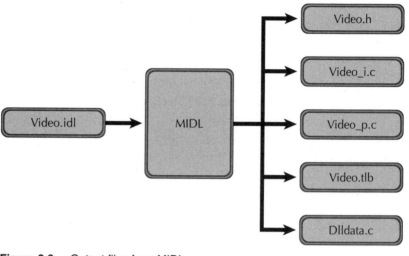

Figure 2.3   Output files from MIDL.

C/C++ Development Files

These files contain C/C++ equivalent declarations for the interfaces and other constructs defined in the IDL file:

Video.h: This header file contains C/C++ declarations for the interfaces and extended data types such as structures, enumerations, etc. Any GUID used in the IDL file (for interfaces, classes, libraries, etc.) is represented as an external variable in this header file. By convention, an interface ID is represented as IID_<InterfaceName>, a class ID is represented as CLSID_<ClassName>, and a library ID is represented as LIBID_<LibraryName>. For our video example, the defined variables look like:

```
EXTERN_C const IID IID_IVideo;
EXTERN_C const IID IID_ISVideo;
EXTERN_C const IID LIBID_VcrLib;
EXTERN_C const CLSID CLSID_VCR;
```

Video_i.c: Contains the actual values of the GUID variables that were declared as extern in the header file. When some piece of code refers to any GUID declared as EXTERN_C in the header file, the code has to be linked with Video_i.obj (the compiler generated object file for Video_i.c) to resolve the symbols.

Type Library Files

The type library file typically has an extension .tlb. For our video example, the output file is Video.tlb.

The type library file has many uses, including the following:

- VB can read the type library and make the interface information available within the development environment.
- With some restrictions that we will cover later, a type library can also be used for marshaling interfaces.
- Visual C++ compiler provides native support to read the type library and generate code to simplify accessing the defined interfaces.

 The Visual Basic development environment provides a tool called Object Browser that lets you view an object's type library information. Saving help strings in the type library ensures that such development environments get to display descriptive information about the interface and its methods.

Proxy-Stub Files

These files contain code for creating a proxy-stub DLL. A proxy-stub DLL is itself a COM server containing COM objects that implement the marshaling logic for the interfaces defined in the IDL file.

Video_p.c: Contains code to create proxy and stub, and to marshal/unmarshal the interfaces defined in file Video.idl.

Dlldata.c: Contains the DLL entry points required by a COM object server.

The proxy-stub code has to be compiled and linked to create the proxy-stub DLL. This DLL has to be registered on both the client and server machine.

IDL FILE STRUCTURE

Now that we know how to process an IDL file, let's see how we go about defining an IDL file.

Broadly speaking, an IDL file is split into three sections: a preprocessor section, an interface section, and the library section.

The Preprocessor Section

The first stage of MIDL processing is to run a C preprocessor on the input file. This means that the familiar C preprocessor directives such as #define, #include, and #if are also available under IDL. Following is an example of a define statement in C that is also a valid IDL statement:

```
#define BUFSIZE 512
```

As macros are *preprocessed*, they are not reproduced in the generated C++ header files. For cases where it is *desirable* for some text to make it through C preprocessing and into the generated C/C++ code, IDL offers a keyword, cpp_quote. The following IDL statement shows its usage:

```
cpp_quote("extern char* g_pszMyName;")
```

The above IDL statement results in generating the following C declaration in the output header file:

```
extern char* g_pszMyName;
```

In the preprocessing section, one can also use the #include directive. This causes the information from the specified file to be preprocessed. In the following IDL statement, definitions from the standard include file, stdio.h, are absorbed into the IDL compilation.

```
#include <stdio.h>
```

All legitimate declarations, including structures and function prototypes, make their way into the generated header file.

For referencing definitions from other IDL files, IDL offers a directive called import. The following IDL statement, for example, will reference the definitions from IDL file wtypes.idl:

```
import "wtypes.idl"
```

When the IDL file containing the statement above is compiled, MIDL will insert an include directive for wtypes.h in the generated header file as shown here:

```
#include "wtypes.h"
```

Note that, unlike the #include directive, the import directive ignores function prototypes.

The Interface Section

One or more interfaces, along with user-defined data types such as structures, enumerators, and even typedefs, can be defined in the interface section.

Note that the preprocessor section and the interface section need not be physically separate in the IDL file. One can mix preprocessor statements with interface declarations if desired.

The Type Library Section

The type library section is identified by the keyword library, as shown below:

```
[
   uuid(318B4AD3-06A7-11d3-9B58-0080C8E11F14),
   helpstring("VCR Type Library")
]
library VcrLib
{
   importlib("stdole32.tlb");
   importlib("stdole2.tlb");

   [
      uuid(318B4AD4-06A7-11d3-9B58-0080C8E11F14),
      helpstring("VCR Class")
   ]
   coclass VCR
   {
      [default] interface IVideo;
      interface ISVideo;
   };

};
```

The library section is a named entry (VcrLib in the above sample) and is uniquely identified by a GUID.

The library section primarily contains a preprocessor subsection, the interface subsection, and a COM class subsection.[3] The preprocessor and the interface subsections are similar to ones described earlier. *Anything that is defined outside the library scope could have been defined within the library*

---

[3] There is also a module subsection. However, it doesn't deserve any attention, as its usage is not relevant to COM programming.

scope, if desired. In fact, the whole IDL file could be one big library section. However, in this case, there will be just one output file—the type library.

The `library` section is what causes the type library to be generated. However, declaring the `library` section is optional. If an IDL file does not contain the `library` section, a type library will not be generated.

Any interface, structure, enumeration, or any such data type that is either defined or referenced within the library section will be saved in the generated type library.

There is one preprocessor directive, `importlib`, which can only be used within the library section. We will examine its usage when we deal with multiple IDL files.

IDL SYNTAX

It is time for us to start designing interfaces. The approach I have taken here is bottoms-up. We will first see how to define interface methods and related issues. Then we will take a look at building interfaces. Finally, we will focus on building the library section.

In order to explore various IDL concepts and issues, I have defined an interface, `IMyExplore`, for our reference. The server class that implements this interface will be referred to as `CMyExplore`. The sample project can be found on the accompanying CD.

Defining Interface Methods

Interface methods are defined within the scope of an interface. The following is an example of an interface defining a method, namely `GetRandomValue`.

```
interface IMyExplore : IUnknown
{
   [helpstring("Obtain a random value")]
   HRESULT GetRandomValue([out] long* pVal);
};
```

An interface method consists of:

1. A return value: Almost always, the return value is an HRESULT.
2. A name: Any valid C-style name can be used.
3. Parameters: A method can have zero or more parameters. Each parameter can have its own list of attributes.

In addition, each method can be optionally annotated with attributes. The most common attribute is helpstring, which is the equivalent of a C language comment.

The following code fragment shows the server-side implementation and the client-side usage of the method GetRandomValue:

```
// Server side implementation
STDMETHODIMP CMyExplore::GetRandomValue(long *pVal)
{
    *pVal = rand();

    return S_OK;
}

// Client side usage
long lVal;
HRESULT hr = pMyExplore->GetRandomValue(&lVal);
```

Directional Attributes

In order for the parameters to be marshaled, the marshaling logic needs to know the semantics of data transfer during the method invocation. The IDL specifies two attributes, [in] and [out], for this purpose. We have already seen them in passing.

- An [in] attribute specifies that the data has to be transferred from the client to the server.
- An [out] attribute specifies that the data has to be transferred from the server to the client.
- An [in, out] combination specifies that the data has to be transferred from the client to the server and back to the client.

IDL method signatures have C-style call-by-value semantics. Therefore, all parameters with the [out] attribute have to be pointers to the type actually returned.

The following example illustrates the use of these attributes:

```
// Interface method definition
HRESULT DirectionDemo(
    [in] long val1,
    [out] long* pVal2,
    [in, out] long* pVal3,
    [out] long* pVal4,
    [in] long val5);
```

```cpp
// Server implementation
STDMETHODIMP CMyExplore::DirectionDemo(long val1, long *pVal2,
  long *pVal3, long *pVal4, long val5)
{
  *pVal2 = val1 + 100;

  *pVal3 = *pVal3 + 200;

  *pVal4 = val5 + 300;

  return S_OK;
}

// Client implementation
void DirectionDemo(IMyExplore* pMyExplore)
{
  cout << "\n\nDirection demo test" << endl;

  long val1 = 1, val2 = 2, val3 = 3, val4 = 4, val5 = 5;
  cout << "Before: " << val1 << ", " << val2 << ", "
    << val3 << ", "
    << val4 << ", "
    << val5 << endl;
  HRESULT hr =   pMyExplore->DirectionDemo(val1, &val2, &val3,
    &val4, val5);
  if (FAILED(hr)) {
    DumpError(hr);
    return;
  }
  cout << "After: " << val1 << ", " << val2 << ", "
    << val3 << ", "
    << val4 << ", "
    << val5 << endl;
}

// Output
Direction demo test
Before: 1, 2, 3, 4, 5
After: 1, 101, 203, 305, 5
```

Besides indicating the direction, the directional attributes also indicate the ownership of the memory allocated. The basic rules of memory management are:

- For an [in] parameter, the memory is allocated and freed by the client.
- For an [out] parameter, the memory is allocated by the server and freed by the client.

- For an [in, out] parameter, the memory is allocated by the client, freed by the server, allocated once again by the server, and finally freed by the client. If possible, the two server-side operations can be combined as one "reallocation" action.

The memory allocations operations are primarily done using COM's memory management APIs that we discussed earlier. The marshaling mechanism uses these APIs when necessary.

Note that not all parameters require us to deal with memory management. Memory management rears its head when we start dealing with arrays and strings, as we will see later in the chapter.

Logical Return Value

Recall our example interface method that returned a random value as output. Let's look at the client code one more time.

```
long lVal;
HRESULT hr = pMyExplore->GetRandomValue(&lVal);
```

The method returns two values—a physical return value of type HRE-SULT, and a logical return value of type long. To indicate that a parameter is the logical return value of a method, IDL supports [retval] as a parameter attribute, as illustrated in the following IDL statement:

```
HRESULT GetRandomValue([out, retval] long* pVal);
```

In environments that support the notion of logical return value, [retval] attribute indicates that the parameter should be mapped as the result of the operation. For example, VB maps the above definition as:

```
Function GetRandomValue() as long
```

The support for native COM within Visual C++ also makes it possible to map the parameter as the result of the operation. Using the native COM support, the client code can simply be written as:

```
long lVal  = pMyExplore->GetRandomValue();
```

Needless to say, there can be only one logical return value for a method, and that the attribute [retval] can be applied only to an [out] type parameter.

Base Data Types

Like any other programming language, IDL has a set of base data types. Table 2.5 provides a description of each of the base data types and their equivalent C++ representation.

TABLE 2.5   IDL Base Data Types

IDL Data Type	Visual C++ Equivalent	Description
void	void	A method with no parameters or a method that does not return a result value
boolean	unsigned char	Indicates TRUE or FALSE
byte	unsigned char	An 8-bit data item
small	char	An 8-bit integer number
short	short	A 16-bit integer number
int	int	A 32-bit integer number on a 32-bit platform
long	long	A 32-bit integer
hyper	_int64	A 64-bit integer
float	float	A 32-bit floating point number
double	double	A 64-bit floating point number
char	unsigned char	An 8-bit data item. Undergoes ASCII-EBCDIC conversion on transmission
wchar_t	unsigned short	16-bit unicode character

A parameter can be specified with any of these base types, or a pointer to a base type. MIDL recognizes these data types as intrinsic and generates marshaling code without requiring extra attributes other than [in] and [out].

Note that unlike C, a pointer to the base type is considered to be a pointer to a single value and not to an array. In order to specify an array, additional parameter attributes are needed. We will cover this later in the chapter.

IDL also allows signed and unsigned versions of all integer data types and pointers to all integer data types.

The base data types have a fixed size and sign. This information is essential for the NDR data format to achieve platform and architectural independence. All base data types, except int, have a well-defined C/C++ translation. Data type `int`, however, is a special case. Its NDR data format is fixed, but its C/C++ translation is dependent on the architecture.

 If possible, avoid using `int` as a data type when designing interfaces. Instead, use short, long, or hyper, as appropriate.

The base data types can be used to define C-style structures and unions. These new data types are referred to as *extended* data types.

String Parameters

In the COM community, there are many definitions of string types. Visual C++ natively supports `char*` and `wchar_t*` string types. Win32 API provides `LPSTR`, `LPWSTR`, and `LPTSTR` string types. The COM SDK provides `OLECHAR*` and `OLESTR` types. IDL supports an extended data type called `BSTR` to deal with strings. Then there are C++ classes called `CComBSTR` and `_bstr_t` available from ATL and Visual C++ environment, respectively.

Let's clear up the confusion surrounding all these definitions.

A string is typically represented as a null-terminated array of `char` type. Win32 SDK defines a macro `LPSTR` to indicate this. For the English language, each character in the string can be represented by exactly one byte. However, there are other regional languages that may require a variable number of bytes (some languages require up to three bytes) to represent a character. Hence, a `char` type string (`LPSTR`) is often referred to as a multibyte string. In practice, the programming community prefers dealing with fixed byte strings. A good compromise was to define a character type that requires exactly two bytes for its representation. Such a character was termed a UNICODE character (also referred to as a wide character). A UNICODE character can deal with most regional languages. As a matter of fact, a UNICODE string can deal with multiple regional languages.

The Microsoft run-time library defines a standard data type called `wchar_t` to indicate a UNICODE character. The Win32 SDK defines a macro, `WCHAR`, to represent a UNICODE character and another macro, `LPWSTR`, to indicate a UNICODE string (which simply maps to data type `wchar_t*`).

To provide source code portability between UNICODE and non-UNICODE builds, the SDK provides two macros—`TCHAR` and `LPTSTR`. These macros map to `WCHAR` and `LPWSTR` under UNICODE builds, and `char` and

LPSTR under non-UNICODE builds. The Win32 SDK also provides macros to represent *constant* strings; these are LPCSTR, LPCWSTR, and LPCTSTR.

Now let's look at the string representation under COM.

Given that a string is an array of characters, it is tempting to assume that a string would get represented as a pointer to char, as in the following example:

```
HRESULT StringParam([in] char* pszString);
```

Not quite. Under IDL semantics, a pointer is assumed to point to a single instance, not to an array of characters. The above IDL statement would result in marshaling only the first character of the string.

To indicate that a parameter is a null-terminated array of characters, IDL introduces an attribute called [string]. Following is an example:

```
HRESULT StringParam([in, string] char* pszString)
```

While a pointer to a char data type can be used as a parameter, the programming community prefers using UNICODE strings. As wchar_t is not defined on many platforms, the COM SDK defined a data type called OLECHAR to represent UNICODE characters. Under Win32 platform, this simply maps to data type wchar_t, as you would expect.

Using OLECHAR as a data type, we can modify our example as:

```
HRESULT StringParam([in, string] OLECHAR* pwszString)
```

The above IDL statement implies that parameter pwszString is a null-terminated UNICODE string.

The following code snippet shows the implementation for the String-Param interface method:

```
STDMETHODIMP CMyExplore::StringParam(OLECHAR *pwszName)
{
  printf("String is %S\n", pwszName);
  return S_OK;
}
```

The following code illustrates its use on Win32 platform using Visual C++:

```
wchar_t* pwszName = L"Alexander, the Great";
HRESULT hr = pMyExplore->StringParam(pwszName);
```

Note that under Visual C++ a UNICODE string can be created using the "L" prefix, as shown above.

The SDK also provides a macro called OLESTR to help developers create a null-terminated UNICODE string. The pointer to such a string is represented by LPOLESTR. Using these two macros, the previous client code can be modified as:

```
LPOLESTR pwszName = OLESTR("Alexander, the Great");
hr = p->StringParam(pwszName);
```

Table 2.6 summarizes string data type definitions under various groups.

TABLE 2.6   String Data Type Definitions

Data Type	VC++ Native	Win32	Generic Win32	COM
Character	char	CHAR	TCHAR	
	wchar_t	WCHAR		OLECHAR
String Representation	"Hello World"	"Hello World"	_T("Hello World")	
	L"Hello World"	L"Hello World"		OLESTR ("Hello World")
String Pointer	char*	LPSTR	LPTSTR	
	wchar_t*	LPWSTR		LPOLESTR
Constant	const char*	LPCSTR	LPCTSTR	
	const wchar_t*	LPCWSTR		LPCOLESTR

There is yet another string type called BSTR that is frequently used as a method parameter. We will cover this string type when we discuss automation.

There is often a need to convert multibyte strings to UNICODE strings and vice-versa. The Win32 SDK provides two APIs, MultiByteToWideChar and WideCharToMultiByte, to achieve this. In reality, however, developers most often end up converting UNICODE strings to portable multibyte type (LPTSTR) and vice-versa. Under non-UNICODE builds, this conversion should call one of the two above-mentioned APIs as appropriate. Under UNICODE builds, however, there is no real need for conversion.

To simplify coding, ATL provides two macros, W2T and T2W, that can be used for string conversions. The following example illustrates the use of one of these APIs:

```
void OutputString(const WCHAR* pwszString)
{
   USES_CONVERSION;        // Should be declared before calling any
                           // ATL conversion macros
   LPTSTR pszString = W2T(pwszString);
   printf("%s\n", pszString);
}
```

As the conversion requires some memory to be allocated to hold the return value, the above-mentioned macros, and many of their variants, internally use a standard run-time routine called _alloca. This routine allocates memory on stack. The cleanup occurs when the calling function returns.

Note that there are two potential problems when using ATL-provided conversion macros.

First, if the macro is used in a C++ exception handling code, as shown below, the current implementation of Visual C++ compiler causes a memory corruption.

```
try {
   ...
}catch(CMyException& e) {
   USES_CONVERSION;
   LPTSTR pszError = W2T(e.GetErrorString());
   DisplayError(pszError);
}
```

Under Visual C++, within the catch block, do not use ATL-defined conversion macros or any other macro that uses _alloca.

The second problem is that ATL just assumes that the memory allocation via _alloca never fails; there is no validity check on the memory pointer returned from _alloca. When such a macro is used within some iteration logic, for example, and the iteration count happens to be a large value, there is a potential of crashing the program. The following code fragment illustrates this behavior:

```
for(int i = 0; i<nRecords; i++) {  // The number of records in the
                                   // database could be in millions
   CMyRecord* p = GetRecord(i);
   LPTSTR pszName = W2T(p->GetName());
   ...
}
```

The reason for the crash is that the memory allocated via _alloca gets freed when the function returns, not when the variable holding the memory location goes out of scope (a popular misconception). Within the for loop in the above code, the process runs out of memory at some point. In this case, _alloca returns NULL. However, ATL still goes ahead and uses the return value, resulting in a potential crash.

Do not use ATL conversion macros in a loop where the iteration count could potentially be very large.

Enumeration Data Type

IDL supports enumerated types with syntax identical to that of their C counterpart, as in the following example:

```
enum MYCOLOR {MYRED, MYGREEN, MYBLUE};
```

The enumeration can be used as a parameter to a method, as in the following example:

```
// Interface method definition
HRESULT GetEnum([out] enum MYCOLOR* pVal);

// Server code
STDMETHODIMP CMyExplore::GetEnum(enum MYCOLOR *pVal)
{
  *pVal = MYRED;
  return S_OK;
}

// Client code
enum MYCOLOR color;
HRESULT hr = pMyExplore->GetEnum(&color);
```

To simplify enum data type declaration, enum definitions can also be used along with C-style typedefs. In this case, we can drop the keyword enum from the interface method declaration, as shown below:

```
typedef enum { MYRED, MYBLUE, MYGREEN } MYCOLOR;

// Interface method definition
HRESULT GetEnum([out] MYCOLOR* pVal);
```

```
// Server code
STDMETHODIMP CMyExplore::GetEnum(MYCOLOR *pVal)
{
  *pVal = MYRED;
  return S_OK;
}
```

```
// Client code
MYCOLOR color;
HRESULT hr = pMyExplore->GetEnum(&color);
```

Note that an enum type variable can be assigned only one value from the possible list of values. It cannot be used to pass a combination of values, as in the following case:

```
// Server code
STDMETHODIMP CMyExplore::GetEnum(MYCOLOR *pVal)
{
  *pVal = MYRED | MYGREEN;
  return S_OK;
}
```

If the value to be returned does not exactly match one of the possible values, the marshaler fails to marshal the value.

If a method intends to pass a combination of enumerated values as a parameter, declare the parameter as a long type, instead of the enum type.

An enum can be uniquely identified by a GUID, if desired, as shown here:

```
typedef
[
  uuid(2B930581-0C8D-11D3-9B66-0080C8E11F14),
] enum {MYRED, MYGREEN, MYBLUE } MYCOLOR;
```

By default, the NDR format for enum is a 16-bit unsigned short. To speed up transmission on 32-bit architectures, it is desirable to have enum values transmitted as 32 bits. IDL defines a v1_enum attribute just for this case:

```
typedef
[
  v1_enum,
  uuid(2B930581-0C8D-11D3-9B66-0080C8E11F14),
] enum {MYRED, MYGREEN, MYBLUE } MYCOLOR;
```

The enumeration and each enumeration constant can have a "help-string" as shown here:

```
typedef
[
  v1_enum,
  uuid(2B930581-0C8D-11D3-9B66-0080C8E11F14),
  helpstring("This is my color enumeration")
] enum {
  [helpstring("This is my red")] MYRED,
  [helpstring("This is my green")] MYGREEN,
  [helpstring("This is my blue")] MYBLUE
}MYCOLOR;
```

The default value for an enumeration starts from zero. If desired, each enumeration item can be assigned an individual value, as shown here:

```
typedef
[
  v1_enum,
  uuid(2B930581-0C8D-11D3-9B66-0080C8E11F14),
  helpstring("This is my color enumeration")
] enum {
  [helpstring("This is my red")] MYRED  = 0x0001,
  [helpstring("This is my green")] MYGREEN = 0x0002,
  [helpstring("This is my blue")] MYBLUE = 0x0004
}MYCOLOR;
```

Structures

An IDL `struct` is almost identical to a C `struct` except for the following differences:

- Each field in an IDL `struct` can have one or more attributes.
- For `structs` that require marshaling, bit fields and function declarations are not permitted.

Following is an example of an IDL `struct`:

```
// Interface Definiton
typedef struct tagMYPOINT
{
  long lX;
  long lY;
}MYPOINT;
```

```
HRESULT StructDemo([out, retval] MYPOINT* pVal);

// Server side code
STDMETHODIMP CMyExplore::StructDemo(MYPOINT *pVal)
{
   pVal->lX = 10;
   pVal->lY = 20;

   return S_OK;
}

// Client side code
MYPOINT pt;
HRESULT hr = pMyExplore->StructDemo(&pt);
```

Like C, an IDL `struct` can contain fields with any valid data type.

Unions

IDL also supports C-style unions of data types. However, in order to be able to properly marshal the union, the marshaler has to know which union member is currently valid (in a union, only one member variable can be valid at a time). IDL solved this problem by associating an integer value with each union member, using a keyword, `case`, as shown below:

```
typedef union tagMYNUMBER {
   [case(1)] long l;
   [case(2)] float f;
}MYNUMBER;
```

When such a union is passed as a method parameter, it is necessary to pass another numeric parameter to indicate which union member is valid. A keyword, `switch_is`, is used for this purpose, as shown here:

```
HRESULT SimpleUnionIn([in] short type,
   [in, switch_is(type)] MYNUMBER num);
```

This numeric parameter is referred to as a *discriminator*.

The following code fragment illustrates the usage:

```
// Server code
STDMETHODIMP CMyExplore::SimpleUnionIn(short type, MYNUMBER num)
{
   long l;
   float f;

   switch(type) {
```

```
    case 1:
      l = num.l;
      break;
    case 2:
      f = num.f;
      break;
    }

    return S_OK;
}

// client side usage
MYNUMBER num;

num.f = 15.0;
pMyExplore->SimpleUnionIn(2, num);

num.l = 10;
pMyExplore->SimpleUnionIn(1, num);
```

It is too easy to make an error when hard-coded numeric values are used for a discriminator. Let's use our knowledge on enumerations and redefine our union:

```
typedef enum tagMYVALUETYPE {
  MYLONG = 1,
  MYFLOAT = 2
}MYVALUETYPE;

typedef union tagMYNUMBER {
  [case(MYLONG)] long l;
  [case(MYFLOAT)] float f;
}MYNUMBER;

// method definition

HRESULT SimpleUnionIn([in] MYVALUETYPE type,
  [in, switch_is(type)] MYNUMBER num);
```

Now, the server-side code as well as the client-side code can avail the enumerator.

Using enumeration for discriminators in union data type simplifies programming.

Encapsulated Unions

From the previous illustration, it is obvious that a union data type and the discriminator always go hand-in-hand as parameters. It seems sensible to bundle these two parameters as one structure, as follows:

```
typedef struct tagMYENUMBER {
  MYVALUETYPE type;

  [switch_is(type)] union {
    [case(MYLONG)] long l;
    [case(MYFLOAT)] float f;
  };
}MYENUMBER;

// Server side code
STDMETHODIMP CMyExplore::EncapsulatedUnionIn(MYENUMBER num)
{
  long l;
  float f;

  switch(num.type) {
  case MYLONG:
    l = num.l;
    break;
  case MYFLOAT:
    f = num.f;
    break;
  }

  return S_OK;
}

// Client side code
MYENUMBER num;

num.type = MYFLOAT;
num.f = 15.0;
pMyExplore->EncapsulatedUnionIn(num);

num.type = MYLONG;
num.l = 10;
pMyExplore->EncapsulatedUnionIn(num);
```

Such a bundled union is referred to as an *encapsulated* or *discriminated* union.

Arrays

Like C, IDL allows you to pass an array of elements as a parameter. Also like C, an array can be specified using array syntax or pointer syntax. However, unlike C, where a pointer can point to a single value or to the beginning of an array, IDL requires a pointer to be annotated with one or more attributes to indicate that it is an array. Such a pointer is referred to as a *sized* pointer.

 Without these special attributes, a pointer will always point to a single value under IDL.

Let's examine how these special attributes are used.

Fixed-Size Arrays.   When the size of the array is already known during the interface method design, the parameter can be specified using fixed-array syntax. Following is an example for sending array data from client to server:

```
// Interface method definition
HRESULT SimpleArrayDemoIn([in] long alVal[100]);

// Server side code
STDMETHODIMP CMyExplore::SimpleArrayDemoIn(long alVal[])
{
   long lLastVal = alVal[99];    // Get data from the last element
                                 // of the array
   return S_OK;
}

// Client side code
long alVal[100];
alVal[99] = 25;    // Set data for the last element of the array
pMyExplore->SimpleArrayDemoIn(alVal);
```

Fixed arrays are easy to use and are optimized for marshaling. The wire representation of the data is identical to the in-memory buffer presented to the server. As the entire content of the array is already in the received buffer, the stub logic is smart enough to use the received buffer memory location as the actual argument to the method. Otherwise, it would have to allocate new memory, copy the received buffer into the memory, pass a pointer to the new memory as the method argument, and free the memory after the method returns.

Variable-Size Arrays.   Fixed arrays are useful when the size of the array is constant and known at the interface design time. However, knowing the size of the array at design time is not always possible.

To allow the size of array to be specified at run time, IDL provides the `size_is` attribute. An array defined this way is known as a conformant array and its size (the number of elements) is called its *conformance*.

The following example shows three stylistic variations of specifying a conformant array:

```
HRESULT ConformantArrayIn([in] long lCount,
    [in, size_is(lCount)] long aVal[];
HRESULT ConformantArrayIn([in] long lCount,
    [in, size_is(lCount)] long aVal[*];
HRESULT ConformantArrayIn([in] long lCount,
    [in, size_is(lCount)] long* aVal;
```

All three styles are equivalent in terms of the underlying NDR format. Any of these methods allow the client to indicate the appropriate conformance and allow the server to use the conformance, as shown in the following code fragment:

```
// Server side code
STDMETHODIMP CMyExplore::ConformantArrayIn(long lCount,
  long alVal[])
{
    long lFirstVal = alVal[0];            // Get data from the first
                                          // element in the array
    long lLastVal = alVal[lCount - 1];    // Get data from the last
                                          // element in the array
    return S_OK;
}


// Client side code
long alVal[100];
alVal[0] = 50;          // Set data for the first element in the array
alVal[99] = 25;         // Set data for the last element in the array
pMyExplore-> ConformantArrayIn(100, alVal);
```

IDL also supports an attribute called `max_is`, a stylistic variation of the `size_is` attribute. While `size_is` indicates the number of elements an array can contain, `max_is` indicates the maximum legal index in an array (which is one less than the number of elements an array can contain). Using the `max_is` attribute, the previous example code could be rewritten as:

```
// interface definition
HRESULT ConformantArrayIn2([in] long lCount,
  [in, max_is(lCount)] long aVal[];
```

```
// Server side code
STDMETHODIMP CMyExplore::ConformantArrayIn(long lCount,
long alVal[])
{
  long lFirstVal = alVal[0];
  long lLastVal = alVal[lCount];        // Get data from the last
                                        // element in the array

  return S_OK;
}
```

```
// Client side code
long alVal[100];
alVal[0] = 50; // Set data for the first element in the array
alVal[99] = 25;  // Set data for the last element in the array
pMyExplore-> ConformantArrayIn2(99, alVal);
```

As with fixed arrays, conformant arrays are marshaling efficient. The received buffer for a conformant array can be passed directly to the method implementation as an argument.

The previous examples showed how to transfer data from a client to a server. A conformant array can also be used for obtaining values from the server. The client passes a potentially empty array to the server and has it filled with useful values, as illustrated in the following example:

```
// interface method
HRESULT ConformantArrayOut([in] long lCount,[out, size_is(lCount)]
  long alVal[]);
```

```
// Server side
STDMETHODIMP CMyExplore::ConformantArrayOut(long lCount, long alVal[])
{
  alVal[0] = 25;                    // Set data for the first element
                                    // in the array
  alVal[lCount-1] = 50;             // Set data for the last element
                                    // in the array

  return S_OK;
}
```

```
// Client side
long alVal[100];
pMyExplore->ConformantArrayOut(100, alVal);
// dump the first and the last element of the array
cout << alVal[0] << ", " << alVal[99] << endl;
```

Wire Efficient Arrays. In the previous example, the client expected the server method to fill in the entire array. But what if the server method cannot fill the entire array?

Consider this scenario: the principal of a school is trying to obtain the student grades as an array of long values:

```
HRESULT GetGrades1([in] long lSize,
    [out, size_is(lSize)] long alGrades[]);
```

Assuming there are no more than 25 students in the class, the principal calls the method as follows:

```
long alGrades[25];                      // A max of 25 students in the class
for(long i=0; i<25; i++){ alGrades[i] = 0;}   // initialize the array to 0
pMyExplore->GetGrades1(25, alGrades);              // make the call
for(i=0; i<25; i++) {cout << alGrades[i] << endl;}     // dump the grades
```

What if the class had less than 25 students? What if there were just five students in the class?

An easy way to solve this problem is to indicate the actual number of students in the class as an [out] value.

```
HRESULT GetGrades2([in] long lSize, [out] long* plActual,
    [out, size_is(lSize)] long alGrades[]);
```

The client code needs slight modifications to deal with the actual number of students:

```
long lActual = 0;
pMyExplore->GetGrades2(25, &lActual, alGrades);
for(i=0; i<lActual; i++) { cout << alGrades[i] << endl;
}
```

This solves the problem. However, we are still not wire efficient. The marshaler doesn't know that only the first five entries in the array have meaningful values. It will still transmit the contents of the entire array on return.

We need to indicate to the marshaler that only some elements of the array should be transmitted. This is accomplished by using the keyword length_is, as shown below:

```
HRESULT GetGrades3([in] long lSize,
    [out] long* plActual,
    [out, size_is(lSize), length_is(*plActual)] long alGrades[]);
```

The client code stays the same as before. However, the marshaler now has enough information to transfer only the required five elements and not the entire array. After receiving these five elements, the client-side proxy code initializes the rest of the elements in the array to zero.

IDL also supports a stylistic variant of length_is known as last_is. Just as size_is and max_is are related, length_is and last_is can be related as follows:

```
length_is(nCount) == last_is(nCount+1)
```

An array specified with the length_is (or last_is) attribute is known as a *varying* array. The value specified using length_is is known as the *variance* of the array. The variance indicates the contents of the array, as opposed to the conformance, which indicates the capacity of the array.

When both the conformance and the variance are used together, as in the above example, the array is known as an *open* array.

Changing Array Index.   The way we defined our GetGrade3 method, the marshaler assumes that the variance of the array is indexed at the first element. In our scenario, the valid grades were from alVal[0] to alVal[4]. What if the grades available at the server were not for the first five students but for the middle five students—alVal[10] to alVal[14]?

IDL solves this problem by defining an attribute, first_is, to indicate the index of the first valid element in a *varying* (or *open*) array. Using this attribute, the method can be redefined as:

```
HRESULT GetGrades4([in] long lSize,
    [out] long* plActual, [out] long* plFirst,
    [out, size_is(lSize), length_is(*plActual),
    first_is(*plFirst)] long alGrades[]);
```

Our client code then becomes:

```
long lActual = 0; long lFirst = 0;
pMyExplore->GetGrades4(25, &lActual, &lFirst, alGrades);
cout << "First is: " << lFirst << endl;
for(i=0; i<lActual; i++) { cout << alGrades[lFirst+i] << endl; }
                            // Dump grades starting from lFirst
```

Finally, consider an extreme scenario. The principal realized that too many students were failing the class. Out of generosity, the principal decided to give each student some extra points. It was decided that this value be passed as the last element of the array, alVal[24].

On the forward trip:

- The size (conformance) of the array is 25.
- The valid number of elements (variance) is 1.
- The index for the first valid element is 24.

On the return trip:

- The conformance of the array is 25.[4]
- The variance of the element is 5.
- The index of the first valid element is 10.

For maximum wire efficiency, the interface method can be defined as follows:

```
HRESULT GetGrades5([in] long lSize,
    [in, out] long* plActual, [in, out] long* plFirst,
    [in, out, size_is(lSize),
    length_is(*plActual), first_is(*plFirst)] long alGrades[]);
```

Developing the client and the server code for the above definition is left as an exercise for the reader.

Resizing an Array.   In all the earlier examples dealing with arrays, the actual size of the array (conformance) was specified by the client. In doing so, the client has to make an assumption about the maximum size of the array. For instance, in the grades example, the principal assumed that the maximum number of students in a class is 25. What if there are more than 25 students in a class?

One way to solve this problem is to define an additional method on the interface to obtain the number of students in the class. The client (the principal) calls this method first, allocates the appropriate amount of memory, and then calls the actual method to obtain the grades. However, this mechanism implies two round trips to the server, which could be expensive. Moreover, there is no guarantee that the number of students cannot change between the first and second method call.

---

[4] The conformance of the array is dictated by the client. The server cannot change it.

If you were a C programmer, your first thought would be to let the server method modify the size of the array. You would then redefine the interface method as follows:

```
HRESULT GetGrades6([out] long* plSize,
    [out, size_is(*plSize)] long alGrades[]);
```

The fact is that the size of the array gets fixed when it is first marshaled. Thus, the server cannot change the size of the array (though it can change the contents of the array). The above line will generate an error during MIDL compilation that the conformance of the array cannot be specified by an out-only value.

How can we then change the size of the array? It turns out that we cannot; well, at least not directly.

What we can do is create a completely new array at the server side and return it to the client. To do so, the method definition has to be changed such that the result is returned as an array.

```
HRESULT GetGrades6([out] long* plCount,
    [out, size_is(,*plCount)] long** palVal);
```

Pay special attention to the comma in the argument list to the size_is attribute. Attribute size_is accepts a variable number of comma-delimited arguments, one per level of indirection. If an argument is missing, the corresponding indirection is assumed to be a pointer to an instance and not an array. In our case, the definition suggests that argument palVal is a pointer to an array. The size of this array will be dictated by the server method.

With the above interface method definition, our server method implementation would be as follows:

```
STDMETHODIMP CMyExplore::GetGrades6(long *plCount, long **palVal)
{
  long lCount = 10;

  // allocate enough memory
  long* alVal = (long*) CoTaskMemAlloc(lCount * sizeof(long));
  for (int i=0;i<lCount; i++) {
    alVal[i] = i + 15;          // Set each value
  }
  *plCount = lCount;            // Set the count
  *palVal = alVal;              // Set the return array

  return S_OK;
}
```

The client code would then become:

```
long* palGrades;
long lCount = 0;
pMyExplore->GetGrades6(&lCount, &palGrades);
for(long i=0; i<lCount; i++)
   { cout << palGrades[i] << endl; }  // dump grades
CoTaskMemFree(palGrades);             // free server-allocated memory
```

Thus, by using an extra pointer indirection, the client no longer has to assume the size of the array.

Pointers

An IDL pointer points to a memory location, just like C. Following are a few examples of pointers:

```
[in]  long*  plVal;    // passing a long value as a pointer

[out] long** pplVal;   // obtaining one element of long* type

[out] BSTR*  pbsVal;   // obtaining one element of BSTR type
```

Unlike C, where a pointer can point to a single value or to the beginning of an array, a pointer under IDL points to a single value unless it is specially attributed to indicate that it is an array. In the above examples, plVal is a pointer to a single long, pplVal is a pointer to a single long*, and pbsVal is a pointer to BSTR.

Recall that in a COM application, the caller and the callee could be running under two separate processes. The same memory location in two processes may contain entirely different pieces of data. Thus, if a pointer is passed as a method parameter from one process, it may point to a memory location with invalid data. Even worse, a valid memory location under one process may point to an inaccessible memory in another process, resulting in an access violation.

COM's solution to this problem is simple. From one process, instead of transmitting the pointer value, transmit the entire contents the pointer is pointing to. In the other process, take this data and recreate the memory just the way the first process was *seeing* it.

When a pointer is used as a method parameter, the marshaler will ensure that the data the pointer points to gets transmitted, no matter how complex is the data structure the pointer is pointing to. Furthermore, if the data structure itself contains a pointer as a member variable, the data pointed by this pointer is transmitted as well. The marshaler goes through the whole data structure recursively and dereferences every non-NULL pointer encountered until there are no more non-NULL pointers to dereference.

This mechanism introduces a new set of problems. Let's examine these problems and see how we can solve them.

For our analysis, we will consider the simple case where the client and the server are running as two separate processes. A more general case would be where the client and the server are in two different contexts (contexts are covered in Chapter 5).

Consider the following simple IDL method definition:

```
HRESULT SetValue([in] long* pValue);
```

If the client were to invoke the method as follows:

```
long lVal = 100;
p->SetValue(&lVal);
```

The proxy code has to ensure that the value 100 gets transmitted to the server, which requires dereferencing the pointer.

What if the client were to invoke the method as follows?

```
p->SetValue(0);
```

If the proxy were to dereference the passed pointer, it would result in an access violation.

The proxy (and the stub) could be smart enough to check for NULL before dereferencing a pointer. But then, should we always force the proxy and the stub to check each and every pointer for NULL? Moreover, what if NULL is indeed a legal value for some cases?

Obviously, there are some cases where a pointer should never be NULL, and other cases where a pointer is allowed to have a NULL value. The interface designer would know of such cases when designing the interface.

To indicate that a pointer must never be NULL, IDL supports the [ref] attribute. Our SetValue method can be redefined as:

```
HRESULT SetValue([in, ref] long* pValue);
```

If the caller now makes the mistake of passing NULL as a parameter, the proxy code will return the error code RPC_X_NULL_REF_POINTER (0x800706f4).[5]

---

[5] MIDL-generated proxy and stub code assume the pointer to be non-NULL if a [ref] attribute is specified. They blindly dereference the pointer, causing an access violation. As the generated proxy/stub code always executes under an exception handler, it traps the access violation and translates it into the error code.

To indicate that a pointer can have a NULL value, IDL supports the [unique] attribute. When this attribute is specified to a pointer, the proxy code does additional checking to see if the passed parameter is NULL. It also inserts a tag in the ORPC packet indicating whether or not a NULL pointer was passed. The stub code examines this tag and, if the tag indicates that a NULL pointer was passed, reconstructs a NULL pointer.

Pointer Defaults.   IDL assumes certain defaults for pointer parameters. To do this, it classifies pointers into two types. The named parameter to a method that is a pointer is referred to as a *top-level* pointer. Any subordinate pointer that is implied by dereferencing a top-level pointer is referred to as an *embedded* pointer.

Consider the following IDL method definition:

```
typedef struct tagMYSTRUCT {
  long lVal1;
  long* plVal2;
}MYSTRUCT;
HRESULT MyMethod([in] long* plVal3,
   [in, out] long** pplVal4, [out] MYSTRUCT* pVal5);
```

In this definition, plVal3 and pVal5 are top-level pointers whereas *pplVal4 and pVal5->plVal2 are embedded pointers.

IDL uses the following logic for any pointer that is not explicitly attributed:

- A top-level pointer is always assumed to be a *ref* pointer.
- A top-level *out*-only pointer *has to be* a *ref* pointer. This is because IDL follows the call-by-value semantics of C: in order for a parameter to be an output parameter, it must have a memory address to hold the output value.
- All embedded pointers are treated as *unique* by default. However, it is good practice to explicitly specify the attributes for embedded pointers. In fact, IDL supports an interface attribute, pointer_default, to specify the default pointer attribute for all embedded pointers.

A Link-List Example.   Let's consider the case of passing a link-list of long values as a method parameter.

The data structure for our link-list is shown below:

```
typedef struct tagMYLONGLIST {
  long lVal;
  struct tagMYLONGLIST* pNext;
}MYLONGLIST;
```

Our link-list consists of a set of elements of type MYLONGLIST. Each element is linked to the next element by the member variable pNext. The last element in the list points to NULL.

In order to enforce that NULL is a legal value for pNext, we need to apply the unique attribute to this member variable.[6]

```
typedef struct tagMYLONGLIST {
  long lVal;
  [unique] struct tagMYLONGLIST* pNext;
}MYLONGLIST;
```

The interface method can be defined as:

```
HRESULT MyLinkList([in] MYLONGLIST* pList);
```

By IDL rules, this definition defaults to:

```
HRESULT MyLinkList([in, ref] MYLONGLIST* pList);
```

To indicate that NULL is a legal value for the parameter itself, we can modify our definition to:

```
HRESULT MyLinkList([in, unique] MYLONGLIST* pList);
```

Following is our server-side and client-side code snippets:

```
// Server-side
STDMETHODIMP CMyExplore::MyLinkList(MYLONGLIST *pList)
{
  long l;
  while(NULL != pList) {
    l = pList->lVal;
    pList = pList->pNext;
  }

  return S_OK;
}

// Client-side
MYLONGLIST lastItem;
lastItem.lVal = 100;
lastItem.pNext = NULL;
```

---

[6] Actually, for our example, the member variable is an embedded pointer and is therefore unique by default. Moreover, for a recursive data-type definition such as this, IDL will not accept the ref attribute, even if you try to force it to be one.

```
MYLONGLIST firstItem;
firstItem.lVal = 200;
firstItem.pNext = &lastItem;

HRESULT hr = pMyExplore->MyLinkList(&firstItem);
```

This will result in transferring the entire link-list as a method parameter.

What if I convert this link-list into a circular list? The only difference between a link-list and a circular list is that the last element of the circular list has to point back to the first element.

Try setting the last item to point to the first item and observe what happens.

```
 . . .
firstItem.lVal = 200;
firstItem.pNext = &lastItem;

lastItem.pNext = &firstItem;
HRESULT hr = pMyExplore->MyLinkList(&firstItem);
```

What you would observe is that the server code was never invoked. If you try to dump the return status code `hr`, it will most likely contain an invalid HRESULT. What happened?

In an attempt to build the wire data, the proxy code recursively started dereferencing the next pointer. As there was no NULL pointer to indicate the termination, the proxy code blindly went into an infinite loop and ran out of stack space. It just so happens that the proxy code runs under a structured exception handler. This prevented the program from crashing. However, the method call failed to go through.

If the proxy code could somehow detect that the pointer it is currently trying to dereference has already been dereferenced, then it can stop further dereferencing. How can we do that?

Detecting Duplicate Pointers.   Consider the following interface method and its client-side code fragment:

```
// Interface method
HRESULT MyMethod([in] long* pl1, [in] long* pl2);

// Client code
long lVal = 10;
p->MyMethod(&lVal, &lVal);
```

In this example, we are passing the same pointer twice. What should the proxy code do in the presence of such duplicate pointers?

The first option would be to do nothing special. In this case, the proxy will treat pl1 and pl2 as two distinct pointers. Not only will the value 10 be transmitted twice, but also the server side will get two pointers pointing to two different locations. What if the semantics of the server method required an equivalence of pointers?

```
STDMETHODIMP CMyExplore::MyMethod(long* pl1, long* pl2)
{
    if (pl1 == pl2) {
        . . .
    }
}
```

In this case, the marshaler would break the semantic contract of the interface method.

To address this problem, IDL allows designers to indicate if the marshaling logic should check for duplicate pointers. Attribute ptr is used for this purpose:

```
HRESULT MyMethod([in, ptr] long* pl1, [in, ptr] long* pl2);
```

When this attribute is specified, the marshaler code will contain extra logic to detect if a pointer has already been used earlier or *aliased*. For all pointers that are aliased, the value is transmitted just once. The server-side stub code will recreate all the pointers. However, they all would point to the same location.

Pointers that use the ptr attribute are called *full pointers*.

Like unique pointers, a full pointer can have a NULL value.

Situations requiring full pointers are rare. However, the full pointer mechanism is useful for solving specific problems such as transmitting a circular list. The stack overflow problem in the previous example can be solved by using a full pointer as follows:

```
// Interface definition
typedef struct tagMYCIRCULARLIST {
    long lVal;
    [ptr] struct tagMYCIRCULARLIST* pNext;
}MYCIRCULARLIST;
HRESULT MyCircularList([in, ptr] MYCIRCULARLIST* pList);
```

```
// Server side code
STDMETHODIMP CMyExplore::MyCircularList(MYCIRCULARLIST *pList)
{
   if (NULL == pList) {
     return S_OK;
   }

   long l;
   MYCIRCULARLIST* pFirst = pList;
   do {
     l = pList->lVal;
     pList = pList->pNext;
   }while(pList != pFirst);
   return S_OK;
}

// Client side code
MYCIRCULARLIST lastItem;
lastItem.lVal = 100;
lastItem.pNext = NULL;

MYCIRCULARLIST firstItem;
firstItem.lVal = 200;
firstItem.pNext = &lastItem;

lastItem.pNext = &firstItem;

HRESULT hr = pMyExplore->MyCircularList(&firstItem);
```

In the above sample code, attribute ptr is used at two locations in the interface definition. Its use for the member variable definition pNext is obvious. Why is it used for the method parameter as well? This is left as an exercise for you (hint: remove the attribute from the method parameter and see what happens. The code is on the CD).

Attributes ref, unique, and ptr are all mutually exclusive, that is, not more than one such attribute can be specified for a pointer. Table 2.7 summarizes the differences between these attributes.

TABLE 2.7   Properties of IDL Pointer Types

Property	ref	unique	ptr
Can be Aliased?	No	No	Yes
Can be NULL?	No	Yes	Yes

Interface Pointers

In the previous section, we looked at marshaling data pointers. COM IDL has native support for marshaling interface pointers (if this could not be done, the whole essence of COM would make no sense).

To pass an interface IFoo as an input parameter, one simply declares it as an [in] parameter of type IFoo*.

```
Interface IBar : IUnknown
{
    HRESULT MyMethod([in] IFoo* pIFoo);
}
```

If the client and the server are in two different contexts, the above method loads the stub for IFoo in the client context, and the proxy for IFoo in the server context.

It may seem odd at first that the stub is getting loaded in the client context and the proxy is getting loaded in the server context, instead of the other way around. The point to remember is that the role of the proxy is to pack the parameter data on an interface method call (from the calling context) and the role of the stub is to unpack the data (in the called context). In our case, when the interface pointer is being handed over to the server, the assumption is that the server will be calling the methods on the interface pointer. In some sense, the server becomes the client and the client becomes the server.

More precisely, in our example case, the client holds the proxy for the IBar interface and the stub for the IFoo interface, and the server holds the stub for the IBar interface but the proxy for the IFoo interface.

An interface pointer passed as an input parameter is always of the unique type, that is, the pointer can have a NULL value, but it cannot be *aliased*.

To obtain an interface pointer to IFoo, one has to declare an out parameter of type IFoo**, as follows:
```
HRESULT MyMethod([out] IFoo** ppIFoo);
```

In this case, the proxy for IFoo gets created in the client code and the stub for IFoo gets created in the server code.

The second case is the most often use-case under COM (recall from the previous chapter that the client obtains an appropriate interface from the server).

Ambiguous Interfaces. Quite often an interface pointer is passed as a pointer to its base interface. Consider, for example, interface IBar derived from interface IFoo. The server returns a pointer to IBar as a pointer to IFoo. The following code illustrates the scenario:

```
//
// IDL definition
//
interface IBar : IFoo
{
  . . .
}
HRESULT MyMethod([out] IFoo** ppIFoo)

//
// Server implementation
//
class CBar : public IBar
{
  . . .
}

STDMETHODIMP CMyServer::MyMethod(IFoo** ppIFoo)
{
  CBar* pBar = CreateBar();
  *ppIFoo = pBar;
  . . .
}
```

When a client invokes MyMethod, the marshaler is not aware that it had to load the proxy/stub for IBar and not IFoo. If the client reinterprets the returned pointer to the IBar type (which it will) and tries to use any method from IBar, the program will behave unpredictably.

For such cases, to make the marshaler aware of the actual interface being passed, we need to provide the marshalar with the identifier of the actual interface. IDL provides the iid_is attribute to accomplish this:

```
HRESULT MyMethod([in] REFIID riid,
  [out, iid_is(riid)] IFoo** ppIFoo)
```

Here, the client is explicitly informing the marshaler that the return type of the interface is of type riid (IID_IBar in our case), allowing the marshaler to load the correct proxy/stub during run time.

Defining IDL Interfaces

A COM interface exposes a group of related functions, analogous to a C++ class definition. The following is an example of an interface definition, IFoo:

```
[
  object,
  uuid(5E7A5F3E-F4F4-11D2-9B37-0080C8E11F14),
  helpstring("This Interface can get and set color of
    the object"),
  pointer_default(unique)
]
interface IFoo : IUnknown
{
  typedef enum { MYRED, MYGREEN, MYBLUE} MYCOLOR;

  HRESULT SetColor([in] MYCOLOR val);
  HRESULT GetColor([out] MYCOLOR* pVal);
};
```

The definition of the interface is marked by the IDL keyword `interface`. This keyword is followed by the logical name of the interface, `IFoo` in our example.

Every COM interface, except interface `IUnknown`, is derived from another interface. Interface `IUnknown` is a special interface and is discussed separately.

Note that IDL doesn't support multiple inheritance; that is, an interface cannot be derived from more than one interface. From our previous chapter, we know why this restriction was placed on the interface definition. However, this has not been a big concern in the COM community. As we will see later, this restriction is only on the interface definition and not on the implementation of the interface, thus providing developers an opportunity to use multiple inheritance. Of course, the programming language being used should support the feature.

The interface body is simply a collection of method definitions and supporting type definition statements. Unlike the C++ class definition that supports the notion of `public` and `private` methods, any method defined in the interface is always a `public` method. (If you really wanted to make a method `private`, why would you put in an interface that, by its definition, gets exposed to the public?)

Interface Attributes

A COM interface can be annotated using the typical IDL attribute syntax; attributes are defined within square brackets and each attribute is separated by a comma.

Every COM interface requires at least two IDL attributes: `object` and `uuid`.

COM-Style Interface.   The first requisite attribute is an `object`. It specifies that the interface is a COM interface. If this attribute is not specified, the interface is assumed to be a DCE RPC interface.

 Never forget to specify the `"object"` attribute when defining a COM interface.

Identification.   The second requisite attribute is `uuid`, a GUID that uniquely identifies the interface. In the case of interfaces, this GUID is referred to as an interface ID or IID. The attribute specification is shown here:

```
uuid(5E7A5F3E-F4F4-11D2-9B37-0080C8E11F14),
```

When an MIDL compiler processes the interface, it gives a C-style symbolic name to the GUID, such as `IID_<interfacename>`. For the `IFoo` interface, the symbolic name is `IID_IFoo`.

Embedded Pointers.   If you recall from the previous section on pointers, each embedded pointer can be explicitly annotated as either `unique`, `ref`, or `ptr`. Instead of annotating each embedded pointer individually, IDL provides an interface-level attribute, `pointer_default`, to indicate the default behavior of any embedded pointer in the interface, as shown here:

```
pointer_default(unique)
```

Providing Helpful Hints.   Quite often it is necessary to provide helpful hints to the developers on what the interface is about and when to use a specific method. The keyword `helpstring` can be used as an interface attribute, as follows:

```
helpstring("This Interface can get and set color of the object"),
```

The Root Interface—`IUnknown`

The COM interface `IUnknown` serves the same purpose as the `IGeneral` interface defined in the previous chapter. If you recall, all interface `IGeneral` did was to maintain the reference count on the interface and to let the client obtain other, more meaningful interfaces from the object. The following is the final version of IGeneral that appeared at the end of the previous chapter:

```
class IGeneral
{
public:
    virtual VRESULT _stdcall Probe(char* pszType,
        IGeneral** ppRetVal) = 0;
    virtual void _stdcall AddReference() = 0;
    virtual void _stdcall Delete() = 0;
};
```

The following is the definition for interface IUnknown, taken from SDK IDL file unknwn.idl:

```
[
    local,
    object,
    uuid(00000000-0000-0000-C000-000000000046),
    pointer_default(unique)
]
interface IUnknown
{
    HRESULT QueryInterface(
        [in] REFIID riid,
        [out, iid_is(riid)] void **ppvObject);
    ULONG AddRef();
    ULONG Release();
}
```

At this point, all the attributes on the interface IUnknown, except the local attribute, should be reasonably clear. Attribute local informs MIDL not to generate any marshaling code for this interface and relaxes COM's requirement that every interface method should return an HRESULT.

Interface IUnknown is functionally equivalent to the class IGeneral defined in the previous chapter. The similarities follow:

- Method QueryInterface is analogous to the IGeneral::Probe method; it returns the requested interface.[7] If the requested interface is not found, the implementation of QueryInterface should return a E_NOINTERFACE error code.

---

[7] Why the interface pointer is returned as void* and not the more intuitive IUnknown* is for legacy reasons.

- Method AddRef is analogous to the IGeneral::AddReference method; it increments the reference count on the underlying object. It should be called for every new copy of a pointer to an interface.
- Method Release is analogous to the IGeneral::Delete method; it decrements the reference count on the underlying object. A reference count of zero indicates that the object is no longer used and that the server is free to release any resources associated with the object.

 The return value from AddRef is the value of the reference count after the increment. It is meant to be used only for diagnostic purposes, as the value is unstable under certain situations.

IUnknown is the root of all COM interfaces. Every other legal COM interface should derive either directly from this interface or from one other COM interface that itself is derived from IUnknown, either directly or indirectly. This means, at the binary level, any COM interface is a pointer to vtbl that has the first three entries as QueryInterface, AddRef, and Release.

The symbolic name of the interface ID for IUnkown is IID_Iunknown, defined as follows:

```
extern "C" const IID IID_IUnknown;
```

This IID, along with many other system-defined IIDs, is provided in the SDK library, uuid.lib. Any COM program, client or server, has to be linked with this library to resolve the COM-defined symbols.

Defining COM Classes

A COM class, or coclass, is a named declaration that represents concrete instantiable type and the potential list of interfaces it exposes. A coclass is typically declared within the scope of a library section. The following is an example of a coclass, MyFoo:

```
[
  uuid(5E7A5F40-F4F4-11D2-9B37-0080C8E11F14),
  helpstring("My Foo Class")
]
coclass MyFoo
{
  interface IFoo;
};
```

The definition of a `coclass` is marked by the IDL keyword `coclass`. This keyword is followed by the logical name of the COM class, `MyFoo` in the above example.

The body of a COM class is simply a list of interfaces the class can potentially expose. Each interface in the list is tagged by the keyword `interface` or `dispinterface`.[8]

 The `coclass` section exposes the *potential* list of interfaces, not the *actual* list. The number of interfaces actually implemented by the COM object could be less, more, or totally different than what is listed in the `coclass` section. This section identifies the interfaces a COM object could potentially support. The client code cannot rely on just this information; it has to go through the usual `QueryInterface` to get the interface(s) it needs.

Like interfaces, a COM class requires a unique identification. This is done by supplying a GUID argument to our all too familiar IDL keyword, `uuid`. When the MIDL compiler processes the `coclass`, it gives a C-style symbolic name to the GUID such as `CLSID_<coclassname>`. For `coclass` `MyFoo` in the previous example, the symbolic name would be `CLSID_MyFoo`.

Defining IDL Libraries

The library section is defined primarily to indicate to the MIDL compiler that a type library needs to be generated. Following is an example of the library definition:

```
[
  uuid(5E7A5F3F-F4F4-11D2-9B37-0080C8E11F14),
  version(1.0),
  helpstring("My Foo 1.0 Type Library")
]
library MyFooLib
{
  importlib("stdole32.tlb");
  importlib("stdole2.tlb");

  [
    uuid(5E7A5F40-F4F4-11D2-9B37-0080C8E11F14),
    helpstring("My Foo Class")
  ]
```

---

[8] `Dispinterfaces` are covered later in the chapter under automation.

```
coclass MyFoo
{
  [default] interface IFoo;
};
};
```

The definition of the library is marked by the IDL keyword `library`. This keyword is followed by the logical name of the library, `MyFooLib` in the above example.

The library body contains definitions and/or references to the interfaces and user-defined data types that need to be saved into the MIDL-generated type library. In addition, the library section can define zero or more `coclass` definitions.

Library Attributes

A COM library can specify attributes using the typical IDL attribute syntax; attributes are defined within square brackets, and each attribute is separated by a comma.

Identification.   As with interfaces, the library is uniquely identified by a GUID using the IDL keyword `uuid`, though in this case the GUID is referred to as a library ID or `LIBID`.   When the MIDL compiler processes the library section, it gives a C-style symbolic name to the GUID such as `LIBID_<libraryname>`. For the library `MyFooLib` in the previous example, the symbolic name would be `LIBID_MyFooLib`.

Version Management.   The generated type library has a major and minor version number. The designer can explicitly specify this version number using the attribute `version`. The major version and minor version are separated by a dot.

Removing Redundancy

As mentioned earlier, any interface definition and data type definition referenced within the scope of the library section will be saved in the type library, even if some of this data has already been saved in some other type library.

For instance, take another look at the library definition for `MyFooLib`. It references `IFoo`, which in turn references `IUnknown`. `IUnknown` references `IID` in its `QueryInterface` method and the IID is an alias for the structure GUID. Therefore, just referencing `IFoo` in the library section causes the definitions for `IUnknown`, as well as GUID, to be saved into the type library.

Definitions such as `IUnkown` and GUID are so commonly used in the IDL files, it doesn't make sense to have the same information being saved in every type library that ever gets created. A better solution would be to create a separate type library for such commonly used definitions.

As a matter of fact, SDK already includes a type library containing all COM system interfaces and data type definitions. The latest version of this type library is 2.0 and is defined in file `stdole2.tlb`. Another standard type library, `stdole32.tlb`, contains automation interfaces (automation is covered in the next section).

In order to exclude definitions that are already present in a different type library, IDL keyword `importlib` can be used. This keyword takes the type library name as an argument.

```
importlib("stdole2.tlb");
```

During IDL compilation, MIDL ensures that any definition found in the specified type library is not saved in the generated type library, thus reducing the type library size.

MIDL shipped with Visual C++ searches for the type library files using the PATH environmental variable (not the INCLUDE path, as you would expect if you were a C++ programmer). This problem has been fixed in the newer versions of Platform SDK (January 2000 or later).

AUTOMATION

One of the goals COM had was to let the component developers select the programming language of their choice. This was a very ambitious goal, given that each language has its own set of data types and that there is no safe mapping between data types from one language to another.

Let's examine these problems in detail and see the solution that COM had to offer.

Basic Data Types

The semantics of many data types are not the same under different languages. For example, data type `char` under Visual C++ has no equivalent match under VB. Data type `short` under Visual C++ is equivalent to data type `integer` under VB. Moreover, there is no uniform definition of data types to deal with date and currency.

COM's solution was to restrict the base data types that will work across all languages. The SDK provides an enumerated type called VARTYPE to precisely define the semantics of each of the automation compatible data types. Table 2.8 lists some important VARTYPEs, their precise IDL definition, and the comparable data type in C++ and VB.

TABLE 2.8   Some Basic Automation Data Types

VARTYPE	IDL Interpretation	Microsoft VC++	Microsoft VB
VT_I2	16-bit, signed	short	Integer
VT_I4	32-bit, signed	long	Long
VT_DATE	Date	DATE (double)	Date
VT_CY	Currency	CY (int64)	Currency
VT_R4	Single precision decimal	float	Single
VT_R8	Double precision decimal	double	Double
VT_UNKNOWN	Interface pointer	IUnknown*	Interface Ref.

Though unsigned data types appear to be automation-compatible (in the sense that MIDL will not complain), they are not supported across all languages.

Do not use unsigned data types if automation is your objective.

Strings

Previously, we saw that the C/C++ language provides adequate support to deal with strings of OLECHARs that are NULL terminated. However, there are other programming languages, such as VB and Java, that prefer length-prefixed OLECHAR strings. To satisfy all the programming communities, the SDK introduced an extended data type called BSTR.

BSTRs are length-prefixed as well as NULL-terminated strings of OLECHARs. The length prefix indicates the number of *bytes* the string consumes (not including the terminating NULL) and is stored as a four-byte integer that immediately precedes the first character of the string. Figure 2.4 shows the string "Hi" as a BSTR.

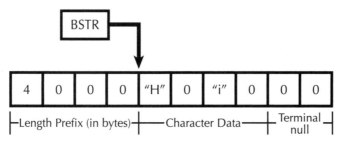

Figure 2.4   BSTR representation of "Hi." Adapted from [Box-98].

From Figure 2.4, it is obvious that one can treat a BSTR as an LPW-STR. However, you cannot treat an LPWSTR as a BSTR. The marshaler packs data using the value specified in the memory preceding the location pointed by the BSTR. If an LPWSTR is used as a BSTR, this memory location could be either an invalid address or would contain a bogus value. This may result in either an access violation (if you are lucky) or huge amounts of bogus data being transmitted.

Never use an LPWSTR as a BSTR (it's okay to use a BSTR as an LPWSTR).

To manage BSTRs, SDK provides several API functions. The SDK documentation describes the API usage in detail. Two important APIs that I will cover here deal with memory allocation issues.

Allocation of BSTR does not go through the COM task memory allocator directly in the sense that APIs such as CoTaskMemAlloc and CoTaskMemFree cannot be used. Instead, COM provides two other APIs, SysAllocString and SysFreeString, to deal with BSTRs. The following are their prototypes:

```
BSTR SysAllocString(const OLECHAR* sz);
void SysFreeString(BSTR bstr);
```

SysAllocString can be used to allocate and initialize a BSTR. Sys-FreeString can be used to free the memory previously allocated via a call to SysAllocString.

You may be wondering how the marshaler knows that BSTRs require special allocation APIs and not the standard task memory allocator APIs. The magic lies in IDL's support for defining wire representation of a data type, BSTR in our case. Al Major covers this topic in detail in [Maj-99].

When a BSTR is passed as an [in] parameter, it is the caller's responsibility to construct the parameter before invoking the method and to free the memory after returning from the method. The following example shows the version of the interface method StringParam revised to use BSTR:

```
// Interface method definition
HRESULT RevisedStringParam([in] BSTR bstrVal);
```

Using this interface method, the client-side code can be modified as:

```
// Client code
LPOLESTR pwszName = OLESTR("Alexander, The Great");

BSTR bstrName = ::SysAllocString(pwszName);
HRESULT hr = pMyExplore->RevisedStringParam(bstrName);
::SysFreeString(bstrName);
```

ATL simplifies using BSTRs by providing a class called CComBSTR. Using this class, the client-side code can be written as:

```
#include <atlbase.h>
...
CComBSTR bstrName = "Alexander, The Great";
HRESULT hr = pMyExplore->RevisedStringParam(bstrName);
```

Note that the client project need not be ATL-based. To use the class CComBSTR, all that is needed is the header file <atlbase.h>.

Similar to ATL, the native COM support under Visual C++ defines another class, _bstr_t, to deal with BSTRs. Following is our client-side code using this class:

```
#include <comdef.h>
...
_bstr_t bstrName = "Alexander, The Great";
HRESULT hr = pMyExplore->RevisedStringParam(bstrName);
```

When a BSTR is passed as an [out] parameter, it is the server's responsibility to allocate the string and the caller's responsibility to free it, as illustrated in the following code snippet:

```
// interface method definition
HRESULT GetString([out] BSTR* pVal);
```

```
                  // server side code
                  STDMETHODIMP CMyExplore::GetString(BSTR *pVal)
                  {
                    *pVal = ::SysAllocString(OLESTR("Alexander, The
                  Great"));
                    if (NULL == *pVal) {
                      return E_OUTOFMEMORY;
                    }

                    return S_OK;
                  }

                  // Client side code
                  BSTR bstrName = NULL;
                  HRESULT hr = pMyExplore->GetString(&bstrName);
                  if (SUCCEEDED(hr)) {
                    // use bstrName
                    ::SysFreeString(bstrName);
                  }
```

Failure to call `SysFreeString` will result in a memory leak. Once again, the ATL class `CComBSTR` can save us from making such a mistake. The destructor of `CComBSTR` automatically calls this API, if need be:

```
// Server side
STDMETHODIMP CMyExplore::GetString(BSTR *pVal)
{
  CComBSTR bstrName = "Alexander, The Great";
  if (NULL == static_cast<BSTR>(bstrName)) {
    return E_OUTOFMEMORY;
  }

  *pVal = bstrName.Detach();
  return S_OK;
}

// Client side
{
  CComBSTR bstrName;
  HRESULT hr = pMyExplore->GetString(&bstrName);
  if (SUCCEEDED(hr)) {
    // use bstrName
  }
} // bstrName gets freed automatically when leaving the scope
```

Unfortunately, class `_bstr_t` doesn't provide the functionality for an instance to be used as an `[out]` parameter.

Should you use CComBSTR or _bstr_t?

Both of them have some distinct advantages.

Class CComBSTR lets you use an instance for an [out] parameter; _bstr_t doesn't.

Class _bstr_t provides reference counting on the instance. Therefore, it is more efficient if its instance is frequently assigned to another instance.

Booleans

The SDK defines a data type called VARIANT_BOOL for dealing with boolean variables. The two possible values for this data type are VARIANT_TRUE and VARIANT_FALSE, which correspondingly map to True and False under VB and VBScript.

Note that IDL defines another data type, boolean, to represent a boolean value. However, this data type is not supported under programming languages other than C/C++ and Java.

To define an automation-compliant boolean parameter, never use boolean or BOOL data types. Always use VARIANT_BOOL.

Variants

Programming languages such as VB and Java support typed data; that is, a variable can be defined to hold a specific data type, as shown in the following VB example:

```
Dim Count as Integer
Count = 10
```

However, scripting languages such as VBScript and Jscript forego this notion of typed data in favor of increased programming simplicity. These *typeless* languages support only one data type called a *variant*. A variant can contain any type of data. When a specific data type is assigned to a variant, or one variant is assigned to another, the run-time system will automatically perform any needed conversion.

Even many typed languages such as VB support variants natively.

The SDK defines a discriminated union to deal with variants. It is called a VARIANT. Each supported data type has a corresponding discriminator value, represented as the VARTYPE. We have seen some of them earlier. Table 2.9 lists some of the frequently used VARTYPEs. For a complete list, check out IDL file wtypes.idl supplied with the SDK.

TABLE 2.9   Variable Types Supported by a VARIANT

Type	Description
VT_EMPTY	has no value associated with it
VT_NULL	contains an SQL style NULL value
VT_I2	2 byte signed integer (short)
VT_I4	4 byte signed integer (long)
VT_R4	4 byte real (float)
VT_R8	8 byte real (double)
VT_CY	64-bit currency
VT_DATE	DATE (double)
VT_BSTR	BSTR
VT_DISPATCH	IDispatch*
VT_ERROR	HRESULT
VT_BOOL	VARIANT_BOOL
VT_VARIANT	VARIANT*
VT_IUNKNOWN	IUnknown*
VT_DECIMAL	16 byte fixed point
VT_UI2	Unsigned short
VT_UI4	Unsigned long
VT_I8	Signed 64-bit int (int64)
VT_UI8	Unsigned 64-bit int
VT_INT	Signed machine int
VT_UINT	Unsigned machine int

To indicate that a variant is a reference, flag VT_BYREF can be combined with the above tags.

A VARIANT can also be represented as a VARIANTARG type. Typically, VARIANTARG is used to represent the method parameters and VARIANT is used to refer to method results.

As with BSTRs, the SDK provides APIs and macros to deal with VARI-ANTs.

A variant has to be initialized before it can be used and has to be cleared after it has been used. The SDK provides the following two APIs for these purposes:

```
void VariantInit(VARIANTARG* pvarg);
void VariantClear(VARIANTARG* pvarg);
```

To understand how to use these APIs, consider a method that accepts a VARIANT as an [in] parameter.

```
HRESULT SetCount([in] VARIANT var);
```

The following code fragment shows how to pass a long value to this method:

```
VARIANT var;
VariantInit(&var);
V_VT(&var) = VT_I4;
V_I4(&var) = 1000;
pMyInterface->SetCount(var);
VariantClear(&var)
```

The SDK also provides many other APIs to manipulate variants, such as copying one variant into another or converting one variant type to another. These APIs are all documented in the SDK.

To simplify manipulating variants, ATL provides a class called CComVariant, and Visual C++ natively provides a class called _variant_t. Using CComVariant, for example, the previously defined code fragment can be simplified as:

```
CComVariant var(1000);
pMyInterface->SetCount(var);
```

As with CComBSTR, the cleanup for CComVariant occurs automatically when the variable goes out of scope.

 If you are not using safe wrapper classes such as CComVariant or _variant_t to deal with variants, make it a practice to call VariantClear before any assignment operation. This will obviate any potential resource leak.

Safe Arrays

Programming languages such as C++ support arrays intrinsically. However, it does so with no index protection, no size limit, and no initialization. An array is just a pointer to a random memory location. Even C++ programmers are reluctant to use raw arrays. Many of them write protected wrapper classes to deal with arrays.

VB on the other hand, provides a more protected way of dealing with arrays; it stores the array bounds and does a run-time check to ensure that the boundaries are not violated.

To deal with arrays safely, the SDK defines a data structure similar to the one that VB uses internally. This data structure is called SAFEARRAY. A SAFEARRAY is an array of other automation-compatible data types. The following example shows how to declare a safe array of BSTRs as a method parameter:

```
HRESULT GetNameList([out, retval] SAFEARRAY(BSTR)* pNameList);
```

Though the above method declaration is automation-compatible, and the marshaler knows how to marshal all the elements of the array, not all languages can deal with safe arrays when declared this way. Our variant data type comes in handy here. A safe array can be passed as a variant, as shown in the following code fragment:

```
// prototype
HRESULT SetNames([in] VARIANT nameList);

// client code
SAFEARRAY *pSA = CreateAndFillSafeArrayWithValidStrings();
VARIANT v; ::VariantInit(&v);
V_VT(&v) = VT_ARRAY | VT_BSTR;
V_ARRAY(&v) = pSA;    //pSA should contain each element of type BSTR
HRESULT hr = SetNames(v);
```

In the above code, each element in the array is of a BSTR type. This is acceptable to typed languages only. The typeless languages cannot deal with an array of BSTRs. If an array is intended to be used from a typeless language, it should be declared as an array of variants, as follows:

```
V_VT(&v) = VT_ARRAY | VT_VARIANT;
V_ARRAY(&v) = pSA;    // pSA should contain each element of type
                      // VARIANT
```

As with BSTRs, the SDK provides a number of API functions for creating, accessing, and releasing safe arrays. Their use is straightforward and is not covered here. To provide programmatic simplification under C++, one can create a wrapper class to deal with safe arrays. For an excellent article on safe arrays, see Ray Djajadinata's article, "Creating a COM Support Class for SAFEARRAY" in *Visual C++ Developer* [Ray-98].

Automation-Compatible Interfaces

If an interface is intended to be used by an automation client, all the methods in the interface should use only the automation-compatible parameters. To ensure this, an interface can be annotated with the oleautomation attribute, as shown below:

```
[
  ...
  oleautomation,
  ...
]
interface IVideo : IUnknown
{
  ...
};
```

Doing so directs MIDL to warn if it encounters any method parameter that is not automation-compatible.

Properties and Methods

We know that any COM object exposes one or more interfaces. We also know that each interface contains a set of predefined functions. Generally speaking, these functions can be classified into two subsets—one that takes some action, and one that obtains or changes the current state of the object. In order to provide a uniform semantic meaning of an automation object across different languages, COM defined the first set of functions as interface *methods* and the second set as interface *properties*.

A method is a member function that specifies an action that an object can perform, such as drawing a line or clearing the screen. A method can take any number of arguments (some of which can be marked as optional), and they can be passed either by value or by reference. A method may or may not have an output parameter.

IDL provides a function level attribute called method to indicate that the function is a method.

A property is a member function that sets or returns information about the state of the object, such as color or visibility. Most properties have a pair of accessor functions—a function to get the property value and a function to set the property value. Properties that are read-only or write-only, however, have only one accessor function.

Table 2.10 shows the attributes available on properties.

TABLE 2.10   Property Attributes

Attribute	Description
propget	obtains the property value
propput	sets the property value
propputref	sets the property value. Value has to be set by reference

Each property or method also requires an identification tag called dispatch identifier or DISPID. The SDK defines DISPID as a value of type long:

```
typedef long DISPID;
```

A DISPID is set on a method using attribute id, as shown in the following example:

```
[id(1), propget] HRESULT GetValue();
```

The SDK predefines many DISPIDs. Their semantics are documented in the SDK. For example, a DISPID of 0 on a property implies that the property is the default value. The behavior is illustrated in the following code fragment:

```
// Interface method definition
[propput, id(0)] HRESULT LastName([in] BSTR newVal);

// VB client usage example 1
person.LastName = "Gandhi"   // Standard way of setting a property

// VB client usage example 2
person = "Gandhi"            // Setting LastName property is simplified
                             // because of id(0)
```

User-defined DISPIDs start from one.

DISPIDs are scoped by the interface. Therefore, two interfaces can use the same value for a DISPID without any interference.

A property can result in two functions—one to get and one to set the property. In this case, both the functions should have the same DISPID.

Specifying DISPIDs is optional. If not specified, a DISPID is automatically assigned.

Run-time Binding

Recall from Chapter 1 that an interface is primarily a `vtbl`-based binary layout. In order for a C++ client to use an interface, its `vtbl` information, and the signature of all the methods, has to be available when the client code is being compiled. The client could invoke only those methods it was made aware of during compilation.

Such a `vtbl`-based binding mechanism works with typed languages such as C++ and VB (using automation-compatible interfaces). However, in general, it is not suitable for automation controllers. Automation controllers do not require the knowledge of any object until the object is created at run time.

What is needed is a mechanism so that an automation controller, or any client, can ask the object at run time if it supports a particular method. If the method is indeed supported, the client would like to know, at run time, the number of parameters and the data type of each parameter so that it can construct the parameter list and invoke the method.

COM provides a way to define an interface that supports such a run-time-binding functionality. However, defining such an interface requires a different IDL syntax; it is declared using the keyword `dispinterface` (short for dispatch interface), as shown in the following example:

```
[
  uuid(318B4AD2-06A7-11d3-9B58-0080C8E11F14),
  helpstring("DISVideo Interface")
]
dispinterface DISVideo
{
  properties:
  methods:
    [helpstring("Obtain the S-Video signal value"), id(1)]
    long GetSVideoSignalValue();
};
```

Note that the COM programming community has adopted the convention of using the prefix 'DI' on the interface name to indicate that it is a `dispinterface` type interface.

But by now we know that COM components can communicate using `vtbl`-based interfaces only. How, then, does the client deal with a `dispinterface`?

It turns out a `dispinterface` is just an abstraction limited to the IDL file. What the client sees is a `vtbl`-based interface. This interface is defined as `IDispatch` in the SDK. The interface definition is shown here:

```
interface IDispatch : IUnknown
{
  HRESULT GetTypeInfoCount( [out] UINT * pctinfo);
  HRESULT GetTypeInfo( [in] UINT iTInfo, [in] LCID lcid,
    [out] ITypeInfo ** ppTInfo);
  HRESULT GetIDsOfNames(
    [in] REFIID riid,
    [in, size_is(cNames)] LPOLESTR * rgszNames,
    [in] UINT cNames,
    [in] LCID lcid,
    [out, size_is(cNames)] DISPID * rgDispId);
  HRESULT Invoke(
    [in] DISPID dispIdMember,
    [in] REFIID riid,
    [in] LCID lcid,
    [in] WORD wFlags,
    [in, out] DISPPARAMS * pDispParams,
    [out] VARIANT * pVarResult,
    [out] EXCEPINFO * pExcepInfo,
    [out] UINT * puArgErr
);
```

Method `GetIDsOfNames` returns the DISPID for the given method name. To invoke a method, the client:

1. obtains the DISPID of the method it is interested in, and
2. calls `IDispatch::Invoke`, passing the DISPID as a parameter. The arguments needed by the method are packed as DISPPARAMS and passed to `Invoke`.

For performance optimization, a client can call `GetIDsOfNames` during compile time. This is referred to as *early binding*. Alternatively, `GetIDsOfNames` could be called during run time, just before the call to `Invoke`. This is referred to as *late binding*.

Run-time binding, early or late, will always be slower than `vtbl`-based binding. If a client is capable of supporting `vtbl`-based binding, such as the one written in C++, why enforce run-time binding?

What would be nice is to satisfy both `vtbl`-based clients as well as clients requiring run-time binding.

So far in our examples we derived our custom interfaces from IUn-known. What if we derive the interfaces from IDispatch instead?

Bingo! You are on the right track. You just laid out the mechanism for defining an interface that has the speed of direct vtbl binding and the flexibility of IDispatch binding. An interface defined this way is referred to as a *dual* interface.

However, there is one small issue that is left; deriving an interface from IDispatch doesn't automatically tell the IDL compiler that the interface is a dual interface. You have to annotate your interface with a dual keyword. The following example shows our interface IVideo defined as a dual interface:

```
[
  object,
  uuid(318B4AD0-06A7-11d3-9B58-0080C8E11F14),
  helpstring("IVideo Interface"),
  dual,
  pointer_default(unique)
]
interface IVideo : IDispatch
{
  [helpstring("Obtain the signal value")]
  HRESULT GetSignalValue([out, retval] long* val);
};
```

The Server Side of the Story.   How does the server code support dispinterface or a dual interface?

In order to support one or more dispinterfaces for an object, the server has to implement IDispatch interface.

The implementation of IDispatch::GetIDsOfNames would return a unique DISPID per method name.

The implementation of IDispatch::Invoke would examine the passed DISPID and would call the appropriate method on the object.

Implementing IDispatch is a very tedious process. Fortunately, ATL simplifies it by providing some C++ template classes. Richard Grimes' book *Professional ATL COM Programming* [Gri-98] discusses this in detail. In the chapters to follow, we will be using ATL wizard to generate IDispatch implementation.

Collections and Enumerations

A topic on automation would not be complete without talking about collections and enumerations.

Automation clients frequently need to deal with sets of objects or variants that should be grouped together. An example of such a collection is a list of files in a subdirectory.

While there is no specific interface to define a collection, there are certain methods that a collection object is expected to implement.

Count

To allow the clients to determine the number of items in the collection, a collection object should implement a Count method. The following is its prototype:

```
HRESULT Count([out, retval] long* count);
```

Item

To fetch a particular item, a method called item should be implemented. The first parameter to the method is the index of the item. The data type for the index is dictated by the implementer and could be numeric, BSTR, or VARIANT.

Enumeration

A collection object should also allow the client to iterate over the items in the set. The following VBScript example shows the usage of such a collection object:

```
'the filelist object has been obtained somehow. Iterate through
'and display the file names
for each file in fileList
  msgbox file.name
next
```

In order to support such an iteration style, the collection object should support a method with a DISPID of DISPID_NEWENUM. This method conventionally is named _NewEnum and returns a pointer to IUnknown, as shown in the following code snippet:

```
[id(DISPID_NEWENUM)] HRESULT _NewEnum(
    [out, retval] IUnknown **ppunk);
```

An underscore preceding any method indicates that the method be hidden. It will not be displayed to users from tools such as VB's auto-statement completion.

DISPID_NEWENUM is defined as −4 in the SDK. If you come across a method that has a DISPID of −4 (or its equivalent—0xFFFFFFFC), it indicates that the method returns an enumeration object.

When this method is called on the object, the object should return a pointer to an interface IEnumVARIANT (defined in the SDK). Interface IEnumVARIANT falls into a category of interfaces called enumeration. These interfaces are typically prefixed as IEnum and are expected to support some methods such as Next and Reset. The semantics of these methods is documented in the SDK.

There are some other optional methods that a collection can support. Charlie Kindel's article on MSDN, "Implementing OLE Automation Collection," [Kin-94] delineates the rules of automation collection fairly clearly.

ATL makes it easy to implement collections and enumerators. See Richard Grimes' article in *Visual C++ Developer's Journal* [Gri-99] for some sample code.

INTERFACES AND MARSHALING

An interface can be marshaled using either the MIDL-generated code or by writing explicit marshaling code.

Marshaling based on MIDL-generated code is referred to as *standard* marshaling.

In some circumstances, the developers may wish to write their own marshaling code. Marshaling based on such code is referred to as *custom* marshaling. For most cases, however, standard marshaling is very performance-efficient.

Standard marshaling could be driven by either the MIDL-generated proxy/stub code or by the MIDL-generated type library.

The proxy/stub code has to be compiled and linked to create the proxy/stub DLL. This DLL acts as a COM server and has to be registered on both the client and the server machine. COM provides a tool called regsvr32.exe that can be used to register or unregister a COM server DLL, as follows:

```
regsvr32.exe myproxystub.dll      // Register the proxy/stub on the
                                  // local machine
regsvr32.exe -u myproxystub.dll   // Unregister it
```

Building a proxy/stub DLL requires some specific compiler switches, a module definition file, and some specific libraries to link with. If you use ATL to create a COM server project, ATL will generate the module definition file and a makefile to build a proxy/stub DLL. If you are not using ATL or if you just want to create proxy/stub DLL for interfaces in a specific IDL file, you can use the `CreatePS` utility I have put on the accompanying CD. This utility generates the module definition file and the makefile to create a proxy/stub DLL, similar to what ATL does.

If type-library-driven marshaling is desired for an interface, the parameters in the interface methods are *restricted* to use automation-compatible type. In addition, the interface should be marked as either `oleautomation` or `dual`. The type library has to be registered on both the client and the server machine. The SDK provides an API, `LoadTypeLibEx`, that can be used to register a type library. If you are using ATL, the wizard generates the registration code for you.

The infrastructure that is responsible for carrying out type-library marshaling is referred to as the *universal marshaler*. It is currently implemented in OLEAUT32.DLL, a DLL supplied by COM.

It is important to understand that marshaling happens on the interface level, not on the object level. An object may support many interfaces. Each interface may have its own marshaling mechanism.

Also note that an interface cannot have more than one marshaling mechanism.

To marshal an interface, register only one entity—either its proxy/stub DLL or its type-library. If you register both, the behavior is unpredictable.

MEMORY MANAGEMENT

We have already covered how directional attributes dictate the role of the client and the server for memory management. To recap:

- For an `[in]` parameter, the memory is allocated and freed by the client.
- For an `[out]` parameter, the memory is allocated by the server and freed by the client.
- For an `[in, out]` parameter, the memory is allocated by the client, freed by the server, allocated once again by the server, and finally freed by the client. If possible, the two server-side operations can be combined as one "reallocation" action.

Memory management APIs are:

- `SysAllocString`, `SysReAllocString`, `SysFreeString`, etc. for BSTRs.
- `VariantInit` and `VariantClear` for VARIANTs.
- `CoTaskMemAlloc`, `CoTaskMemReAlloc`, and `CoTaskMemFree` for raw memory.

To demonstrate the use of memory management APIs, I will define two IDL structures; the first structure contains two BSTRs and a VARIANT, and the second structure contains an array of the first structure.

```
typedef struct tagMYLEADER {
  BSTR bsFirstName;
  BSTR bsLastName;
  VARIANT vTitle;
}MYLEADER;

typedef struct tagMYLEADERS {
  long lElements;
  [size_is(lElements)] MYLEADER* pData;
}MYLEADERS;

// Interface method
HRESULT GetMyLeaders([out] MYLEADERS* pDataArray);
```

The following code fragment shows how the memory is allocated at the server side and deallocated at the client side:

```
// Server code
STDMETHODIMP CMyExplore::GetMyLeaders(MYLEADERS *pDataArray)
{
  pDataArray->lElements = 2;

  // raw allocation
  pDataArray->pData =
    (MYLEADER*) ::CoTaskMemAlloc(2 * sizeof(MYLEADER));

  // BSTR allocations
  pDataArray->pData[0].bsFirstName=SysAllocString(L"Mohandas");
  pDataArray->pData[0].bsLastName=SysAllocString(L"Gandhi");

  // BSTR allocation in VARIANT
  VARIANT& v0 = pDataArray->pData[0].vTitle;
  ::VariantInit(&v0);
```

```
  V_VT(&v0) = VT_BSTR;
  V_BSTR(&v0) = ::SysAllocString(L"Mahatma");

  // BSTR allocations
  pDataArray->pData[1].bsFirstName=SysAllocString(L"Winston");
  pDataArray->pData[1].bsLastName=SysAllocString(L"Churchil");
  // BSTR allocation in VARIANT
  VARIANT& v1 = pDataArray->pData[1].vTitle;
  ::VariantInit(&v1);
  V_VT(&v1) = VT_BSTR;
  V_BSTR(&v1) = ::SysAllocString(L"Sir");

  return S_OK;
}


// Client code fragment
MYLEADERS leaders;

HRESULT hr = pMyExplore->GetMyLeaders(&leaders);
...

// Free memory
for(i=0; i<leaders.lElements; i++) {
  MYLEADER* pLeader = &leaders.pData[i];
  ::VariantClear(&pLeader->vTitle);   // freed BSTR in the variant
  ::SysFreeString(pLeader->bsFirstName);     // freed BSTR
  ::SysFreeString(pLeader->bsLastName);      // freed BSTR
}
::CoTaskMemFree(leaders.pData);           // freed raw allocation
```

The above code fragment used raw APIs for BSTRs and VARIANTs. To make the code less susceptible to human errors, one can use wrapper classes such as CComBSTR and CComVariant provided by ATL.

ORGANIZING MULTIPLE IDL FILES

Often times, a COM developer has to deal with multiple IDL files.

Consider the scenario where several VCR manufacturers got together and defined an interface for video signals, IVideo.

Now all the VCR manufacturers can get back to work and create their own IDL file defining the interface. However, this is not practical; some manufacturers can make a mistake in defining the interface. Moreover, if the interface had to be extended, every manufacturer will have to edit their respective IDL file.

In fact, COM defines many data types and core system interfaces, including IUnknown, that would cause a maintenance nightmare if not defined at one place.

Ideally (or is it IDLly?), the interface should be defined in one file. Any other IDL file should be able to reference the interface from this file.

Now that the case for multiple IDL files is made, you already know from a previous section that you need to use the import keyword to access the definitions from a different IDL file.

Many COM-defined core interfaces are in SDK files oaidl.idl and ocidl.idl. It is very common to see these two files imported at the beginning of an IDL file. Tools such as ATL wizard will import these two files in the IDL file (rather blindly, but that's okay).

```
import "oaidl.idl";
import "ocidl.idl";
```

In order to prevent duplication of definitions in a type library, you will need to judiciously use the importlib keyword. If you use ATL wizard, it will importlib SDK-defined type libraries, stdole2.tlb and stdole32.tlb, in the library section.

```
importlib("stdole32.tlb");
importlib("stdole2.tlb");
```

Blindly importlibing these two type libraries is perfectly okay. In fact, you should always do so. Depending on your needs, you may wish to importlib additional type libraries.

PUTTING IT ALL TOGETHER

It is time for us to convert our C++ interfaces defined in the previous chapter into IDL interfaces. We will define two interfaces, IVideo and ISVideo, create a library section, and define a COM class for our VCR.

Step 1: Create a file, video.idl, using notepad or your favorite editor.

Step 2: Access information from SDK-defined IDL files, as follows:

```
import "oaidl.idl";
import "ocidl.idl";
```

Step 3: Define interface block for Ivideo, as follows:

```
[ .
]
interface IVideo : IUnknown
{
};
```

Step 4: Add interface attributes. The required ones are object and uuid. However, it is good practice to add helpstring and pointer_default as well.

```
[
   object,
   uuid(318B4AD0-06A7-11d3-9B58-0080C8E11F14),
   helpstring("IVideo Interface"),
   pointer_default(unique)
]
```

You will have to run guidgen.exe to obtain the GUID for the interface.

 If you use guidgen.exe to obtain a GUID, leave it running until you obtain all the GUIDs. This way, all the GUIDs used in a project will have contiguous values, and it makes it easy to identify them.

However, you will need to run guidgen.exe on NT4. On Windows 2000, the algorithm used to generate GUIDs is different; it no longer generates contiguous GUIDs.

Step 5: Add the interface methods.

The following class shows our final C++ interface that appeared at the end of the previous chapter:

```
class IVideo : public IGeneral
{
public:
   virtual VRESULT _stdcall GetSignalValue(long* pRetVal) = 0;
};
```

The following is the equivalent IDL interface representation:

```
interface IVideo : IUnknown
{
   HRESULT GetSignalValue([out] long* val);
};
```

Step 6: Add method attributes.

I am adding just one attribute—helpstring—as follows:

```
interface IVideo : IUnknown
{
  [helpstring("Obtain the signal value")]
  HRESULT GetSignalValue([out] long* val);
};
```

Step 7: Repeat steps 3 through 6 for interface ISVideo. Following is the final definition of interface ISVideo.

```
[
  object,
  uuid(318B4AD1-06A7-11d3-9B58-0080C8E11F14),
  helpstring("ISVideo Interface"),
  pointer_default(unique)
]
interface ISVideo : IUnknown
{
  [helpstring("Obtain the S-Video signal value")]
  HRESULT GetSVideoSignalValue([out, retval] long* val);
};
```

Step 8: Define the library block, as follows:

```
[
]
library VcrLib
{

};
```

Step 9: Add library attributes. The required attribute is uuid. However, it is a good idea to also add the version number and helpstring.

```
[
  uuid(318B4AD2-06A7-11d3-9B58-0080C8E11F14),
  version(1.0),
  helpstring("VCR Type Library")
]
```

Step 10: Add importlib statements for SDK type libraries, as follows:

```
library VcrLib
{
  importlib("stdole32.tlb");
  importlib("stdole2.tlb");
};
```

Step 11: Add `coclass` block within the library scope, as follows:

```
[
]
coclass VCR
{
};
```

Step 12: Define `coclass` attributes. The required attribute is `uuid`. However, adding helpstring as well is a good idea.

```
uuid(318B4AD3-06A7-11d3-9B58-0080C8E11F14),
helpstring("VCR Class")
```

Step 13: List the interfaces we plan to expose in the `coclass` scope, as follows:

```
interface IVideo;
interface ISVideo;
```

We are done. Following is the IDL file we just created in its entirety.

```
// File Video.idl

import "oaidl.idl";
import "ocidl.idl";

[
  object,
  uuid(318B4AD0-06A7-11d3-9B58-0080C8E11F14),
  helpstring("IVideo Interface"),
  pointer_default(unique)
]
interface IVideo : IUnknown
{
  [helpstring("Obtain the signal value")]
  HRESULT GetSignalValue([out, retval] long* val);
};

[
  object,
  uuid(318B4AD1-06A7-11d3-9B58-0080C8E11F14),
  helpstring("ISVideo Interface"),
  pointer_default(unique)
]
interface ISVideo : IUnknown
{
  [helpstring("Obtain the S-Video signal value")]
  HRESULT GetSVideoSignalValue([out, retval] long* val);
};
```

```
[
  uuid(318B4AD2-06A7-11d3-9B58-0080C8E11F14),
  version(1.0),
  helpstring("VCR Type Library")
]
library VcrLib
{
  importlib("stdole32.tlb");
  importlib("stdole2.tlb");

  [
    uuid(318B4AD3-06A7-11d3-9B58-0080C8E11F14),
    helpstring("VCR Class")
  ]
  coclass VCR
  {
    interface IVideo;
    interface ISVideo;
  };

};
```

SUMMARY

In this chapter, we examined various goals that the COM committee had in defining the Interface Definition Language (IDL). We looked at various IDL constructs that are used in defining interfaces and are responsible for generating the marshaling logic. In defining interfaces, we looked at issues such as network efficiency and the ability to work with languages other than C++. We examined the rules of memory allocations and learned how to correctly use various APIs dealing with memory management. Finally, we converted interface definitions defined in the previous chapter from C++ abstract base classes to IDL interfaces.

This chapter covered a reasonable amount of information on IDL. Those wishing to learn more about interface design should read Al Major's book, *COM IDL and Interface Design* [Maj-99].

In the next chapter, we will take the newly defined interfaces and build our first COM server.

REFERENCES

[Kin-94]   Charlie Kindel, "Implementing OLE Automation Collection," Microsoft Developer Network, 1994. *http://msdn.microsoft.com/library/techart/msdn_collect.htm*

[Gri-99]   Richard Grimes, "ATL 3.0's Enumerator and Collection Templates," *Visual C++ Developer's Journal*, vol. 2, no. 2, April 1999.

[Pro-99]   Jeff Prosise, "Wicked Code," Microsoft Systems Journal, vol. 14, no. 5, May 1999. *http://msdn.microsoft.com/library/periodic/period99/wicked0599.htm*

[Box-98]   Don Box, *Essential COM*, Addison Wesley, ISBN 0-201-63446-5, 1998.

[Maj-99]   Al Major, et al. *COM IDL and Interface Design*, Wrox Press, ISBN 1861002254, February 1999.

[Ray-98]   Ray Djajadinata, "Creating a COM Support Class for SAFEARRAY," *Visual C++ Developer*, November 1998.

[Gri-98]   Richard Grimes, *Professional ATL COM Programming*, Wrox Press, ISBN 1-861001-4-01, 1998.

Components

$\mathbf{I}$n the previous chapter, we learned the techniques of defining interfaces. Once we have defined the interfaces, the next step is to create the COM component that implements the defined interfaces. In this chapter we look at various aspects of implementing a COM server. We will use the C++ code that we developed in Chapter 1 and turn it into COM-style C++ code. The focus is on understanding why and how features are implemented in COM, and learning the terminology used in COM-based component development. We will explore several ways to reuse a third-party component's functionality. The primary goal of this chapter is to make you understand the intrinsics of COM-based client and server development. A secondary goal is to make you feel comfortable in developing COM components using Active Template Library (ATL) and developing client code using ATL, as well as using native COM support provided by Visual C++.

FROM C++ TO COM—A QUICK TOUR

In Chapter 1, we defined non-COM interfaces `IVideo` and `ISVideo` using C++. In Chapter 2, we turned them into COM-style interfaces. Now, we will use the non-COM C++ implementation from Chapter 1 and turn it to COM-based C++ code. As you will see, programming in COM is not that difficult. After all, we did lay the foundation of COM in Chapter 1.

Implementing Interfaces

Let's begin by converting the definition of class `CVcr` from our non-COM implementation. The following code fragment shows the class as defined at the end of Chapter 1:

```
// File vcr.h

#include "Video.h"

class CVcr : public IVideo, public ISVideo
{
public:
  CVcr(void);
  ~CVcr();

  // IGeneral interface
  VRESULT _stdcall Probe(char* pszType, IGeneral** ppRetVal);
  void _stdcall AddReference();
  void _stdcall Delete();

  // IVideo interface
  VRESULT _stdcall GetSignalValue(long* pRetVal);

  // ISVideo interface
  VRESULT _stdcall GetSVideoSignalValue(long* pRetVal);

private:
  long m_lCurValue;
  int m_nCurCount;
  long m_lRefCount;
};
```

To COMify this class, we need to do the following:

- convert methods to use COM-style return values and calling conventions
- replace IGeneral method declarations with corresponding IUnknown method declarations.

Use COM Calling Conventions

To use COM-style calling conventions, we can use COM SDK-defined macros that were discussed in the previous chapter. Following are two simple rules to help you with the macro usage:

Rule 1: If the interface method returns an HRESULT (as almost all methods do), use the STDMETHOD(FuncName) macro.

For example, consider the following IVideo method:

```
HRESULT GetSignalValue([out, retval] long* val);
```

This interface method will have the following C++ style method declaration:

```
STDMETHOD(GetSignalValue)(long* pRetVal);
```

Rule 2: If the interface method returns a type other than HRESULT, use the
`STDMETHOD_(Type, FuncName)` macro.

For example, consider the `AddRef` method for interface `IUnknown`:

```
ULONG AddRef();
```

This interface method will have the following C++ style method declaration:

```
STDMETHOD_(ULONG, AddRef)();
```

Declare IUnknown Methods

We will replace the `IGeneral` methods with the corresponding `IUnknown`
methods. The equivalent methods for `Probe`, `AddReference`, and `Delete`
are `QueryInterface`, `AddRef`, and `Release`, respectively.

```
STDMETHOD(QueryInterface)(REFIID iid, void** pp);
STDMETHOD_(ULONG, AddRef)();
STDMETHOD_(ULONG, Release)();
```

After making the necessary changes, the following is the revised C++
class definition:

```
// File vcr.h

#include "Video.h"

class CVcr : public IVideo, public ISVideo
{
public:
  CVcr(void);
  ~CVcr();

  // IUnknown interface
  STDMETHOD(QueryInterface)(REFIID iid, void** pp);
  STDMETHOD_(ULONG, AddRef)();
  STDMETHOD_(ULONG, Release)();

  // IVideo interface
  STDMETHOD(GetSignalValue)(long* plVal);

  // ISVideo interface
```

```
STDMETHOD(GetSVideoSignalValue)(long* plVal);

private:
  long m_lCurValue;
  int m_nCurCount;
  long m_lRefCount;
};
```

 Even though the IDL interface definition does not allow multiple inheritance, there is no restriction on the implementation to support it, as can be seen in the above code.

Method Implementation

Let's now turn the non-COM implementation of C++ class methods from Chapter 1 into a COM-based C++ implementation.

To indicate COM-style implementation for a method, we use STD-METHODIMP macros discussed in Chapter 2. The usage rules are similar to those for STDMETHOD.

Also, as the return values are of type HRESULT now, we need to change our return code definitions to HRESULTs. The SDK defines many standard HRESULT values, along with their explanation, in the header file winerror.h. The ones that are currently of interest to us are S_OK and E_UNEXPECTED. The value S_OK indicates that the function call succeeded. Value E_UNEXPECTED indicates a failure in the code. For now, I will use E_UNEXPECTED to also indicate an internal error. Later in the chapter, I will show you how to use custom HRESULTs.

Except for the method QueryInterface, converting the rest of the methods is fairly straightforward. The following code shows the final implementation of these methods:

```
// File vcr.cpp
#include "Vcr.h"

CVcr:: CVcr()
{
  m_lCurValue = 5;
  m_nCurCount = 0;
```

```
    m_lRefCount = 0;
}

CVcr::~CVcr()
{
}

STDMETHODIMP_(ULONG) CVcr::AddRef()
{
  return (++m_lRefCount);
}

STDMETHODIMP_(ULONG) CVcr::Release()
{
  ULONG lRetVal = (--m_lRefCount);
  if (0 == lRetVal) {
    delete this;
  }
  return lRetVal;
}

STDMETHODIMP CVcr::GetSignalValue(long* pRetVal)
{
  if (m_nCurCount >= 5 || m_nCurCount < 0) {
    return E_UNEXPECTED;
  }

  m_nCurCount++;
  if (5 == m_nCurCount ) {
    m_lCurValue = 5;
    m_nCurCount = 1;
  }

  long lReturnValue = m_lCurValue;
  m_lCurValue += 10;
  *pRetVal = lReturnValue;
  return S_OK;
}

STDMETHODIMP CVcr::GetSVideoSignalValue(long* pRetVal)
{
  if (m_nCurCount >= 5 || m_nCurCount < 0) {
    return E_UNEXPECTED;
  }

  m_nCurCount++;
  if (5 == m_nCurCount ) {
```

```
        m_lCurValue = 5;
        m_nCurCount = 1;
    }

    long lReturnValue = m_lCurValue;
    m_lCurValue += 20;
    *pRetVal = lReturnValue;
    return S_OK;
}
```

If you compare this code to the one in Chapter 1, the only difference you will see is that of method signatures and return values. The rest of the code is identical.

The last method to be converted is Probe. The following code fragment shows the non-COM implementation as it appeared in Chapter 1:

```
VRESULT CVcr::Probe(char* pszType, IGeneral** ppRetVal)
{
    *ppRetVal = NULL;
    if (!stricmp(pszType, "general")) {
        *ppRetVal = static_cast<IVideo*>(this);
    }else
    if (!stricmp(pszType, "video")) {
        *ppRetVal = static_cast<IVideo*>(this);
    }else
    if (!stricmp(pszType, "svideo")) {
        *ppRetVal = static_cast<ISVideo*>(this);
    }

    if (NULL != (*ppRetVal)) {
        AddReference();
        return V_OK;
    }

    return V_NOINTERFACE;
}
```

Converting this method to the IUnknown method, QueryInterface, requires a few changes:

- The string comparison stricmp has to be replaced by interface ID comparison. The SDK provides an API, IsEqualIID, to compare two GUIDs.
- If the requested interface is not found, the return value has to be indicated as E_NOINTERFACE, another standard HRESULT value defined in winerror.h.

The revised implementation is shown below:

```
STDMETHODIMP CVcr::QueryInterface(REFIID iid, void** ppRetVal)
{
   *ppRetVal = NULL;

   if (IsEqualIID(iid, IID_IUnknown)) {
     *ppRetVal = static_cast<IVideo*>(this);
   }else
   if (IsEqualIID(iid, IID_IVideo)) {
     *ppRetVal = static_cast<IVideo*>(this);
   }else
   if (IsEqualIID(iid, IID_ISVideo)) {
     *ppRetVal = static_cast<ISVideo*>(this);
   }

   if (NULL != (*ppRetVal)) {
     AddRef();
     return S_OK;
   }

   return E_NOINTERFACE;
}
```

We just finished implementing the class that supports the interfaces. What remains to be done is adding a mechanism that would let the client instantiate this class and obtain the requested interface pointer.

Instantiation Logic

If you recall from Chapter 1, we defined a function, CreateVCR, that enabled the client to obtain an instance of CVcr. The following is the code fragment taken from Chapter 1:

```
VRESULT _stdcall CreateVCR(char* pszType, IGeneral** ppRetVal)
{
   *ppRetVal = NULL;

   CVcr* pVcr = new CVcr;
   if (NULL == pVcr) {
     return V_OUTOFMEMORY;
   }

   VRESULT vr = pVcr->Probe(pszType, ppRetVal);
   if (V_FAILED(vr)) {
     delete pVcr;
   }

   return vr;
}
```

In order to make this function available outside the DLL, recall that it was declared as an export function in the module definition file, vcr.def:

```
; File VCR.DEF

LIBRARY    VCR.DLL

EXPORTS
  CreateVCR
```

COM employs a similar technique to let the client access an object from the server. In its case, however, it mandates that the export function be called DllGetClassObject. Following is its prototype:

```
STDAPI DllGetClassObject(REFCLSID rclsid, REFIID riid, LPVOID* ppv);
```

The second and third parameters correspond to the two parameters we used for CreateVCR—parameter riid specifies the interface that the client is interested in, and the interface pointer is returned in parameter ppv (as with IUnknown::QueryInterface, we are still stuck with LPVOID* as return type for legacy reasons). What's the first parameter for? As we will see later, a DLL can host multiple classes. The first parameter represents the CLSID of the class the client is interested in. For our implementation, this CLSID should match the GUID specified in the coclass definition of the IDL file Video.idl. If there is no match, then the implementation needs to return another standard HRESULT error code—CLASS_E_CLASSNOTAVAILABLE—to the client.

If the instance creation fails because of limited memory resources, COM requires that another standard HRESULT error code, E_OUTOFMEMORY, be used as a return value.

Here is our new implementation:

```
STDAPI DllGetClassObject(REFCLSID rclsid, REFIID riid,
  LPVOID* ppv)
{
  if (!IsEqualIID(rclsid, CLSID_VCR)) {
    return CLASS_E_CLASSNOTAVAILABLE;
  }

  CVcr* pVCR = new CVcr;
  if (NULL == pVCR) {
    return E_OUTOFMEMORY;
  }

  HRESULT hr = pVCR->QueryInterface(riid, ppv);
```

```
if (FAILED(hr)) {
    delete pVCR;
}

return hr;
}
```

In the above implementation, each call to DllGetClassObject returns a new instance. Though this is considered illegal under COM, let's ignore it for the moment. We will revisit this issue in the next section.

Where are the variables CLSID_VCR, IID_IVideo, and IID_ISVideo defined? If you recall from Chapter 2, when the IDL file Video.idl is compiled using MIDL, two of the generated files were Video.h. and Video_i.c. The first file defines these variables as external constants and the second file specifies the actual storage. File Video.h needs to be included in any C++ source module that refers to either of these constants or to any of the interfaces defined in the IDL file. File Video_i.c should be included just once in some source module.

```
#include "Vcr.h"
#include "Video_i.c"
```

Failure to include Video_i.c will result in the linker reporting unresolved external symbols when the object files are linked to create the final executable. If it is included more than once, the linker will complain about duplicate symbol definitions.

The version of MIDL that is shipped with Visual C++ 6.0 or the SDK is capable of generating code that eliminates the need for using Video_i.c in the implementation. The generated output contains another form of declaration for GUIDs that make it possible to obtain the GUID using __uuidof, a keyword provided by Visual C++ compiler. If you make the following changes in the previous code, you can remove the inclusion of Video_i.c from the source code.

1. Replace references to IID_IVideo and IID_ISVideo __uuidof(IVideo) and __uuidof(ISVideo), respectively.

2. Replace references to CLSID_VCR with__uuidof(VCR).

This technique works if your reference is limited to interfaces and coclasses. The current version of MIDL does not generate a similar declaration for type library ID (LIBID). Therefore, the __uuidof keyword cannot be used with LIBIDs.

The last thing that remains is the creation of a module-definition file. We need to *export* DllGetClassObject. The difference to be noted is that this function, and some other functions that we will discuss later, are being exported only to be used by the COM infrastructure. Client programs access such a function indirectly (through COM). Therefore, such a function should be declared as PRIVATE.

```
; Module-Definition File Vcr.Def

LIBRARY    "MyVcr.DLL"

EXPORTS
    DllGetClassObject   PRIVATE
```

The keyword PRIVATE ensures that the function can only be called through the Win32 API GetProcAddress. If the caller attempts to call this function directly, the linker will not be able to resolve the function symbol.

This concludes our move from non-COM C++ to COM C++. Compile and link the code, and we've got our DLL-based COM server for VCR.

Now let's convert our TV client code to use the COM mechanism. As it turns out, this part is even easier.

The TV Client

The following is the main logic of the TV client code as it appeared at the end of Chapter 1:

```
int main(int argc, char* argv[])
{
  ISVideo* pSVideo = NULL;
  VRESULT vr = CreateInstance("vcr.dll",
    "svideo", reinterpret_cast<IGeneral**>(&pSVideo));
  if (V_FAILED(vr)) {
    ReportError(vr);
    return 1;
  }

  UseSVideo(pSVideo);
  pSVideo->Delete();
  return 0;
}
```

If you recall, function CreateInstance went through LoadLibrary, GetProcAddress, and CreateVCR calls to fetch the needed interface pointer. COM SDK provides this same functionality in an API known as CoGetClassObject. The following is its prototype:

```
STDAPI CoGetClassObject(REFCLSID rclsid, DWORD dwClsContext,
   COSERVERINFO* pServerInfo, REFIID riid, LPVOID* ppv);
```

Most of the parameters to CoGetClassObject are equivalent in meaning to the CreateInstance function:

- Parameter rclsid identifies the class object to be loaded (as opposed to the name of the DLL in the CreateInstance function).
- Parameter riid identifies the interface that the client is interested in.
- Parameter ppv is the return value. Similar to QueryInterface, this function returns a void* for legacy reasons.

The two parameters that do not have any equivalence in function CreateInstance are dwClsContext and pServerInfo.

- Parameter dwClsContext indicates the type of COM server to load. So far, we have been developing DLL-based COM servers. As we will see later, a COM server could be set to run in the same process space as the client or as a separate process. Since we do not care about the server type at this point, we will specify CLSCTX_ALL for dwClsContext, indicating that we can deal with any type of server.
- Parameter pServerInfo can be used to specify the machine where the COM server should load and execute. For now, we will specify a NULL value, indicating that we are interested in obtaining the server from the local machine.

The other obvious changes are replacing data type VRESULT with HRESULT and function ReportError with its equivalent function, DumpError, which we implemented in Chapter 2. The following is our revised code:

```
int main(int argc, char* argv[])
{
  ISVideo* pSVideo = NULL;
  HRESULT hr = ::CoGetClassObject(CLSID_VCR, CLSCTX_ALL, NULL,
    IID_ISVideo, reinterpret_cast<void**>(&pSVideo));
  if (FAILED(hr)) {
    DumpError(hr);
```

```
      return 1;
   }

   UseSVideo(pSVideo);
   pSVideo->Release();
   return 0;
}
```

What remains to be done is the initialization of the COM system. In order to use COM, the SDK mandates that a client initialize the COM system before making any COM-related calls and reset the system back to its uninitialized state after all the COM-related calls have been made. It defines the following APIs for this purpose:

```
HRESULT CoInitialize(LPVOID pvReserved);     // initialize COM
HRESULT CoUninitialize();                     // uninitialize COM
```

The parameter to `CoInitialize` is reserved for future use. It should be set to NULL for now.

If a client forgets to call `CoInitialize`, most other COM calls (including `CoGetClassObject`) will return the error code CO_E_NOTINI-TIALIZED (0x800401F0).

If `CoUninitialize` is not called, some resources that the COM system had acquired will not be freed, causing a resource leakage in the client's process.

With these two changes in place, the revised client code is as follows:

```
int main(int argc, char* argv[])
{
   ::CoInitialize(NULL);
   ISVideo* pSVideo = NULL;
   HRESULT hr = ::CoGetClassObject(CLSID_VCR, CLSCTX_ALL, NULL,
      IID_ISVideo, reinterpret_cast<void**>(&pSVideo));
   if (FAILED(hr)) {
      DumpError(hr);
      ::CoUninitialize();
      return 1;
   }

   UseSVideo(pSVideo);
   pSVideo->Release();
   ::CoUninitialize();
   return 0;
}
```

Compile and link the code.

```
cl tv.cpp ole32.lib.
```

 Many COM APIs, including `CoInitialize`, `CoUninitialize`, and `CoGetClassObject`, are implemented in the SDK library ole32.lib. This library should always be linked with the client code.

Let's run the TV executable and see what happens.

Here is the output of our run:

```
Class not registered - 0x80040154
```

What happened was that the call to `CoGetClassObject` failed. The COM infrastructure doesn't know where the implementation for class `CLSID_VCR` is.

We know the implementation is in `MyVcr.dll` because we were the ones to implement it. However, unless we provide this information to the COM infrastructure, it will never know the whereabouts of the server.

Let's look at how COM expects us to provide this information.

The COM+ Catalog

The configuration information of a COM class, including the file name of the DLL that implements the COM class, has to be stored in some persistent database so that, when `CoCreateInstance` is called, the COM system can load the DLL on the client's behalf. This database is referred to as the COM+ Catalog. COM+ provides a component to manage the catalog, appropriately called the Catalog Manager. Windows 2000 provides a configuration management visual tool called the Component Services Snap-in that internally communicates with the Catalog Manager.

The process of adding COM class-specific entries to the catalog is referred to as *registering* the class. The reverse process, that is, removing the class specific information, is called *unregistering* the class.

We will learn more about the Catalog Manager in Chapter 5. For this chapter, the point of interest is that the Catalog Manager mandates that a Windows registry key, `HKEY_CLASSES_ROOT\CLSID\{<CLSID>}\InprocServer32`, be used to store DLL file name information. The default value for this subkey contains the full path to the DLL to be loaded.

Ideally, a COM component should be registered using the Catalog Manager API. However, many legacy components bypass the Catalog Manager and insert the needed registry keys by some other means (the concept of Catalog Manager was not available prior to Windows 2000). Such a component is considered a *non-configured* component. For our discussion in this chapter, it is sufficient for us to use a non-configured component.

The registry entries can be modified either programmatically or through the OS-provided tool called `regedit.exe`. Using `regedit.exe`, one can modify the entries either through the user-interface or through an ASCII file containing the information in a specific format.

We will add the needed entries for our COM server using `regedit.exe` for now. Later in the chapter we will see how to do this programmatically.

The following text shows the needed entries in a format that `regedit.exe` can use:

```
REGEDIT4

[HKEY_CLASSES_ROOT\CLSID\{318B4AD3-06A7-11d3-9B58-
0080C8E11F14}\InprocServer32]
@="D:\\BookExamples\\Chapter04-ComServer\\01\\MyVcr.dll"
```

The first entry in the registry file, REGEDIT4, specifies that the syntax of the file should follow the Windows convention.

Add this information to the registry using the tool `regedit.exe`, as follows:

```
regedit.exe MyVcr.reg
```

Once this information is registered, the COM infrastructure now has enough information to know which DLL file to load for `CLSID_VCR`. If you run the TV client program once again, it will work this time.

Let's recap.

- We converted the C++ implementation from Chapter 1 into COM-style implementation.
- We replaced function `CreateVCR` with function `DllGetClassObject`.
- In the client code, we replaced the call to `CreateInstance` with a call to `CoGetClassObject`.

- We added COM initialization/uninitialization logic in the client code.
- We registered the COM server information.

In our drive to quickly convert the plain C++ code to COM-style C++ code, we left a few questions unanswered:

- How can we house multiple classes in a DLL?
- Why did we say that our implementation of `DllGetClassObject` is not legal under COM?

It's time to revisit our C++ code and fill in the missing gaps.

REVISITING C++ CODE

Multiple Classes in a Server

The DLL that we created is a *housing* for the implementation of class `CVcr`—a class that implements the interfaces associated with `CLSID_VCR`. Such a DLL is referred to as a COM server. If you think about it, there is no reason why a COM server cannot house more than one class. In fact, in many cases it makes sense to house a number of related classes together.

COM supports this notion of a server supporting multiple classes.

If we support multiple classes in one server, the question that then arises is, which instance of the class should `DllGetClassObject` return? This is where the first parameter to `DLLGetClassObject` makes sense. Depending on the specified CLSID, the implementation knows which instance to return.

At this point, it would be a good idea to recap some of the terminology used under COM:

- An interface is an abstract definition for communication between a client and a server. In our case, we have two such interfaces—`IVideo` and `ISVideo`.
- An implementation is a concrete data type that supports one or more interfaces by providing program code for each of the interface methods. In our case, it is the C++ class, `CVcr`.
- A COM object, or just an object, is an instance of the implementation. In our case, it would be "`new CVcr`."

- A software vendor who develops a COM server can publish the interfaces it supports by way of defining one or more `coclasses` in the
  IDL file. A `coclass` (or a COM class) is a named declaration that represents concrete instantiable type and the potential list of interfaces it
  exposes. In our case, it is the IDL declaration "`coclass VCR`." All
  that is known about a `coclass` is its CLSID and the potential list of
  interfaces it supports.

Multiple Instances of a Class

Consider the following scenario.

Our TV customers are demanding *picture-in-picture* capability. With
this ability, the TV can display information from two different sources at the
same time. In our case, it essentially boils down to the client being able to
create two instances of the VCR class.

Cool! You say. All we need to do is to call `CoGetClassObject` two
times, one for each source, as shown below:

```
ISVideo* pSVideoSource1 = NULL;
HRESULT hr = ::CoGetClassObject(CLSID_VCR, CLSCTX_ALL, NULL,
   IID_ISVideo, reinterpret_cast<void**>(&pSVideoSource1));

ISVideo* pSVideoSource2 = NULL;
hr = ::CoGetClassObject(CLSID_VCR, CLSCTX_ALL, NULL, IID_ISVideo,
   reinterpret_cast<void**>(&pSVideoSource2));
```

You are thinking in the right direction. However, recall what goes on when
`CoGetClassObject` is called. First, `LoadLibrary` is called, followed by
`GetProcAddress`, which gets the memory address of the `DllGetClassOb-
ject` function. Finally, function `DllGetClassObject` is invoked which in
turn searches for the specified CLSID.

Look at the problem we are trying to solve—we just want multiple
instances of the same class to be created. For efficiency, we do not want
`LoadLibrary`, `GetProcessAddress`, and search-for-`CLSID` to be called
multiple times.

If `CoGetClassObject` would return an object (specific to the requested
CLSID) that supports a mechanism to create instances of the class, our problem is solved. We could just call `CoGetClassObject` once and *cache* the
returned object. Each time a new instance is desired, we can ask the cached
object (via some interface) to create a new instance of the class.

This intermediate object that lets you create instances of the actual implementation class is called the *class object*.

Class Object

A class object implements the instance-less functionality of the specified CLSID. As I mentioned earlier, it is desired that this object be cached and reused by COM. Therefore, it does not make sense to have multiple instances of this object. Therefore, COM mandates that a class object be a singleton, that is, it can have just one instance.

Even though a class object is technically a "COM object", it is a special kind of object. It should be viewed as a vehicle to get to the more meaningful object—the one that implements the interfaces you wish to use.

If you recall the earlier implementation of DllGetClassObject, the "class object" and our "COM object" were the same. This is not considered illegal. What is illegal is that we are creating a new instance of the class object each time DllGetClassObject is called, thus violating the singleton rule.

How can you ensure that DllGetClassObject returns the same object each time it is called? I know what you are thinking—just define a static variable to store the class object as shown here:

```
STDAPI DllGetClassObject(REFCLSID rclsid, REFIID riid,
  LPVOID* ppv)
{
  if (!IsEqualIID(rclsid, CLSID_VCR)) {
    return CLASS_E_CLASSNOTAVAILABLE;
  }

  static CVcr* g_pVCR = NULL;

  if (NULL == g_pVCR) {
    g_pVCR = new CVcr;
    if (NULL == g_pVCR) {
      return E_OUTOFMEMORY;
    }
    g_pVCR->AddRef();        // Keep the pointer alive for
                             // server lifetime
  }

  HRESULT hr = g_pVCR->QueryInterface(riid, ppv);

  return hr;
}
```

With this logic, the class object is allocated just once—the first time `DllGetClassObject` is called.

 The above code makes an extra call to `AddRef`. The class object has to stay alive during the lifetime of the server. If the reference count were not incremented artificially, the object would get deleted after the clients have released references to the object. In that case, the next call to `DllGetClassObject` will return a pointer to an invalid memory location.

Now let's turn our attention to the client code. Our TV code makes two calls to `CoGetClassObject` in order to support picture-in-picture. However, there is a problem here—as the objects being returned are the same, both the displayed images will be identical. It is quite likely that you would like to see two different images. After all, you paid extra bucks to get the picture-in-picture feature.

The problem is, in writing our server code, we treated the class object and the implementation object as one and the same. Not only should we separate the two, but we should also provide a mechanism on the class object to return a new implementation object. This way, the TV client can get the class object (just once) and request it to create two new instances (or as many as it wants) of the `SVideo` source.

Class Factories

Obviously, the class object has to support a new interface that would let the client create new instances of the implementation class. COM SDK defines a standard interface called `IClassFactory` that a class object can support. Following is its definition taken from SDK-supplied file `unknwn.idl`. For clarity, I have removed some unneeded information.

```
[
  object,
  uuid(00000001-0000-0000-C000-000000000046),
  pointer_default(unique)
]
interface IClassFactory : IUnknown
{
  HRESULT CreateInstance(
    [in, unique] IUnknown * pUnkOuter,
    [in] REFIID riid,
    [out, iid_is(riid)] void **ppvObject);

  HRESULT LockServer([in] BOOL fLock);
};
```

The method that is of interest is `CreateInstance`. It has three parameters:

- The first parameter is used for something called *aggregation*. We will talk about aggregation in a later section. For now, we will specify NULL as its value to indicate that we are not interested in aggregation.[1]
- The second parameter is the IID of the interface. In our case, this is `IID_ISVideo`.
- The third parameter is the return value; it returns a pointer to the newly created instance.

Let's implement our class object logic.

Following is the C++ class definition of the class object:

```cpp
class CVcrClassObject : public IClassFactory
{
public:
  CVcrClassObject();
  ~CVcrClassObject();

  // IUnknown interface
  STDMETHOD(QueryInterface)(REFIID iid, void** pp);
  STDMETHOD_(ULONG, AddRef)();
  STDMETHOD_(ULONG, Release)();

  // IClassFactory interface
  STDMETHOD(CreateInstance)(IUnknown* pUnkOuter, REFIID riid,
    void** ppV);
  STDMETHOD(LockServer)(BOOL fLock);

private:
  long m_lRefCount;
};
```

The class has to support two interfaces—the first is the ubiquitous interface `IUnknown` (we know we always have to support this), and the second one is `IClassFactory`.

Implementing `IUnknown` basically amounts to using boilerplate code. You can cut and paste code from the `CVcr` implementation. Just remember to

---

[1] Recall from Chapter 2 that the `[unique]` attribute on a method parameter makes it possible to specify NULL as a valid value.

change the `QueryInterface` code to support `IUnknown` and `IClassFac-`
`tory`. That code is not shown here. You can find it on the CD.

Following is the implementation for the `IClassFactory` method
`CreateInstance`:

```
STDMETHODIMP CVcrClassObject::CreateInstance(
  IUnknown* pUnkOuter,
  REFIID riid,
  void** ppV)
{
  *ppV = NULL; // always initialize the return value

  if (NULL != pUnkOuter) {
    // we don't support aggregation
    return CLASS_E_NOAGGREGATION;
  }

  CVcr* pVCR = new CVcr;
  if (NULL == pVCR) {
    return E_OUTOFMEMORY;
  }

  HRESULT hr = pVCR->QueryInterface(riid, ppV);
  if (FAILED(hr)) {
    delete pVCR;
  }
  return hr;
}
```

The second `IClassFactory` method, `LockServer`, is currently of no
interest to us. We just return a standard HRESULT error code, `E_NOTIMPL`,
to indicate that the logic has not been implemented for the method.

```
STDMETHODIMP CVcrClassObject::LockServer(BOOL fLock)
{
  return E_NOTIMPL;
}
```

We now need to modify the `DllGetClassObject` code to use
`CVcrClassObject`.

```
STDAPI DllGetClassObject(REFCLSID rclsid, REFIID riid,
  LPVOID* ppv)
{
  if (!IsEqualIID(rclsid, CLSID_VCR)) {
    return CLASS_E_CLASSNOTAVAILABLE;
```

```
  }

  static CVcrClassObject* g_pVCRClassObject = NULL;

  if (NULL == g_pVCRClassObject) {
    g_pVCRClassObject = new CVcrClassObject;
    if (NULL == g_pVCRClassObject) {
      return E_OUTOFMEMORY;
    }

    // Keep the pointer alive for server lifetime
    g_pVCRClassObject->AddRef();
  }

  HRESULT hr = g_pVCRClassObject->QueryInterface(riid, ppv);

  return hr;
}
```

This completes the changes required for the server code.

Now let's modify the TV client code to create new instances from the class object. Following is the revised code. For brevity, I have removed error-checking logic.

```
int main(int argc, char* argv[])
{
  ::CoInitialize(NULL);
  IClassFactory* pCF = NULL;
  ::CoGetClassObject(CLSID_VCR, CLSCTX_ALL, NULL,
    IID_IClassFactory, reinterpret_cast<void**>(&pCF));

  ISVideo* pSVideoSource1 = NULL;
  pCF->CreateInstance(NULL, IID_ISVideo,
    reinterpret_cast<void**>(&pSVideoSource1));

  ISVideo* pSVideoSource2 = NULL;
  pCF->CreateInstance(NULL, IID_ISVideo,
    reinterpret_cast<void**>(&pSVideoSource2));

  // Done with class factory
  pCF->Release(); pCF = NULL;

  // For now, assume the following two calls are
  // executing simultaneously
  UseSVideo(pSVideoSource1);
  UseSVideo(pSVideoSource2); // Picture-in-picture
```

```
    pSVideoSource1->Release();
    pSVideoSource2->Release();

    ::CoUninitialize();
    return 0;
}
```

We are done defining the important concepts and implementing the sample code. At this point, I would like you to recall the meaning of the following terms: Interface, COM class (`coclass`), C++ implementation class, COM object, class object, and class factory. If you feel you are not clear on any of these terms, please read the previous section once again. These terms are fundamental to understanding the COM programming model (not to mention the rest of the book).

Let's look at some of the optimizations we can do.

Optimizations

If you examine the client code, it is obvious that a class object itself is not that meaningful; it is just a way of getting to a more meaningful object—the object implementing the desired interface. Therefore, it makes sense to combine the capabilities of `CoCreateClassObject` and `CreateInstance` into one function, thereby saving one roundtrip to the server. The SDK provides an API, `CoCreateInstance`, to do just this:

```
STDAPI CoCreateInstance(REFCLSID rclsid, LPUNKNOWN pUnkOuter,
    DWORD dwClsContext, REFIID riid, LPVOID* ppv);
```

Using this API, the TV code can be written as:

```
int main(int argc, char* argv[])
{
  ::CoInitialize(NULL);
  ISVideo* pSVideoSource1 = NULL;
  ::CoCreateInstance(CLSID_VCR, NULL, CLSCTX_ALL, IID_ISVideo,
    reinterpret_cast<void**>(&pSVideoSource1));

  ISVideo* pSVideoSource2 = NULL;
  ::CoCreateInstance(CLSID_VCR, NULL, CLSCTX_ALL, IID_ISVideo,
    reinterpret_cast<void**>(&pSVideoSource2));

  // For now, assume the following two calls are
  // executing simultaneously
  UseSVideo(pSVideoSource1);
  UseSVideo(pSVideoSource2); // Picture-in-picture
```

```
    pSVideoSource1->Release();
    pSVideoSource2->Release();

    ::CoUninitialize();
    return 0;
}
```

Let's recap what we have achieved so far in this section.

We realized that a class object should really be a singleton. However, in order to be able to create newer COM objects (instances of the implementation class), the class object should support the `IClassFactory` interface. The client can then call `CoGetClassObject` followed by `CreateInstance`, or can combine them into just one operation, `CoCreateInstance`.

Note that COM does not mandate that a class object support the `IClassFactory` interface. COM monikers, for example, require a different interface on the class objects.[2] However, if interface `IClassFactory` is not supported on the class object, `CoCreateInstance` will fail with error code REGDB_E_CLASSNOTREG (0x80040154).

Two problems still need to be addressed. The first one has to do with the way we chose to publish our class information, and the second one deals with memory consumption and leakage.

Storing Configuration Information

If you recall, the way we registered our server code was by adding an entry in the Windows registry specifying the path name of the server. There are two problems with this approach:

- Each time the DLL is moved to a different directory, one has to edit the registry entry manually and type in the new path name. Not only is this a pain in the neck, it is also error-prone.
- If the DLL is removed from the machine, one has to remember to delete the stale registry entries; that is, manually unregister the class.

Windows provides APIs to obtain the path name of a running executable as well as to add/delete registry entries. If this registration process is

---

[2] Covering COM monikers is outside the scope of this book.

pushed to the COM server, the server itself can then handle registering/unregistering programmatically.[3]

COM expects a COM server[4] to implement two functions to handle self-registration.

```
STDAPI DllRegisterServer(void);    // register yourself
STDAPI DllUnregisterServer(void); // unregister yourself
```

Let's implement the first function. This requires obtaining the path name of the DLL programmatically.

Under Windows, a DLL loaded into a process space can obtain its own path name by calling a Win32 API `GetModuleFileName`. Following is its prototype:

```
DWORD GetModuleFileName(HINSTANCE hInst, LPTSTR lpFilename,
    DWORD nSize );
```

Each loaded DLL in the process space is assigned a value, called a module handle, which is unique within the process. By specifying the module handle as the first parameter, the DLL path name can be obtained programmatically.

In order to call this function from a DLL, the DLL needs to know its own module handle. How can the DLL get its own module handle?

A DLL can implement an optional function called `DllMain`.[5] The operating system calls this function and passes the module handle as a parameter when the DLL is loaded for the first time within a process. This gives the DLL a chance to copy the module handle in a global location so that the value can be accessed from other DLL functions, as shown here:

---

[3] Registering a DLL file path using explicit code is counter-intuitive to the main theme that permeates through COM+—that of using "out-of-band" attributes instead of "in-band" explicit code. However, in the spirit of easy migration of legacy COM code to COM+, COM+ 1.0 made an exception for the file path as well as a few other attributes.

[4] The COM servers we refer to are all DLL-based, which is what COM+ promotes. In the era of classic COM, a server could be a stand-alone executable.

[5] A DLL has to have `DllMain` function. However, if this function is not implemented explicitly, the linker uses the default implementation (that just returns S_OK) provided in the standard run-time library.

```
static HINSTANCE g_hInstance = NULL;

// DLL Entry Point
BOOL WINAPI DllMain(HINSTANCE hInstance, DWORD dwReason,
  LPVOID /*lpReserved*/)
{
  if (dwReason == DLL_PROCESS_ATTACH)
  {
    g_hInstance = hInstance;
  }
  return TRUE;                    // ok
}
```

Here is the code for registering the DLL. The registry manipulation APIs such as `RegCreateKey` and `RegSetValueEx` are documented in the Win32 SDK.

```
HRESULT AddRegistryEntry(LPCTSTR pszSubKey, LPCTSTR pszValueName,
  LPCTSTR pszValue)
{
  HKEY hSubKey = NULL;
  LONG lRetVal =
    ::RegCreateKey(HKEY_CLASSES_ROOT, pszSubKey, &hSubKey);
  if (ERROR_SUCCESS != lRetVal) {
    return HRESULT_FROM_WIN32(lRetVal);
  }

  int len= lstrlen(pszValue) + 1;    //include terminating NULL char
  lRetVal = ::RegSetValueEx(hSubKey, pszValueName, 0, REG_SZ,
    reinterpret_cast<const BYTE*>(pszValue), len);
  ::RegCloseKey(hSubKey);
  return HRESULT_FROM_WIN32(lRetVal);
}

// DllRegisterServer - Adds entries to the system registry
STDAPI DllRegisterServer(void)
{
  TCHAR szPath[MAX_PATH];
  ::GetModuleFileName(g_hInstance, szPath,
    sizeof(szPath)/sizeof(TCHAR));
  HRESULT hr = AddRegistryEntry(
"CLSID\\{318B4AD3-06A7-11d3-9B58-0080C8E11F14}\\InprocServer32",
    "", szPath);
  return hr;
}
```

The registry entry that `DllRegisterServer` adds is the same as the one we previously added using `rededit.exe`.

Unregistering a server is even easier—we just need to delete the registry key `CLSID\{318B4AD3-06A7-11d3-9B58-0080C8E11F14}` and the subkeys underneath.

 The API to delete a Windows registry key, `RegDeleteKey`, expects that the key (or the subkey) being deleted has no child subkeys. Therefore, one has to recursively delete the child subkeys first.

Here is the final code for unregistering the DLL. Given that we do not have any subkeys to delete, the code is straightforward.

```
// DllUnregisterServer - Removes entries from the system registry

STDAPI DllUnregisterServer(void)
{
  long lRetVal = ::RegDeleteKey(HKEY_CLASSES_ROOT,
"CLSID\\{318B4AD3-06A7-11d3-9B58-0080C8E11F14}\\InprocServer32");
  if (ERROR_SUCCESS != lRetVal) {
    return HRESULT_FROM_WIN32(lRetVal);
  }
  lRetVal = ::RegDeleteKey(HKEY_CLASSES_ROOT,
    "CLSID\\{318B4AD3-06A7-11d3-9B58-0080C8E11F14}");
  return HRESULT_FROM_WIN32(lRetVal);
}
```

We now need to export the `DllRegisterServer` and `DllUnregisterServer` functions, similar to what we did for `DllGetClassObject`. Following is the revised module-definition file:

```
; Module-Definition File Vcr.Def

LIBRARY     "MyVcr.DLL"

EXPORTS
   DllGetClassObject          PRIVATE
   DllRegisterServer          PRIVATE
   DllUnregisterServer        PRIVATE
```

The OS includes a program called `regsvr32.exe` to deal with DLL registration. To register a DLL, supply the DLL path name as the argument:

```
regsvr32 MyVcr.dll
```

To unregister a DLL, specify -u as a switch:

```
regsvr32 -u MyVcr.dll
```

One can easily guess that `regsvr32.exe` just loads the specified DLL and invokes one of the two registration functions. Implementing such a program is left as an exercise for you.

Memory Cleanup

Let's reexamine our class object creation code:

```
static CVcrClassObject* g_pVCRClassObject = NULL;
g_pVCRClassObject = new CVcrClassObject;
if (NULL == g_pVCRClassObject) {
  return E_OUTOFMEMORY;
}
g_pVCRClassObject->AddRef();
```

Recall that we bumped up the reference count to ensure that the class object does not get deleted during the lifetime of the server. However, when the server is no longer in use, it is our responsibility to release the class object. Otherwise, we will have a memory leakage.

How does COM determine that a server is no longer in use? I will answer this in the next section. For now, the important thing to note is, when the server is no longer in use, COM unloads the DLL.

Recall that function `DllMain` was being called when the DLL gets loaded. This same function is also called when the DLL is getting unloaded, giving us the perfect opportunity to release the class object. Following is the code:

```
static CVcrClassObject* g_pVCRClassObject = NULL;

// DLL Entry Point
extern "C" BOOL WINAPI DllMain(HINSTANCE hInstance,
  DWORD dwReason, LPVOID /*lpReserved*/)
{
  if (DLL_PROCESS_ATTACH == dwReason) {
    g_hInstance = hInstance;
  }else
  if (DLL_PROCESS_DETACH == dwReason) {
    if (NULL != g_pVCRClassObject) {
      g_pVCRClassObject->Release();
    }
  }

  return TRUE;   // ok
}
```

Note that I had to move the static variable `g_pVCRClassObject` to the file level scope, as two different functions, `DllGetClassObject` and `DllMain`, need to use the same variable.

As much as you dislike using global variables, they are an unavoidable evil sometimes. However, the list of global variables seems to be increasing in our case. First, we had one global variable—`g_hInstance`. Now we've added `g_pVCRClassObject`.

One improvement we can do is to group all global parameters under one structure (or class) and have just one global variable for the whole structure, as shown here:

```
// File MyModule.h

#pragma once              // Visual C++ optimization to avoid loading
                          // a header file multiple times

class CVcrClassObject;    // forward declaration

struct MYMODULEINFO
{
  MYMODULEINFO()
  {
    hInstance = NULL;
    pVCRClassObject = NULL;
  }

  HINSTANCE hInstance;
  CVcrClassObject* pVCRClassObject;
};

extern MYMODULEINFO g_MyModule;
```

While we are in this good programming practices mode, I would like to introduce the notion of one standard include file. The idea is that there are many project-specific include files that get used frequently but change infrequently. All such header files can be referenced through just one header file. Any other source module in the project would then need to include this one header file, besides any other header file it may need. Using such a technique has a couple of advantages:

- Any macro that has to be defined project-wide can be defined at one place.
- Microsoft's compiler can "precompile" this header just once, thereby reducing project build time.

If you have been programming in Microsoft's world, you would know that such a file is typically named `StdAfx.h`. Here is our version of this file:

```
// File StdAfx.h

#pragma once

#define WIN32_LEAN_AND_MEAN

#include <windows.h>
#include <ole2.h>
#include "MyModule.h"
```

File `windows.h` is needed for using any Win32 API and `ole2.h` is needed for using any COM API. Until now, they were getting referenced automatically through the MIDL-generated file `Video.h`. Here, we reference them explicitly.

Macro `WIN32_LEAN_AND_MEAN` can be defined to exclude rarely used header files referenced in `windows.h`. This speeds up compilation time.

When to Unload a DLL?

The problem of releasing the class object is fixed. However, in this process, we overlooked an important aspect. Earlier, I conveniently sneaked in the text that when the server is no longer is use, the COM library unloads the DLL. But how does the COM library know a server is not in use?

The COM library mediated the process of delivering a class object from the client to the server. However, it does not know how many COM objects the client created, for example, by calling the `IClassFactory::Create-Instance` method. As long as the client has a reference to even one object, the server has to stay loaded. Therefore, the COM library cannot just arbitrarily unload the server.

The COM library may not know the number of server objects that have outstanding references, but the server sure does. After all, it is the server that is issuing objects to the client. Therefore, it makes sense that the COM library asks the server to see if it is fine to unload.

The COM specifications define that a server implement a function called `DllCanUnloadNow`. The function should return `S_OK` code if it is okay to unload the DLL. Otherwise, the return code should be `S_FALSE`.

```
STDAPI DllCanUnloadNow(void)
{
   return (AnyOutstandingReference()) ? S_OK : S_FALSE;
}
```

To keep track of the outstanding references, a typical technique is to use a global counter (yet another global variable), as shown here:

```
struct MYMODULEINFO
{
   MYMODULEINFO()
   {
      hInstance = NULL;
      pVCRClassObject = NULL;
      lCount = 0;
   }

   HINSTANCE hInstance;
   CVcrClassObject* pVCRClassObject;
   ULONG lCount;
};
```

Using this counter, function DllCanUnloadNow can be implemented as:

```
STDAPI DllCanUnloadNow(void)
{
   return (g_MyModule.lCount==0) ? S_OK : S_FALSE;
}
```

The variable needs to be incremented each time an object is created and decremented each time an object is deleted. What better place than the object constructor and destructor to add this logic?

```
CVcr:: CVcr()
{
   . . .

   g_MyModule.lCount++;
}

CVcr::~CVcr()
{
   . . .

   g_MyModule.lCount-;
}
```

We also need to add a similar logic to the class object code. After all, a class object is a COM object. It can have outstanding references as well.

However, keeping track of outstanding references for a class object is a little tricky. The problem is, the server will always keep the class object alive by bumping up the reference count to one initially. If the count logic is added in the constructor, as we did for class CVcr, the global object count will never become zero. Hence, a call to DllCanUnloadNow will always return S_FALSE, and the server will never be unloaded.

For a cached object such as the class object, we know that the object reference count will be one if there are no clients holding the object. Otherwise, the reference count will be two or more. For such an object, we can move our global object count logic into the reference count code, that is, within the implementation of the AddRef and Release methods, as shown below:

```
STDMETHODIMP_(ULONG) CVcrClassObject::AddRef()
{
  long lRetVal = (++m_lRefCount);
  if (lRetVal == 2) {
    // a client is requesting for a AddRef
    g_MyModule.lCount++;
  }
  return lRetVal;
}

STDMETHODIMP_(ULONG) CVcrClassObject::Release()
{
  ULONG lRetVal = (—m_lRefCount);
  if (1 == lRetVal) {
    // all clients have released the references
    g_MyModule.lCount—;
  }else
  if (0 == lRetVal) {
    delete this;
  }
  return lRetVal;
}
```

There is still one more problem that we need to address. A client releases an object by calling the method Release. This call goes directly to the server, not through the COM library. Therefore, when a client releases the last object it is holding from a server, the COM library still is not aware that the server can potentially be freed.

The COM SDK defines an API, CoFreeUnusedLibraries, that the clients can call at strategic locations in their code to unload any COM servers that are no longer in use. The COM library keeps a list of each DLL server that has been loaded, either directly (using CoGetClassObject) or indi-

rectly (using `CoCreateInstance`). When `CoFreeUnUsedLibraries` is
called, it walks through the list and unloads a DLL, if it is okay to do so. Following is the pseudo-logic for the implementation:

```
for each DLL-handle in the list
{
  pFnCanUnloadNow = GetProcAddress(handle, "DllCanUnloadNow");
  HRESULT hr = (*pfnCanUnloadNow)();
  if (S_OK == hr) {
    FreeLibrary(handle);
    Remove handle from the list.
  }
}
```

Call `CoFreeUnusedLibraries` at some strategic places in your client
code. This causes the unused COM DLLs to be unloaded from the address
space of the process, thus reducing some memory footprint.

Optimizations

Calling `CoFreeUnusedLibraries` unloads all the servers that are *currently*
not in use. Note the emphasis on *currently*. There are cases when a client
releases all the objects from a server but may need to instantiate objects once
again from the same server at a later time. This will result in loading the
server (the DLL) once again.

Loading and unloading a DLL can get expensive in terms of performance. What is desired is the ability to prevent a specific server from getting
unloaded even if the server is not currently in use.

It turns out that the COM designers had already thought of this problem
when designing the `IClassFactory` interface.

Recall that this interface had a method called `LockServer` that we
never really implemented. The code is shown here:

```
STDMETHODIMP CVcrClassObject::LockServer(BOOL fLock)
{
   return E_NOTIMPL;
}
```

A client can call this method to keep a server from getting unloaded.
Parameter `fLock`, if `TRUE`, indicates that the server be kept in memory. A
`FALSE` value indicates that it is okay to unload it.

The implementation can be tied very well with our global counter variable. So far, we were only using it for keeping the object count. However, there is no reason not to use the same global variable for the `LockServer` method. The following is such an implementation:

```
STDMETHODIMP CVcrClassObject::LockServer(BOOL fLock)
{
   if (TRUE == fLock) {
      g_MyModule.lCount++;
   }else {
      g_MyModule.lCount-;
   }

   return S_OK;
}
```

It is the client's responsibility, of course, to call `LockServer(TRUE)` and `LockServer(FALSE)` in a pair. Otherwise, the DLL will always stay in memory.

Congratulations! You just finished writing a complete DLL-based COM server that adheres to all the COM rules.

Now let's reorganize the implementation code a little to make it more manageable.

Code Cleanup

If you recall, our global variable `g_MyModule` has three data members that are publicly accessible. The structure is shown here for your review:

```
struct MYMODULEINFO
{
   MYMODULEINFO()
   {
      hInstance = NULL;
      pVCRClassObject = NULL;
      lCount = 0;
   }

   HINSTANCE hInstance;
   CVcrClassObject* pVCRClassObject;
   ULONG lCount;
};
```

The first thing I would like to do is mark these data members as private. And while I am at it, I would also like to change the structure definition to a class definition, as shown here:

```
// File MyModule.h
#pragma once
class CVcrClassObject;        // forward declaration
class CMyModule
{
public:
  CMyModule();
  ~CMyModule();
    ...
private:
  HINSTANCE m_hInstance;
  CVcrClassObject* m_pVCRClassObject;
  LONG m_lCount;
};
extern CMyModule g_MyModule;

// File MyModule.cpp

CMyModule::CMyModule()
{
  m_hInstance = NULL;
  m_pVCRClassObject = NULL;
  m_lCount = 0;
}

CMyModule::~CMyModule()
{
  _ASSERT (NULL == m_pVCRClassObject);
  _ASSERT (0 == m_lCount);
}
```

Data member `m_hInstance` needs to be initialized once the execution begins, but it should be accessible anytime during the execution:

```
HRESULT CMyModule::Init(HINSTANCE hInst)
{
  m_hInstance = hInst;
  return S_OK;
}

HINSTANCE CMyModule::GetModuleInstance()
{
  return m_hInstance;
}
```

The idea behind defining method `Init` is to isolate all the initialization logic to just one method.

Data member `m_lCount` is used as a global counter:

```
LONG CMyModule::Lock()
{
  return ++m_lCount;
}

LONG CMyModule::Unlock()
{
  return —m_lCount;
}

LONG CMyModule:: GetLockCount ()
{
  return m_lCount;
}
```

The final data member `m_pVCRClassObject` is used to create a class object. I will define a new method, `CMyModule::GetClassObject`, and move the logic from `DllGetClassObject` to this method.

```
HRESULT CMyModule::GetClassObject(REFCLSID rclsid, REFIID riid,
  LPVOID* ppv)
{
  if (!IsEqualIID(rclsid, CLSID_VCR)) {
    return CLASS_E_CLASSNOTAVAILABLE;
  }

  if (NULL == m_pVCRClassObject) {
    m_pVCRClassObject = new CVcrClassObject;
    if (NULL == m_pVCRClassObject) {
      return E_OUTOFMEMORY;
    }

    // Keep the pointer alive for server lifetime
    m_pVCRClassObject->AddRef();
  }

  return m_pVCRClassObject->QueryInterface(riid, ppv);
}
```

The extra reference on the class object has to be released on execution termination. I will define another method, `CMyModule::Term`, and move the logic from `DllMain` to this method:

```
void CMyModule::Term()
{
  if (NULL != m_pVCRClassObject) {
    m_pVCRClassObject->Release();
    m_pVCRClassObject = NULL;
  }
  _ASSERT (0 == m_lCount);
}
```

Similar to the method Init, which isolated all the initialization logic to just one method, the method Term can be used to isolate all the termination logic.

Finally, I would like to move all the registration logic from DllRegisterServer and DllUnregisterServer to class CMyModule.

```
// RegisterServer - Adds entries to the system registry

HRESULT CMyModule::RegisterServer(void)
{
  // Remove old entries first
  UnregisterServer();

  // Add New entries
  TCHAR szPath[MAX_PATH];
  ::GetModuleFileName(m_hInstance, szPath,
    sizeof(szPath)/sizeof(TCHAR));
  HRESULT hr = AddRegistryEntry(
"CLSID\\{318B4AD3-06A7-11d3-9B58-0080C8E11F14}\\InprocServer32",
    "", szPath);
  return hr;
}


// UnregisterServer - Removes entries from the system registry

HRESULT CMyModule::UnregisterServer(void)
{
  DeleteRegistryKey(HKEY_CLASSES_ROOT,
    "CLSID\\{318B4AD3-06A7-11d3-9B58-0080C8E11F14}");
  return S_OK;
}
```

The following code shows the final representation of class CMyModule:

```
class CMyModule
{
public:
  CMyModule();
  ~CMyModule();
```

```cpp
    // Initialize the object
    HRESULT Init(HINSTANCE hInst);

    // Cleanup the object
    void Term();

    // HINSTANCE access
    HINSTANCE GetModuleInstance(){return m_hInstance; }

    // Global count access
    LONG Lock();
    LONG Unlock();
    LONG GetLockCount(){ return m_lCount; }

    // Class object access
    HRESULT GetClassObject(REFCLSID rclsid, REFIID riid,
      LPVOID* ppv);

    // Registration routines
    HRESULT RegisterServer();
    HRESULT UnregisterServer();

    // Registry helper
    static HRESULT AddRegistryEntry(LPCTSTR pszSubKey,
      LPCTSTR pszValueName,
      LPCTSTR pszValue);
    static HRESULT DeleteRegistryKey(HKEY hKeyParent,
      LPCTSTR pszSubKey);

private:
  HINSTANCE m_hInstance;
  CVcrClassObject* m_pVCRClassObject;
  LONG m_lCount;
};
```

As the public data members are now declared as private, we will need to touch the rest of the server code to use appropriate methods instead of accessing data members directly. The following code snippet shows one such source file. This code defines all the entry points for the DLL.

```cpp
// File VcrDll.cpp

#include "StdAfx.h"

// DLL Entry Point
extern "C" BOOL WINAPI DllMain(HINSTANCE hInstance,
  DWORD dwReason, LPVOID /*lpReserved*/)
{
```

```
    if (DLL_PROCESS_ATTACH == dwReason) {
      g_MyModule.Init(hInstance);
    }else
    if (DLL_PROCESS_DETACH == dwReason) {
      g_MyModule.Term();
    }

    return TRUE;   // ok
}

// Returns the requested interface for the requested clsid
STDAPI DllGetClassObject(REFCLSID rclsid, REFIID riid,
  LPVOID* ppv)
{
    return g_MyModule.GetClassObject(rclsid, riid, ppv);
}

// DllRegisterServer - Adds entries to the system registry
STDAPI DllRegisterServer(void)
{
    return g_MyModule.RegisterServer();
}

// DllUnregisterServer - Removes entries from the system registry
STDAPI DllUnregisterServer(void)
{
    return g_MyModule.UnregisterServer();
}

// Used to determine whether the DLL can be unloaded by OLE
STDAPI DllCanUnloadNow(void)
{
    return (g_MyModule.GetLockCount()==0) ? S_OK : S_FALSE;
}
```

We now have code that is more readable and easier to manage. Also, if we add a little more abstraction, we can use the same global class with every COM server that we write. This class isolates the mechanism to register, unregister, obtain the class object, and keep the global reference count.

Let's step back and start dissecting how COM objects are implemented.

IMPLEMENTING COM OBJECTS

Once the interfaces have been designed and a `coclass` has been declared, the next step is to programmatically implement the support for the interfaces. In this section, we will revisit the code developed in the earlier section, and examine various aspects of implementation in detail. We will continue to use C++ for implementing the code as it is a widely used programming language.

The reason for the popularity of C++ language in implementing a COM server is perhaps because supporting multiple interfaces in a C++ class can easily be achieved by using the language's support for multiple inheritance.

Using Multiple Inheritance

We know that a COM object frequently has to support multiple interfaces. C++ language support for multiple inheritance makes it convenient to support multiple interfaces on a class. All that is needed is to declare each interface as a base class of the implementation class, as shown below:

```
class CVcr : public IVideo, public ISVideo
{
   ...
};
```

There are many other ways to support multiple interfaces. Multiple inheritance is by far the most commonly used technique.

Recall that an interface contains nothing but pure virtual methods. A class cannot be instantiated if it contains pure virtual methods. Therefore, we will need to declare all the pure virtual methods from interfaces `IVideo` and `ISVideo`, and their base interface, `IUnknown`, as concrete methods on the class, as follows:

```
class CVcr : public IVideo, public ISVideo
{
public:
  // IUnknown interface
  STDMETHOD(QueryInterface)(REFIID iid, void** pp);
  STDMETHOD_(ULONG, AddRef)();
  STDMETHOD_(ULONG, Release)();
```

```
// IVideo interface
STDMETHOD(GetSignalValue)(long* plVal);

// ISVideo interface
STDMETHOD(GetSVideoSignalValue)(long* plVal);

...
};
```

Let's see how we can implement these methods.

Implementing the Root Interface

A COM object is always required to support the IUnknown interface. To recap, this interface has two functionalities:

- Manage the lifetime of the object using a reference-counting mechanism.
- Lets a client navigate from one interface to another via the QueryInterface method.

The SDK does not provide a default implementation for IUnknown. Instead, in order to ensure trouble-free interaction within COM components, the COM specifications precisely define rules for reference counting as well as for querying an interface. Based on these rules, the object implementer is free to implement the three IUnknown methods using whatever logic that makes sense for the specific object. The rules should be followed strictly.

Reference Counting Rules

In dealing with interface pointers, the server and the client both have some responsibilities towards the lifetime of the object. Here are the rules that apply:

Rule #1: Reference counting does not apply to a NULL interface pointer.
As a matter of fact, any method call on a NULL interface pointer will typically result in a program crash with an "access violation" error message.

Rule #2: AddRef and Release typically go together.
For every call to AddRef, there should be a call to Release at some point later.

Rule #3: If an interface pointer is obtained, either via a COM API or an interface method, the callee should call AddRef before returning

the interface and the caller should call `Release` once done with the interface pointer.

Consider our previous TV client example. We called a COM API, `CoCreateInstance`, that returned an `ISVideo` interface pointer. In this case, it can be assumed that a successful return from this API would have incremented the reference count up. It is now the responsibility of the TV client to release it once it is done with the interface.

```
ISVideo* pSVideoSource1 = NULL;
::CoCreateInstance(CLSID_VCR, NULL, CLSCTX_ALL,
IID_ISVideo,
  reinterpret_cast<void**>(&pSVideoSource1));

...


pSVideoSource1->Release();
```

Releasing an interface pointer informs the server that the caller is not interested in using the same pointer anymore. Making any method calls on such an interface pointer may result in unexpected behavior (the underlying object could already have been deleted).

It is a good idea to set the pointer to NULL once it is released.

```
pSVideoSource1->Release(); pSVideoSource1 = NULL;
```

Rule #4: If an interface pointer is copied, the reference count should be incremented by calling `AddRef`.

Consider, for example, the following line of code:

```
ISVideo* pSVideoNew = pSVideoSource1;
```

As a new copy of `ISVideo` interface pointer is made, a call to `AddRef` should be in order, as shown here:

```
pSVideoNew->AddRef();
```

Remember that both the variables, `pSVideoSource1` and `pSVideoNew`, need to be released at some point.

In a large project, it is easy to forget calling `Release` on an object or calling `AddRef` when copying an object. Essentially, any one of the above four reference counting rules can be broken easily. ATL provides a template class, `CComPtr`, to help eliminate such programming mistakes. This class wraps the actual interface pointer and ensures that the rules of reference counting are maintained. The programmer would not need to explicitly call `AddRef` or `Release` on the object. We will see how to use this class later in the chapter.

When copying an interface pointer, there are special cases when the redundant calls to `AddRef` and `Release` can be optimized away. This requires special knowledge about the relationship between two or more interface pointers. One such example is when we know that an interface pointer will last longer than its copy. Examine the following code fragment:

```
void UseSVideo(ISVideo* pSVideo)
{
  long val;
  VRESULT vr;
  for(int i=0; i<10; i++) {
    vr = pSVideo->GetSVideoSignalValue(&val);
    if (V_FAILED(vr)) {
      ReportError(vr);
      continue;
    }
    cout << "Round: " << i << " - Value: " << val << endl;
  }
}

int main(int argc, char* argv[])
{
  . . .
  ISVideo* pSVideoSource1 = NULL;
  ::CoCreateInstance(CLSID_VCR, NULL, CLSCTX_ALL, IID_ISVideo,
    reinterpret_cast<void**>(&pSVideoSource1));
  . . .
  UseSVideo(pSVideoSource1);
  . . .
  pSVideoSource1->Release();
  . . .
}
```

When function `UseSVideo` is called, interface pointer `pSVideoSource1` is copied to `pSVideo`. However, variable `pSVideo` will get destroyed before pSVideoSource1 is released. In this case, there is no need to call AddRef and Release on variable pSVideo.

In the above case, the special relationship between the two memory locations was very obvious. In general, finding such relationships is not easy. Spending time to find such relationships may not be worth it. The benefits of removing calls to AddRef and Release are fairly insignificant. Moreover, removing these calls with an assumed relationship is a debugging nightmare when the assumption turns out to be incorrect. Not to mention how poorly it reflects on your company when the customer finds a crash.

When in doubt, even slightly, use AddRef and Release on an interface pointer copy.

Reference Count Implementation

We have seen reference count implementation in Chapter 1. This is just a remake in COM-style programming.

The class that implements the interfaces maintains a member variable of data type long, as follows:

```
class CMyImpl : public IInterface1, IInterface2, ...
{
public:
   ...
private:
   ...
   long m_lRefCount;
};
```

The count has to be initialized to zero in the object construction:

```
CMyImpl:: CMyImpl()
{
   ...
   m_lRefCount = 0;
}
```

Method AddRef increments the count:

```
STDMETHODIMP_(ULONG) CMyImpl::AddRef()
{
   return ++m_lRefCount;
}
```

Method `Release` decrements the count. If the count reaches zero, there are no more outstanding references to the object, implying that the object is not needed anymore. A typical implementation deletes itself.

```
STDMETHODIMP_(ULONG) CMyImpl::Release()
{
  ULONG lRetVal = −m_lRefCount;
  if (0 == lRetVal) {
    delete this;
  }
  return lRetVal;
}
```

This reference counting implementation is so generic that one can easily write a C++ template to implement this functionality. As we will see later, Microsoft's ATL does just this (and much more).

Relationship Between Interfaces

COM uses a standard technique for visually representing objects. Figure 3.1 shows the representation for our VCR class.

Figure 3.1 adheres to COM's philosophy of separating interfaces from implementation and hiding implementation details of the object. All that is known for an object is the potential list of interfaces the object exposes. For the VCR object, they are `IVideo`, `ISVideo`, and `IUnknown`.

`IUnknown` method `QueryInterface` (generally referred to as QI in the COM community) is the means by which a client can obtain one interface from another on the same object. However, COM places certain requirements on the relationship between all the interfaces an object exposes through

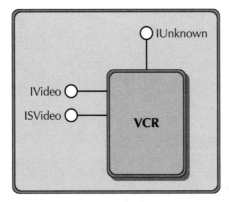

Figure 3.1   Representation of an object.

`QueryInterface`. As we will see shortly, these requirements simplify the client's use of an object.

As every object is expected to implement interface `IUnknown`, `QueryInterface` for `IID_IUnknown` should never fail on an object.

Interfaces are Symmetric. In order to obtain a specific interface, a client should not be concerned with which interface to acquire first.

For example, in our TV-VCR code, in order to obtain the `ISVideo` interface pointer, the TV client should be able to acquire any of the three interfaces first and then QI its way to the `ISVideo` interface.

To facilitate this, COM mandates that QI should be symmetric. That is, if interface `IVideo` is obtained through `ISVideo`, then interface `ISVideo` can be obtained through interface `IVideo`. This symmetry can be represented as follows:

```
If QI(IX) ➤ IY then
QI (QI(IX) ➤ IY) ➤ IX
```

Interfaces are Transitive. A client should not be forced to obtain all interfaces of an object in a specific sequence.

In our TV-VCR sample, the client should not be forced to obtain `IUnknown`, `IVideo`, and `ISVideo` in a specific order. Instead, all interfaces should be treated as peers. If this were not the case, the TV client would have to code specific QI sequences to obtain a specific interface pointer.

To facilitate this, COM mandates that QI should be transitive. That is, if interface `ISVideo` can be obtained from `IVideo`, and `IVideo` can be obtained from `IUnknown`, then `ISVideo` can be obtained directly from `IUnknown`. This transitivity can be represented as follows:

```
If QI(QI(IX) ➤ IY) ➤ IZ then
QI(IX) ➤ IZ
```

Interfaces are Reflexive. A client should be able to obtain the same interface from an existing interface pointer.

In our TV-VCR sample, if the client has a pointer to `ISVideo`, he or she should be able to QI this pointer to obtain additional `ISVideo` pointers.

To understand why this is important, consider the following code fragment:

```
extern void UseSignal(IUnknown* pUnk);

int main()
{
   ...
   ISVideo* pSVideo = ObtainSVideoInterface();
   UseSignal(pSVideo);
   ...
}
```

When a strongly typed interface (such as ISVideo) is passed as its base type parameter (such as IUnknown), the called function (UseSignal) loses information about the original type forever. It would be counterintuitive if the original type information could not be regained inside the function, as shown here:

```
void UseSignal(IUnknown* pUnk)
{
   ISVideo* pSVideo;
   hr = pUnk->QueryInterface(IID_ISVideo, (void**)
&pSVideo);
   ...
}
```

To facilitate this, COM mandates that a QI request through an interface pointer must always succeed if the requested type matches the type of pointer to make the request. This can be represented as:

```
QI(IX) ➤ IX
```

Consistent Set of Interfaces.   The set of interfaces supported by an object should not change during the lifetime of the object. If QI returns S_OK for interface IX, it must always return S_OK for interface IX during the lifetime of the object. If QI returns E_NOINTERFACE for interface IX, it must always return E_NOINTERFACE during the lifetime of the object. Recall that the lifetime of the object is governed by the number of outstanding references on the object. The object is alive as long as there is at least one outstanding interface pointer on the object.

If this consistency restriction is not maintained, one of the earlier specified rules will break down.

The consistency restriction is placed on the object (the instance of the class) and not on the class itself. Two different objects of the same class can individually use some state or temporal information to decide the set of interfaces each will support during its lifetime.

Also note that the supported set of interfaces is fixed only for the lifetime of the object, not forever. It is legal, for example, for the implementer to support additional interfaces in a new version of the COM server.

Unique Object Identity. A client may wish to determine if two interface pointers point to the same object.

To facilitate this, COM mandates that a QI for IUnknown should return the *same pointer value* for each request. A client can then determine if two interface pointers point to the same object identity, as shown in the following code fragment:

```
bool IsItTheSameObject(ISVideo* pSVideo, IVideo* pVideo)
{
  IUnknown* pUnk1 = NULL;
  HRESULT hr = pSVideo->QueryInterface(IID_IUnknown,
    (void**) &pUnk1);
  _ASSERT (SUCCEEDED(hr));
  IUnknown* pUnk2 = NULL;
  hr = pVideo->QueryInterface(IID_IUnknown, (void**) &pUnk2);
  _ASSERT (SUCCEEDED(hr));
  bool bRetVal = (pUnk1 == pUnk2);
  pUnk1->Release(); pUnk2->Release();
  return bRetVal;
}
```

The notion of object identity is a fundamental concept that is used by the COM remoting architecture to efficiently represent interface pointers on the network.

Now that we understand all the requirements placed on a QI implementation, let's reexamine our own implementation.

Typical QI Implementation

The following is the QI implementation for the TV-VCR sample:

```
STDMETHODIMP CVcr::QueryInterface(REFIID iid, void** ppRetVal)
{
  *ppRetVal = NULL;
```

```
if (IsEqualIID(iid, IID_IUnknown)) {
  *ppRetVal = static_cast<IVideo*>(this);
}else
if (IsEqualIID(iid, IID_IVideo)) {
  *ppRetVal = static_cast<IVideo*>(this);
}else
if (IsEqualIID(iid, IID_ISVideo)) {
  *ppRetVal = static_cast<ISVideo*>(this);
}

if (NULL != (*ppRetVal)) {
  AddRef();
  return S_OK;
}

return E_NOINTERFACE;
}
```

For each interface that is supported, the "this" pointer is statically cast to the interface type and returned.

Returning interface IUnknown is a special case. Simply static-casting the object to IUnknown, as shown below, will result in a compiler error:

```
*ppRetVal = static_cast<IUnknown*>(this);
```

The problem is that there are two paths to IUnknown in the vtbl layout, as both the interfaces, IVideo and ISVideo, are derived from IUnknown. With a static-cast such as the one above, the compiler does not know which path to choose. We can cast "this" to IVideo specifically and help the compiler to pick one path.

 Typecasting this to ISVideo would have worked as well, as the implementation of IUnknown is the same for both IVideo and ISVideo. However, what should not be done is typecasting to IVideo at one time and to ISVideo at another time during the lifetime of the object, as it breaks the object identity rule.

In order to isolate the logic of converting "this" to IUnknown, it is a good idea to define a method on the class to return the IUnknown pointer:

```
IUnknown* CVcr::GetUnknown()
{
  return static_cast<IVideo*>(this);
}
```

Let's recap what we learned in this section.

A COM object has to follow certain rules for counting the references as well as maintaining the relationship between the interfaces it exposes. We discussed how to implement `IUnknown` methods that would obey these rules.

It is left as an exercise to the reader to prove that the DLL server that was implemented in the earlier section follows these rules.

The code that we wrote to implement `QueryInterface` can easily be converted to a template so that it can be used with any class implementation. This is what ATL does. Let's see how.

ATL is Our Friend

If you examine the code that we have developed so far, you will see that there is a lot of grunge work that you have to do in order to implement a COM object:

- For every COM object, you have to implement `IUnknown` logic—reference-counting as well as support for querying an interface.
- For every COM object, you have to implement a class object (that itself is a COM object). You typically will have to support an `IClass-Factory` interface for your class object.
- You need to keep track of every COM object that has an outstanding reference using a global counter.
- You have to implement the registration logic for the COM server.

All this work may very well defocus you from your main implementation logic.

With a little more thought, one can isolate this grunge work into a separate piece of code, then reuse this code for the next COM object or COM server to be implemented.

It turns out that ATL already does this for you. ATL is a set of template-based C++ classes with which you can easily create COM objects. The code has been written with efficiency and compactness in mind.

Let's see how we can leverage ATL in our code.

Standard Include Files

The core ATL logic is defined in two header files, `atlbase.h` and `atlcom.h`. File `atlcom.h` relies on a global variable, `_Module`, to be defined by the developer. This variable should be of type ATL class `CComModule` or its derivative. As you may have guessed, class CComModule is the replacement for our earlier defined class CMyModule, and variable _Module is the replacement for our defined variable g_MyModule.

The standard header file for a project should contain the above two header files and the global variable _Module declared as external:

```
// File StdAfx.h

#pragma once

#define WIN32_LEAN_AND_MEAN
#define _ATL_MIN_CRT
#define _USRDLL

#include <atlbase.h>
extern CComModule _Module;
#include <atlcom.h>
```

The macro _ATL_MIN_CRT instructs ATL to minimize the use of the C run-time library. If this macro is defined, ATL defines its run-time functions such as malloc, free, operator new, and operator delete. It even defines run-time startup code—_DLLMainCRTStartup for in-process servers and WinMainCRTStartup for out-of-process servers.[6] By default, ATL assumes the code being developed is for out-of-process servers. Macro _USRDLL instructs ATL to use _DLLMainCRTStartup as the startup.

Though most of the code provided by ATL is template-based and is defined in header files, some supplementary code is defined in source files. One such source file is atlimpl.cpp. This file needs to be referenced just once in the project, typically done in a standard source file, StdAfx.cpp:

```
// File StdAfx.cpp    (source file that includes just the
//          standard includes)

#include "StdAfx.h"
#include <atlimpl.cpp>
```

Registration Logic

Instead of hard-coding the registration information, as we did earlier, ATL requires that this information be moved to a text file in a script format that

---

[6] Out-of-process COM servers are supported as legacy components under COM+.

ATL understands. This file typically has `.rgs` extension. The following list-
ing shows the registration script for our COM object:

```
HKCR
{
  NoRemove CLSID
  {
    ForceRemove {318B4AD3-06A7-11d3-9B58-0080C8E11F14}
    {
      InprocServer32 = s '%MODULE%'
    }
  }
}
```

You should consult the ATL documentation for the format of the script.
You should also read Craig McQueen's "Using the ATL Registry Component" [Mcq-98] for a good introduction. In the above text fragment, we are
indicating that the `InprocServer32` entry be added under the key
`HKEY_CLASSES_ROOT\CLSID\{OurCLSID}`. The keyword `ForceRemove`
indicates that the specified subkey should be deleted and recreated before
adding any entries. The keyword `NoRemove` indicates that the entries should
be added to the specified subkey without actually deleting the subkey first.

The definition is typically added as a resource into the resource file
associated with the project, as follows:

```
// File Resource.h
#define IDR_VCR 100

// File MyVcr.rc
#include "Resource.h"

IDR_VCR  REGISTRY DISCARDABLE  "Vcr.rgs"
```

For more information on using resource files, check the SDK documentation.

A remaining piece of logic is to associate the resource `IDR_VCR` with the
implementation class `CVcr`. Using macro `DECLARE_REGISTRY_RESOURCEID`
does the trick, as shown here:

```
// File vcr.h

#include "Resource.h"
...

class CVcr :
  ...
{
public:
  ...
```

DECLARE_REGISTRY_RESOURCEID(IDR_VCR)
```
  ...
};
```

Let's revise our `CVcr` class to support interfaces `IVideo` and `ISVideo` using ATL.

Implementation Class Logic

ATL breaks the implementation for `IUnknown` into two distinct code pieces:

- An internal piece that implements the core `IUnknown` logic: the methods are called `InternalQueryInterface`, `InternalAddRef`, and `InternalRelease`.
- A wrapper code that just turns around and calls the internal code.

The internal piece is implemented in a class called `CComObjectRoot`. Any ATL-based COM implementation class needs to be derived from this class (or its variants such as `CComObjectRootEx`), as shown here:

```
// File vcr.h

#include "Resource.h"
#include "Video.h"

class CVcr :
  ...
  public CComObjectRoot,
  ...
{
  ...
};
```

Finally, method `InternalQueryInterface` needs to be informed of the list of interfaces the class supports. The list is sandwiched between

BEGIN_COM_MAP and END_COM_MAP macros. Each interface that is supported is specified using the COM_INTERFACE_ENTRY macro, as shown below:

```
class CVcr :
  public IVideo,
  public ISVideo,
  public CComObjectRoot,
  ...
{
public:
  ...

BEGIN_COM_MAP(CVcr)
  COM_INTERFACE_ENTRY(IVideo)
  COM_INTERFACE_ENTRY(ISVideo)
END_COM_MAP()


  ...
};
```

Note that interface IUnknown is implicitly assumed to be a supported interface and hence should not be specified in the interface map.

Class Object Support

Each implementation class has to be tied to a class object that will let us create an instance of the implementation class. If you recall, our old implementation defined a class CVcrClassObject (that supported method CreateInstance to create instances) for this purpose. ATL pushes instance creation logic to the implementation class itself. To use ATL's mechanism, each implementation class is required to have the class CComCoClass in its base class list. This class contains the instance creation logic.

The following code shows class CVcr revised to use ATL:

```
// File vcr.h

#include "Resource.h"
#include "Video.h"

class CVcr :
  public IVideo,
  public ISVideo,
  public CComObjectRoot,
  public CComCoClass<CVcr, &CLSID_VCR>
{
```

```
public:
  CVcr();
  ~CVcr();

DECLARE_REGISTRY_RESOURCEID(IDR_VCR)

BEGIN_COM_MAP(CVcr)
  COM_INTERFACE_ENTRY(IVideo)
  COM_INTERFACE_ENTRY(ISVideo)
END_COM_MAP()

  // IVideo interface
  STDMETHOD(GetSignalValue)(long* plVal);

  // ISVideo interface
  STDMETHOD(GetSVideoSignalValue)(long* plVal);

private:
  long m_lCurValue;
  int m_nCurCount;
};
```

Note that CVcr is still an abstract class in that it does not define IUnknown methods. Therefore, the following line of code will fail to compile:

```
CVcr* pVcr = new CVcr;
```

ATL defines the IUnknown methods in a template called CComObject. Not only does this class implement the logic of the IUnknown interface, but it also helps in keeping track of the number of outstanding objects (via the Lock and Unlock methods). Using this template, an instantiable class of CVcr can be declared as CComObject<CVcr>, as illustrated in the following line of code:

```
CComObject<CVcr>* pVcr = new CComObject<CVcr>;
```

The above line of code will not fail during compilation.

Of course, ATL suggests that the object be created in a slightly different way:

```
CComObject<CVcr>* pVcr = CComObject<CVcr>::CreateInstance();
```

Why the second form of coding is better than the first one is left as an exercise for the readers (hint: check the ATL documentation for the FinalConstruct method).

Just one more bit left—knowing that there could be many implementation classes in a COM server, ATL requires the classes be specified in a list so that when `DllGetClassObject` is called, ATL can search for the requested class object in the list.

Such a list has to be specified as a sandwich between `BEGIN_OBJECT_MAP` and `END_OBJECT_MAP` macros. Each coclass that is being exposed should be defined using the `OBJECT_ENTRY` macro, as shown below, for our VCR class:

```
// File VcrDll.cpp

#include "StdAfx.h"
#include "Video.h"
#include "Video_i.c"
#include "Vcr.h"

BEGIN_OBJECT_MAP(ObjectMap)
  OBJECT_ENTRY(CLSID_VCR, CVcr)
END_OBJECT_MAP()
```

The map declared here should be passed as a parameter to the initialization method of the global instance, `_Module`, as shown here:

```
// DLL Entry Point
extern "C" BOOL WINAPI DllMain(HINSTANCE hInstance,
  DWORD dwReason, LPVOID /*lpReserved*/)
{
  if (DLL_PROCESS_ATTACH == dwReason) {
    _Module.Init(ObjectMap, hInstance, NULL);
  }else
  if (DLL_PROCESS_DETACH == dwReason) {
    _Module.Term();
  }

  return TRUE;   // ok
}
```

That's it. By using ATL, we got rid of our class factory implementation code, our registration code, and our `IUnknown` implementation code without sacrificing any efficiency or flexibility. The revised code is much easier to read and maintain.

Is there ever a reason not to use ATL? There is no reason, unless you like inflicting pain on yourself and other team members. That said, however, it is important to understand the fundamentals of COM programming and what goes on under the hood of ATL. This chapter is here to explain the fundamentals to you and will continue to use non-ATL code. However, I will demonstrate the use of ATL whenever appropriate.

TEAR-OFF INTERFACES

An object may support a large number of interfaces. In some scenarios, some of the interfaces are used rarely (for example, for backward compatibility) or transiently.

In order to reduce the overhead of such rarely used interfaces, a developer may not choose to support them in the object implementation. Instead, when the request for such an interface is made (via `QueryInterface`, for example), the `vtbl` for the interface is dynamically constructed and returned. The last `Release` on the interface will destroy this `vtbl`.

Such a technique is referred to as a tear-off, as a new interface is "torn off" on demand, that is, constructed and destroyed on the fly.

Note that this technique potentially returns different physical results for identical `QueryInterface` requests. However, this does not break the component model as long as the tear-off interface honors all the rules of `IUnknown`, such as object-identity, symmetry, etc.

Academically, a tear-off is a clever technique that manipulates the loophole in COM's specifications. However, as we will see in a later chapter, this technique breaks down if the interface has to be marshaled, for example, across a process boundary.

Implementing a tear-off interface is left as an exercise for the reader.

At this point, we completely understand the rules of COM object implementation. Let's explore the possibility of reusing third-party components and its impact on the design.

REUSING COMPONENTS

Consider the following scenario. In our TV-VCR sample, component VCR supports `IVideo` and `ISVideo` interfaces. Things were working great for our VCR manufacturer, that is, until the electronics manufacturer consortium decided to publish a new interface, `IComponentVideo`. This new interface happens to provide superior picture quality. The following is its definition:

```
[
  object,
  uuid(318B4AD4-06A7-11d3-9B58-0080C8E11F14),
  helpstring("IComponentVideo Interface"),
  pointer_default(unique)
]
interface IComponentVideo : IUnknown
{
  [helpstring("Obtain the signal value")]
  HRESULT GetCVideoSignalValue([out, retval] long* val);
};
```

A bold startup company, ComponentVideo.com, went ahead and developed a new COM component that provides the IComponentVideo interface.

Our original VCR manufacturer has grown fat. As with any big company, management realizes that it cannot move fast. Its only choice is to collaborate with the startup company. Source code reuse is not an option as the two companies have different coding standards and perhaps prefer using different programming languages. So the only choice is to use the startup's component at the binary level (as an executable). The trick, however, is to hide from the customers the information that a third-party component is involved.

There are two ways to achieve this goal—containment and aggregation. Let's look at each of them in detail.

Containment

An easy way to accomplish the company's goal of reusing a third-party component, while hiding the fact from the customers, is to create an instance of the third-party component and internally maintain the interface pointer. This mechanism is referred to as containment—one component contains pointers to interfaces on the other component. In this respect, the containing component is simply a client of the contained component. In COM terminology, the containing component is referred to as the outer component and the contained component as the inner component. Figure 3.2 illustrates this concept.

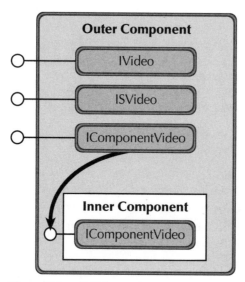

Figure 3.2   COM containment.

The outer component supports the same interface as that of the inner component. However, the implementation explicitly forwards the method calls to the inner component. Such an implementation for our CVcr class is shown below:

```
class CVcr : public IVideo, public ISVideo, IComponentVideo
{
public:
  CVcr(void);
  HRESULT Init();
  ~CVcr();

  // IUnknown interface
  ...

  // IVideo interface
  ...

  // ISVideo interface
  ...

  // IComponentVideo interface
  STDMETHOD(GetCVideoSignalValue)(long* plVal);
```

```
private:
  ...
  IComponentVideo* m_pComponentVideo;
};

CVcr:: CVcr()
{
  ...

  m_pComponentVideo = NULL;
}

HRESULT CVcr::Init()
{
  HRESULT hr = ::CoCreateInstance(
    CLSID_ComponentVCR,
    NULL,
    CLSCTX_ALL,
    IID_IComponentVideo,
    reinterpret_cast<void**>(&m_pComponentVideo));

  return hr;
}

CVcr::~CVcr()
{
  if (NULL != m_pComponentVideo) {
    m_pComponentVideo->Release();
  }

  ...
}

STDMETHODIMP CVcr::QueryInterface(REFIID iid, void** ppRetVal)
{
  ...
  if (IsEqualIID(iid, IID_IComponentVideo)) {
    *ppRetVal = static_cast<IComponentVideo*>(this);
  }
  ...
}

HRESULT CVcr::GetCVideoSignalValue(long* pRetVal)
{
  _ASSERT (NULL != m_pComponentVideo);
  return m_pComponentVideo->GetCVideoSignalValue(pRetVal);
}
```

Note that the interface method GetCVideoSignalValue gets forwarded to the inner component's implementation. In general, for every interface method, the outer component has to define a *wrapper* method that simply turns around and calls the appropriate method on the inner component.

The TV client can obtain the IComponentVideo interface from the VCR in the same way as it normally does, that is, using either CoCreateInstance or QueryInterface, as shown here:

```
int main(int argc, char* argv[])
{
   ::CoInitialize(NULL);
   IComponentVideo* pCVideo = NULL;
   HRESULT hr = ::CoCreateInstance(CLSID_VCR, NULL, CLSCTX_ALL,
      IID_IComponentVideo, reinterpret_cast<void**>(&pCVideo));
   if (FAILED(hr)) {
      DumpError(hr);
      ::CoUninitialize();
      return 1;
   }

   UseCVideo(pCVideo);

   pCVideo->Release();

   ::CoUninitialize();
   return 0;
}

void UseCVideo(IComponentVideo* pCVideo)
{
   long val;
   HRESULT hr;
   for(int i=0; i<10; i++) {
      hr = pCVideo->GetCVideoSignalValue(&val);
      if (FAILED(hr)) {
         DumpError(hr);
         continue;
      }
      cout << "Round: " << i << " - Value: " << val << endl;
   }
}
```

There are two issues with containment:

- For each method in the inner component, the outer component has to implement a wrapper. For a component with potentially thousands of methods, this may become a nuisance.
- If the inner component adds a new interface that could be useful to the client, the client never gets to see it, unless the code of the outer component is modified to incorporate the new interface methods.

These issues may or may not be a problem for the developer of the outer component. If all that is needed is *isolation* from the inner component, with exposure to specific methods, containment is a good technique for component reusability.

Aggregation

Looking at our implementation for containment, an optimization pops into your mind right away—why bother writing wrappers for each interface method of the inner component? Why not just return the interface pointer to the inner component if a request for the interface is made, as shown in the following code:

```
STDMETHODIMP CVcr::QueryInterface(REFIID iid, void** ppRetVal)
{
   ...
  if (IsEqualIID(iid, IID_IComponentVideo)) {
    return m_pComponentVideo->QueryInterface(
      IID_IComponentVideo, ppRetVal);
  }
   ...
}
```

A simple trick, and we save lots of wrapper code. We deserve a pat on the back.

Such a mechanism of component reusage, where the outer component passes the inner component's interface pointer directly to the client, is called *aggregation*. Figure 3.3 illustrates this concept.

Don't gloat too much, however. The code fragment shown earlier violates a number of QueryInterface rules.

Consider the scenario where the client obtains two interface pointers from the VCR object—ISVideo and IComponentVideo. Note that, in our

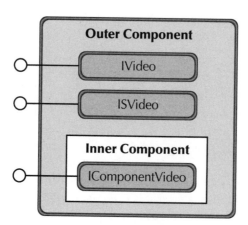

Figure 3.3   COM aggregation.

server implementation, QI for ISVideo will go through the outer component and IComponentVideo will go through the inner component.

- The object identity rule says that a QI for IUnknown on both the interface pointers should return the same pointer. However, as the QI on ISVideo goes through the outer component and the QI on IComponentVideo goes through the inner component, the returned IUnknown pointers are different. This violates the object identity rule.

- If a QI for IVideo is made on the ISVideo interface pointer, it succeeds. However, if a QI for IVideo is made on the IComponentVideo pointer, it fails. This violates the symmetry rule.

The crux of the problem is that the client sees two different unknowns—the inner IUnknown and the outer IUnknown. Each IUnknown implements its own QI and reference counting logic.

The client should see only one object identity, the identity of the outer component, and should never see the inner component's unknown. The inner and outer component should cooperate with each other in convincing the client that there is only one unknown and that an interface pointer on the inner component belongs to the outer component.

As the client may get a direct interface pointer to the inner component, the inner component should just delegate all the IUnknown calls to the outer component.

```
class CInnerComponent : public IUnknown
{
private:
  IUnknown* m_pOuter;
public:
  STDMETHOD(QueryInterface)(REFIID iid, void** pp)
  {
    return m_pOuter->QueryInterface(iid, pp);
  }
  STDMETHOD_(ULONG, AddRef)()
  {
    return m_pOuter->AddRef();
  }
  STDMETHOD_(ULONG, Release)()
  {
    return m_pOuter->Release();
  }
  ...
};
```

Such an implementation of IUnknown, which delegates all three method calls to some other implementation of IUnknown, is referred to as the *delegating* unknown.

There is still a catch in our aggregation logic. Consider the case when the client queries the outer object for an interface that belongs to the inner object. In this case, the outer object will forward the request to the inner object, which in turn delegates it back to the outer object. The process will get into a cycle that cannot be broken.

What this means is, when it comes to QueryInterface, the outer component cannot use the *delegating* unknown from the inner component. The inner component needs to provide a second implementation of the unknown—an implementation that does not delegate calls back to the outer component.

Implementing the Inner Component

There are several ways to provide two distinct implementations of IUnknown from a single object. The most commonly used technique is for the inner component to implement two IUnknown interfaces. The *non-delegating* unknown implements IUnknown for the inner component in the usual way. The *delegating* unknown forwards IUnknown method calls to either the outer unknown (if aggregated) or the *non-delegating* unknown (if not aggregated).

The *non-delegating* IUnknown methods can be declared as three *internal* methods, as shown here:

```
class CComponentVcr : public IComponentVideo
{
public:
      ...
  // Non-delegating IUnknown calls
  STDMETHOD(InternalQueryInterface)(REFIID iid, void** ppv);
  STDMETHOD_(ULONG, InternalAddRef)();
  STDMETHOD_(ULONG, InternalRelease)();
};
```

However, a non-delegating unknown is still an IUnknown type, and therefore has to satisfy the vtbl requirements of IUnknown.

One way to achieve the vtbl requirements is to have a member variable that maintains the binary layout of IUnknown, as shown in the following code fragment:

```
class CComponentVcr : public IComponentVideo
{
public:
  ...
  class CNDUnknown : public IUnknown
  {
  public:
    ...
    CComponentVcr* Object(); // helper function

    STDMETHOD(QueryInterface)(REFIID iid, void** ppv)
    {
      return Object()->InternalQueryInterface(iid, ppv);
    }

    STDMETHOD_(ULONG, AddRef)()
    {
      return Object()->InternalAddRef();
    }

    STDMETHOD_(ULONG, Release)()
    {
      return Object()->InternalRelease();
    }
  };
  CNDUnknown m_NDUnknown;
  ...
};
```

In the above code, the helper method CNDUnknown::Object needs to return the pointer to the CComponentVcr instance. A simple C trick that can be used is to reconstruct the pointer to the CComponentVcr instance based on the knowledge that the member variable m_NDUnknown has a fixed memory that is offset from the beginning of its parent class, as shown here:

```
class CNDUnknown : public IUnknown
{
public:
  ...
  CComponentVcr* Object()
  {
    return reinterpret_cast<CComponentVcr*>(
      reinterpret_cast<BYTE*>(this) -
        offsetof(CComponentVcr, m_NDUnknown));
  }
  ...
```

The *non-delegating* implementation of IUnknown, that is, methods InternalQueryInterface, InternalAddRef, and InternalRelease, are similar to the ones we have seen many times in earlier examples. The only difference is that, when requested for IUnknown, QueryInterface returns a pointer to the *non-delegating* IUnknown, and not "this." The code fragment is shown below:

```
STDMETHODIMP CComponentVcr::InternalQueryInterface(REFIID iid,
  void** ppRetVal)
{
  *ppRetVal = NULL;

  if (IsEqualIID(iid, IID_IUnknown)) {
    *ppRetVal = static_cast<IUnknown*>(&m_NDUnknown);
  }else
  if (IsEqualIID(iid, IID_IComponentVideo)) {
    *ppRetVal = static_cast<IComponentVideo*>(this);
  }

  if (NULL != (*ppRetVal)) {
    reinterpret_cast<IUnknown*>(*ppRetVal)->AddRef();
    return S_OK;
  }

  return E_NOINTERFACE;
}

STDMETHODIMP_(ULONG) CComponentVcr::InternalAddRef()
{
  return (++m_lRefCount);
}
```

```
STDMETHODIMP_(ULONG) CComponentVcr::InternalRelease()
{
  ULONG lRetVal = (-m_lRefCount);
  if (0 == lRetVal) {
    delete this;
  }
  return lRetVal;
}
```

The logic for *delegating* unknown implementation is straightforward. A member variable can be used to obtain the desired indirection to the actual `IUnknown` implementation.

```
class CComponentVcr : public IComponentVideo
{
private:
  IUnknown* m_pUnkActual; // actual unknown to be invoked

public:
  // IUnknown interface (delegating IUnknown)
  STDMETHOD(QueryInterface)(REFIID iid, void** ppv)
  {
    return m_pUnkActual->QueryInterface(iid, ppv);
  }

  STDMETHOD_(ULONG, AddRef)()
  {
    return m_pUnkActual->AddRef();
  }

  STDMETHOD_(ULONG, Release)()
  {
    return m_pUnkActual->Release();
  }
}
```

Variable `m_pUnkActual` needs to point to either the outer unknown (in case of aggregation) or to the non-delegating unknown (if used as a stand-alone object). The code below defines an initialization method on the object. The parameter passed is the pointer to the outer object, in the case of aggregation, or `NULL`, if used as a stand-alone object.

```
class CComponentVcr : public IComponentVideo
{
public:
  HRESULT Init(IUnknown* pUnkOuter);
  ...
};
```

```
HRESULT CComponentVcr::Init(IUnknown* pUnkOuter)
{
  if (NULL == pUnkOuter) {
    m_pUnkActual = &m_NDUnknown;
  }else {
    m_pUnkActual = pUnkOuter;
  }
  return S_OK;
}
```

So how would a component know if it is being instantiated as a stand-alone object or as an inner object? Obviously, this information has to be available in the `IClassFactory::CreateInstance` method so that the implementation can construct the object appropriately.

COM designers had already considered the possibility of component reuse using aggregation. Recall that the `IClassFactory::CreateInstance` method had three parameters:

```
HRESULT CreateInstance([in] IUnknown* pUnk, [in] REFIID riid,
  [out, iid_is(riid)] void** ppv);
```

So far, we took the first parameter for granted and just passed a NULL value. Now, it is time for us to pass a non-NULL value as the first parameter.

COM specifies that, if `IClassFactory::CreateInstance` is invoked with a desire to aggregate, the first parameter should be a pointer to the outer object.

Recall that in the case of aggregation, the inner component needs to return a pointer to the non-delegating unknown. Also recall that, in our implementation of `InternalQueryInterface`, we return a non-delegating unknown only if the requested interface is `IID_IUnknown`. Otherwise, we would need to create a non-delegating `vtbl` layout for every interface that is requested.

To ease the development pain, COM further mandates that, in the case of aggregation, the requested interface be restricted to `IID_IUnknown`. That is, if the first parameter to `CreateInstance` is non-NULL, the second parameter *has* to be `IID_IUnknown`.

These specifications apply not only to `IClassFactory::CreateInstance`, but also to its corresponding API function, `CoCreateInstance`.

With these specifications, our function `CreateInstance` can be implemented as follows:

```
STDMETHODIMP CComponentVcrClassObject::CreateInstance(
  IUnknown* pUnkOuter,
  REFIID riid,
  void** ppV)
{
  *ppV = NULL; // always initialize the return value

  if ((NULL != pUnkOuter) && (IID_IUnknown != riid) ) {
    return E_INVALIDARG;
  }

  CComponentVcr* pVCR = new CComponentVcr;
  if (NULL == pVCR) {
    return E_OUTOFMEMORY;
  }

  HRESULT hr = pVCR->Init(pUnkOuter);
  if (FAILED(hr)) {
    delete pVCR;
    return hr;
  }

  hr = pVCR->InternalQueryInterface(riid, ppV);
  if (FAILED(hr)) {
    delete pVCR;
  }
  return hr;
}
```

Note that what we return is the *non-delegating* version of the unknown. If a stand-alone object is created, this is certainly appropriate. If an aggregate is being created, this is necessary to ensure that the inner object is AddRefed, not the outer object.

ATL's Support for Implementing the Inner Component.   By default, ATL assumes that a component will support aggregation. If the support for aggregation is not desired, it can be turned off by using an ATL-supplied macro, DECLARE_NOT_AGGREGATABLE, as shown in the following code fragment:

```
class CVcr : ...
{
  ...

DECLARE_NOT_AGGREGATABLE(CVcr)
  ...
};
```

Implementing the Outer Component

Let's examine the implementation details of the outer component.

As you would expect, the outer component has to maintain a pointer to the IUnknown interface of the inner component.

```cpp
class CVcr : public IVideo, public ISVideo
{
public:
  CVcr(void);
  HRESULT Init();
  ~CVcr();
  ...
private:
  ...
  IUnknown* m_pUnkInner;
};
```

The inner component can be instantiated during some initialization call and can be released in the destructor, as shown here:

```cpp
CVcr:: CVcr()
{
  ...
  m_pUnkInner = NULL;
}

HRESULT CVcr::Init()
{
  HRESULT hr = ::CoCreateInstance(
    CLSID_ComponentVCR,
    GetRawUnknown(),
    CLSCTX_ALL,
    IID_IUnknown,
    reinterpret_cast<void**>(&m_pUnkInner));

  return hr;
}

CVcr::~CVcr()
{
  if (NULL != m_pUnkInner) {
    m_pUnkInner->Release();
  }
  ...
}
```

When the client queries the interface that is supported by the inner component, the outer component can just forward the request to the inner component:

```
STDMETHODIMP CVcr::QueryInterface(REFIID iid, void** ppRetVal)
{
  ...

  if (IsEqualIID(iid, IID_IComponentVideo)) {
    return m_pUnkInner->QueryInterface(iid, ppRetVal);
  }
  ...
}
```

Now you can pat yourself on your back. We just finished writing a
COM server that supports aggregation.

ATL Support for the Outer Component.   ATL simplifies the
grunge work of dealing with the inner components. Following are the steps:

Step 1: Add a member variable to hold the inner component.

```
class CVcr : ...
{
  ...
private:
  CComPtr<IUnknown> m_spUnkInner;
};
```

Step 2: Add the COM_INTERFACE_ENTRY_AUTOAGGREGATE macro to the
        interface map.

```
class CVcr : ...
{
  ...
BEGIN_COM_MAP(CVcr)
  COM_INTERFACE_ENTRY(IVideo)
  COM_INTERFACE_ENTRY(ISVideo)
  COM_INTERFACE_ENTRY_AUTOAGGREGATE(__uuidof(IComponentVideo),
    m_spUnkInner.p, __uuidof(ComponentVCR))
END_COM_MAP()
};
```

Step 3: Add the DECLARE_GET_CONTROLLING_UNKNOWN macro to the class.

```
class CVcr : ...
{
  ...
DECLARE_GET_CONTROLLING_UNKNOWN ()
};
```

That's it. With just three simple steps, ATL can automatically manage the inner component.

Aggregation Gotchas

In the previous code fragment, note that the initialization method of the outer object AddRefs the inner object. According to the reference counting rules, this is the right thing to do. However, in our code, the initialization method of the inner object does not AddRef the outer object, even though it duplicates the pointer to the outer object. This violates our reference counting rule #4. However, there is a reason behind the logic. Had the inner object called AddRef on the outer object, the reference count of the outer object would never go to zero, even after the client has released all the references to the object. Thus, the outer object, and therefore the inner object, will always stay in memory.

To avoid such an unbroken cycle in the case of aggregation, COM explicitly mandates that the outer object hold a reference-counted pointer to the inner object's non-delegating unknown and the inner object hold a non-reference-counted pointer to the IUnknown of the outer object.

What about violating the reference counting rule? Well, the above relationship between the outer and inner object is covered under the special knowledge clause of reference counting: as the lifetime of the inner object is a proper subset of the lifetime of the outer object, it is safe for the inner object not to reference-count the outer object.

A similar reference counting problem occurs when the inner object needs to communicate with the outer object. In order to do so, the inner object needs to call QueryInterface through the controlling IUnknown. This results in AddRefing the outer object. If the inner object holds the returned interface pointer as a data member, we once again get into an unbroken cycle.

To avoid such a problem, the inner object should acquire and release the interface pointer on demand, holding on to the pointer only as long as it is needed, as illustrated in the following code snippet:

```
STDMETHODIMP CInner::SomeMethod()
{
  ISomeInterface* pY = NULL;
  m_pUnkOuter->QueryInterface(IID_ISomeInterface, (void**) &pY);
  Use(pY);
  pY->Release();
}
```

Knowing that the lifetime of the inner object is less than the lifetime of the outer object, you can play another trick—acquire and release the pointer once at initialization time, but continue to hold the pointer as a data member.

```
STDMETHODIMP CInner::Initialize()
{
  m_pUnkOuter->QueryInterface(IID_ISomeInterface,
    (void**) &m_pY);
  m_pY->Release();
  // m_pY still points to the valid object.
  // Use it whenever needed.
}
```

However, this is a dangerous trick to play. If the outer object implements the requested interface as a tear-off interface, the call to Release will destroy the tear-off object, leaving variable m_pY pointing to an invalid object.

ERROR REPORTING

Recall our implementation of the ISVideo interface method GetSVideoSig-nalValue. If a member variable exceeded a limit, which could happen only if we had some implementation problem, we returned an SDK-defined error code E_UNEXPECTED. The following code fragment shows the relevant lines:

```
// File Vcr.cpp

HRESULT CVcr::GetSVideoSignalValue(long* pRetVal)
{
  if (m_nCurCount >= 5 || m_nCurCount < 0) {
    return E_UNEXPECTED;
  }
  ...
}
```

If the client receives this error code and runs it through the DumpError method defined in Chapter 2, the error displayed would be "catastrophic failure." This error doesn't convey much to either the client or the developer, as it could have been generated by any of the layers between the client and the server (such as the COM library, the COM marshaling mechanism, the ORPC channel, etc.).

Instead of returning such a generic error message, it makes more sense to return an error code that is meaningful in the context of the ISVideo interface alone. This is where the custom HRESULTs (from Chapter 2) come into picture.

A custom HRESULT can be defined in the IDL file using the familiar MAKE_HRESULT macro, as shown here:

```
// File Video.idl

cpp_quote("#define VCR_E_INTERNALERROR \
  MAKE_HRESULT(SEVERITY_ERROR, FACILITY_ITF, 0x200 + 1)")
```

Keyword cpp_quote causes MIDL to emit the specified string into the generated header file.

The GetSVideoSignalValue code can be modified to return this new HRESULT value.

```
// File Vcr.cpp

HRESULT CVcr::GetSVideoSignalValue(long* pRetVal)
{
  if (m_nCurCount >= 5 || m_nCurCount < 0) {
    return VCR_E_INTERNALERROR;
  }
  ...
}
```

The client can now check if the error code is specifically from the object, as follows:

```
// File tv.cpp

int main(int /*argc*/, char* /*argv*/[])
{
  ::CoInitialize(NULL);
  DoIt();
  ::CoUninitialize();
  return 0;
}

void DoIt()
{
  ISVideo* pSVideo = NULL;
  HRESULT hr = ::CoCreateInstance(CLSID_VCR, NULL, CLSCTX_ALL,
    IID_ISVideo, reinterpret_cast<void**>(&pSVideo));
  if (FAILED(hr)) {
    DumpError(hr);
    return;
  }
```

```
  long val;
  hr = pSVideo->GetSVideoSignalValue(&val);
  if (SUCCEEDED(hr)) {
    cout << "Value: " << val << endl;
    return;
  }

  // The call failed
  if (HRESULT_FACILITY(hr) == FACILITY_ITF) {
    cout << "ISVideo specific error: 0x" << hex << hr << endl;
  }else {
    DumpError(hr);
  }
}
```

Recall from Chapter 2 that a custom HRESULT is meaningful only in the context of the interface. If two interfaces define the same custom HRE-SULT, it will not cause any problems.

A last bit of information on custom HRESULTs—a custom HRESULT need not always return failure codes. It can also return success codes using SEVERITY_SUCCESS.

At this point, I would like to temporarily deviate from the main topic and bring your attention to a bug in our TV client code.

If you observe the code, you will see that we forgot to call Release on the pSVideo interface pointer, not just at one place, but at two places.

Such a programming mistake, however, cannot be completely elimi-nated, at least for us humans. What would be nice is if the pointer automati-cally released itself when it goes out of scope.

Writing such a *smart* pointer class is not that difficult. However, it turns out that ATL has already done this for us. It defines a template called CComPtr that a client can use with minimal code changes. Our revised TV client code, using CComPtr, is as follows:

```
// File tv.cpp

...
#include <atlbase.h>
...
void DoIt()
{
  CComPtr<ISVideo> spSVideo;
  HRESULT hr = ::CoCreateInstance(CLSID_VCR, NULL, CLSCTX_ALL,
    IID_ISVideo, reinterpret_cast<void**>(&spSVideo));
```

```
  if (FAILED(hr)) {
    DumpError(hr);
    return;
  }

  long val;
  hr = spSVideo->GetSVideoSignalValue(&val);
  if (SUCCEEDED(hr)) {
    cout << "Value: " << val << endl;
    return;
  }

  // The call failed
  if (HRESULT_FACILITY(hr) == FACILITY_ITF) {
    cout << "ISVideo specific error: 0x" << hex << hr << endl;
  }else {
    DumpError(hr);
  }
}
```

The variable spSVideo will release itself, if it is not NULL, when it goes out of scope.

Note that I changed the variable name from pSVideo to spSVideo. This follows the convention I have adopted throughout the book (and in real life) whenever I use a smart pointer.

Visual C++ natively supports a smart pointer class called _com_ptr_t that is similar in functionality to CComPtr. To create a specialized version of an interface, Visual C++ defines a macro called _COM_SMARTPTR_TYPEDEF. The following code, for example, declares the _com_ptr_t specialization ISVideoPtr.

```
_COM_SMARTPTR_TYPEDEF(ISVideo, __uuidof(ISVideo));
```

Visual C++ defines _com_ptr_t specialization for many standard interfaces. In addition, it can generate specialization for an interface defined in a type-library using a pre-processor directive called import. The usage of this directive is shown later in the section.

 Always use smart pointers to make your code more robust.

We can now return to our main topic of error reporting.

A custom HRESULT by itself is still not very descriptive to the client. What would be nice is if the object returns a descriptive text to the client.

Using C++ style exceptions as a possibility can be ruled out. Recall from Chapter 1 that there is no binary standard for them.

To address this problem, COM defines an interface, IErrorInfo, that the server can use to set extended error information and the client can use to retrieve it. The interface divides the extended error information into five fields:

- The IID of the interface that sets the error information.
- The source responsible for setting the error information. This field is typically filled with the class name of the object.
- The textual description of the error.
- The Windows help filename, if any, that documents this error.
- The Windows help context ID for this error.

The server code may implement an object that supports IErrorInfo, populate its fields, and call a COM API SetErrorInfo to set the extended error information. Following is the prototype for SetErrorInfo:

```
HRESULT SetErrorInfo([in] DWORD dwReserved,
    [in] IErrorInfo* pEI);
```

COM provides a default implementation of IErrorInfo that can be instantiated using the COM API function CreateErrorInfo. Following is its prototype:

```
HRESULT CreateErrorInfo([out] ICreateErrorInfo** ppCEI);
```

The API returns an object that supports an additional interface, ICreateErrorInfo. This interface defines methods to populate the above-mentioned fields. Note that not all fields need to be populated. The server may choose to leave some fields empty.

The following server side code fragment shows how the default implementation of IErrorInfo can be used to set the error information:

```
void CVcr::Error(REFIID iid, LPOLESTR pszDesc)
{
  // Create error information
  CComPtr<ICreateErrorInfo> spCEI;
  HRESULT hr = ::CreateErrorInfo(&spCEI);
  _ASSERT (SUCCEEDED(hr));
  hr = spCEI->SetGUID(iid);
  _ASSERT (SUCCEEDED(hr));
```

```
hr = spCEI->SetSource(OLESTR("My VCR"));
_ASSERT (SUCCEEDED(hr));
hr = spCEI->SetDescription(pszDesc);
_ASSERT (SUCCEEDED(hr));

// Make error information available to the client
CComPtr<IErrorInfo> spEI;
hr = spCEI->QueryInterface(IID_IErrorInfo, (void**) &spEI);
_ASSERT (SUCCEEDED(hr));
hr = ::SetErrorInfo(0, spEI);
_ASSERT (SUCCEEDED(hr));
}
```

The following code fragment shows how our server client can use the above method to set the error information:

```
HRESULT CVcr::GetSignalValue(long* pRetVal)
{
  if (m_nCurCount >= 5 || m_nCurCount < 0) {
    Error(IID_IVideo, OLESTR("Count is out of range"));
    return VCR_E_INTERNALERROR;
  }
  ...
}
```

With this logic, the client can now obtain the extended error information using the COM API GetErrorInfo. Following is its prototype:

```
HRESULT GetErrorInfo([in] DWORD dwReserved,
  [out] IErrorInfo** ppEI);
```

While calling GetErrorInfo will return some error information, the client unfortunately does not know if it is some stale information left over as a result of calling some other COM API or some other interface method on some other object.

To ensure that the error information originated as a result of calling the specific interface on the object, COM mandates that the client first ask the object if it supports error information by querying it for a standard interface IsupportErrorInfo. Following is its definition:

```
interface ISupportErrorInfo: IUnknown
{
  HRESULT InterfaceSupportsErrorInfo( [in] REFIID riid);
}
```

Method InterfaceSupportsErrorInfo can be used to further confirm if the object supports error information on a specific interface.

The following TV client code fragment illustrates the use of obtaining extended error information:

```
void DoIt()
{
  ...
  // The call on ISVideo failed
  ...
  // Check if the object supports extended error information
  CComPtr<ISupportErrorInfo> spSEI;
  hr = spSVideo->QueryInterface(IID_ISupportErrorInfo,
    (void**) &spSEI);
  if (FAILED(hr)) {
    return; // error info not supported
  }

  // Check if error info is available for ISVideo interface
  hr = spSEI->InterfaceSupportsErrorInfo(IID_ISVideo);
  if (S_OK != hr) {
    return; // error info not supported on ISVideo
  }

  // Get the error information and display
  CComPtr<IErrorInfo> spEI;
  hr = ::GetErrorInfo(0, &spEI);
  if (FAILED(hr)) {
    return; // failed for some obscure reason
  }

  CComBSTR bsDesc;
  hr = spEI->GetDescription(&bsDesc);
  if (FAILED(hr)) {
    return; // failed for some obscure reason
  }

  USES_CONVERSION;
  cout << "Extended error info: " << W2T(bsDesc) << endl;
}
```

Obtaining descriptive text requires a lot of coding. Fortunately, the code can easily be encapsulated in a utility function. However, Visual C++ has added native COM support to deal with this situation in the form of a class called _com_error. The following code fragment shows our revised DumpError logic using this class:

```
void DumpError(_com_error& e)
{
  if (HRESULT_FACILITY(e.Error()) == FACILITY_ITF) {
    cout << "ISVideo specific error: 0x"
      << hex << e.Error() << endl;
  }else {
    cout << e.ErrorMessage() << endl;
  }

  // Extended error, if any
  _bstr_t bsDesc = e.Description();
  if (NULL != (LPCTSTR) bsDesc) {
    cout << "Extended error info: "
      << (LPCTSTR) bsDesc << endl;
  }
}
```

To use the native COM support, a function that fails typically throws an exception of type _com_error. Using the exception mechanism, our main entry function can be rewritten as follows:

```
int main(int /*argc*/, char* /*argv*/[])
{
  ::CoInitialize(NULL);
  try {
    DoIt();
  }catch(_com_error& e) {
    DumpError(e);
  }

  ::CoUninitialize();
  return 0;
}
```

What about the actual DoIt code?

In order to fully utilize the potential of native COM support, the compiler has added a new directive called import that takes a filename as an argument. The filename could be a type-library file or an executable file containing a type library.

```
#import "Video.tlb" no_namespace
```

Upon this directive, the compiler reads the type library and generates wrapper classes for all the interfaces encountered. These wrapper classes implement methods that throw a _com_error exception on failures.

Attribute no_namespace turns off the namespace scoping on the generated classes. Consult the online documentation for other attributes.

With the native COM support enabled, our `DoIt` method can be rewritten as follows:

```
void DoIt()
{
  ISVideoPtr spSVideo(__uuidof(VCR));
  long val = spSVideo->GetSVideoSignalValue();
  cout << "Value: " << val << endl;
}
```

It is worth comparing this code with the earlier written code that was based on raw method calls. The code based on native COM support is very small and easy to maintain.

We are done (finally). Now we know how to develop COM-based servers and clients, and we have picked up a few good tips on using ATL as well as native COM support provided by Visual C++.

SUMMARY

In this chapter, we looked at how to implement COM servers and COM clients.
Implementing a COM server requires the following:

- For every COM class (`coclass`), an implementation class has to be developed. The implementation class supports one or more interfaces.
- The implementation class should also support `IUnknown` and should abide by the rules of `QueryInterface`.
- For every coclass, a class object has to be created. The class object typically supports interface `IClassFactory` to let the clients create instances of the implementation class.
- The server code has to implement logic for registering and unregistering the server.
- The server code has to deal with the lifetime management of the objects it creates.

We saw that the framework provided by ATL takes care of most of the grunge work.

A COM server can also reuse a third-party component using containment or aggregation. We looked at how ATL simplifies developing a component that supports aggregation.

In developing a COM client, the client has to follow certain rules of reference counting. We saw how ATL, as well as Visual C++ native COM support, can simplify client programming.

Finally, we looked at how to provide better error messages from the server to the client.

This chapter and the previous chapters built the foundation of COM, which is also the foundation of COM+. It is very difficult to determine where COM ends and COM+ begins. Any COM-related technology could also be referred to as COM+ technology. Hence, I may interchange the terms COM and COM+. At places where I explicitly wish to indicate a COM technology prior to Windows 2000, I will refer to it as *classic* COM.

In the chapters to follow, we will look at the facilities provided by COM+ in developing enterprise systems.

REFERENCES

[Mcq-98]   Craig McQueen, "Using the ATL Registry Component," Visual C++ Developer, October 1998. *http://msdn.microsoft.com/library/periodic/period98/ Vcd1098.htm*

[Gri-98]   Richard Grimes, *Professional ATL COM Programming*, Wrox Press, ISBN 1-861001-4-01, 1998.

[Box-98]   Don Box, *Essential COM*, Addison Wesley, ISBN 0-201-63446-5, 1998.

[Rec-99]   Brent Rector and Chris Sells, *ATL Internals*, Addison Wesley, ISBN 0-201-69589-8, 1999.

[Rog-97]   Dale Rogerson, *Inside COM*, Microsoft Press, ISBN 1-57231-349-8, 1997.

The Extension

Essence of COM+

$\mathbf{I}$n the previous chapters, we built the foundation of the component object model. By providing the ability to link components dynamically and by standardizing the communication interface between the components to a binary level, we provided a way for software developers to reuse code without regard to the compiler or programming language.

Although COM provides a good infrastructure for developers to create software products, it does not alleviate the problems of developing enterprise systems—applications that are used in large organizations such as banks, airlines, insurance companies, and hospitals. The development complexity arises from the extra enterprise-level requirements such as scalability, robustness, security, transaction support, etc.

In order to meet these requirements, enterprise application designers tend to develop their own in-house software infrastructure. Thus, developing enterprise systems not only becomes a slow process, but also consumes resources for development and maintenance, for what is essentially a generic infrastructure problem.

COM+ is an advanced COM run-time environment that provides solutions to many generic infrastructure problems, including those previously mentioned. It is an integral part of Windows 2000 operating system.

In this chapter, we examine in detail the requirements for enterprise systems and get an overview of the services provided by COM+ to facilitate developing enterprise systems.

ENTERPRISE SYSTEMS

An enterprise system typically consists of different programs on different computers interacting with each other. It is a large application, at least compared to a single desktop application, and typically integrates with databases. These applications are generally used in large organizations, and are accessed by hundreds of clients simultaneously.

Historically, developing enterprise systems has been a very long and very expensive process. This is primarily because of the requirements developers had to meet. Let's examine some of those requirements.

Security

Almost all enterprise applications care about security issues. Following are some security requirements:

- The application has to ensure that only authorized users can access the system.
- Some people have more privileges than others in accessing the system. The application has to maintain a table of individuals and their roles in accessing the system.
- The application has to authenticate the users, that is, verify that the users are indeed the ones they claim to be.
- If any sensitive information is being sent from one computer to another, the application has to provide some level of data encryption to prevent hackers from tapping the wire. The level of encryption increases with the sensitivity of the information.

Scalability

An enterprise system has to be designed such that hundreds of clients can access it concurrently, yet each client request should be serviced in a reasonable amount of time. Some requirements are as follows:

- The client load can frequently cause the application to outgrow a single computer. The application should provide some form of load balancing between multiple computers.
- If a database is frequently accessed, the application has to cache data, such as back-end tables in memory, to improve performance.

- In case of distributed computing, the application should continue to work even if the remote computer is not accessible.
- Frequently, just one instance of an application component is not enough to handle the client load. For such cases, the application has to create a *pool* of multiple instances of the component.

Sharing Resources

A resource such as a database table or some in-memory state of a component is often shared among many subsystems of an enterprise system. In such cases, the requirements are as follows:

- If two subsystems, or two instances of the same component, try to modify a resource concurrently from multiple threads, it may produce some inconsistency in the state of the resource. The application has to ensure the consistency of the data, perhaps by ensuring that only one subsystem can modify the data at a time.
- The application has to be designed such that a deadlock does not occur when two subsystems wait on each other for releasing a resource.

Transactions

An enterprise application typically deals with multiple databases. A transaction may require more than one database to be updated. However, if the update succeeds on one database and fails on another, the system may get into an inconsistent state. The possibility of this happening is pretty good, considering that the databases may reside at geographically dispersed locations, and given that power and network outages are facts of life.

A transaction must be such that it entirely succeeds or entirely fails. However many different operations the transaction involves, either everything must be updated successfully or nothing should be updated. This all-or-nothing proposition of a transaction is called *atomicity*.

Besides atomicity, a transaction has to meet three other requirements: consistency, isolation, and durability. These requirements are typically referred to as ACID rules (A = Atomicity, C = Consistency, I = Isolation, and D = Durability).

An enterprise system has to treat various operations across multiple databases as a single transaction and ensure the integrity of the system by meeting the ACID rules.

THREE-TIER ARCHITECTURE

A paradigm that has emerged as a standard for corporate application development has been the two-tier model. The first tier is the user's application and the second tier is the data source. A common two-tier architecture is the client/server model. Under this model, the second tier (the server) accesses a database management system such as SQL Server, and the first tier (the client) does the needed data processing and presents the information to the user.

The incredible explosion of the Internet has caused a revolution in the way information has to be made available to users. The users now expect to get the information and applications they need from a single location, the browser. The traditional client/server model cannot meet this challenge. The data processing logic, the transactional logic, the synchronization logic, etc., cannot just be embedded at the user application level. What is needed is to separate the presentation logic from the data processing logic. The data processing logic, commonly referred to as the business logic, can then provide a centralized resource management functionality across multiple clients. This three-tier architecture, enhanced for Internet applications, is depicted in Figure 4.1.

There are a variety of approaches for implementing all the layers, depending on the choice of data access layer, the types of clients, the developer's choice of tools and technology, and the communication mechanism between different layers. Although developers can implement their own mechanisms, it is ultimately better to choose a mechanism that reduces maintenance.

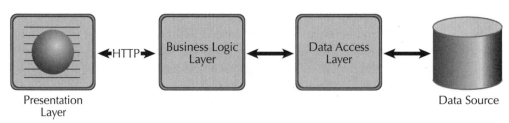

Figure 4.1   Internet three-tier architecture.

Windows DNA

To simplify three-tier enterprise-level application development, Microsoft has defined a technology termed Windows Distributed interNet Applications Architecture, or Windows DNA. Windows DNA describes those Microsoft technologies that provide a complete, integrated n-tier development model, and those services that developers require to build scalable and dependable enterprise-level systems on Windows platform.

The DNA architecture consists of three logical tiers corresponding to each layer of the three-tier architecture, as shown in Figure 4.2.

The presentation services tier is the application front end. This tier is responsible for gathering information from the users, sending the information to the business services tier, receiving the results from the business services, and presenting them to the users. The applications in this tier can be devel-

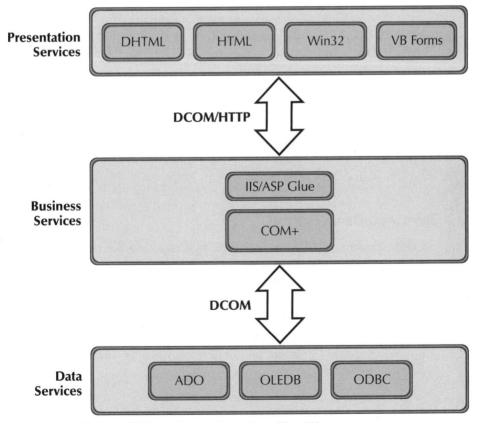

Figure 4.2   Windows DNA services. Adapted from [Fer-99].

oped either as rich clients or thin clients. A rich client uses VB forms or Win32 services directly. A thin client (one that targets a browser) uses HTML or DHTML along with some client-side and some server-side scripting, if needed.

The business services tier is responsible for receiving input from the presentation tier, interacting with the data services tier, performing the application's business operations, and sending the information back to the presentation tier.

For supporting thin-client-based applications, Microsoft provides a web server called Internet Information Server (IIS). To support server-side scripting, Microsoft provides another technology called Active Server Pages (ASP). ASP is typically bundled with IIS.

The data services tier is the only tier that deals directly with the data, which usually resides in a relational database such as SQL Server. This tier is responsible for the storage, retrieval, and general maintenance of the data.

In order to standardize data access mechanisms across various database servers, Microsoft has defined technologies such as Open Database Connectivity (ODBC) and a more recent one, OLE DB. In order to simplify the usage model, Microsoft has built another technology on top of OLE DB called Active Data Object (ADO).

The long-term vision of Windows DNA is to simplify all three tiers by providing infrastructural support at each level [ARM-99]. The current focus, however, is to provide infrastructure at the business services tier, and to some extent at the data services tier, in the form of COM+. Let's move on to explore what COM+ is all about.

COM+ = SIMPLIFIED DEVELOPMENT

COM+ extends COM's run-time environment to provide infrastructure for developing enterprise-level applications. It specifically addresses the problems of the business tier in the three-tier model. This is an integral part of the Windows 2000 operating system. As many of the tedious, grungy details of run-time services are moved into the operating system, the developers are free to focus on higher-level problems and their solutions.

Let's quickly examine the services provided by COM+. In the later chapters, we will cover these services in detail.

Administrative Control

Traditionally, a lot of configuration details of an application are embedded in the application itself. As an example, an application can explicitly check to ensure that its caller belongs to the administrative group. Such a control should really belong to the actual administrator of the application, and not the application itself.

COM+ provides a distinction between the main logic of the program and its configuration. It defines a standard location, called the COM+ Catalog, to store configuration information for each application. A developer can use declarative programming attributes, outside the scope of the application, to define the default configuration settings. However, an administrator can change these settings either programmatically or by using a COM+ provided tool called the Component Services Snap-in.

Transaction Services

Currently, many commercially available database servers meet the requirements of a transaction. Such a server typically buffers the changes made to a specific database until the client tells it to *commit* the changes. At this point, all the changes are applied to the database in question.

Although the database server takes care of each database individually, there is no standardized technique to coordinate operations among distributed databases, and among distributed components. Developing such a code is extremely hard, as well as resource-consuming.

COM+ provides an easy way to treat operations across distributed databases and components as a single transaction. It simplifies the way an individual operation votes towards the outcome of a transaction.

A transaction, however, need not always deal with a database. It may involve a non-database-related operation such as sending an e-mail. In case the transaction fails, sending the e-mail should be aborted.

COM+ provides a mechanism to let the developers define one or more operations that can participate in a transaction. Using this mechanism, for example, you can develop code to access a legacy database as part of a distributed transaction.

Security Services

As mentioned earlier, an enterprise system requires many security primitives such as authenticating a user, ensuring that the user is authorized to access the specific part of the system, providing encryption when data is transmitted over the wire, etc. COM+ provides all these services.

Enterprise applications often go beyond the basic security primitives. They require that the access to a specific part of the system be based on logical groupings of users, called roles. COM+ lets a developer define user roles for an application. Note that these user roles are not the same as the user groups that one can create using Windows' User Manager. A Windows user group defines the resources that the group-users can access at the operating system level. A user role under COM+ is defined at the application level. It defines the specific parts of the application the users (under the role) have access to.

COM+ provides an easy way for administrators to associate existing user accounts (or user groups) with a particular role. For situations that are too complex to be handled administratively, COM+ provides a way for developers to programmatically define the security logic.

Under distributed systems, it is sometimes required that component B act on behalf of its caller component A when accessing another component C, where all three components reside on different machines. Such a requirement is called *user delegation*. Implementing user delegation is not an easy task and requires some low-level support from the operating system. Here, once again, COM+ (and Windows 2000) comes to the rescue.

Synchronization Services

Under distributed systems, certain critical portions of the components need protection against the possibility of concurrent access from multiple threads. Writing code to do this is not only expensive in terms of time and money, but it is also extremely difficult to get it right.

COM+ offers various levels of synchronization primitives to protect resources from concurrent access. Depending on the level of desired scalability, and the quality of the code, either the developer or the administrator can choose an appropriate synchronization level for the application. For situations that are too complex to handle administratively, COM+ defines programmatic ways to define synchronization logic.

For serializing calls to an object, classic COM required the Windows message queue. However, because of the way the architecture was implemented, any time a client made a call to such an object, it required a thread-switch, which tends to be expensive. COM+ defines a new synchronization paradigm which controls concurrent access and doesn't require a thread switch or the Windows message queue.

Queued Components

The development model under classic COM is based on procedural interaction. A client connects to a component, queries the appropriate interface, and makes synchronous method calls on the returned interface. The following code example illustrates this behavior. The code fragment credits a user account with 100 dollars. It uses a remote component for updating the account balance.

```
// Get the account manager object from the machine "PVTEST00"
COSERVERINFO serverInfo;
serverInfo.pwszName = OLESTR("PVTEST00");
...

MULTI_QI mqiEntry;
mqiEntry.pIID = &IID_IUnknown;
...

HRESULT hr = CoCreateInstanceEx(
    __uuidof(AccountMgr),
    ...,
    &serverInfo,
    1,
    &mqiEntry),
...

IAccountMgrPtr spAccountMgr = mqiEntry.pItf;
mqiEntry.pItf->Release();
spAccountMgr->Credit(CComBSTR("Pradeep"), 100);
spAccountMgr = NULL; // release the object
```

Under such a model, the life cycle of the client is tightly coupled with the component. An RPC connection is maintained between the client and the account manager. This model is easy to program. The client assumes that the component is loaded and running throughout the interaction.

The program fails, however, if the remote object is not reachable. Perhaps the network was down at the time the call was made.

An alternative to such a synchronous programming technique is to use another technique called *message-based programming*.

In a message-based application, the client and the component are separated by time. Therefore, their life cycles are decoupled. This gives the application developer flexibility in the area of scalability and availability. If the component is not available, the client application can still execute.

Of course, developing a message-based distributed application requires a lot of plumbing. Microsoft provides this plumbing in the form of a technology called Microsoft's Message Queue Server (MSMQ).

COM+ simplifies message-based programming further by hiding the details of messaging with a service called Queued Components. The developers continue to develop the components in the same way they always did, with a couple of exceptions that we will cover later.

Here's how the process works. When the client instantiates a queued component, the run-time service actually creates a local proxy object called a *recorder*. As the client makes method calls, the recorder simply records them (into a MSMQ message). When the client releases the last reference to the object, the message is passed to the actual server via MSMQ. A special service running on the server then de-queues the message and instantiates the component using another proxy called the *player*. The player interacts with the component, as if it was the actual client, and plays the stored method calls. If a call fails during the operation, the message is placed back into the queue, at which point the developer has several options to deal with the message, based on the services provided by MSMQ.

Event Service

Traditionally, events or callbacks between a component and any associated clients are handled as follows:

- The component defines an interface that it will use for callbacks.
- The client implements an object supporting this interface. Such an object is referred to as a *sink*.
- The client registers the sink with the component.
- The component invokes an appropriate method on the sink.
- When no longer needed, the client can unregister the sink.

Note that the conventional sense of client and component reverses their roles when talking about events. As the component is making the method call, it becomes the client and the actual client becomes the server. In this regard, COM+ uses the term "publisher" for the component that will publish or provide information, and the term "subscriber" for the module that intends to receive such information.

A major drawback with the traditional publisher/subscriber model is that their life cycles are tightly coupled (because of COM's RPC-based implementation). Another drawback is that to multicast information, that is, to inform all the subscribers simultaneously, requires a lot of low-level code.

The COM+ events model significantly upgrades the traditional event model. It decouples the tight binding between the client and the server by providing an intermediary object called the *event class*. The actual event interface is implemented by this event class, making it look like a subscriber to the publisher. When a publisher wants to fire an event, it creates an instance of the event class, calls the appropriate method, and releases the interface. The run-time service then determines how and when to notify the subscribers.

As in the case of queued components, the lifetime of the publisher and the subscriber have been decoupled. If a subscriber is not active when an event occurs, the run-time event service can activate the subscriber and pass the information along.

Object Pooling

Under classic COM, a client instantiates a component, uses it, and releases it when done. Under some cases, object instantiation may take a considerable amount of time. To handle such situations, it may be a good idea to maintain a set of component instances loaded in memory so that they are immediately available for use by the client application.

Recall from Chapter 3 that a client instantiates an object using CoCreate-Instance API. Therefore, just creating a pool of objects is not enough. The COM+ run-time service has to intercept the object creation call and ensure that the object is fetched from the pool. Similarly, when the client releases the object, the COM+ run-time service has to ensure that the object is returned back to the pool.

An object needs a way to know when it is being activated or deactivated so that it can initialize its state or release the resources that it has been holding. COM+ specifies a standard interface, IObjectControl, that a class can implement to receive these notifications.

Object pooling support is needed for building large, scalable applications. However, some of the most precious resources in an enterprise application are its database connections. COM+ (along with ODBC and OLE DB) supports connection pooling (more precisely, pooling of database connections), which allows applications to create and destroy database connections on an as-needed basis without significant performance penalty.

Just-In-Time (JIT) Activation

In classic COM applications, objects are often created at startup and maintained (via reference counting) throughout the lifetime of the application. This practice tends to improve performance, as the application has a ready reference to all the objects whenever it needs to use them. However, it makes inefficient use of server resources.

JIT activation is another service provided by COM+ whereby the actual instances of an object are activated just prior to the first call made on them and are deactivated immediately after they finish their work.

Under JIT activation, when the client creates an object, the COM+ service creates a standard proxy and returns it to the client. The actual object is activated (a new instance created or an instance fetched from the pool of objects) only when the client makes the first call on the object.

When the actual object informs COM+ that it is done with the job it was supposed to do, COM+ releases the reference to this actual server-side object. If object pooling is enabled and the object agrees to go back to the object pool, COM+ puts it back into the pool.

The base client, however, is still holding a reference to the object (via its proxy). When the client makes another call, a server side object once again gets activated.

Together with object pooling, JIT activation can provide a high degree of scalability. More importantly, as we will see later, JIT can enforce transactional correctness with the greatest possible speed.

Remote Deployment

Prior to COM+, there was no easy way to install and register a COM server from the local machine to one or more remote machines. To install an application, administrators either walked up to each machine or used tools such as the Microsoft System Management Server (SMS).

COM+ provides an easy way for administrators to group one or more COM servers as one application and create an installable package file for the application. This package file can then be placed on a network shared drive, and from the local machine, an administrator can instruct each remote machine to install the application contained within the package. Once installed, an administrator can also uninstall an application remotely.

SUMMARY

Developing enterprise systems requires many infrastructural features such as scalability, robustness, security, transaction support, etc., to be implemented. Historically, developing enterprise systems required a significant amount of time and resources.

COM+, an advanced COM run-time environment that is packaged with Windows 2000, provides solutions to many generic infrastructure problems. The services provided by COM+ facilitate developing enterprise systems.

In the chapters to follow, we will examine each of the COM+ services in detail.

REFERENCES

[Arm-99]   Tom Armstrong, "COM + MTS = COM+," *Visual C++ Developers Journal*, vol. 2, no. 1, February/March 1999.

[Fer-99]   Dan Fergus, "Windows 2000: The Overview," *Visual C++ Developers Journal*, vol. 2, no. 5, November/December 1999.

[Box-99]   Don Box, "House of COM," *Microsoft Systems Journal*, vol. 14, no. 5, May 1999. *http://msdn.microsoft.com/library/periodic/period99/com0599.htm*

[Sha-99]   Bruce Shankle, "Find Recombinant Success with Windows DNA," *Microsoft Internet Developer*, vol. 4, no. 3, March 1999. *http://msdn.microsoft.com/ library/periodic/period99/dna.htm*

CHAPTER 5

COM+ Programming Model

In Chapter 4, we saw that COM+ offers a slew of services such as synchronization, transaction, queuing, and security. Developers can leverage one or more of these services to build enterprise systems.

A component has to be configured to indicate to COM+ the specific COM+ services it is interested in using. When a client creates an object of such a configured component, COM+ sets up the requested services for the object.

Essentially, the configuration settings on a COM object dictate certain run-time requirements for the object. These run-time requirements for a COM+ object are collectively referred to as the object's context.

In this chapter, we look at how to specify the configuration settings for a component and where COM+ stores the configuration information. We then examine how COM+ ensures that an object is created in a context that is compatible with its configuration settings. Finally, we look at different ways to use an object in a different context.

ATTRIBUTE-BASED PROGRAMMING

Before we get deeper into the COM+ programming model, let's answer one important question, "Why should I use COM+ services when I can provide the same functionality in my code?"

Sure you can. You are a competent Jedi programmer and the "Force" is with you. However, an even more important question one must ask is, "Is it worth doing it?"

Consider a simple scenario. You have developed a component that is not thread-safe (thread-safety issues are covered in the next chapter). To protect the internal state of the component, you wish to serialize access to the component, that is, set it up so that only one client can access it at any given time. To achieve this, you can use Win32 APIs that provide resource locking. Using these APIs, you would:

1. Lock the component when a client request comes in, so that no other client can access it.
2. Carry out the task requested by the client.
3. Release ownership of the component by unlocking it.

The locking and unlocking APIs need to be called within each interface method of the component. Therein lies some problems.

Problem #1: The more code you have to write and maintain, the more development costs you incur.

Problem #2: The more methods you have in your component, the more chances you have of making a human mistake. You may forget to call the resource-locking APIs in a method or two. Worse, you may call the API to lock the resource but forget to call the API to unlock it when returning from a method. This would deny access to your component throughout its process lifetime.

In general, having the platform provide a service is preferable to writing it yourself for the following reasons:

1. It reduces development cost. You can focus on your business needs instead of focusing on infrastructural issues.
2. It reduces the amount of code you have to write, thus reducing the chances of making a coding mistake. For example, if the platform provides the serialization mechanism, it would require zero lines of code in your application, virtually eliminating the chance of writing buggy lines of serialization-related code.
3. It usually reduces the number of page faults within your application, as many applications are sharing the same infrastructural code.
4. By decoupling the infrastructural functionality from the code, the platform vendor has more freedom to improve the underlying implementation without breaking your code. For example, the next release of the platform may have improved the speed/performance of the serialization logic. Your component can benefit from this improvement without requiring any code changes.

What if the platform implementation itself is buggy?

As the platform is providing an infrastructure that is potentially shared by many applications, it is very likely that the platform will have gone through more testing than the average piece of application code. Bugs will be reduced over time, resulting in a very stable platform code.

How do we decouple the functionality from the code?

To make it convenient for developers, COM+ requires that a COM class be declared using "out-of-band" attributes instead of "in-band" explicit code. Recall from Chapter 2 that a similar technique was used for defining interfaces using IDL. This formalization of declarative programming using attributed classes is fundamental to the COM+ programming model.

Obviously, the attributes for the class have to be stored somewhere so that COM+ infrastructure can access them and provide the needed services to the instances of the class. Let's investigate this further.

The COM+ Catalog

COM+ stores all the configuration information of a component in a persistent storage referred to as the *COM+ Catalog*. To manage this catalog, COM+ provides a component appropriately called the *Catalog Manager*.

In designing the catalog, due consideration was given to ensure easy migration of component DLLs that were based on classic COM. This required that the Catalog Manager control the Windows registry key HKEY_CLASSES_ROOT. Recall from Chapter 3 that classic COM mandates that a component DLL export two functions, DllRegisterServer and DllUnregisterServer. The first function is expected to add certain entries under the Windows registry key HKEY_CLASSES_ROOT and the second function is expected to clean them up.

What are the entries that are needed under the Windows registry key? We will answer this in the next section. Let's first answer another question—where should we store the newer attributes needed for a configured component?

The Windows registry database is already cluttered with all kinds of data—COM as well as non-COM related. Therefore, it makes more sense to use a separate database that stores only COM+ related attributes. This auxiliary configuration database is currently referred to as RegDB.

The interaction of the Catalog Manager with both the databases, RegDB and Windows registry, is depicted in Figure 5.1.

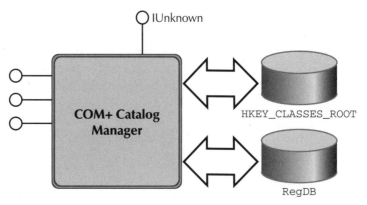

Figure 5.1   The COM+ Catalog Manager.

At activation time, CoCreateInstance inspects the catalog to determine which (if any) additional services the component needs and ensures that the newly created object receives the services it requested.

Only those components that are explicitly installed into the catalog can avail COM+ services. These components are called *configured components*. If a component bypasses the Catalog Manager to register itself, it is called a *non-configured* or a *legacy* component.

Configuring a Component

There are two ways to configure a component:

1. Explicitly program against the Catalog Manager interfaces.
2. Use a visual tool called the Component Services Snap-in that comes with Windows 2000.

We will explore the first option in Chapter 12. For now, let's examine the second option.

Figure 5.2 shows a snapshot of the Component Services Snap-in.

The main administrative unit of COM+ is called an *application*. A COM+ application is a collection of components that work together and share certain configuration settings. These attributes are applied across all the components within an application.

Configuration attributes are not just limited to the application level. Components within an application, their interfaces, and their interface meth-

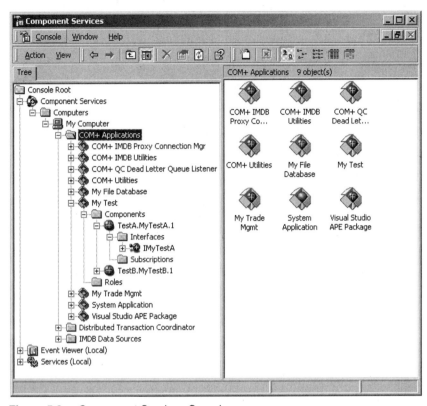

Figure 5.2   Component Services Snap-in.

ods all have specific attributes associated with them, and can be configured individually.

To enforce some form of access control, an application can also define a list of user roles. A user role is a symbolic category of users, as defined by the developer of the application, for the purpose of determining access permissions to the application's resources. We will cover user roles in Chapter 7 when we discuss security.

Typically, a software vendor creates one or more applications during installation. When an application is installed, the system automatically applies certain default attribute settings to the application (and the components underneath). The installation program can change some of these settings programmatically. However, using the Component Services Snap-in, the administrator can modify some of these settings, at any time, thus enabling the administrator to fine-tune the application's execution environment.

When an application is installed, it can be configured to run in the same address space as the client. Such an application is called a *library* application.

While a *library* application makes sense from a performance point of view, it also implies that an ill-written or a malicious component may corrupt the address space of its client. Likewise, a "crash" in the client code may adversely affect the server. To protect the client and the server from each other, the application can be specified to run in its own process address space. An application marked to run in a separate address space is called a *server* application.

 Classic COM supports two types of servers—a DLL-based server and an EXE-based server. Under COM+, however, only a DLL-based server can avail COM+ services. EXE-based servers are still supported, but they have to run as non-configured components. An EXE-based server can avail COM+ services indirectly by accessing a configured component.

When the client activates a component using `CoCreateInstance` for example, the COM+ library inspects the catalog to determine the services requested by the component at the application level, as well as at the underneath levels, and ensures that the new object receives the services it requested.

If the requested component belongs to a server application, COM+ creates a surrogate process and loads the component in the surrogate process. As we will see later, COM+ launches an executable called `DllHost.exe` to run the surrogate process.

Note that under COM+ 1.0 a component cannot belong to more than one application. Otherwise, COM+ cannot resolve the resulting attribute ambiguities.

 A future release of COM+ will support the notion of specifying multiple CLSIDs for a COM class. In effect, the same binary can be treated as multiple components, each of which can be configured individually.

The release will also support the notion of public and private components. Under COM+ 1.0, a component is *public* in the sense that any component from any application can access the component. In the future release, if a component is marked as *private*, only those component that belong to the same application can access the component.

Table 5.1 shows the attributes that are applicable to an application. The table also indicates if an attribute is applicable to a server-type application, a library-type application, or both.

Table 5.1   Application Attributes

Attribute	Available Choices	Library, Server, or Both
Description	Text up to 500 characters long	Both
Authorization (Access Check)	None, Process Level, Process + Component Level	Both
Authentication	Enable, Disable	Library
Authentication Level	None, Connect, Call, Packet, Packet Integrity, Packet Privacy	Server
Impersonation Level	Anonymous, Identity, Impersonate, Delegate	Server
Security Identity	Interactive user, Specific user	Server
Queuing	Non-queued, Queued, Queued + Listener	Server
Process Shutdown	Never, n minutes after idle	Server
Debugger	Command to launch the debugger	Server
Change Permission	Attributes can/cannot be changed	Both
Delete Permission	Application can/cannot be deleted	Both
Compensating Resource Manager (CRM)	Enable, Disable	Server
Enable 3GB Support	Enable, Disable	Server

Attributes that are related to security, queuing, and CRM require an in-depth study and will be covered in later chapters. Here is an explanation of the other attributes:

- **Process Shutdown:** If a server application is used frequently, it is desirable to let the application run even when it is idle, that is, no client is currently using the application. The motivation is simple—if the application runs all the time, any new client will be served immediately. The drawback, however, is that an idle application still wastes some CPU resources and may hold some other system resources. An engineering trade-off is to set the application to shut down if it stays idle for a specified period.

- **Support for 3GB Memory:** By default, a per-process address limit is 2G under Windows OS on 32-bit processors (such as Intel Pentium class processors). For applications that are I/O intensive, such as database management systems, the use of a larger process space can provide considerable performance benefits as time-intensive I/O access to media is reduced. If 3GB support is enabled, the OS reduces the potential

RAM allocated to Windows NT kernel from 2GB to 1GB, and provides the extra RAM to the application. This feature, of course, is meaningful only for computers that have more than 2GB of physical RAM.

- **Debugger Support:** Debugging a library application is straightforward—as the DLL runs in-process with the client application a developer can start debugging the client application and step into the component DLL code. A server application, on the other hand, runs in a separate process space (the surrogate process) than the client application. Though there is a way to attach to a running process and debug it, chances are you will miss the initialization logic by the time you attach to the process. COM+ facilitates debugging a server application. If the debugger support option is enabled and a debugger path is specified, COM+ spawns the debugger and attaches the server process to the debugger.

 Once COM+ spawns the debugger, the debugger doesn't automatically proceed with the program execution. This gives you a chance to set the break points in your code.

- **Change Permission:** The developer of an application knows what settings are best for the application and will set them accordingly during installation. To ensure that no one can change the settings accidentally, the designer can turn the change-permission flag off. If this permission is turned off, the administrators of the application have to explicitly turn the flag on before they can tweak any other attributes.
- **Delete Permission:** Some applications, once installed, are deemed very important for the overall functioning of the system. To ensure that no one can accidentally delete the application, its developers, or an administrator, can turn this flag off. In this case, one has to explicitly turn the permission on to be able to delete the application.

Attributes can also be specified at the component, interface, and interface method level. These attributes are primarily related to transactions, security, queuing, etc., and will be discussed in later chapters.

Component Initialization

Quite often an object that is being activated needs to be initialized with some administratively specified values. For example, if a component requires connecting to a database, the administrator of the component may need to specify the

exact DSN for the database (in case of ODBC connection), or the machine/user-
name where the database server is running (in case of OLE DB connection). To
facilitate this customization for a component, the Component Services Snap-in
provides an option for the administrator to specify an initialization string for the
component. During activation time, COM+ passes this string to the object.

If the component requires multiple values to be specified, all the values
have to be combined into a single initialization string, perhaps separated by
commas. The format of the initialization string is dictated (and documented)
by the component vendor.

How is the initialization string passed to the object?

A component that wishes to receive an initialization string is required
to implement a standard interface, `IObjectConstruct`. The following is its
definition:

```
IObjectConstruct : IUnknown
{
  HRESULT Construct([in] IDispatch *pCtorObj);
};
```

When the object is activated, COM+ calls `IObjectConstruct::Con-
struct` method that the object implements and passes the string in the form of
a pointer to an interface `IObjectConstructString`. The following is the
definition of `IObjectConstructString` interface:

```
IObjectConstructString : IDispatch
{
  [propget] HRESULT ConstructString([retval][out] BSTR *pVal);
}
```

The object can obtain the initialization string by calling `IObjectCon-
structString::ConstructString` method, as illustrated in the follow-
ing code snippet:

```
class CMyServer : ...
{
  ...

private:
  CComBSTR m_bsInitString;
};

STDMETHODIMP CMyServer::Construct(IDispatch* pDisp)
{
  CComPtr<IObjectConstructString> spConstructString;
```

```
HRESULT hr = pDisp->QueryInterface(&spConstructString);
_ASSERT (SUCCEEDED(hr));
hr = spConstructString->get_ConstructString(&m_bsInitString);
_ASSERT (SUCCEEDED(hr));
return hr;
}
```

You may be wondering why `IObjectConstruct::Construct` method doesn't just specify BSTR as a parameter. This would certainly simplify server-side programming. I guess in the future releases of COM+, Microsoft intends to support additional interfaces on the object that is passed as a parameter to `IObjectConstruct::Construct` method. Passing a generic `IDispatch` pointer as a parameter gives them this flexibility without breaking the existing code base.

Developer-Specified Attributes

Many attributes, such as those that are security related, are best chosen at deployment time and are thus configurable through the Catalog Manager, either through an installation program or manually by an administrator. However, there are certain attributes, such as those related to transaction and concurrency, that only a developer can correctly determine. Such attributes are best specified as static resources or data inside the component DLL. The Component Services Snap-in, for example, does not provide any user interface to change such attributes.

Attributes under Windows Registry

As with classic COM components, COM+ requires that a component DLL export two functions—`DllRegisterServer` and `DllUnregisterServer`. When a component DLL is added to an application under the Catalog Manager, the Catalog Manager automatically invokes `DllRegisterServer`, giving the component a chance to add the needed entries to the Windows registry. When a component is removed, the Catalog Manager invokes `DllUnregisterServer`, letting the component clean up its registry entries.

Though the developer can add any kind of information to the Windows registry, there are a few entries, as follows, that are important for COM+:

- `HKEY_CLASSES_ROOT\CLSID\{<CLSID>}\InprocServer32`: The default value of this registry subkey must be the complete file path to the DLL serving the component as identified by its `CLSID`.

- HKEY_CLASSES_ROOT\CLSID\{<CLSID>}\InprocServer32\ ThreadingModel: This registry value indicates the type of apartment (apartments are covered in Chapter 6) the component can live in. The possible choices are apartment, free, both, or neutral.[1]

Though a CLSID can identify a class uniquely, it is hard for humans to remember. To identify an object, a human-readable version of CLSID is preferred. This identifier is referred to as the programmatic identifier or PROGID. A PROGID is typically represented as <vendor>.<component>.<version> as in Word.Application.8. A CLSID can also have a version-independent PROGID.

- HKEY_CLASSES_ROOT\CLSID\{<CLSID>}\ProgID: The default value of this registry subkey specifies the PROGID for the component.

A PROGID makes it easy to identify a component. However, instance creation still requires a CLSID. Programming languages such as VB hide this by letting you instantiate an object using the PROGID. Behind the scenes, VB obtains the CLSID for the given PROGID using an API CLSIDFromProgID.

- HKEY_CLASSES_ROOT\<ProgID>\CLSID: The default value of this registry subkey specifies the CLSID of the component. This entry helps CLSIDFromProgID map a PROGID back to its CLSID.

The above-mentioned entries should be programmatically added to the registry when DllRegisterServer is invoked. It is up to the developer to define a technique for accessing this data within the program code. The technique that ATL uses is to define the registry entries in a specific format in a file and bind the content of this file as a static resource into the component's DLL (see Chapter 3).

Type Library-Based Attributes. The SDK lets some attributes be defined in the library section of the IDL. The following IDL example specifies a transaction setting called TRANSACTION_REQUIRED on the component class AccountMgr.

---

[1] Technically, it is okay to leave this entry blank. In this case, COM uses a threading model called Main Thread Apartment. However, this is a legacy case and should not be used.

```
[
  uuid(C9CF273D-EDED-4BD1-9DE6-559559BF001D),
  version(1.0),
  helpstring("AccountMgmt 1.0 Type Library")
]
library ACCOUNTMGMTLib
{
  importlib("stdole32.tlb");
  importlib("stdole2.tlb");

  [
    uuid(0AC21FA4-DB2A-474F-A501-F9C9A062A63E),
    helpstring("AccountMgr Class"),
    TRANSACTION_REQUIRED
  ]
  coclass AccountMgr
  {
    [default] interface IAccountMgr;
  };
};
```

Recall from Chapter 2 that attributes defined under the library section get saved into the type library when the IDL file is compiled. This type library can be stored either as a stand-alone file or within the component DLL as a static resource. In the former case, when the component DLL is added to an application through the Catalog Manager, the type library file should also be added to the application.

At this point, it should be reasonably clear how a component is configured at development and deployment time. Now let's look at how COM+ ensures that the services requested by a component are available to the component's objects throughout their lifetime.

COM+ CONTEXT

The configuration settings at all levels—application, component, interface, and interface method—essentially specify certain run-time requirements for a COM+ object. For example, a component might be (or might not be) interested in participating in a transaction. The component might be interested in using the synchronization or the security services provided by COM+. All these run-time requirements for the component's object are collectively referred to as the object's context. The context represents the environment in which the COM+ object lives, the sea in which it swims.

An object's context is created and attached to the object by COM+ during the object activation. This context remains fixed and immutable until the object is deactivated.

I have deliberately chosen the words object activation and deactivation, as opposed to object creation and destruction. As these terms are used quite frequently throughout the remainder of the book, it is important to understand their precise meaning.

Activating an object would really have been synonymous with creating an object, if not for *object pooling*, a feature provided by COM+. If object pooling is enabled on a component, a pool of objects is created upfront (the minimum and maximum sizes are configurable attributes on the component). When a client requests an object, using CoCreateInstance for example, the object is fetched from the pool. When the client releases the object, the object goes back to the pool. Pooling objects improves performance in some cases.

Object activation implies either fetching an object from the pool (if object pooling is enabled on the component) or creating a new object. Likewise, object deactivation implies either returning the object to the pool (if object pooling is enabled) or destroying the object.

Let's get back to our context (pun intended).

Earlier, I said that an object's context is created and attached to an object when COM+ activates an object. Well, I lied about the creation of an object context *every* time an object is activated. Actually, COM+ checks if a compatible context exists in the process space. If one is found, this context is attached to the object. Only if a compatible context is not found does COM+ create a new context and attach it to the object. Thus, as different components can be configured with different requirements, a process often contains more than one context. Some configuration settings allow an object to reside in a shared context with other like-minded objects—these objects are geared to swim in the same sea. Other configuration settings force an object to swim in a private sea that no other object can swim in. This is illustrated in Figure 5.3.

This brings us to an important question—what if the object's activator has a context that is incompatible with that of the object?

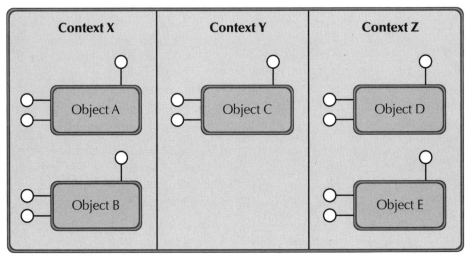

Figure 5.3   Contexts within a process.

Contexts and Interception

An object can live only within its context—it is geared to swim only in a specific sea. Clearly, the object cannot just be created in a different sea. The incompatible environment will produce unexpected behavior.

The mechanism that COM+ uses to solve this problem is called *interception*. Instead of creating the actual object in the incompatible context, COM+ automatically creates a proxy that is geared to swim in the new sea. The proxy implements the same interfaces as the real object. This mechanism provides COM+ the ability to intercept method calls on the proxy.

Following is the basic interception algorithm:

1. The configuration settings on a component dictate its run-time requirements or its context.
2. At activation time, COM+ checks if the activator (that is, the code that called `CoCreateInstance`) has a context that is compatible with the component's configuration.
3. If the activator's context is compatible, the object is activated in the activator's context, that is, the activator gets a raw reference to the object.
4. If the activator's context is not compatible, COM+ switches to a context that is compatible (it may have to create a new context if one doesn't already exist), and activates the object in this context. COM+ then

creates a proxy to this object in the activator's context and returns this proxy to the activator.

5. In case of a raw reference, no interception takes place. A method call invoked by the client goes directly to the method implementation logic.

6. In case of a proxy reference, each time the client invokes a method on the proxy, COM+ intercepts this method call, switches the run-time environment to the context that is compatible with the object, executes the call, switches the run-time environment back to the client's context, and returns the value.

Figure 5.4 illustrates this behavior. Here object C belongs to context Y. When it tries to activate object E whose component settings are compatible with context Z, COM+ creates object E in context Z and a proxy to object E in context Y. COM+ then returns a pointer to this proxy to object C.

This simple interception algorithm is the key to ensuring that the services the component requested are available to the object(s).

I am using the term "proxy" very loosely. Technically speaking, the incompatible context gets a *proxy manager* that loads an *interface proxy* for each actual interface being queried on the actual object. The proxy manager acts as the client-side identity of the object. The interface proxy translates method invocations into ORPC calls. To maintain the correct identity relationships, the interface proxies are aggregated into the proxy manager's identity.

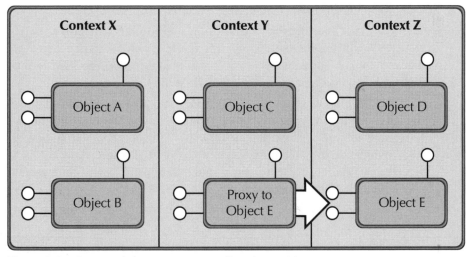

Figure 5.4   Intercepting cross-context calls using proxies.

Also note that object activation is not the only case when a proxy might get created. A proxy could also be created when an interface pointer is passed from one context to another via some interface method call. Once again, COM+ will take care of creating the proxy.

There is one exception to the above-mentioned interception algorithm. An object from a non-configured component is always activated in the activator's context, provided the threading model of the component matches the apartment type of the activator. Threading models and apartments are covered in the next chapter.

At this point, it should be reasonably clear that the activator gets either a raw reference to the activated object (in case of compatible contexts) or a proxy (in case of incompatible contexts). This now brings us to the next question— can this obtained reference (either raw or proxy) be shared with other contexts?

Consider the case when the activator gets a raw reference. This implies that the object resides in the current context and depends on the current run-time environment for proper operation. The current sea is the only sea it can swim in. If this raw reference were shared with another context, for example, by using a global variable to store the reference, and if the other context were to use the raw reference, the object's method would execute without the benefit of the interception, that is, the context that is used during method execution is that of the caller, not that of the object. This will result in completely unpredictable behavior. For example, if the object relied on some transaction service or security service to be available during method execution, it may not get one. Worse yet, it may get the caller's settings (which may be completely different). Almost all configured services would malfunction if the call were processed in the wrong context.

Now let's consider the case when the activator gets the proxy. At first glance, it would appear that sharing a proxy across contexts is okay. After all, it is just a proxy. The actual object still resides in the right sea. COM+ would still be able to intercept the calls on the proxy.

Not so fast. The proxy that is returned by any API or method call is configured to run a certain set of interception services based on the differences between the object's context and the context where the proxy was first initialized. Simply put, even the proxy is geared to swim in a specific sea. Passing this proxy to another context is not guaranteed to work, as this third context may need a different set of interception services.

One could argue that a proxy should be smart enough to work from any context. However, this would make the proxy implementation very inefficient. There is yet another problem. Developers rarely wish to distinguish between the raw reference and the proxy. Had we had such a smart proxy, developers would then need to treat it differently than raw references.

So, how do you pass object references (either raw or proxy) from one context to another?

COM allows interface pointers to be marshaled across context boundaries. Marshaling an interface pointer transforms the interface pointer into a block of memory suitable for transmitting to any context on the network. The importing context can unmarshal this block of data, that is, decode it to obtain an object reference that is suitable to swim in the new sea.

The SDK provides two APIs, `CoMarshalInterface` and `CoUnmarshal-Interface`, to marshal an interface pointer from one context and unmarshal it in another context, respectively. In general, application programmers rarely deal with marshaling APIs themselves, as the most common cases of marshaling interface pointers are handled by COM implicitly. These cases are:

1. when an object is activated and the activator's context is incompatible with the component configuration, and
2. when a reference is passed as an interface method parameter from one context to another.

In both cases, COM does the needed marshaling and unmarshaling automatically.

The only time explicit marshaling is needed is if a reference is passed from one context to another using a mechanism other than the interface method call, such as by means of a global variable. In such cases, the developers have to explicitly marshal and unmarshal the interface pointer. In the next chapter, we will examine one such case and show the usage of the marshaling APIs mentioned earlier. We will also look at another facility provided by COM+ called the Global Interface Table (GIT) to simplify marshaling logic.

Interception and Performance

Recall from the previous section that when a method call is made on a proxy, COM+ intercepts the call, switches the run-time environment to the context that is compatible with the real object, executes the call, and switches the run-time environment back to the caller's context on return. If need be, the call stack is serialized, that is, the method parameters are marshaled, and an OS thread switch is performed.

In terms of performance, OS thread-switching is the most expensive operation, followed by call-stack serialization. The rest of the interception services are not as expensive.

Much thought went into designing the proxies in order to make the cross-context method calls as efficient as possible. In general, the smaller the delta between the caller's context and the real object's context, the lower the performance cost. A proxy runs only those interception services a boundary crossing requires. If OS thread-switching or call-stack serialization is not needed, it will be avoided, and the stack frame can simply be shared across the context boundary. Of course, if the method contains an object reference as a parameter, it would have to be marshaled.

OBJECT CONTEXT

We know very well by now that each object under COM+ has a context associated with it. This context maintains the run-time requirements for all the like-minded objects. An obvious question that arises is, is there a way for an object to avail its context information and perhaps change some run-time state?

Under COM+, each context in a process has a unique COM object that represents it. This object is called the object context (OC). Each OC is uniquely identified by a GUID, referred to as the context-ID.

Objects can access their context's OC by calling the `CoGetObject-Context` API. Following is its prototype:

```
WINOLEAPI CoGetObjectContext(/*IN*/ REFIID riid, /*OUT*/ LPVOID * ppv);
```

The first parameter to the API is the requested interface on the OC. The interfaces that are of interest to us are `IID_IObjectContextInfo`, `IID_IObjectContextActivity`, and `IID_IObjectContextState`.[2] The methods on these interfaces are explained in Tables 5.2, 5.3, and 5.4, respectively.

---

[2] There is yet another interface, `IID_IObjectContext`, that has been left for backward compatibility with Microsoft Transaction Server (MTS). However, the newer interfaces replace the functionality of this old interface.

Table 5.2 `IObjectContextInfo` **Interface Methods**

Method	Description
GetContextId	Returns the GUID that uniquely identifies the context to which the object belongs
GetActivityId	Returns the GUID that uniquely identifies the synchronization activity to which the object belongs
IsInTransaction	Indicates whether the object is or is not part of a transaction
GetTransaction	Returns the `ITransaction` interface of the transaction to which the object belongs
GetTransactionId	Returns the GUID that uniquely identifies the transaction to which the object belongs

Table 5.3 `IObjectContextActivity` **Interface Methods**

Method	Description
GetActivityId	Returns the GUID that uniquely identifies the synchronization activity to which the object belongs

Table 5.4 `IObjectContextState` **Interface Methods**

Method	Description
SetDeactivateOnReturn	Informs COM+ that it is okay to deactivate the object when the calling method returns. Meaningful if just-in-time activation (JIT) is enabled
GetDeactivateOnReturn	Returns a boolean value that indicates if the object is set to be deactivated on return. Meaningful if JIT is enabled
SetMyTransactionVote	Lets the object set its vote (as a boolean flag) when the object participates in a transaction
GetMyTransactionVote	Returns the current transaction vote setting

Activity-related methods are discussed in detail in Chapter 6 (Concurrency). Transaction-related methods are discussed in detail in Chapter 8 (Transactions). JIT-related methods are discussed in Chapter 11 (Scalability).

This leaves us with just one method to discuss, `GetContextId`. This method returns the GUID that identifies the context. The following code snippet shows how to use this method:

```
STDMETHODIMP CMyTestA::DoIt()
{
  CComPtr<IObjectContextInfo> spCI;

  HRESULT hr = ::CoGetObjectContext(IID_IObjectContextInfo,
    reinterpret_cast<void**>(&spCI));
  _ASSERT (SUCCEEDED(hr));

  GUID contextid;
  hr = spCI->GetContextId(&contextid);
  _ASSERT (SUCCEEDED(hr));


  ...
  return S_OK;
}
```

Default Context

When one object activates another object, COM+ checks to see if the activator's context is compatible with the activatee's configuration and, if required,
sets up proper interception services. Getting the context information is not a
problem when the activator happens to be an object of a configured component. Each object has a context attached to it, that COM+ can retrieve. However, there are cases when the activator is either an object from a
non-configured component or not an object at all (such as a stand-alone client
program). The following code snippet shows a stand-alone program activating a configured component's object:

```
int APIENTRY WinMain(HINSTANCE hInstance,
              HINSTANCE hPrevInstance,
              LPSTR    lpCmdLine,
              int      nCmdShow)
{
  ::CoInitialize(NULL);      // Initialize the COM system.
  IMyTestBPtr sp;
  HRESULT hr = sp.CreateInstance(__uuidof(MyTestB));
  if (SUCCEEDED(hr)) {
    sp->DoIt();
  }
  ...
}
```

When `CoCreateInstance` is called on the `MyTestB` COM class,
COM+ needs to match the context of the activator with the configuration of
the class `MyTestB`. But what is the context of the activator in this case?

In order to facilitate context lookup, COM+ provides a notion of *default context*. A default context has the semantics of classic COM: it doesn't store any transaction, synchronization, or security-related attributes. As a matter of fact, the OC for the default context does not even support any of the context-related interfaces (try writing a small test program to get any of the context-related interfaces). The only reason this context exists is so that it can hold objects of a non-configured class.

Here is how it works:

Each executing program (process) consists of one primary thread (executing `WinMain`) and perhaps some worker threads. A thread indicates its interest in using COM by calling the API `CoInitializeEx`. Following is its prototype:

```
WINOLEAPI CoInitializeEx(/*IN*/ LPVOID pvReserved,
  /*IN*/ DWORD dwCoInit);
```

The first parameter for this API is reserved for future use. The second parameter indicates the type of apartment the thread would like to enter into. Apartments are covered in the next chapter. An apartment type basically dictates how the threads dispatch the calls. There are two values for this parameter—`COINIT_APARTMENTTHREADED` and `COINIT_MULTITHREADED`. This value is typically decided during development time.

The COM SDK requires you to define one of the following two macros before including `<windows.h>`. This makes the prototype for `CoInitializeEx` API available to the compiler.

```
#define _WIN32_DCOM

#define _WIN32_WINNT 0x0500
```

If the apartment type is fixed as `COINIT_APARTMENTTHREADED`, the developer can use a simplified variation of the API, `CoInitialize`. The following is its prototype.

```
WINOLEAPI CoInitialize(/*IN*/ LPVOID pvReserved);
```

`CoInitialize(Ex)` has to be called before most other COM APIs can be called (including `CoCreateInstance`). When `CoInitialize(Ex)` is called, COM+ initializes the COM library and attaches an appropriate default context to the thread (there is one default context for each apartment type). The only information that the context contains is the apartment type.

The thread continues to reside in the default context until the thread wishes to leave the context (and thereby terminating its use of any COM services) by calling another API, CoUninitialize. The following is its prototype:

```
void CoUninitialize();
```

CoUninitialize should be called once for each successful call to CoIntializeEx or CoInitialize.

According to Microsoft documentation, if the parent thread has called CoInitialize(Ex), the child threads need not call the API. However, I have made it a practice to call CoInitialize(Ex) and CoUninitialize APIs, respectively, at the start and at the exit of any thread that I spawn.

So, when an object of MyTestB is being activated, COM+ first checks to see if MyTestB is a configured class. If it is a configured class, then, by definition, the default context will not match the configuration of the class. Hence, COM+ activates the object in a compatible context and returns a proxy pointer to the client.

If MyTestB is a non-configured class, COM+ checks to see if the threading model of the class is compatible with the default context (essentially the apartment type) of the activator. If it is, then COM+ activates the object in the default context of the activator. Otherwise, COM+ activates the object in the default context of a compatible apartment and returns a proxy pointer to the client.

In the above example, the activator was assumed to be a stand-alone program. A similar logic holds if the activator is an object of a configured class. The non-configured object being activated runs either in the activator's context, if the threading model is compatible, or in the default context of a compatible apartment.

CALL CONTEXT

When servicing a method call, the object may want to get more information about its caller. One reason is to check the caller's credentials.

The object context stores information only about the context of the object. It doesn't store the caller's information.

To address this problem, COM+ defines and associates a context to the current method call. A method can obtain this *call context* by calling the API CoGetCallContext. The following is its prototype:

```
WINOLEAPI CoGetCallContext( /*IN*/ REFIID riid,
  /*OUT*/ void **ppInterface );
```

A call context supports many interfaces. Parameter `riid` specifies the IID of the requested interface. The interfaces that are of interest to us are `IServerSecurity` and `ISecurityCallContext`. We will cover both these interfaces in detail in Chapter 7.

OBJECT ACTIVATION

Now that we understand how contexts and interception work, let's look at the mechanism of object activation.

Object activation is handled by a COM+ provided service called the Service Control Manager (SCM). When a client requests that an object be activated using `CoCreateInstance(Ex)` or `CoGetClasObject`, for example, the SCM locates and loads the appropriate component, and hands the client an interface pointer to the raw object or to its proxy, as the case may be.

Object activation reduces to three basic scenarios:

1. The activator and the component are both on the local machine, and the component belongs to a library application. In this case, the activated object will run in-process with the activator.
2. The activator and the component are both on the same machine and the component belongs to a server application. In this case, the activated object will run out-of-process with the activator.
3. The component is on a remote machine. In this case, the component can only be specified to belong to a server application.

Let's examine each of these cases in detail.

In-Process Activation

A client creates an instance by calling the API `CoCreateInstance`. This API was covered in Chapter 3. The following prototype is reprinted for your convenience:

```
STDAPI CoCreateInstance(REFCLSID rclsid, LPUNKNOWN pUnkOuter,
  DWORD dwClsContext, REFIID riid, LPVOID* ppv);
```

If the run-time requirements of the object being activated are the same as that of the activator, the activator gets a raw reference to the actual object, as shown in Figure 5.5.

If the run-time requirements of the object being activated do not match that of the activator, the SCM creates a proxy-stub pair for the object and sets up one or more interception policies on the client side as well as on the server side. The proxy and the stub communicate with each other using the ORPC channel (see Chapter 2). The overall communication mechanism is illustrated in Figure 5.6.

The interception policies are set up based on the delta between the contexts of the client (activator) and the server object. The policies on the client side are invoked when a method is called, and again after it returns. The policies on the server side are invoked when the call first arrives at the server side, and again before it leaves. These policies provide whatever interception services were requested by the server object. For example, if the server object has requested for synchronization service, the server-side policy might acquire a lock on entry and release the lock when it exits.

For intraprocess communication, the ORPC channel uses the most efficient communication transport.

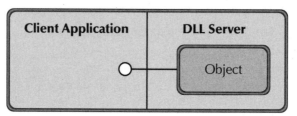

Figure 5.5   In-process activation (compatible context).

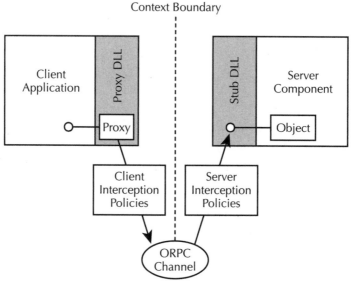

Figure 5.6   Cross-context communication.

Out-of-Process Activation (Local Host)

Here, the requested component belongs to a server application. The client still uses CoCreateInstance (or its friends such as CoGetClassObject) to activate the object. In this case, however, the SCM creates a surrogate process (called DllHost.exe) and loads the component in the surrogate process. The rest of the mechanism is similar to that of cross-context communication explained earlier and represented in Figure 5.6. The only difference is that the transport used by the ORPC channel is LRPC (Lightweight RPC). LRPC is a Microsoft proprietary variant of RPC which has the exact same calling syntax as the DCE RPC run time but is optimized to reduce data copying and eliminate access to the networking code altogether.

Remote Activation (Distributed Computing)

In order to activate a component remotely, the name of the remote machine has to be specified during instance creation. As CoCreateInstance API does not have any provision for this, the SDK defines an extended variant of this API called CoCreateInstanceEx. The following is its prototype:

```
HRESULT CoCreateInstanceEx(
    REFCLSID rclsid,              //CLSID of the object to be created
    IUnknown *punkOuter,          //If part of an aggregate,
                                  //the controlling IUnknown
    DWORD dwClsCtx,               //CLSCTX values
    COSERVERINFO *pServerInfo,    //Machine on which the object
                                  //should be instantiated
    ULONG cmq,                    //Number of MULTI_QI structures
                                  //in pResults
    MULTI_QI *pResults            //Array of MULTI_QI structures
);
```

The COSERVERINFO structure is primarily used to identify a remote machine. Machines are identified using the naming scheme of the network transport. By default, all UNC ("\\MYDEV" or "MYDEV") and DNS names ("mydev.pvhome.local" or "15.65.87.252") are allowed.

A secondary use of the COSERVERINFO structure is to specify a different security protocol or a different client identity during object activation. This type of use is covered in Chapter 7.

As round trips can be very expensive, CoCreateInstanceEx makes it possible to obtain a number of interface pointers (using MULTI_QI structure) in just one API call.

The following function code shows how to instantiate a remote object and obtain an `IUnknown` interface pointer to it. This code is available on the CD.

```
HRESULT
CPLCreateInstance(
  LPCOLESTR pwszMach,     // [in] Remote machine
  const CLSID& clsId,     // [in] Class ID
  IUnknown** ppOut,       // [out, retval] instance handle
  DWORD dwClsCtx          // [in] CLSCTX values
  )
{
  *ppOut = NULL;
  COSERVERINFO serverInfo;
  serverInfo.dwReserved1 = 0;
  serverInfo.pwszName = const_cast<LPOLESTR>(pwszMach);
  serverInfo.pAuthInfo = NULL;
  serverInfo.dwReserved2 = 0;
  MULTI_QI mqiEntry;
  mqiEntry.pIID = &IID_IUnknown;
  mqiEntry.pItf = NULL;
  mqiEntry.hr = 0;

  HRESULT hr = ::CoCreateInstanceEx(clsId,
    NULL,
    dwClsCtx,
    &serverInfo,
    1,
    &mqiEntry);

  if (FAILED(hr)) {
    return hr;
  }

  _ASSERT (NULL != mqiEntry.pItf);
  *ppOut = mqiEntry.pItf;

  return hr;
}
```

The mechanism of setting up proxy-stub and interception policies is similar to that of out-of-process activation (Figure 5.6). The only difference is that, to communicate with a remote host, the ORPC channel prefers using Transmission Control Protocol (TCP) on Windows 2000 and User Datagram Protocol (UDP) on Windows NT 4.0.

Executing in a Different Context

Using Activator's Context

We know that if an object being activated has a configuration that does not match the activator's context, the object is activated in a different context. However, there are occasions when a component does not require any configured service of its own but would rather use the configured services of its activator. This could be useful for some utility components. It is also useful for components that do not support cross-context marshaling, or have very stringent performance requirements.

COM+ supports a configuration option that a developer can select to ensure that the object can only be activated within the context of its activator. If for some reason the creator's context has been configured in such a way that it can't support the new object, CoCreateInstance will fail and return the error CO_E_ATTEMPT_TO_CREATE_OUTSIDE_CLIENT_CONTEXT.

If CoCreateInstance succeeds, all calls on the new object will be serviced in the activator's context. This holds true even if the references to the new object are passed to other contexts.

Activating an object of a configured class using the activator's context looks very similar to activating an object of the non-configured component. However, there is a subtle difference in the activation mechanisms. In the former case, the object is guaranteed to use the activator's context. If this cannot be accomplished because the activator's context is not compatible with the class configuration, COM+ returns error code CO_E_ATTEMP_TO_CREATE_OUT-SIDE_CLIENT_CONTEXT. In the latter case, if the object cannot run in the activator's context, COM+ will activate it in an appropriate default context and will return a proxy to the activator.

What if an object wants to run in the context of *any* of its callers?

Using a Caller's Context

A component implementor may decide that the component does not require any COM+ services. Instead, the implemntor goes through great lengths to ensure that the component's object is capable of residing in any context. However, it is impossible for the clients to know that such access is safe for a particular object; so all cross-context interface pointer sharing must be established using an explicit marshaling technique. This means that access to an in-process object could still be occurring via (somewhat expensive) ORPC calls.

Unlike clients, objects do know if they are safe to be used as raw references in any context. Such objects have the opportunity to bypass the standard marshaling technique provided by COM and implement their own custom marshaling.

A little background on custom marshaling is in order.

By default, when `CoMarshalInterface` is first called on an object (this happens automatically when an interface is first requested from a different context), COM+ asks the object if it wishes to handle its own cross-context communication. This question comes in the form of a `QueryInterface` request for the `IMarshal` interface. Most objects do not implement the `IMarshal` interface and fail this `QueryInterface` request. This indicates to COM+ that the objects are perfectly happy letting COM+ handle all communications via ORPC calls. Objects that do implement this interface are indicating that the object implementor would prefer handling all cross-context communications via a custom proxy.

Components that implement custom marshaling cannot be installed as a configured component.

For an object that wishes to run in the context of its caller, the object implementor could use custom marshaling to easily bypass the stub manager and simply serialize a raw pointer to the object into the marshaled object reference. The custom proxy implementation could simply read the raw pointer from the marshaled object reference and pass it to the caller in the importing context. The client would still pass the interface pointer across the context boundary by calling `CoMarshalInterface` (either explicitly or automatically by COM). However, the custom proxy will end up returning the raw reference into the new context. Although this technique will work perfectly for intraprocess marshaling, it will fail miserably for interprocess marshaling (recall from Chapter 2 that a raw address pointer from one process space cannot simply be used in another process space). Fortunately, when the marshaling request comes to the object (via `IMarshal::MarshalInterface`), the marshaling context is passed as a parameter (see MSHCTX flags in the SDK documentation). The object implementation can simply delegate to the standard marshaler for any marshaling context other than `MSHCTX_INPROC`.

As the behavior just described is useful for a large class of objects, COM provides an aggregatable implementation of `IMarshal` that accomplishes what was just described. This implementation is called the Free

Threaded Marshaler (FTM) and can be created using the `CoCreate-FreeThreadedMarshaler` API call.

```
HRESULT CoCreateFreeThreadedMarshaler(IN LPUNKNOWN punkOuter,
   OUT LPUNKNOWN *ppunkMarshal);
```

A class that wishes to use the FTM typically aggregates an instance during the instantiation time. The following code snippet shows how it can be done within an ATL class:

```
// CMyTestD
class ATL_NO_VTABLE CMyTestD :
   ...
{
public:
  CMyTestD()
  {
    m_pUnkMarshaler = NULL;
  }
  ...

    HRESULT FinalConstruct()
    {
       return CoCreateFreeThreadedMarshaler(
   GetControllingUnknown(), &m_pUnkMarshaler.p);
}

void FinalRelease()
{
  m_pUnkMarshaler.Release();
}

CComPtr<IUnknown> m_pUnkMarshaler;
...
};
```

Recall from Chapter 3 that, to support aggregation, the `QueryInterface` method has to be modified, as shown in the following code snippet:

```
STDMETHODIMP CMyTestD::QueryInterface(REFIID riid, void** ppv)
{
  // Check for usual IIDs first
  if (riid == IID_IUnknown || riid == ... || riid == ...) {
    do the necessary casting and return S_OK
  }

  // now check for IID_IMarshal
```

```
if (riid == IID_IMarshal) {
  return m_pUnkMarshaler->QueryInterface(riid, ppv)
}
return S_FALSE; // requested interface not found
}
```

Fortunately, the ATL wizard makes it very convenient to generate all the needed logic. When the wizard is run, one of the options on the `Attributes` tab is `Free Threaded Marshaler`. If this option is selected, the wizard will aggregate the FTM into your ATL class.

Once a component is implemented with FTM support, the object will always run in its caller's context, irrespective of which context the object was activated in. Figure 5.7 illustrates this *context-neutrality* of such an object.

In Figure 5.7, object E is shared between context Y and Z. Compare this to Figure 5.4 to see the difference between a context-sensitive object and a context-neutral object.

 You must think very carefully before using FTM. If absolute care is not taken, it will result in unpredictable results. For example, if the object being FTMed contains an interface pointer to another object that is configured to run in a specific context, a call on this interface pointer may get executed in the wrong context.

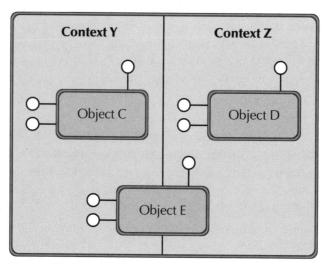

Figure 5.7   Context neutrality.

SUMMARY

In this chapter, we saw that the COM+ programming model is based on defining "out-of-band" attributes on a COM+ application. This lets the administrator of the application control its behavior. The configuration settings are stored in the COM+ catalog.

When an object is activated, COM+ ensures that the object runs in an appropriate context and correctly sets it up to receive the services it had requested. By providing a comprehensive interception mechanism, COM+ ensures that this run-time environment of the object is maintained during the lifetime of the object.

An object from a non-configured component runs in a default context.

A context is represented by a unique COM object called the object context (OC). The SDK provides APIs to let an object access its context's OC.

Finally, we looked at how an object can use the activator's context or the caller's context.

A few of the configuration attributes were examined in detail in this chapter. In the chapters to follow, we will examine many other important attributes.

REFERENCES

[She-99]   George Shepherd, "COM+ Interception and Contexts," *Visual C++ Developers Journal*, vol. 2, no. 3, July/August 1999.

[Box-99a]   Don Box, "Windows 2000 Brings Significant Refinements to the COM+ Programming Model," *Microsoft Systems Journal*, May 1999. *http://msdn.microsoft.com/ library/periodic/period99/complusprog.htm*

[Box-99b]   Don Box, "House of COM—Are Contexts Real?" *Microsoft Systems Journal*, September 1999. *http://msdn.microsoft.com/library/periodic/ period99/com0999.htm*

[Pla-99]   David Platt, *Understanding COM+*, Microsoft Press, 1999.

[Box-97]   Don Box, *Essential COM*, Addison Wesley, ISBN 0-201-63446-5, December 1997.

CHAPTER 6

Concurrency

$\mathbf{I}$n the previous chapter, we saw that COM+ classes can be configured with a variety of run-time requirements. We defined "context" as a set of run-time requirements of an object. One such run-time requirement is concerned with the concurrency management of the object. Under Windows OS, a process can execute multiple threads concurrently, each of which carries out a specific task. Developing a multithreaded application requires careful designing. In this chapter, we look at various issues involved with multithread programming and examine the infrastructure provided by COM+ to simplify developing components that are safe from concurrent access. Finally, we look at different techniques to design components that make efficient use of the COM+ synchronization infrastructure.

MULTITHREAD PROGRAMMING

First, a little background on processes and threads...

A thread is the basic unit to which the Windows operating system allocates processor time. A process, that is, a single instance of a running application, consists of at least one thread of execution known as the *primary thread*. A thread can execute just one task at a time. To perform multiple tasks concurrently, a process can create multiple threads. Even though only one thread can execute at any time,[1] the Windows OS preemptively switches execution from one thread to another. The switching is so fast that all the threads appear to run at the same time.

---

[1] More specifically, thread execution is processor-based. A multiprocessor machine can have multiple threads executing simultaneously.

All the threads within a process share the virtual address space and global variables of that process. However, each thread has its own stack. Therefore, when a thread is executing, any program variables that are created on the stack are local to the thread.

Often times, it is necessary to maintain thread-specific data. However, a static or global variable cannot be used for this purpose because it has the same value across all the threads. To address this problem, the OS provides a feature called *thread local storage* (TLS). With TLS, you can create a unique copy of a variable for each thread.

The Win32 SDK provides APIs that deal with thread creation, manipulation, and synchronization. The SDK also provides comprehensive documentation on their usage.

With this brief background information, let's develop a simple application that demonstrates the use of Win32 APIs in creating and manipulating threads. As we go along in the chapter, we will pick up other thread-related information that we need to know.

A Simple Example

The objective of this example is to illustrate the technique of creating and using threads in a program. In this simple example, the main thread will create a secondary thread that computes the product of two numbers. The main thread will just wait until the secondary thread completes the computation, whereupon the main thread will display the computed value.

The code for this example can be found on the CD.

The SDK provides two APIs, `CreateThread` and `ExitThread`, to create a thread or terminate the thread, respectively. Following are their prototypes:

```
HANDLE CreateThread(
    LPSECURITY_ATTRIBUTES lpThreadAttributes, //pointer to security
                                              //attributes
    DWORD dwStackSize,                // initial thread stack size
    LPTHREAD_START_ROUTINE lpStartAddress,    // pointer to thread
                                              // function
    LPVOID lpParameter,                  // argument for new thread
    DWORD dwCreationFlags,                    // creation flags
    LPDWORD lpThreadId                //pointer to return thread ID
);

VOID ExitThread(DWORD dwExitCode);                 // Exit a thread.
```

Parameter `lpStartAddress` is an application-defined function that serves as the starting address for a thread. When the application-defined function returns, or explicitly calls `ExitThread`, the thread terminates.

The thread function takes a single argument. Parameter `lpParameter` specifies the value for this argument.

Note that only one argument can be passed to the thread function. The current example, however, requires three logical arguments—the two numbers whose product needs to be computed and a return variable that holds the computed value. The easiest way to solve this problem is to create a data structure containing the three variables and pass a pointer to an instance of the structure as the argument to the function, as shown in the following code snippet:

```
struct MYPARAM {
    int nVal1;
    int nVal2;
    int nProduct;
};

int APIENTRY WinMain(HINSTANCE hInstance,
    HINSTANCE hPrevInstance,
    LPSTR lpCmdLine,
    int nCmdShow)
{
    // Step 1: Initialize the data to be passed to the thread
    MYPARAM data;
    data.nVal1 = 5;
    data.nVal2 = 7;
    data.nProduct = 0;

    // Step 2: Create and run the thread
    DWORD dwThreadID;
    HANDLE hThread = ::CreateThread(NULL, 0, MyThreadProc,
        &data, 0, &dwThreadID);
    if (NULL == hThread) {
        MessageBox(NULL, _T("Cannot create thread"), NULL,
MB_OK);
        return 1;
    }
    ...
}
```

In this code snippet, the function that will be executed by the thread is `MyThreadProc`. The implementation for this function follows:

```
DWORD WINAPI MyThreadProc(LPVOID pData)
{
   ::Sleep(30 * 1000); // Sleep for 30 seconds (for our test)
   MYPARAM* pParam = reinterpret_cast<MYPARAM*>(pData);
   pParam->nProduct = pParam->nVal1 * pParam->nVal2;
   return 0;
}
```

Note that the thread function definition requires the argument to be of type LPVOID. Consequently, the argument has to be reinterpreted to whatever it represents within the function scope. In the example, the parameter is reinterpreted as a pointer to MYPARAM data structure.

The WinMain thread now waits for the secondary thread to quit. This can be done by calling the Win32 API WaitForSingleObject on the handle that was returned by the earlier call to CreateThread, as shown below:

```
// Step 3: Wait for the thread to quit
::WaitForSingleObject(hThread, INFINITE);    // wait infinitely
```

Once the thread quits, the parent thread has to clean up the thread resource by calling a Win32 API, CloseHandle:

```
// Step 4: Release the thread handle
::CloseHandle(hThread); hThread = NULL;
```

The computed value is ready to be displayed:

```
// Step 5: Display the product
TCHAR buf[100];
_stprintf(buf, _T("The product is %d"), data.nProduct);
::MessageBox(NULL, buf, _T("Compute Product"), MB_OK);
```

Tada! We just finished writing our first multithreaded application.

Although one can use the SDK APIs directly to create and manipulate threads, it is more convenient to wrap the APIs in a C++ class. As part of the CPL toolkit, I have developed a C++ abstract base class, CCPLWinThread, to simplify dealing with threads. Following is its definition. For clarity, I have removed some methods that are not relevant to the current discussion.

```
class CCPLWinThread
{
public:
   CCPLWinThread();                     // Constructor
   HRESULT Init();                      // Initializer
   virtual ~CCPLWinThread();            // Destructor
```

```
HRESULT StartThread();          // Start the thread
bool IsThreadActive();          // Check if the thread is running
void StopThread();              // Stop the thread

// Wait for the thread to quit
// (within the specified timeout interval)
bool WaitForCompletion(DWORD dwTimeOut = INFINITE);

protected:
virtual void Proc() = 0;        // The thread entry point
...
};
```

To use this class, you have to create a derived class, add your methods and data members to the class, and implement the virtual method `Proc`, the entry point for the thread.

The following class definition captures the same essence of the secondary thread as our earlier example:

```
class CMyProductThread : public CCPLWinThread
{
public:
    int m_nVal1;
    int m_nVal2;
    int m_nProduct;

    void Proc()
    {
       m_nProduct = m_nVal1 * m_nVal2;
    }
};
```

During run time, the primary thread would create an instance of this class, set the appropriate data members, and call the `StartThread` method, as shown below:

```
int APIENTRY WinMain(HINSTANCE hInstance,
    HINSTANCE hPrevInstance,
    LPSTR lpCmdLine,
    int nCmdShow)
{
    // Step 1: Create an instance and initialize it
    CMyProductThread myThread;       myThread.Init();

    // Step 2: Initialize the data to be passed to the thread
    myThread.m_nVal1 = 5;
    myThread.m_nVal2 = 7;
```

```
// Step 3: Start the thread
myThread.StartThread();

// Step 4: Wait for the thread to quit
myThread.WaitForCompletion();

// Step 5: Display the product
TCHAR buf[100];
_stprintf(buf, _T("The product is %d"), myThread.m_nProduct);
::MessageBox(NULL, buf, _T("Compute Product"), MB_OK);

    return 0;
}
```

As can be seen, the steps are similar to those used in the earlier code snippet, except that the thread creation, destruction, and cleanup (closing the thread handle, etc.) has been abstracted in the CCPLWinThread class.

Abstracting thread creation and destruction buys us one more thing. It turns out that if a thread intends to use any C run-time (CRT) library methods, it is better to use the thread manipulation routines provided by the run-time library, such as _beginthreadex and _endthreadex. This eliminates some memory leaks [Ric-96]. Depending on whether the project intends to use the run-time library, the developers can modify the class implementation. The scope of code changes are isolated to just one class.

Get familiar with class CCPLWinThread. As we go along in this chapter, we will continue to add more functionality to this class.

Now let's look at some of the problems associated with multithreaded programming.

Multithreading Issues

Multithreading is a powerful technique that can improve the performance and responsiveness of your application. At the same time, multithreading introduces some complexities into your code that, if not properly attended during the design and development cycle, may lead to a disaster.

Shared Data Conflicts

If two threads have access to the same variable (more precisely, the same memory location), updating the variable from both the threads may leave the variable's value in an inconsistent state. Consider, for example, the following code:

```
extern int g_nCount;        // a global variable
...
g_nCount = g_nCount + 10;
```

On most processors, this addition is not an atomic instruction, that is, the compiler would generate more than one instruction of machine code for the above statement. On the Intel x86 architecture, the following lines of machine language instructions were generated:[2]

```
mov eax, DWORD PTR ?g_nCount@@3HA          ; g_nCount
add eax, 10                                ; 0000000aH
mov DWORD PTR ?g_nCount@@3HA, eax          ; g_nCount
```

If both the threads executed this sequence, we would expect that the value of g_nCount would be 20 more than it was before any thread executed it. However, if one thread gets preempted by the OS after having executed the first mov instruction, the other thread will pick up the same value of g_nCount as the first thread, both will add 10 onto that value, and when the result is stored back, the final value of g_nCount is higher by just 10.

Shared data conflicts may manifest themselves in a number of ways. In fact, even if only one thread updates the data and the other threads just read it, the data may still get into an inconsistent state. For example, let's say a C structure is being shared between multiple threads. The structure contains a list of names (as string pointers) and a variable, count, that indicates the total number of items in the list. Let's say a thread updates the structure by removing a name from the list and then adjusts the variable count to reflect the new total. If the thread is preempted before count is updated, a different thread will pick the wrong value of count and will try to use a string pointer that has already been deleted. This, in all likelihood, will result in an access violation.

If a memory location (or any other resource) will be accessed concurrently from more than one thread, the developer has to provide some explicit mechanism to synchronize access to such a shared resource.

Fortunately, the Win32 SDK provides many primitives such as critical sections, mutexes, semaphores, and events to achieve synchronization between threads. The first three primitives are generally used to provide mutual exclusion to some shared resource, that is, allow only one thread to access the resource at any given time. The fourth primitive is typically used to send a signal to a thread. The thread can then act upon this signal and take action.

Thread Affinity

Under the Win32 system, certain resources have thread affinity, that is, such resources can only be used by a specific thread. Some examples follow:

---

[2] The code was compiled without any optimization flags turned on.

Critical sections and mutexes have thread affinity. For example, you cannot enter a critical section on one thread and leave the critical section from another thread.

A TLS by definition has thread affinity. A TLS from one thread is not available in any other thread.

All Windows user-interface (UI) related objects, such as window handles, Windows messages, etc., have thread affinity. A Windows message is a structure of type MSG. A message can be posted to a window handle using PostMessage API. The message goes in an MSG queue associated with the thread that created the window handle. In order to receive and process a message from the message queue, a developer has to set up a window procedure (WndProc) and a message pump.[3] A message pump uses some variant of the following code:

```
MSG msg;
While (GetMessage(&msg, 0, 0, 0)) {
  DispatchMessage(&msg);
}
```

One of the fields in the MSG structure is the window handle for which the message was intended. Function call DispatchMessage dispatches the received message to the WndProc associated with this window handle.

Because of the thread affinity of Windows messages, the thread that created the window handle should also be the thread that implements the message pump. As a matter of fact, GetMessage can receive messages for the current thread only (the thread that called the function).

Deadlocks

If two threads wait on each other to release a shared resource before resuming their execution, a deadlock condition occurs. As all the threads participating in a deadlock are suspended and cannot, therefore, release the resources they own, no thread can continue execution. As a result, the application hangs.

Incorrect Use of a Synchronization Object

When a synchronization object is used to guard a shared resource, a typical sequence of operations is as follows:

---

[3] Interaction of a thread and its message queue can be found in WIN32 SDK documentation or in any standard Windows programming book.

1. Lock the synchronization object

2. Use the shared resource

3. Unlock the synchronization object

If the developer forgets to unlock the synchronization object after locking it, the resource would become inaccessible to any other thread.

A more serious problem occurs when the thread is terminated abnormally. The SDK provides an API, TerminateThread, to kill a thread. When this API is called, the target thread has no chance to execute any user-mode code and its initial stack is not deallocated. This can result in the following problems:

- If the target thread has entered a critical section, the critical section will not be released. Thus, some resource may become inaccessible to other threads.
- If the target thread is executing certain kernel level calls when it is terminated, the kernel state for the thread's process could be inconsistent.
- If the target thread is manipulating the global state of a shared DLL, the state of the DLL could be destroyed, affecting other users of the DLL.

In general, threads should not be killed abnormally. A better approach is to send a signal (the "event" synchronization primitive can be used here) to the thread. Of course, the thread procedure should periodically check for this event and return gracefully from the procedure if the event has been fired.

The StopThread method on the CCPLWinThread class does just this. It triggers an event represented by the member variable, m_hStopEvent. The implementor of the thread procedure has to check for this event periodically by calling a method on the class, Wait, as shown below:

```
void Proc()
{
  for(;;) {
      HANDLE hWait = this->Wait(1000);    // check for stop request
                                          // for 1000 milliseconds

    if (hWait == m_hStopEvent) {
      return;
    }

    ... // do something
  }
}
```

Method `Wait` need not wait for just the stop-event synchronization handle. You can add other synchronization handles to wait for by calling `CCPLWinThread`'s method, `AddHandleToWaitGroup`.

Performance

Using more threads doesn't always translate into greater performance for a couple of reasons:

- Each thread consumes some system resources. If the resources available to the OS decrease, the overall performance degrades.
- Thread-switching is a very expensive operation. The OS has to save the thread-context (the register values, etc.) of the executing thread and load the thread-context of the new thread.

Now that we understand the basics of multithread programming and the problems associated with it, let's see what COM has to offer to help us simplify developing a thread-safe component.

APARTMENTS

The extent of thread-safe code varies from application to application. At one extreme there are legacy applications that are not at all thread-safe. At the opposite end of the spectrum are well-crafted applications that make sophisticated use of the thread synchronization primitives. Then there are other applications that have special threading constraints, such as dependency on TLS or use of user-interface primitives.

An application should still be able to use components from another application without re-architecting its own synchronization strategy.

To facilitate transparent use of an object irrespective of its threading strategy, COM treats an object's concurrency constraints as yet another run-time requirement. The developer of the component decides on the threading strategy, or the *threading model,* as it is formally referred to.

Recall from Chapter 5 that any run-time requirement of an object becomes part of the object's context. It is possible that many contexts in a process share the same concurrency constraints. COM+ groups contexts of similar concurrency constraints into an abstraction called an *apartment.* The primary role of an apartment is to help COM+ determine which threads in the process are allowed to dispatch interface method calls in a particular context.

A process contains one or more apartments, and an apartment contains one or more contexts. This is illustrated in Figure 6.1.

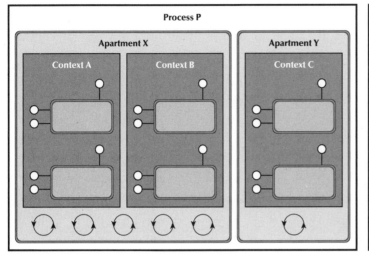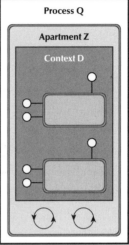

Figure 6.1   Contexts, apartments, and processes. Adapted from [Box-99].

Note that a context resides in exactly one apartment; no two apartments share the same context. If an object reference needs to be passed from one apartment to another, it is implicit that the reference has to be passed from one context to another. And we already know from Chapter 5 that such a reference has to be marshaled, either explicitly or via COM+ support.

 Those of you who have been programming in classic COM know that a reference does not need marshaling when passed within the same apartment. This is different under COM+. There may be many contexts within the same apartment. If a reference is being passed from one context to another context, the reference has to be marshaled, even if the contexts belong to the same apartment.

A thread enters an apartment by calling a COM API, CoInitial-izeEx. The following is its prototype:

```
WINOLEAPI CoInitializeEx(/*IN*/ LPVOID pvReserved,
    /*IN*/ DWORD dwCoInit);
```

The first parameter for this API is reserved for future use. The second parameter indicates the type of apartment the thread would like to enter into.

Once a thread enters an apartment, it cannot enter another apartment without leaving the current apartment first.

To leave the current apartment, the thread can call another COM API, `CoUninitialize`. The following is its prototype:

`void CoUninitialize();`

For proper cleanup, `CoUninitialize` should be called once for each successful call to `CoIntializeEx`.

 It is important to understand that a thread is not an apartment. A thread enters and leaves an apartment. Only objects (along with their context objects) reside in an apartment.

COM+ defines three types of apartments an object can reside in:

1. Single-threaded apartments (STA)
2. Multithreaded apartments (MTA)
3. Thread-neutral apartments (TNA)

Let's examine each of these in detail.

Single-Threaded Apartments (STA)

As the name implies, only one thread can execute in an STA. More precisely, there is only *one* specific thread associated with an STA and this is the only thread that can *ever* execute in the STA. As a result, all the objects that reside in the STA will never be accessed concurrently.

Because of this thread affinity, STAs are good for:

- Objects that use TLS as intermediate storage between method calls.
- Objects that do not have any protection (synchronization support) for their member data and therefore would like to avoid any shared data conflict.
- Objects dealing with user interfaces.

When a thread calls `CoInitializeEx` passing the `COINIT_APART-MENTTHREADED` flag, COM+ creates a new STA and associates that STA with the thread. All objects that are subsequently created in the new STA will receive their calls only on this specific thread.

To enter an STA, COM provides a simplified variation of `CoInitial-izeEx`, `CoInitialize`, that developers can use. The following is its prototype:

```
WINOLEAPI CoInitialize(/*IN*/ LPVOID pvReserved);
```

Each thread within a process that calls `CoInitialize` (or `CoInitializeEx` with `COINIT_APARTMENTTHREADED` flag) gets a new STA. Therefore, a process may contain many STAs.

When the thread calls `CoUnintialize`, the STA gets torn down.

Multithreaded Apartments (MTA)

In an MTA, multiple threads can execute concurrently.

When a thread calls `CoInitializeEx`, passing `COINIT_MULTI-THREADED` value as the apartment type, COM creates an MTA for the process, if one does not already exist. This thread, and any other thread that subsequently calls `CoInitializeEx` passing `COINIT_MULTITHREADED` as the apartment type, will use the same MTA. Therefore, a process can have at most one MTA.

Any object that is created in the MTA can receive its method calls from any MTA thread in the process. COM does not serialize method calls to the object. As method calls can be executed concurrently, the object should implement its own synchronization logic for guarding member and global data. In addition, as any MTA thread could invoke the object's method, no thread-specific state may be stored in the object (by using TLS, for example).

As the synchronization logic is applied at the implementation level, the developer gets to fine-tune the synchronization mechanism, resulting in a higher level of performance. Of course, the higher performance comes at the expense of more complexity in the code since the developer has to address the issues related to multithreaded programming.

When the last thread that is using the MTA leaves it (by calling `CoUninitialize`), the apartment gets torn down.

Thread-Neutral Apartments (TNA)

Recall from our earlier discussion that no two apartments share the same context. Therefore, a cross-apartment method call automatically implies a cross-context call. Combining this fact with our knowledge of cross-context marshaling from Chapter 5, we can state that if the caller's thread is in a different apartment than that of the object, the caller would get a proxy to the object.

When the caller thread makes a method call to the proxy, COM+ would intercept and dispatch the call to an appropriate thread in the object's apartment. We will cover this architecture in detail in the next section. The important point to note here is that if an object resides in an STA or an MTA, a cross-apartment method call on the object requires a thread switch. And we know from our earlier discussion that a thread switch is a very expensive operation.

This performance problem can be solved if a thread-neutral apartment is used instead of an STA or an MTA. Under TNA, the client always receives a lightweight proxy. When a method call is made on this proxy, COM+ switches to the object's context without causing a thread switch.

Unlike STA and MTA, a thread cannot enter or leave a TNA. Only objects can reside in a TNA.

Also note that there can be only one TNA in a process (similar to MTA).

The TNA is the preferred apartment for objects that do not have any thread affinity. As we will see in a later section, under TNA, the developer can still choose between providing its own fine-grain synchronization logic or letting COM+ serialize the method calls to an object.

You may be thinking that TNA seems similar to the FTM that we covered in the previous chapter. After all, both of them execute incoming calls in the caller's thread. The difference is that a TNA-based object has its own apartment (and context). An FTM-based object does not have a context of its own; it uses the caller's context. The FTM is used if an object has reasons to use the caller's context. The TNA is preferred for all other cases.

CONFIGURATION SETTINGS

A component's implementors decide the threading strategy (the apartment type) to be used by the component. However, an approach based on the component calling `CoInitializeEx` cannot be used. A component is built as an in-process server (a DLL)—the client will have already called `CoInitializeEx` by the time an object gets created.

The approach taken by COM+ was that each COM class defines its threading model in the Windows registry key. Recall from Chapter 5 that the COM+ Catalog Manager controls the Windows registry key, `HKEY_CLASSES_ROOT\CLSID`, and that COM+ expects the implementors to add the requisite registry entries in the export function `DllRegisterServer` and to clean up the entries in the export function `DllUnregisterServer`.

The threading model for a CLSID is specified under the following registry value:

```
HKEY_CLASSES_ROOT\CLSID\{<CLSID>}\InprocServer32\ThreadingModel
```

There are five possible values for the `ThreadingModel` registry entry, as follows:

- `ThreadingModel="Apartment"` indicates that the object can be created (and executed) only in an STA.
- `ThreadingModel="Free"` indicates that the object can be created (and executed) only in an MTA.
- `ThreadingModel="Both"` indicates that the object can be created either in an STA or MTA. COM+ uses the apartment type of the client to create the object. Of course, the object will execute only in the apartment it is created in.
- `ThreadingModel="Neutral"` indicates that the object can be created (and executed) only in a TNA.
- The absence of a `ThreadingModel` entry represents a legacy case. It implies that the object can run only on the main STA. The main STA is defined as the first STA to be initialized in the process.

The interaction between apartments, context, objects, and threads has been a source of tremendous confusion among the COM community. Let me see if I can clear up some of the confusion:

- An apartment is nothing but a group of contexts sharing the same concurrency requirements.
- An object never enters or leaves an apartment. The object is created in an apartment (more specifically, in a context within an apartment) based on the `ThreadingModel` registry entry. The object lives and dies in the apartment.
- A thread enters and leaves an apartment. A thread can enter only one apartment at a time. Once a thread enters an apartment, it gets associated with the default context for the apartment (default contexts are covered in Chapter 5).
- The TNA is a special apartment that has meaning only for the objects. A thread can never enter or leave a TNA.

- If the client's apartment is not compatible with that of the component's threading model, COM+ silently creates the object in a compatible apartment and returns a proxy to the client.
- If the object's apartment is either an STA or an MTA, a cross-apartment call will result in a thread switch. If the object's apartment is a TNA, the thread switch is not needed for the cross-apartment call.
- If the client's apartment is compatible with that of the component, there are two cases to be addressed.
    1. If the client's context is the same as that of the created object, the client gets a raw reference to the object.
    2. If the contexts are not the same, the client gets a proxy. However, there is no thread switch involved during cross-context calls, as the contexts are part of the same apartment.
- If an object spawns a thread (using `CreateThread`, for example), the resulting thread does not inherit the context of the parent object. The thread can enter an apartment, thereby getting the default context for the apartment.

Component implementors that do not mark a threading model for their classes can ignore threading issues, as their DLL will be accessed from only one thread, the main thread.

Implementors that mark their classes as "`Apartment`" are indicating that any object that is created can be accessed only from one thread for the lifetime of the object. This implies that there is no need to protect the state of an individual instance. However, it is possible to have multiple instances of the COM class in the same process (on different threads, of course). Therefore, if these multiple instances share some resource, the resource still needs to be protected from multiple accesses.

`ThreadingModel="Both"` implies that the object should be created in the same apartment as that of the client. A client, irrespective of its apartment state, does not require a thread switch while making a method call on the object. This by far is the most efficient case. However, if the object interface is marshaled and passed to another apartment, a cross-apartment call will still result in a thread switch.

`ThreadingModel="Neutral"` is similar to "both" in the sense that a method call never requires a thread switch. The added advantage is that if the object interface is marshaled and passed to another apartment, a cross-apartment call *also* does not require a thread switch. Although a case can be made that `ThreadingModel="Both"` is a bit more efficient than `"Neutral"` under some circumstances (the client gets a raw pointer, not the proxy), the performance difference is negligible. Moreover, an implementor can specify additional synchronization settings with `ThreadingModel="Neutral"` as we will see later. Hence, under COM+, this is the preferred threading model for components that do not require any thread-affinity.

`ThreadingModel="Free"` results in some code simplification under classic COM. Under classic COM, there is no need to explicitly marshal a reference between two threads within the same apartment. If a class is marked as `"Free"`, any instance created for the class resides in the MTA and could be accessed by a secondary MTA thread directly, even if the instantiation came from an STA-based client. Under COM+, however, two threads within an apartment may belong to different contexts, and passing a reference from one thread to another may still require explicit marshaling. Therefore, `ThreadingModel="Neutral"` is preferred over `ThreadingModel="Free"` under COM+.

 If you do not wish to use any of the COM+ services for a component and would like to avoid explicit marshaling between the threads, you can install the component as non-configured and set the `ThreadingModel` to `"Free"`.

Activities

Earlier, I indicated that the preferred threading model for components that do not require any thread affinity is `Neutral`. This configuration setting on the component forces COM+ to create the object in a TNA.

As multiple threads can concurrently access a TNA object, the implementors still need to deal with multithreading issues and explicitly use defensive multithreaded programming techniques.

But what about those developers who would rather focus on business needs and not worry about multithreaded programming?

To provide synchronized access to an object, COM+ provides a generic solution called *activity-based synchronization.*

An activity is a collection of one or more contexts that share concurrency characteristics. An activity may cross processes as well as machine boundaries. Within an activity, concurrent calls from multiple threads are not allowed, that is, COM+ provides intrinsic call serialization across all the contexts in an activity.

As shown in Figure 6.2, a context within a process may at most belong to one activity, but many contexts may not belong to an activity at all. Contexts that do not belong to an activity (such as the default context of an apartment) get no intrinsic call serialization, that is, any thread in the context apartment can enter the context at any time. Of course, if the context belongs to an STA, then no more than one thread will ever access the context.

At first glance, an activity and an STA appear to be the same thing. However, an activity is far more powerful than an STA. It can span multiple processes and machines although, as you will see later, COM+ weakens the concurrency guarantees when an activity spans multiple processes.

An object can reside in any of the following activities:

- Creator's activity
- New activity
- No activity

Component implementors specify the activity the component should belong to by means of a configurable attribute called synchronization. Figure 6.3 shows various synchronization values that can be set on a component.

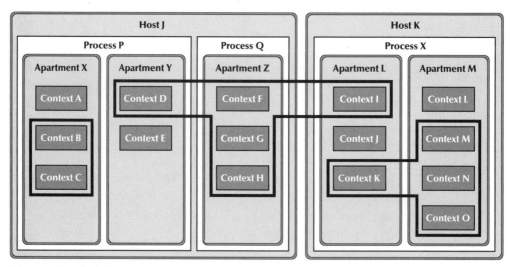

Figure 6.2   Activities.

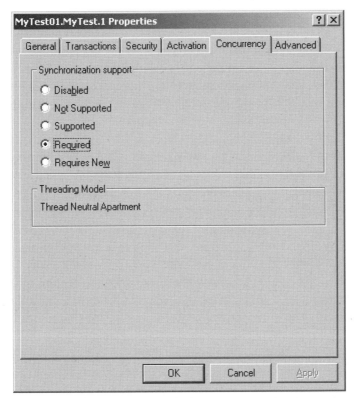

Figure 6.3 Synchronization settings on a component.

Following is an explanation of the various synchronization settings:

- **Disabled**: Any synchronization-related overhead for the component is eliminated.
- **Not Supported**: The object has no interest in either starting its own activity or being part of its creator's activity.
- **Supported**: The object doesn't care for the presence or absence of its creator's activity. If the creator belongs to an activity, the object will enter this activity. Otherwise, no new activity will be created.
- **Required**: The object has to be part of an activity. If its creator belongs to an activity, the object will enter this activity. Otherwise, the object will start a new activity.
- **Requires New**: The object will always start a new activity, independent of its creator's activity status.

Note that the `ThreadingModel` attribute of a component dictates *which* threads in an apartment can dispatch calls to an object, whereas the `synchronization` attribute dictates *when* a thread can dispatch calls to the object. The `synchronization` attribute is largely independent of the `ThreadingModel` attribute, although some combinations of the two are incompatible. For example, components that have `ThreadingModel="Apartment"` require either `Synchronization="Required"` or `Synchronization="Required New"`.

By setting `ThreadingModel="Neutral"` and `Synchronization="Required"`, one can get a variation of a TNA that allows any thread to call into the object, but only one thread can call at any given time. Such a configuration is often referred to as the *rental-threading* model.

To ensure that no two threads can enter an activity concurrently, COM+ allocates a process-wide lock for each activity. When a proxy tries to enter a context in an activity, the proxy's interceptor attempts to acquire ownership of the lock. If the lock is available, the call proceeds. If not, the caller waits until it can get ownership of the lock. Once the method call returns to the interceptor, the lock is released, potentially allowing the next caller to enter the activity.

While the above mechanism ensures that only one thread can enter an activity at a time, it doesn't prevent the possibility of a deadlock. Consider for example, two objects, A and B, that belong to two different activities on two different machines. Consider the case of nested method calls where the client calls a method on A, A calls a method on B, and B calls a method on A. When the client calls a method on A's proxy, the proxy's interceptor locks A's activity. Object A then proceeds to call a method on B. This is a blocking call waiting for the response from B. Now, B tries to enter A's activity. But A's activity is already locked. We now have a situation where the call from A to B is blocked and the call from B to A is blocked. A deadlock, indeed! This scenario can easily be extended to any number of objects making a chain of calls on the same call stack.

To prevent such deadlocks, COM defines the notion of *causality*, which you can think of as the logical ID of a stack of nested calls. Due to the synchronous nature of method invocations, causality has a single logical thread of control throughout the network, despite the fact that several physical threads may be used to service the calls.

Causality begins when a thread makes a method call on the proxy. COM generates a causality ID and tags it to this method call and to all the subsequent nested calls from object to object, even across host machines. An activity gets locked in the context of a causality ID. If an incoming call arrives while an activity is locked, COM checks if the causality ID of the incoming call matches that of the one that locked the activity. If the IDs match, COM lets the call be serviced. If the incoming call is from a different causality, COM correctly blocks its entrance to the activity. Thus, by allowing reentrancy from the same caller, COM solves the deadlock problem.

APARTMENTS AND STANDARD MARSHALING

All along in this chapter I have mentioned several times that a cross-apartment access to an STA or MTA object requires a thread switch. It is interesting to learn how COM implements an apartment and why a cross-apartment call results in a thread switch. As most objects elect to use standard marshaling for cross-apartment (and cross-context) access, I will focus on the same.

We know from Chapters 2 and 5 that, if the client and the objects are in two different apartments, the client gets a proxy to the object. More specifically, the client gets a *proxy manager* that loads an *interface proxy* for each interface queried on the object. When a method call is made on the interface proxy, the interface proxy marshals the parameter information into an ORPC message and sends it over the ORPC channel to the interface stub. The interface stub receives the ORPC message, unmarshals it, and invokes the appropriate interface method on the object.

While communicating over the ORPC channel, COM uses the most efficient transport protocol available based on the type of importing (client's) and exporting (object's) apartment.

If the importing apartment is on a different host, COM uses RPC as the transport protocol. An RPC thread cache is started in the exporting apartment's process. This thread cache waits for incoming connection requests. When a request comes in, the thread cache will dispatch a thread to service the request and continue to wait for additional requests. When the thread is done servicing the request, it will return back to the thread cache.

If the importing apartment is on the same host but in a different process, COM uses lightweight RPC (LRPC) as the transport protocol. LRPC is a Microsoft proprietary variant of RPC which has the exact same calling syntax as the DEC RPC run time (thus, the seamless interchangeability), but is optimized to reduce data copying and eliminate access to the networking code altogether.

If the importing apartment is in the same process, COM can bypass the RPC thread cache and use the caller's thread directly to service the request.

In summary, the thread that services the incoming request could be one from the RPC thread cache or could be the client's thread itself. The thread will dispatch the call to the object's apartment, wait for a response, and return the response back to the client.

Now let's see how the calls are dispatched to the actual apartment.

Dispatching Calls to an STA

If the incoming call originates from a different host, we know that the call has to be dispatched using a thread from the RPC thread cache. However, an STA has its own thread to work with. No other threads can enter an existing STA.

We therefore need a way to communicate between the RPC thread and the STA thread. Here is what COM does.

To enter the STA and dispatch a call to the STA's thread, the RPC thread packs the ORPC message into a Windows message and posts it (using PostMessage) to the STA thread's MSG queue.

From our earlier discussion, we know that in order to process a message from a message queue we need a window handle, a WndProc, and a message pump.

COM takes care of providing the window handle and the WndProc. It creates an invisible window for each thread that enters an STA. The WndProc of this window receives the message posted by the RPC thread and passes the embedded ORPC message to the stub. The interface stub processes the ORPC message in the context of the STA thread.

Developers have to take care of implementing the message pump. Each STA thread should implement a message pump.

Figure 6.4 illustrates the call dispatching sequence in an STA.

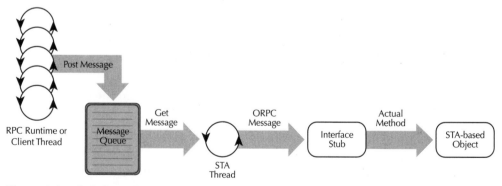

Figure 6.4   Call dispatching sequence in an STA. Adapted from [Box-98].

If the incoming call originates from the same host but from a different process, a special transport is used that bypasses the RPC thread cache and calls `PostMessage` from the thread of the caller. This is because Windows lets you post a message from a different process on the local machine, but not on a remote machine.

If the incoming call originates from the same process but from a different apartment, the ORPC channel can directly use the client thread to post a message.

Obviously, if the call originates from the same STA apartment, the call will be processed directly, bypassing the message queue. There is no need to switch the thread.

From a programming perspective, two important points are to be noted:

- A cross-apartment call into an STA *always* results in a thread switch.
- An STA requires a message pump to process incoming requests.

The second point deserves a little more attention.

The message pump in the STA is not just used for processing incoming ORPC requests, but can also be used for any non-COM-related window messages (recall that an STA thread is an ideal candidate for UI processing). In either case, if an interface method call takes a considerable time to execute, no incoming ORPC requests would be processed and the UI would appear to be frozen. Therefore, any interface method in an STA should not do a blocking wait (using `WaitForSingleObject`, for example). Moreover, if the method is expected to take a considerable time to execute, then it should implement some variant of the message pump in the method implementation code. For example, at some strategic points in the code, the method could check if a new message has arrived in the queue and dispatch that message.

The same holds true when an STA thread makes either a cross-apartment method call into an MTA or into a different process method call. Recall that when such a method call is made, the proxy sends an ORPC message and waits for an ORPC response. The call is blocked until a response is received. A blocking call such as this would prevent incoming messages on the MSG queue to be serviced.

To be able to process the incoming messages, the ORPC channel uses a different thread to wait for the ORPC response (the thread gets created when the caller first receives the proxy). As the caller's thread cannot be released until a response is received, the channel puts the caller's thread in an internal message pump. This internal message pump serves:

- the incoming ORPC requests (as Windows messages)
- normal non-COM-related Windows messages
- the ORPC response message from the thread waiting for the ORPC response

Having an internal message pump in the ORPC channel also solves the problem of potential deadlock when an STA thread makes a cross-apartment method call, and the method turns around and tries to enter the STA thread (this deadlock problem is similar to the one we described earlier for activities). While the cross-apartment method call is still waiting for an ORPC response, the nested call can now reenter the STA.

Dispatching Calls to an MTA

After knowing how STA calls are dispatched, learning how a call is dispatched to an MTA is a piece of cake.

If the incoming call originates from a different host or from a different process on the same host, a thread from the RPC thread cache services the request. It enters the object's apartment and passes the ORPC message to the stub.

If the call originates from an STA within the same process, it is equivalent to the case we covered earlier where an STA thread makes an outgoing call into an MTA. One of the threads from the RPC cache enters the MTA, passes the ORPC message to the stub, receives the ORPC response, and posts it as a Windows message back to the STA thread.

If the call originates from an MTA within the same process, the ORPC channel uses the caller's thread to enter the MTA and process the request. No thread switch is required.

Dispatching Calls to a TNA

Dispatching calls to a TNA is even simpler.

If the call originates from a different host or from a different process on the local host, the dispatching mechanism is similar to that of an MTA. A thread from the RPC thread cache enters the TNA and passes the ORPC message to the interface stub.

If the call originates from a different apartment within the same process, the ORPC channel uses the caller's thread to enter the TNA. There is no thread switch involved. The only performance hit is that the lightweight interceptor has to set up the proper context before entering the TNA and then reset it upon exiting.

If the object is configured to run under a rental apartment, all the other ORPC requests are blocked once a thread enters a TNA.

When an outgoing call is made from the TNA, it is done on either an STA or MTA thread, depending upon where the call originated. The same call dispatching rules apply as discussed earlier. The fact that the call was routed through a TNA is of no consequence. For example, if the call originated from an MTA, through a TNA, to an MTA (in the same process), the ORPC channel will use the original caller's thread to execute the method.

CROSS-CONTEXT ACCESS

In Chapter 5, I made the case that an interface pointer, either raw or proxy, should always be marshaled when passed from one context to another. I also noted that application programmers rarely deal with marshaling because COM handles the most common cases of interface pointer marshaling implicitly. Explicit marshaling is only needed when a reference to an object is shared outside the scope of an interface method call. COM provides APIs to explicitly marshal and unmarshal interface pointers.

Let's put these marshaling APIs to use.

You may be wondering why I am talking about interface marshaling in a chapter on concurrency management instead of in Chapter 5 which dealt with contexts. Well, it is just convenient to demonstrate marshaling across apartments. After all, cross-apartment access does imply cross-context access.

The SDK provides two APIs, `CoMarshalInterface` and `CoUnmarshalInterface`, to marshal and unmarshal an interface pointer, respectively. Following are their prototypes:

```
STDAPI CoMarshalInterface(
    IStream *pStm,          //Pointer to the stream used for marshaling
    REFIID riid,            //Reference to the identifier of the interface
    IUnknown *pUnk,         //Pointer to the interface to be marshaled
    DWORD dwDestContext,    //Destination context
    void *pvDestContext,    //Reserved for future use
    DWORD mshlflags         //Reason for marshaling
);

STDAPI CoUnmarshalInterface(
    IStream * pStm,         //Pointer to the stream
    REFIID riid,            //Reference to the identifier of the interface
    void ** ppv             //Address of output variable that receives
                            //the interface pointer requested in riid
);
```

The first API, CoMarshalInterface, marshals a context-relative object reference to context-neutral byte streams. These byte streams can be passed to any other contexts.

The second API reads the byte stream and creates a proxy in the caller's context.

Let's write a program to demonstrate the usage of these APIs.

Using the ATL wizard, I will generate a free-threaded component MyTest that supports an interface IMyTest. This interface has a method DoIt whose implementation just returns S_OK.

```
STDMETHODIMP CMyTest::DoIt()
{
   return S_OK;
}
```

The client program has two threads. The main thread enters an MTA and creates an object of class MyTest.

```
int WinMain(...)
{
   // Enter MTA
   ::CoInitializeEx(NULL, COINIT_MULTITHREADED);

   // Create an object and get IMyTest interface
   IMyTestPtr spTest(__uuidof(MyTest));
   ...
}
```

The secondary thread runs in an STA. It calls the interface method DoIt on the object that was created by the main thread.

```
class CMyThread : public CCPLWinThread
{
public:
   IMyTestPtr m_spTest;

   void Proc()
   {
     try {
       m_spTest->DoIt();
     }
     catch(_com_error& e) {
       ReportError(e);
     }
   }
};
```

The main thread creates the secondary thread, passes the interface pointer to the secondary thread, starts it, and waits for it to finish.

```
CMyThread myThread; myThread.Init();
myThread.SetApartmentToEnter(COINIT_APARTMENTTHREADED);

// Pass the interface pointer to the thread without marshaling
myThread.m_spTest = spTest;

// Start the thread and wait for the thread to quit
myThread.StartThread();
myThread.WaitForCompletion();
```

Note that I haven't used any marshaling APIs yet. Let's run the client program and see what happens.

The call to `DoIt` in the secondary thread fails with an error, `RPC_E_WRONG_THREAD`, which stands for "the application called an interface that was marshaled for a different thread."

So just passing raw interface pointers between two apartments (therefore, two contexts) doesn't work.

 This experiment was designed to bring forth this error. Sometimes, passing an interface pointer from one context to another without explicit marshaling may seem to work. However, there is no guarantee that the services provided by COM will function correctly.

Now let's modify our code to use the marshaling APIs.

The following code snippet shows how an interface pointer can be marshaled into a global handle:

```
HGLOBAL MyMarshalInterface(IMyTestPtr spTest)
{
   // Create an IStream pointer on a dynamally allocated global
memory
   IStreamPtr spStream;
   HRESULT hr = ::CreateStreamOnHGlobal(0, FALSE, &spStream);
   VERIFYHR(hr);

   // Marshal the interface pointer into the stream
   hr = ::CoMarshalInterface(spStream,
      __uuidof(IMyTest),
      spTest,
      MSHCTX_INPROC,
```

```
   0,
   MSHLFLAGS_NORMAL);
VERIFYHR(hr);

// obtain the handle to the global memory and return it
HGLOBAL hRetVal;
hr = ::GetHGlobalFromStream(spStream, &hRetVal);
VERIFYHR(hr);
return hRetVal;
}
```

While making a call to `CoMarshalInterface`, a developer can specify the distance of the destination context as a) within the same process, b) in a different process on the local machine, or c) on a different machine. COM uses this information as a hint for creating an efficiently marshaled packet. For our example, I specified `MSHCTX_INPROC` to indicate that the importing context is within the same process.

`CoMarshalInterface` also supports the notion of single-time unmarshaling or multiple-time unmarshaling. If the object reference is marshaled using the `MSHLFLAGS_NORMAL` flag, it is referred to as *normal marshaling* or *call marshaling*. The semantics of normal marshaling imply one-time unmarshaling only. Normal marshaling also has a timeout period within which if the unmarshaling doesn't occur, the data becomes invalid. Under *table marshaling*, the marshaled information is written to a globally available table, where it can be retrieved by multiple clients and unmarshaled multiple times. And there is no timeout period associated with it.

The case of interface marshaling within a process is so common that the SDK defines a simplified variation of the marshaling APIs, `CoMarshalInterThreadInterfaceInStream` and `CoGetInterfaceAndReleaseStream`. Using these APIs is straightforward and is left as an exercise for the reader.

Global Interface Table (GIT)

In the preceding code, the object reference was marshaled using *normal marshaling* semantics. Under *normal marshaling*, the data becomes invalid after it has been unmarshaled once. It is often desirable to marshal a pointer from one thread and have multiple threads (perhaps from different contexts) unmarshal the interface pointer when needed. Though *table marshaling* can be used to achieve this, for reasons beyond the scope of this book, table marshaling doesn't work if the interface pointer to be marshaled happens to be a proxy.

To solve the problem of making an interface pointer accessible to multiple contexts, COM introduces a facility called the Global Interface Table (GIT).

The GIT is a process-wide table that contains marshaled interface pointers that can be unmarshaled multiple times. This is semantically equivalent to
table marshaling, except that it works for raw references as well as proxies.

The GIT supports an interface `IGlobalInterfaceTable` that has
methods to add, retrieve, or remove one or more interface pointers. When an
interface pointer is added to the GIT, it returns a DWORD cookie (called the
GIT cookie). If this cookie is published to other contexts by some means, each
interested context can retrieve the interface pointer using this cookie as a key.

The following code snippet shows how the `ITest` interface pointer
from our example can be added to the GIT:

```
DWORD MyMarshalInterfaceInGIT(IMyTestPtr spTest)
{
  // Create an instance of GIT
  IGlobalInterfaceTablePtr spGIT;
  HRESULT hr = ::CoCreateInstance(CLSID_StdGlobalInterfaceTable,
    0,
    CLSCTX_INPROC_SERVER,
    __uuidof(IGlobalInterfaceTable),
    (void**) &spGIT);

  // Add our interface pointer to GIT
  DWORD dwCookie;
  hr = spGIT->RegisterInterfaceInGlobal(spTest,
    __uuidof(IMyTest), &dwCookie);
  return dwCookie;
}
```

COM provides a standard implementation of the GIT as an in-proc
component with CLSID, `CLSID_StdGlobalInterfaceTable`. The implementation is completely thread-safe.

The code above obtains the `IGlobalInterfaceTable` interface
pointer from the standard implementation, registers the `IMyTest` interface
pointer with the GIT, and returns the generated cookie.

Any other context within the process can use the generated cookie to
unmarshal the interface pointer and get a proxy, as shown in the following
code snippet:

```
IMyTestPtr MyUnmarshalInterfaceFromGIT(DWORD dwCookie)
{
  // Create an instance of GIT
  IGlobalInterfaceTablePtr spGIT;
  HRESULT hr = ::CoCreateInstance(CLSID_StdGlobalInterfaceTable,
    0,
```

```
    CLSCTX_INPROC_SERVER,
    __uuidof(IGlobalInterfaceTable),
    (void**) &spGIT);

  IMyTestPtr spTest;
  hr = spGIT->GetInterfaceFromGlobal(dwCookie,
    __uuidof(IMyTest), (void**) &spTest);
  return spTest;
}
```

The above example created an instance of the GIT on an as-needed basis. In typical applications, a single process-wide instance is created just once at the startup.

DEVELOPING THREAD-SAFE COM CODE

At this point, we have a good understanding of multithreaded programming issues as well as the intricacies of COM apartments and marshaling. So let's take a look at some common techniques to develop apartment-safe and thread-safe code.

Shared Data Conflicts

Earlier, I mentioned that if a memory location or any other resource will be accessed concurrently from more than one thread, the developer has to provide some explicit mechanism to synchronize access to such a shared resource.

Using a Main STA

The most convenient solution is to let COM synchronize the access by not specifying the ThreadingModel attribute on the class. This forces COM to create all the objects in the main STA. As only one thread will ever access the main STA, there is no sharing of data between multiple threads.

While this solution works, there is a performance penalty. Every method call has to be marshaled back to the main STA thread.

Using an STA

The next best thing to do would be to mark the ThreadingModel as Apartment. COM places each object provided by the component in an STA, thereby achieving serialization on each object.

While this protects the state of the object from concurrent access, any data that is shared among multiple objects is not protected. This is because objects from the components can be created in multiple STAs. Multiple STA threads can access a shared data concurrently. It is the responsibility of the developer to use proper synchronization primitives to protect shared data.

Let's see how we can use a Win32 synchronization primitive to protect a shared resource.

Perhaps the most efficient Win32 synchronization primitive is a critical section. To lock access to a resource, a thread should enter a critical section. Once done using the resource, the thread should unlock access to the resource by leaving the critical section.

ATL provides a class, CComAutoCriticalSection, that simplifies the usage of a critical section. Here is how you can protect a global variable, g_nCount, using this class.

The first step is to declare a global variable of type CComAutoCriticalSection, as shown below:

```
CComAutoCriticalSection g_myCS;
long g_nCount = 500;
```

Each time g_nCount is accessed, Lock and Unlock methods on CComAutoCriticalSection should be called, as illustrated in the following code snippet:

```
STDMETHODIMP CMyCount::GetCount(long *plCount)
{
  g_myCS.Lock();
  *plCount = g_nCount;
  g_myCS.Unlock();

  return S_OK;
}

STDMETHODIMP CMyCount::IncrementCount(long nValue)
{
  g_myCS.Lock();
  g_nCount += nValue;
  g_myCS.Unlock();

  return S_OK;
}
```

Any number of variables can be grouped together and accessed within just one critical section. Mutually exclusive groups of variables may be enclosed in separate critical sections to provide a finer level of granularity.

Recall from Chapter 3 that the class factory that is returned via `DllGetClass-Object` is a global singleton and is typically created on the first call to `Dll-GetClassObject`. As `DllGetClassObject` can be invoked concurrently from two different STA threads, the creation of the class factory object has to be protected. Fortunately, ATL does this for us.

A similar condition applies to the `DllGetUnloadNow`, the function that keeps track of outstanding object references via a global variable. Once again, ATL provides thread-safe implementation of this function.

Though a critical section is quite efficient, Win32 provides a simpler and more efficient mechanism for synchronizing access to a single variable of data type LONG. The mechanism uses the `InterlockedXX` family of APIs. Using these APIs, for example, our code can be simplified as follows:

```
STDMETHODIMP CMyCount::GetCount(long *plCount)
{
   *plCount = g_nCount;

   return S_OK;
}

STDMETHODIMP CMyCount::IncrementCount(long nValue)
{
   ::InterlockedExchangeAdd(&g_nCount, nValue);

   return S_OK;
}
```

The `InterlockedXX` functions are used only if the value needs to be modified, not if the value just needs to be read.

In my CPL toolkit, I have provided a class, `CCPLWinAtomicCounter`, that abstracts `Interlocked` APIs. You can use a variable of this class type as a regular LONG variable, except that it is protected from shared access:

```
CCPLWinAtomicCounter g_nCount;
...
STDMETHODIMP CMyCount::GetCount(long *plCount)
{
  *plCount = g_nCount;

  return S_OK;
}

STDMETHODIMP CMyCount::IncrementCount(long nValue)
{
  g_nCount += nValue;

  return S_OK;
}
```

Using Activities

If the class code does not have any thread affinity, another approach would be to mark the class as Synchronization=Required. This will result in only one thread accessing the object at any time. This case is similar to STA; although the state of the object is protected implicitly, any shared data between multiple objects needs to be protected explicitly.

The activity logic fails when two threads try to enter the same activity from two different processes. An activity is locked only process-wide; not machine or domain wide. This decision was made on the premise that the cost associated with providing a fully distributed activity protection out-weighs its benefits. As a result, if two objects A and B from two different processes are part of the same activity, and calls A::X and B::Y are made on them from different threads, it is entirely possible that the two calls will execute concurrently. Worse yet, if objects A and B were to call each other, a deadlock would almost certainly ensue as X and Y would be part of two different causalities and would not be considered nested calls.

To avoid such a problem, multiple clients should not share an object, especially across process boundaries. If two different clients need to access the same piece of data, they should do so by creating two distinct object identities that access the same data state.

Using a TNA or an MTA

Now we are getting ready to get our hands dirty. Instead of relying on COM to provide synchronization, we are indicating that we will provide our own complete synchronization solution.

Using an MTA or a TNA, two method calls on an object can execute concurrently. Therefore, not only the state of the global data needs protection, even the state of the object specific data has to be protected from concurrent access.

In Chapter 3, we used a LONG variable to keep track of the reference count on an object:

```
STDMETHODIMP_(ULONG) CVcr::AddRef()
{
  return (++m_lRefCount);
}

STDMETHODIMP_(ULONG) CVcr::Release()
{
  ULONG lRetVal = (--m_lRefCount);
  if (0 == lRetVal) {
    delete this;
  }
  return lRetVal;
}
```

While the code served its purpose in explaining the concept of reference counting, it is not thread-safe under the MTA or TNA. The shared variable, m_lRefCount, needs protection in case the two methods execute concurrently. A standard technique is to use InterlockedIncrement and InterlockedDecrement APIs for reference counting. Fortunately, once again ATL-generated code rescues us from this labor.

How about protecting the state of an individual object?

Synchronization primitives such as a critical section or a mutex can be used to protect data. However, one has to be careful using these primitives. Improper use or careless use can spell trouble. Let's see how.

The code fragment below shows a simple ATL-based implementation class that supports an interface to set a person's first and last name.

```
class CPerson :
  . . .
{
  . . .
// IPerson
public:
  STDMETHOD(LockAccess)();
  STDMETHOD(SetFirstName)(/*[in]*/ BSTR bsFirstName);
  STDMETHOD(SetLastName)(/*[in]*/ BSTR bsLastName);
  STDMETHOD(UnlockAccess)();
```

```
private:
  CComAutoCriticalSection m_CS;
  CComBSTR m_bsFirstName;
  CComBSTR m_bsLastName;
};

STDMETHODIMP CPerson::LockAccess()
{
  m_CS.Lock();
  return S_OK;
}

STDMETHODIMP CPerson::SetFirstName(BSTR bsFirstName)
{
  m_bsFirstName = bsFirstName;
  return S_OK;
}

STDMETHODIMP CPerson::SetLastName(BSTR bsLastName)
{
  m_bsLastName = bsLastName;
  return S_OK;
}

STDMETHODIMP CPerson::UnlockAccess()
{
  m_CS.Unlock();
  return S_OK;
}
```

The goal is to let the client explicitly lock access to the object's state before updating the first and the last name, and unlocking the access after finishing the update.

While the code looks simple and the logic looks clean, there is a major problem with the code. It, in all likelyhood, won't work under an MTA.

Recall that, under an MTA, an incoming call is serviced by an arbitrary thread from the RPC thread cache. The call to LockAccess may be serviced by one RPC thread and the call to UnlockAccess may be serviced by another RPC thread. The problem is, the synchronization primitives such as critical sections and mutexes have thread affinity. One cannot lock a critical section on one thread and unlock it in some other thread.

So, let's get smarter—lock the access and update the data within the same call. The following code fragment shows the revised logic:

```
STDMETHODIMP CPerson::SetName(BSTR bsFirstName, BSTR bsLastName)
{
  m_CS.Lock();
  m_bsFirstName = bsFirstName;
  m_bsLastName = bsLastName;
  return S_OK;
}
```

This is much better. Right?

Except for one little problem—we forgot to call Unlock on the critical section. As a result, the resource stays locked. Another call to method Set-Name, or any other method call that accesses the data members, may come on a different RPC thread and will get blocked trying to lock the resource.

While the case shown above is a trivial one, it is easy to make such a mistake in a complex software code. For example, if a method has many return paths, the developer can overlook calling Unlock on one of the return paths.

There is yet another possibility of human error. Once the developers decide to associate a synchronization primitive with some resource, that resource should never be accessed without locking the primitive first. In a complex component with hundreds of methods that access some internal data, it is easy to forget locking the resource in one or two methods. And the bug will go undetected. The C++ compiler can only catch syntactic errors; it cannot catch a logical error.

To eliminate the possibility of making such logical errors, I have developed a template class, CCPLWinSharedResource, that makes a resource safe from concurrent access. The data that needs to be protected can be specified as a parameter to the template. Any valid C data type or structure can be passed as a parameter. The following code fragment shows how to declare a thread-safe variable using this template class:

```
class CPerson :
  ...
private:
  struct PERSONINFO {
    CComBSTR bsFirstName;
    CComBSTR bsLastName;
  };

  CCPLWinSharedResource<PERSONINFO> m_Info;
};
```

In this code, the PERSONINFO structure is embedded within the variable m_Info. The only way to access the structure is by taking ownership of m_Info. This is done by declaring a local variable of type CCPLWinShare-dResource<T>::GUARD, as shown below:

```
STDMETHODIMP CPerson::SetName(BSTR bsFirstName, BSTR bsLastName)
{
  CCPLWinSharedResource<PERSONINFO>::GUARD guard(m_Info);
  PERSONINFO& info = guard;

  info.bsFirstName = bsFirstName;
  info.bsLastName = bsLastName;

  return S_OK;
}
```

Internally, CCPLWinSharedResource uses a critical section to protect data. By declaring the local variable of type CCPLWinSharedResource<PER-SONINFO>::GUARD, the critical section is locked. The lock is released when the local variable goes out of the scope.

Using the CCPLWinSharedResource template removes the possibility of human errors we discussed earlier, as follows:

- The compiler will not let you access the embedded data directly. To access the data, you have to declare a local variable of GUARD type. This will result in locking the resource.
- The resource will be unlocked automatically when the variable goes out of scope. You do need to explicitly unlock it.

The template class is part of the CPL toolkit and is included on the CD.

Handling Reentrancy

We know that when an outgoing call is made from an STA, COM creates a message pump inside the channel while waiting for the ORPC response. Besides processing any non-COM-related Windows messages, the message pump also services any incoming ORPC requests (as Windows messages).

Servicing incoming ORPC requests while making an outgoing call makes the STA code reentrant.

By default, the channel will allow all the incoming ORPC requests to be serviced while the client thread waits for an ORPC response. However, COM provides a way to install a custom message filter for the thread. A message filter is a per-STA COM object that implements an interface IMessage-Filter. A developer can install a custom message filter using the COM API

CoRegisterMessageFilter. Implementing a message filter is relatively straightforward and is left as an exercise for the readers.

Note that message filters are unique to STAs. As there are no concurrency guarantees for the MTA, COM doesn't provide any support for reentrancy. It is up to the developers to handle reentrancy issues.

One problem with reentrancy under MTAs is the possibility of a deadlock. Consider the case when an outbound method call to another object is made from an MTA while holding a physical lock and the other object calls back into the MTA, as shown in the following code fragment:

```
STDMETHODIMP CPerson::GetName(BSTR* pbsFirstName,
  BSTR* pbsLastName)
{
  m_CS.Lock();
  *pbsFirstName = m_bsFirstName.Copy();
  *pbsLastName = m_bsLastName.Copy();
  m_CS.Unlock();
  return S_OK;
}


STDMETHODIMP CPerson::SetName(BSTR bsFirstName, BSTR bsLastName)
{
  m_CS.Lock();

  m_bsFirstName = bsFirstName;
  m_bsLastName = bsLastName;

  // inform another object of the name change
  m_spAdmin->NameChange(this);

  m_CS.Unlock();
  return S_OK;
}


STDMETHODIMP CAdmin::NameChange(IPerson* pPerson)
{
  CComBSTR bsFirstName, bsLastName;
  pPerson->GetName(&bsFirstName, &bsLastName);
  return S_OK;
}
```

When CPerson::SetName is called, the method locks the resource, updates the name, and calls CAdmin::NameChange to inform the CAdmin object of the name change. When the CAdmin object calls back into CPerson::GetName, a thread from the RPC thread cache services the call. As the resource is already locked on the outgoing thread, a deadlock occurs.

There are many ways to deal with such deadlocks. The developers have to deal with them on a case-by-case basis. For example, in the above code, a little rearrangement of the code could avoid the deadlock. The revised code snippet is shown below:

```
STDMETHODIMP CPerson::SetName(BSTR bsFirstName, BSTR bsLastName)
{
  m_CS.Lock();

  m_bsFirstName = bsFirstName;
  m_bsLastName = bsLastName;

  m_CS.Unlock(); // unlock the resource first

  // inform another object of the name change
  m_spAdmin->NameChange(this);

  return S_OK;
}
```

Another possibility of avoiding deadlocks is to configure a component to run under an activity. In this case, COM provides infrastructural support to prevent deadlocks, as we covered earlier in the chapter. However, if your object will run under an activity, be very careful of using any explicit synchronization mechanism in your code. If the activity spans multiple processes, though there is just one logical thread, there is a possibility that multiple physical threads could enter an activity, and your synchronization mechanism may result in a deadlock.

Note that deadlocks are not limited to MTAs. As TNAs too are reentrant, there is a possibility of a deadlock here.

Waiting for an Event

We know that, in an STA, if an interface method call takes considerable time to execute, no incoming ORPC requests will be processed. Furthermore, since no UI-related Windows messages would get processed, the UI will appear to freeze. Therefore, any interface method in an STA should never do a blocking wait (using `WaitForSingleObject` or `WaitForMultipleObjects`, for example). Moreover, if the method is expected to take a considerable time to execute, then the method should implement some variant of the message pump.

What if you *do* have to wait for an event to be signaled?

To handle this problem, the SDK provides an API called `CoWaitFor-MultipleHandles`. This function is similar in functionality to its Win32 counterpart `WaitForMultipleObjectsEx`. The difference is that this function internally runs a message pump, besides waiting for an event to be signaled. The function also uses the calling thread's message filter to control how pending calls will be handled.

`CoWaitForMultipleHandles` can be used with any apartment type. The function is smart enough to recognize if the current apartment is an MTA and, if so, disables the message pump. If the apartment is an STA or TNA, the message pump remains enabled.

The CPL toolkit class `CCPLWinThread` (on the CD) uses `CoWaitForMultipleHandles` internally. I have also included a program on the CD to demonstrate the use of `CoWaitForMultipleHandles`.

You may be wondering why we need message pumps under TNA. Recall that a method call from an STA can directly enter a TNA. Therefore, any class that is implemented under a TNA is subject to the same rules as that of an STA. Like STA, if an interface method takes considerable time to execute under a TNA, the implementation should introduce a message pump.

Sharing State Across Multiple Objects

Many times it is desirable to share one or more properties (values) across many objects within a process. For example, an application may control the feature-set it exposes to the customers by means of a license key. Each component within the application may individually wish to control the feature-set by accessing the license key.

If all the objects that are interested in sharing the properties belong to the same COM server, the problem can be easily solved. A global variable can be used to contain each property that needs to be shared. Of course, the global variables need to be protected from concurrent access.

The technique of using global variables, however, will not work if the properties need to be shared across various components (COM servers). The data segment (where the global variables are stored) for each DLL is generally private to the DLL. Therefore, a global variable from one component cannot be accessed directly from another component.

One way to get around this problem is to ensure that all the global variables reside within one component. All other components can access the properties by means of an interface on the first component.

COM Singleton

The above-mentioned technique can be improvised by ensuring that the component that holds the properties is a *singleton*, that is, the class factory for the COM class returns the same object each time the client calls CoCreateInstance (or other similar APIs). This eliminates the need for using global variables to store properties.

ATL makes it very convenient to develop a singleton COM class. It requires that just one macro, DECLARE_CLASSFACTORY_SINGLETON, be added to the implementation.

The following code snippet shows a singleton COM server that exposes an interface to access a property called LicenseKey:

```
// File MySingleton.h

class CMySingleton :
  ...
{
  ...

BEGIN_COM_MAP(CMySingleton)
  COM_INTERFACE_ENTRY(IMySingleton)
END_COM_MAP()

DECLARE_CLASSFACTORY_SINGLETON(CMySingleton)

// IMySingleton
public:
  STDMETHOD(get_LicenseKey)(/*[out, retval]*/ BSTR *pVal);
  STDMETHOD(put_LicenseKey)(/*[in]*/ BSTR newVal);

private:
  // variable to hold the license key
  CCPLWinSharedResource<CComBSTR> m_bsLicenseKey;
};

// File MySingleton.cpp

STDMETHODIMP CMySingleton::get_LicenseKey(BSTR *pVal)
{
  CCPLWinSharedResource<CComBSTR>::GUARD guard(m_bsLicenseKey);
```

```
    CComBSTR& bsLicenseKey = guard;
    *pVal = bsLicenseKey.Copy();

    return S_OK;
}


STDMETHODIMP CMySingleton::put_LicenseKey(BSTR newVal)
{
    CCPLWinSharedResource<CComBSTR>::GUARD guard(m_bsLicenseKey);
    CComBSTR& bsLicenseKey = guard;
    bsLicenseKey = newVal;

    return S_OK;
}
```

Using this singleton class, one object (from one component) can set the license key property. Some other object (from a different component within the same process) can obtain the license key, as shown in the following code snippet:

```
// One object sets the value
IMySingletonPtr spSingleton;
HRESULT hr = spSingleton.CreateInstance(__uuidof(MySingleton));
if (FAILED(hr)) {
  _com_issue_error(hr);
}
spSingleton->LicenseKey = "MyMagicNumber1234";
...
// Some other object gets the value
IMySingletonPtr spSingleton;
HRESULT hr = spSingleton.CreateInstance(__uuidof(MySingleton));
if (FAILED(hr)) {
  _com_issue_error(hr);
}
ConstructFeatureListBasedOnLicenseKey(spSingleton->LicenseKey);
```

Though COM singleton is a widely acceptable programming idiom, it has a few deficiencies and, in some cases, has a high potential of breaking the COM model [Box-99]. A better strategy is to separate the code from the shared state. In this case, the COM object itself is not a singleton. However, all the objects of the COM class share the same state.

Avoid implementing singletons in COM as much as possible. If you do have to implement one, be aware of the problems associated with it.

Shared Property Manager

Sharing properties among multiple objects in a thread-safe manner is such a common programming task that COM+ provides a COM class called the shared property manager (SPM) that lets multiple clients access shared data without the need of complex programming. The SPM model consists of the following three interfaces:

- Interface ISharedProperty is used to set or retrieve the value of a property.
- Interface ISharedPropertyGroup is used to group related properties together. This interface lets one create or access a shared property.
- Interface ISharedPropertyGroupManager is used to create shared property groups and to obtain access to existing shared property groups.

The following code snippet demonstrates setting and retrieving a shared property using the SPM. The property is referred to as "Key" and is contained within the "LicenseInfo" group.

```
#import "c:\winnt\system32\comsvcs.dll" // Import the type
                                        // library for the SPM
using namespace COMSVCSLib;

void CreateLicenseKeyPropertyAndSetItsValue()
{
  // Instantiate the SPM
  ISharedPropertyGroupManagerPtr spGroupMgr;
  spGroupMgr.CreateInstance(
    __uuidof(SharedPropertyGroupManager));

  // Create a group called "LicenseInfo"
  long lIsoMode = LockSetGet;   // lock each property individually
  long lRelMode = Process;      // Do not destroy the group
                                // till the process quits
  VARIANT_BOOL bExists;         // Return value to indicate if
                                // the group already exists
```

```
  ISharedPropertyGroupPtr spGroup =
    spGroupMgr->CreatePropertyGroup("LicenseInfo",
    &lIsoMode, &lRelMode, &bExists);

  // Create a property called "Key"
  ISharedPropertyPtr spProperty =
    spGroup->CreateProperty("Key", &bExists);

  // Set the property value
  spProperty->Value = "MyMagicNumber1234";
}

void ObtainLicenseKey()
{
  // Instantiate the SPM
  ISharedPropertyGroupManagerPtr spGroupMgr;
  spGroupMgr.CreateInstance(
    __uuidof(SharedPropertyGroupManager));

  // Get the "LicenseInfo" group
  ISharedPropertyGroupPtr spGroup =
    spGroupMgr->GetGroup("LicenseInfo");

  // Get the "Key" property
  ISharedPropertyPtr spProperty = spGroup->GetProperty("Key");

  // Use the property
  ConstructFeatureListBasedOnLicenseKey (spProperty->Value);
}
```

 Shared properties can be shared only by the objects running within the same process. Therefore, if you want instances of different components to share properties, you have to install the components in the same COM+ application. Moreover, if the base client also wants to access the shared properties, the COM+ application has to be marked as the library application so that the base client as well as the components can run in the same process space.

SUMMARY

In this chapter, we looked at various issues involved with multithreaded programming. We saw that protecting an object from concurrent access requires complex programming. To simplify component development, COM+ offers a choice of threading strategies to developers. To deal with the threading strategy used by a component, COM+ defines the notion of apartments. The type of apartment dictates the way calls are dispatched to the apartment.

To provide synchronized access to an object, COM+ provides activity-based synchronization.

Finally, we looked at various techniques to develop thread-safe code that leverages the infrastructure provided by COM+.

REFERENCES

[Ric-96]   Jeffrey Richter, "Win32 Q & A," *Microsoft Systems Journal*, March 1996.
http://msdn.microsoft.com/library/periodic/period96/SFFF.htm

[Box-98]   Don Box, *Essential COM*, Addison Wesley, ISBN 0-201-63446-5, 1998.

[Box-99]   Don Box, "House of COM," *Microsoft Systems Journal*, May 1999.
http://msdn.microsoft.com/library/periodic/period99/com0599.htm

Security

Windows 2000 is a secure operating system. The security offered by the operating system protects the local machine from any unauthorized operation performed by a user. Each secured resource under the operating system can be configured to allow access to some users while denying access to others.

However, COM's ability to invoke servers, especially from remote machines, raises security issues such as the verification of client's credentials and how to validate that the client is privileged to perform an operation on a secured resource.

Security is also a concern for clients. A client may have good reasons not to trust the server, and therefore may wish to hide its credentials from the server.

COM+ provides support to address client-side and server-side security issues. In this chapter we will look at how we can leverage this support in developing secure applications.

THE COM+ SECURITY MODEL

Although COM is supposed to be platform-independent, it is not possible for us to completely ignore the security model of the underlying operating system. Consequently, before we delve into a detailed discussion of the many issues concerning the COM+ security model, I shall review the basics of the Windows NT security system. However, I will consciously try to keep the details to a minimum and cover only those aspects that are relevant to our current discussion.

Windows NT Security System Basics

Under Windows NT (Windows 2000 is based on NT technology), each user or group is referred to as an account[1] and is uniquely identified by a *security identifier*, or SID. Each time an account is added to the system, the system generates an SID and assigns it to the new account. Built-in accounts such as LocalSystem and Administrator have predefined SIDs.

Windows NT is also a highly secure operating system. Most of the objects in the system such as NTFS files, registry keys, processes, threads, etc., can be configured so that they are accessible only by selected accounts. Such objects are referred to as *securable objects*. Each securable object has a *security descriptor* (SD). Among other things, a security descriptor contains:

- An owner SID that identifies the current owner of the object. An owner can always access the object.
- A *discretionary access list*, or DACL, that determines which accounts can access the object and which accounts are specifically denied access to the object.

The DACL is at the heart of NT security. The entries in this list are called *access control entries* (ACEs). Figure 7.1 shows the layout of the ACE.

An ACE consists of three parts: an ACE header, a SID, and an access mask. The ACE header determines whether the access is allowed or denied. The SID identifies a single user or group (account) for which the access is allowed or denied. The access mask determines the level of access that is allowed or denied. For example, the DACL for an NTFS file can contain an ACE entry that indicates that user Smith is denied access for writing to the file. Figure 7.2 shows an example of such a DACL.

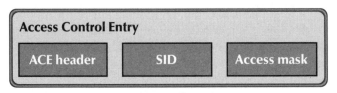

Figure 7.1   The layout of the ACE.

---

[1] NT 4.0 introduced a new term, trustee, to represent an account.

ACCESS_DENIED_ACE_TYPE	User Smith	FILE_WRITE_DATA
ACCESS_ALLOWED_ACE_TYPE	Group Programmers	GENERIC_ALL
. . .	. . .	. . .
. . .	. . .	. . .

Figure 7.2   An example of a DACL.

The order of ACE entries in the DACL is important. For example, consider the case where "smith" belongs to a group called "hackers." Let's say the DACL for a file contains two ACES: one that denies access to the "hackers" group and the other that allows access to "smith." If the latter ACE is present before the former ACE in the DACL, user "smith" gets the access to the file. Just reversing the order would deny access to "smith."

Also note that an SD may not contain a DACL at all, indicating that the object does not need any protection. On the other hand, an SD with an empty DACL indicates that no one is allowed access to the object. Be careful not to confuse these two cases.

Only the owner of a securable object can access its SD to add or delete ACEs.

How does the system determine if a process can access a securable object? The key lies in another NT entity—the *access token*.

When you log on to an NT system, the system gives you an access token. Among other things, the access token contains:

- The user SID, identifying who you are.
- The list of each group that you belong to.

Under NT, each process runs within the security context of a user. The process gets attached to the access token of the account that created the process (by calling `CreateProcess`) or the access token of the account that was passed as a parameter to `CreateProcessAsUser`.

When the process accesses any securable object, the system calls match the accounts from the process' access token against the entries in the DACL of the securable object and determine if the access should be allowed or denied.

To be more precise, it is not the process but a thread within the process (either the primary thread or any other spawned thread) that accesses the securable object. Under NT, however, the system provides the ability to execute a thread in a security context different from that of the process that owns the thread. This is called *impersonation*. So, when a thread accesses a secured object, the system checks if the thread is under impersonation. If it is, the system uses the access token of the impersonating user. Otherwise, the access token of the owner process is used for an access check.

A process itself is a securable object, and therefore has its own security descriptor. By default, its DACL specifies access only to the user represented by the access token of the process. If other users must access the object, the owner of the process can add ACEs to the DACL that grants access to a group of users.

I have included a program on the CD that dumps the security descriptor of a process. This code can be slightly modified to dump the security descriptor for any securable object.

The most visible part of the security system is the password. Giving away the password will compromise the security of the whole system. When sensitive data such as passwords are transferred over the wire, the user should inform the underlying transport provider to take extra precaution to ensure data security.

Do not give out your passwords.

For more information on NT security, read Marshall Brain's *Win32 System Services* [Bra-94]. Another good reference to look at is *Professional DCOM Programming* by Richard Grimes [Gri-97].

Now, let's look at various security issues that COM addresses.

Security Issues Under COM

Activation Control

We need to ensure that sensitive applications cannot be launched by just anyone. For example, let's say a company has developed a component to review and change employee salaries. It makes sense that only the managers should be able to launch such a component.

COM provides a mechanism to specify who is permitted to launch the application. This is referred to as *activation control*.

An administrator chooses accounts (users or groups) that are allowed or denied permission to start the application on the local computer.

The administrator can also define system-wide launch permissions used by COM when an application does not provide its own launch permissions.

An activation control setting is meaningful only for classic COM applications. COM+ applications use a different mechanism called *role-based security* that will be described later.

Access Control

Preventing unauthorized persons from launching the application isn't enough. A malicious user, for example, can still connect to an already launched application and access its services.

To solve this problem, COM provides a mechanism to control access to the component's objects. The *access control* determines who is permitted to access the component's objects.

Similar to launch permission settings, an administrator selects users or groups that are allowed or denied permission to access the component's objects.

The administrator can define system-wide access permission used by COM when an application does not provide its own access permissions.

The access control setting is meaningful only for classic COM applications. COM+ applications use role-based security.

Authentication Control

When a client makes a connection to the server, the server must be able to verify that the client is who it says it is. Otherwise, for example, an employee could fake himself as a manager, access the employee salary component that we talked about earlier, and give himself a nice little raise.

The process of identifying the caller is called authentication. In association with the underlying security support provider (SSP), COM can authenticate the caller. SSPs are covered later in the chapter.

Authentication also provides data security. When a client calls a method on a remote server object, the method call parameters get transmitted over the wire. To protect this data from the hackers, authentication can be set at various levels, encryption being one such option. These levels are indicated by `RPC_C_AUTHN_LEVEL_xxx` constants, defined in the SDK header file `<RpcDce.h>`.

The possible authentication levels—from lowest to highest security—along with their description, are shown in Table 7.1.

Table 7.1   COM+ Authentication Levels

Level	Constant	Description
Default	`RPC_C_AUTHN_LEVEL_DEFAULT`	The underlying SSP provides the default value.
None	`RPC_C_AUTHN_LEVEL_NONE`	No authentication.
Connect	`RPC_C_AUTHN_LEVEL_CONNECT`	Authenticates the client only when the client first connects to the server.
Call	`RPC_C_AUTHN_LEVEL_CALL`	Authenticates the client at the beginning of each remote call.
Packet	`RPC_C_AUTHN_LEVEL_PKT`	Authenticates that the data is received from the expected client.
Packet Integrity	`RPC_C_AUTHN_LEVEL_PKT_INTEGRITY`	Authenticates and verifies that data has not been tampered with in transit.
Packet Privacy	`RPC_C_AUTHN_LEVEL_PKT_PRIVACY`	Method call parameters are encrypted before transmission. The server authenticates, verifies, and decrypts the data.

Note that while each successive authentication level adds more security, it is done at the expense of decreased performance.

Identity Control

The identity control specifies the security credentials under which the component will execute. This could either be the security credentials of the interactive user (the user who is currently logged on to the computer), or a specific user account configured for this purpose.

An application is launched under the security context of the specified identity. This security context is used when the application tries to access resources, such as files or databases, or makes calls to other applications.

There are two important things to keep in mind when specifying the identity:

- If the application is set to run under the interactive users' identity, the server will fail to run if there is no interactive user logged on to the system. While this is an extremely good feature for debugging an application, you should generally avoid using an interactive users' identity for production code.
- The COM SCM calls Win32 APIs `LogonUser` and `CreateProcess-AsUser` to launch the COM server using the specified account. Therefore, the account specified should have a "Log on as a Batch Job" privilege. Otherwise, activation requests will fail.

Sometimes it is desired that the server use the client's credentials during the method call to access a local resource. COM provides a mechanism to enable such *impersonation* during the method call.

Sometimes it is also desirable for the server to impersonate the client's security context when accessing a network resource or making outgoing calls to other servers (on other machines). This is called *delegation*. With the help of the underlying SSP, COM can support delegation.

The SDK defines each impersonation level by using `RPC_C_IMP_LEVEL_xxx` constants. Table 7.2 describes each impersonation level.

Table 7.2   COM+ Impersonation Levels

Level	Constant	Description
Default	`RPC_C_IMP_LEVEL_DEFAULT`	The underlying SSP provides the default value.
Anonymous	`RPC_C_IMP_LEVEL_ANONYMOUS`	The client is anonymous to the server. The server cannot obtain the client's identification information nor can it impersonate the client.
Identify	`RPC_C_IMP_LEVEL_IDENTIFY`	The server can obtain the client's identification information and can impersonate the client to do ACL checks.
Impersonate	`RPC_C_IMP_LEVEL_IMPERSONATE`	The server can impersonate the client. While impersonating, the server can access only those resources available on the server's machine.
Delegate	`RPC_C_IMP_LEVEL_DELEGATE`	The server can impersonate the client. The server can access network resources as well as make outgoing calls on the client's behalf.

Impersonation levels can also be used to protect the client from untrustworthy components. From the client's point of view, anonymous-level impersonation is the most secure, as the component can neither obtain any client credentials nor act on its behalf. With each successive level, a component is granted further liberties with the client's security credentials.

A few points to note about the impersonation levels:

- RPC_C_IMP_LEVEL_ANONYMOUS is not supported for remote calls. If specified, the impersonation will automatically be promoted to RPC_C_IMP_LEVEL_IDENTIFY.
- RPC_C_IMP_LEVEL_DELEGATE is not supported by Windows NT LAN Manager SSP (NTLMSSP). Kerberos SSP supports it.
- Impersonation level and authentication levels are largely independent of each other. However, to impersonate a client, the client has to be authenticated. Therefore, authentication level RPC_C_AUTHN_LEVEL_NONE cannot be used when an impersonation other than anonymous is desired.
- RPC_C_IMP_LEVEL_IDENTIFY is the default impersonation level when the OS is first installed.

Role-Based Security

Under COM+, roles provide a flexible and extensible security configuration model. A role is a symbolic name that identifies a logical group of users that share the same security privilege. This is conceptually similar to a user group in Windows NT (or Windows 2000); the difference being that a user group is global across a Windows NT domain, while roles are configured for specific COM+ applications.

When a COM+ application is deployed, the administrator can create certain roles (for the application) and bind those roles to specific users and user groups. For our salary component example, the administrator can create roles such as "Managers" and "Employees" and bind specific users (or user groups) to the roles. The administrator can then specify which role(s) can access the application. The administrator can fine-tune the access at the per-component, per-interface, or even per-method level.

Essentially, roles provide protection for the code; they control access to methods that can be called by clients of a COM+ application. Role membership is checked whenever a client attempts to call a method exposed by a component in an application. If the caller is in a role assigned to the method it is calling, the call succeeds. Otherwise, the call fails and returns E_ACCESSDENIED.

Security Service Providers (SSPs)

Why does COM need its own security model? Windows is considered to be a secure operating system platform. Why can't COM components simply take advantage of that security model?

COM could have used Windows' security model. However, COM requires a security model that can be supported on all platforms on which COM+ services are available.

Moreover, COM's dependency on RPC binds it to use many features of RPC security infrastructure.

The solution was to define a higher-level abstraction—one that is based on the security provided by the operating system as well as the underlying RPC security mechanisms. This higher-level security model insulates (or tries to insulate) component developers from the specific security mechanisms so that components can benefit from newer security services without needing to change the code.

To obtain such a flexible security model wherein newer security services can be availed automatically, COM defined an API set, the Security Support Provider Interface (SSPI), that isolates everything the user sees from the systems that actually handle security.

A vendor can develop a DLL that implements SSPI. This DLL is referred to as a Security Service Provider (SSP). Though the vendor has to implement SSPI, it is free to use whatever mechanism it wants to enforce security.

Figure 7.3 shows the security architecture in COM+.

Prior to Windows 2000, only one SSP was available—NTLMSSP. This SSP uses the NTLM authentication protocol that employs a challenge-response mechanism to authenticate clients. In the challenge-response mechanism, the server issues a challenge that consists of sending some data to the client. The client uses an encoded version of the user's password to encrypt this data. This encrypted data is then sent back to the server. The server decrypts the data and compares it with the original data. If the data is identical, the user is authenticated.

Note that the user's password is never sent across the network using NTLMSSP. For this reason, the server cannot use *delegation* to access network resources or to make outgoing calls to servers on other machines.

Windows 2000 offers a newer SSP that implements the Kerberos v5 network authentication service. NTLMSSP is still available under Windows 2000. However, Kerberos SSP is the default SSP.

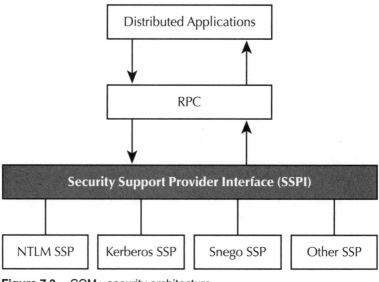

Figure 7.3   COM+ security architecture.

Kerberos is a more sophisticated authentication protocol than NTLM, and supports features such as mutual authentication (client and server can both authenticate each other) and delegation of security information from one machine to another. For an in-depth discussion of the Kerberos security protocol, see David Chappell's article on Kerberos [Cha-99]. For our discussion, it is relevant to know that Kerberos SSP supports delegation while NTLMSSP does not.

The client and the server applications have to choose a specific SSP to communicate. In a mixed environment where some machines only have NTLMSSP and others have Kerberos SSP, it becomes problematic to programmatically choose an SSP. To solve this problem, Microsoft RPC provides a pseudo-SSP called the Simple GSS-API Negotiation Mechanism (Snego) SSP. Snego SSP does not provide any actual authentication feature. It just helps applications select a real SSP.

Besides the above three SSPs, Windows 2000 RPC supports many other SSPs. Each SSP offers its service in the form of what is called a package. Each package is identified by a specific RPC_C_AUTHN_xxx constant. Table 7.3 describes some of those security packages.

Table 7.3   Security Packages In Windows 2000

Description	Constant
No authentication	RPC_C_AUTHN_NONE
DCE private key	RPC_C_AUTHN_DCE_PRIVATE
DCE public key	RPC_C_AUTHN_DCE_PUBLIC
Snego	RPC_C_AUTHN_GSS_NEGOTIATE
NTLM	RPC_C_AUTHN_WINNT
Kerberos	RPC_C_AUTHN_GSS_KERBEROS
Microsoft SChannel	RPC_C_AUTHN_GSS_SCHANNEL
Microsoft MSN	RPC_C_AUTHN_MSN
COM+ security blanket negotiation to pick a default	RPC_C_AUTHN_DEFAULT

The list of packages installed on a system can be obtained using `EnumerateSecurityPackages` API. The API also returns the capabilities of each package. The CD contains a program, `EnumSSP`, that will dump the information for each installed SSP on the local machine.

A security package is also referred to as the authentication service.[2]

Some SSPs, such as DCE SSP, are capable of using an authorization service to perform authorization checking. The SDK defines `RPC_C_AUTHZ_xxx` constants for authorization services. They are listed in Table 7.4.

Table 7.4   Authorization Services

Constant	Description
RPC_C_AUTHZ_NONE	No authorization.
RPC_C_AUTHZ_NAME	Authorization is based on the client's principal name.
RPC_C_AUTHZ_DCE	Authorization is based on the client's DCE privilege attribute certificate (PAC) information.
RPC_C_AUTHZ_DEFAULT	The default authorization service for the current SSP is used.

A server can specify the authorization service to use. However, as the most commonly used SSPs, NTLM and Kerberos, do not utilize any autho-

---

[2] Technically, an SSP provides a security package. However, for most intents and purposes, an SSP, a security package, and an authentication service are one and the same.

rization service, the server typically specifies `RPC_C_AUTHZ_NONE` (or `RPC_C_AUTHZ_DEFAULT` that results in `RPC_C_AUTHZ_NONE`) as the authorization service.

Security Blankets

Under COM, the client specifies some security settings and the server specifies some settings. The collection of parameters that govern how security is handled between the client and the server is called the *security blanket*. A security blanket basically consists of the following parameters:

- The authentication service, that is, the security package to be used (Table 7.3).
- The authorization service to be used (Table 7.4).
- The principal name of the client.
- The authentication level to be used (Table 7.1).
- The impersonation level to be used (Table 7.2).
- The privileged information of the client application.
- Various authentication capabilities such as mutual authentication and cloaking. These capabilities are defined using the `EOAC_xxx` constants provided by the SDK (covered later).

While most parameters are specified exclusively by either the client or the server, there are some parameters that can be specified by both the client and the server. To select the appropriate settings, COM+ undergoes a negotiating process appropriately called the *security blanket negotiation*. The security blanket negotiation occurs when COM+ first instantiates a proxy. During the negotiation, COM picks up an authentication service that is available to both the client and the server. COM+ also chooses an authorization service and principal name that works with the selected authentication service. For the authentication level, COM+ uses the higher level of the client-side and server-side settings. The impersonation level is the one specified by the client. The server cannot specify the impersonation level. However, remember that the server itself can act as a client to another server, in which case it gets to specify all the client-side settings.

Once the default security blanket is computed, its values are assigned to the newly created proxy. These new values affect all calls made on the proxy, that is, until the client overrides the value programmatically by calling the `IClientSecurity::SetBlanket` API (covered later).

Now that we understand the security issues involving COM and the security model provided by COM, let's examine how we can explicitly specify various security settings.

In general, COM+ provides reasonable values for the default security setting so that an application can be developed and installed without considering any security aspects. However, there are situations when the default values are not adequate and you have to explicitly specify the security settings.

COM+ security settings can be neatly subdivided into two groups: declarative security and programmatic security. Declarative security can be used to override the default security. It reduces the amount of code that you have to write. For a finer control (and more pleasure for us geeks), you can handle security programmatically, thereby overriding both the default and the declarative security settings.

Let's begin by examining the declarative security.

DECLARATIVE SECURITY

As with many other aspects of COM+, an administrator can configure COM+ security setting by manipulating the COM+ catalog. Though COM+ security settings can also be handled programmatically, manipulating the catalog gives the administrator more flexibility in terms of customizing the security environment.

The COM+ catalog can be manipulated either programmatically or by using the Component Services Snap-in. We will use the latter approach for our current discussion. Manipulating the COM+ catalog programmatically is covered in Chapter 12.

Declarative security can be further divided into default settings and application-specific settings.

Default Settings

Default settings are used for those components that do not provide their own settings. These settings are local to a computer and can be changed using the properties dialog box of a computer. The properties dialog box is shown in Figure 7.4.

As shown in Figure 7.4, the default settings include default protocols, default security, and default properties.

The default protocols property page lists the set of network protocols (such as TCP/IP, NETBEUI, etc.) available for distributed computing on the

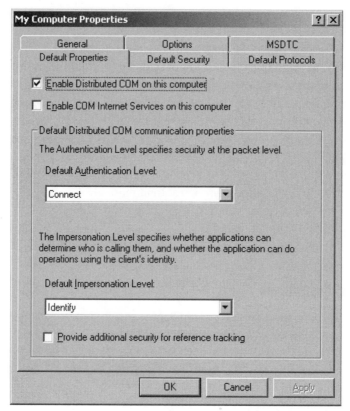

Figure 7.4   Default COM+ settings.

machine. The ordering of the protocols reflects the priority in which a client application[3] will use them. When the client application initiates connection to the server application, it uses the first protocol on the list for the connection. If the server machine does not support the same protocol, the connection will time out. The client uses the next protocol on the list until it eventually succeeds.

By default, Windows 2000 uses TCP/IP as the top protocol and Windows NT 4.0 uses NETBEUI (UDP) as the top protocol.

Consider the scenario where a client application on an NT 4.0 machine communicates with a server application on a Windows 2000 machine. Assume

---

[3] The term client application is used loosely here. It is the underlying RPC infrastructure that needs to use the network protocol.

that the client machine supports UDP and TCP (in that order) whereas the server machine supports only TCP. The client application tries to connect to the server using UDP, unaware that the server does not support it. The application waits until the connection eventually times out (after 30 to 60 seconds) before it tries the second protocol on the list. Changing the order of protocols on the client machine so that the first protocol on the list is the one that the server supports could dramatically improve the initial connection time.

Classic COM applications can be individually configured to use a specific protocol sequence using DCOMCNFG.EXE, a system-supplied program. There is no such configuration option for COM+ applications.

The default security property page can be used to configure the default launch and access permissions for a classic COM application. The administrator can explicitly allow or deny permissions to selected users or groups. When the OS is installed, the default launch permissions are for administrators, the system account, and the interactive user account. The default access permission list is empty indicating that everyone is denied access to a classic COM application. A classic COM application can override the default security settings by using DCOMCNFG.EXE.

Note that the default access and launch permissions do not affect COM+ applications.

The "Default Properties" property page lets the administrator set the default authentication and impersonation options on a machine-wide basis. These properties are valid for both classic COM as well as COM+ applications as long as the values are not overridden programmatically during run time.

The "Enable Distributed COM on this computer" is the main switch for DCOM. If this box is not checked, all remote calls to and from the machine are rejected. This option is enabled by default.

The "Enable COM Internet Service on this computer" option determines whether COM+ Internet Services (CIS, also known as DCOM over HTTP) is available on the machine. This option is disabled by default. Enabling this option allows DCOM to operate over the Internet in the presence of most proxy servers and firewalls. Covering CIS is beyond the scope of this book, but more information about CIS can be found in MSDN article "COM Internet Services" [Lev-99].

The "Default Authentication Level" setting specifies the authentication level used on the system. The possible authentication levels are shown in Table 7.1.

The "Default Impersonation Level" setting specifies the base impersonation level that clients running on the system will grant to the servers.

The "Provide additional security for reference tracking" option helps keep track of the distributed reference count on the computer. The SDK defines this option as EOAC_SECURE_REFS authentication capability. This option is disabled by default. When enabled, an object and its stub exist as long as there is at least one client that has a reference to this object, even though some other client may call one too many Releases on the object. Though this option protects the server from a malicious client, it comes at the expense of decreased performance.

Application-Specific Settings

The focus of this section is for COM+ application settings. Classic COM applications specify their security needs through a system provided utility, DCOMCNFG.EXE. For more information on DCOMCNFG settings, see *Professional DCOM Programming* by Richard Grimes [Gri-97].

Identity

A server application can be configured to run under the identity of a specific user account. Figure 7.5 shows the identity setting for the application.

The application can be made to run under the interactive user account or a specific user account. Windows uses the credentials of the selected user when accessing a securable object, that is, if the calling thread is not under impersonation.

Roles

An administrator can define one or more roles to be used with the application and assign users and groups to each role. Note that the application may be shipped with some pre-defined roles. However, it is still the administrator's responsibility to assign accounts to each role.

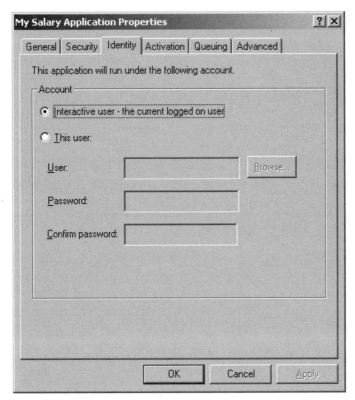

Figure 7.5   Identity settings for a server application.

Security Settings

Figure 7.6 shows the security setting property page for the application.

Assigning accounts to a role does not automatically enable access checking. The administrator also needs to enable the "Enforce access checks for this application" option.

Access checks can be performed at the process level or at the component level. When the second option is selected, the administrator can associate specific roles at the components level, the interfaces level, and the interface methods level. At these finer levels, not only can COM+ do explicit role checking, it can also make an interface IServerCallContext available within the context of a method call. We will see how to use this interface later in the chapter.

The administrator can also specify the authentication level and the impersonation level to be used for the client-server communication. The

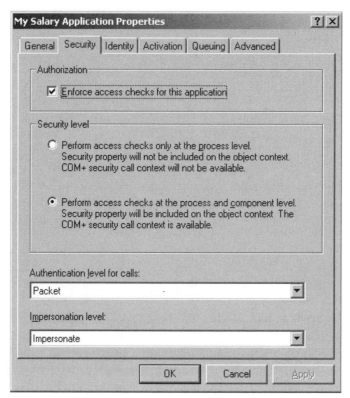

Figure 7.6   Security settings for a COM+ application.

impersonation level setting is used only when the application's object acts as a client to some other object.

Though many security settings can be configured declaratively, there are certain features of a COM/COM+ security model that can be accessed only via COM interfaces. For example, a server can only impersonate a client programmatically. Also, there are cases when a client has to specify a security setting during run time. For example, when passing sensitive information such as a credit card number, the client may wish to temporarily boost the authentication level to packet-level encryption.

Let's look at how we can deal with security programmatically.

SERVER-SIDE SECURITY PROGRAMMING

When the client makes a method call to the server, COM creates a call context and makes it available to the server. *Do not confuse the call context with the object context (actually the object's context object) that was covered in Chapter 5.* Note the following differences:

- The context object represents the context of the server object. Its lifetime is tied to the lifetime of the server object. The call context represents the context of the method call. It is valid only for the duration of the method call.
- The context object is obtained using the CoGetObjectContext API.
  . The call context is obtained using the CoGetCallContext API.

There are only two interfaces that deal with security on the server side, IServerSecurity and ISecurityCallContext.

IServerSecurity is used by a component to identify and/or impersonate a client. The following code shows the IDL definition of this interface:

```
interface IServerSecurity : IUnknown
{
   HRESULT QueryBlanket (
      [out]   DWORD      *pAuthnSvc,
      [out]   DWORD      *pAuthzSvc,
      [out]   OLECHAR    **pServerPrincName,
      [out]   DWORD      *pAuthnLevel,
      [out]   DWORD      *pImpLevel,
      [out]   void       **pPrivs,
      [in,out] DWORD     *pCapabilities );

   HRESULT ImpersonateClient();

   HRESULT RevertToSelf();

   BOOL IsImpersonating();
}
```

The stub implements the IServerSecurity interface, so there is no reason to implement this interface unless you are using custom marshaling.

To obtain a pointer to the IServerSecurity interface, the server can call the CoGetCallContext API within a method call, as shown below:

```
         STDMETHODIMP CMyServer::SomeMethod()
         {
           CComPtr<IServerSecurity> spSec;
           HRESULT hr =
         ::CoGetCallContext(__uuidof(IServerSecurity),
             (void**) &spSec);
           ...
         }
```

 `CoGetCallContext` can be called only from the thread invoked by a client (as a result of some method call).

Also note that if you spawn a secondary thread in your server code, there is no call context available to the thread. A call to `CoGetCallContext` will fail.

The `IServerSecurity::QueryBlanket` method is used to obtain the security blanket of the call context. The following code fragment shows how to dump various parameters of the security blanket. This code can be found on the CD. For brevity, I have removed the error checking logic from the code:

```
void DisplaySecurityBlanket()
{
  CComPtr<IServerSecurity> spSec;
  ::CoGetCallContext(__uuidof(IServerSecurity),(void**) &spSec);

  DWORD dwAuthnSvc, dwAuthzSvc, dwAuthnLevel,
     dwImpLevel, dwCapabilities;
  OLECHAR* pPrincipalName = NULL;
  RPC_AUTHZ_HANDLE hPrivs;
  hr = spSec->QueryBlanket(
     &dwAuthnSvc,
     &dwAuthzSvc,
     &pPrincipalName,
     &dwAuthnLevel,
     &dwImpLevel,
     &hPrivs,
     &dwCapabilities);

  _bstr_t bsDisplay = _T("Principal name: ");
  if (NULL == pPrincipalName) {
    bsDisplay += "(Unknown)";
  }else {
    bsDisplay += pPrincipalName;
    ::CoTaskMemFree(pPrincipalName); pPrincipalName = NULL;
```

```
}

bsDisplay += "\nPrivilege name: ";
if (NULL == hPrivs) {
  bsDisplay += "(Unknown)";
}else {
  bsDisplay += reinterpret_cast<LPCWSTR>(hPrivs);
}

TCHAR buf[256];
_stprintf(buf, _T("\ndwAuthnSvc=%d, dwAuthzSvc=%d,
  dwAuthnLevel=%d, dwImpLevel=%d, dwCapabilities=%d"),
  dwAuthnSvc, dwAuthzSvc, dwAuthnLevel,
  dwImpLevel, dwCapabilities);
bsDisplay += buf;
::MessageBox(NULL, bsDisplay, _T("Security blanket"), MB_OK);
}
```

The following points should be noted about the `QueryBlanket` method:

1. The principal name returned via `pPrincipalName` is the account under which the server application is running. The client's principal name can be obtained via the `pPrivs` parameter but only if the authentication service being used is either NTLM or Kerberos.
2. The current implementation of COM (under Windows 2000) does not return the correct impersonation level (via `dwImpLevel` parameter).

To impersonate a client, `ImpersonateClient` can be called. To restore the thread back to its original security context, `RevertToSelf` can be called. If `RevertToSelf` is not called explicitly after calling `ImpersonateClient`, COM automatically calls `RevertToSelf` when the method returns.

The server can also check if it is currently under impersonation by calling `IsImpersonating` API.

Finally, to simplify dealing with the `IServerSecurity` interface, COM provides several helper functions, as shown in Table 7.5.

Table 7.5 `IServerSecurity` **Helper Functions**

Method	Helper Function
QueryBlanket	CoQueryClientBlanket
ImpersonateClient	CoImpersonateClient
RevertToSelf	CoRevertToSelf
IsImpersonating	(none)

Interface `IServerSecurity` is available for components based on classic COM as well as COM+ configured components. COM+ configured components can also avail another interface, `ISecurityCallContext`, by calling `CoGetCallContext`, as shown in the following code snippet:

```
STDMETHODIMP CMyServer::SomeMethod()
{
   CComPtr<ISecurityCallContext> spSec;
   HRESULT hr =
      ::CoGetCallContext(_uuidof(ISecurityCallContext),
        (void**) &spSec);
   ...
}
```

Interface `ISecurityCallContext` is available only for COM+ configured components. In addition, the application should be marked to check access roles at the process and the component levels.

The following code shows the IDL definition for `ISecurityCall-Context`.[4]

```
ISecurityCallContext : IDispatch
{
  [propget] HRESULT Count([out, retval] long *plCount);
  [propget] HRESULT Item([in] BSTR name,
    [out, retval] VARIANT *pItem);
  [propget] HRESULT NewEnum([out, retval] IUnknown **ppEnum);
  HRESULT IsCallerInRole([in] BSTR bstrRole,
    [out, retval] VARIANT_BOOL *pfInRole);
  HRESULT IsSecurityEnabled(
```

---

[4] The current SDK does not provide the IDL file for COM+ services interfaces. The header file `<comsvcs.h>` defines this interface. I worked my way back to construct the interface definition.

```
    [out,retval] VARIANT_BOOL *pfIsEnabled);
  HRESULT IsUserInRole([in] VARIANT *pUser, [in] BSTR bstrRole,
    [out, retval] VARIANT_BOOL *pfInRole);
};
```

To understand how this interface can be used, let's develop a component that manages employee salary. The component implements the following interface:

```
interface IEmployeeSalary : IDispatch
{
  HRESULT GetSalary([in] BSTR bsEmployeeName,
    [out, retval] long *pVal);
  HRESULT UpdateSalary([in] BSTR bsEmployeeName,
    [in] long newVal);
};
```

Let's define a COM+ server application and add this component to the application. Let's also define two roles, Managers and Employees. The Managers role can access and update the salary for an employee. The Employees role can only access the salary. Logically, it makes sense to declaratively associate both roles with the GetSalary method and only the Managers role with the UpdateSalary method.

This declarative role association has just one problem: any employee can access any other employee's salary information. This is clearly not acceptable. However, declarative programming does have its limitations. You need to programmatically add the logic to ensure that a caller can view only its salary information and nobody else's. The following code snippet demonstrates how ISERVerSecurityContext can be used to validate the current caller's account identification against the bsEmployeeName parameter and grant access to the salary information:

```
STDMETHODIMP CEmployeeSalary::GetSalary(BSTR bsEmployeeName, long *pVal)
{
  CComPtr<ISecurityCallContext> spSec;
  ::CoGetCallContext(__uuidof(ISecurityCallContext),
    (void**) &spSec);

  VARIANT_BOOL bFlag;
  hr = spSec->IsCallerInRole(CComBSTR("Managers"), &bFlag);
  if (VARIANT_TRUE == bFlag) { // managers always have access
    *pVal = 100000;
    return S_OK;
  }
          // the caller must be in "Employees" role
```

```
// (as set declaratively on the method).
// Get the original caller account name

_bstr_t bsCaller = GetOriginalCaller(spSec);

if (0 != wcscmp(bsCaller, bsEmployeeName)) {
  // A different employee
  return E_ACCESSDENIED;
}

// validated the account
*pVal = 80000;

return S_OK;
}
```

COM+ classifies all the information that is available on the security call context into different collections of properties. To deal with these collections, COM+ defines three types of collection objects—SecurityIdentity, SecurityCallers, and SecurityCallContext. Recall from Chapter 2 that a collection object typically supports two methods, Count and Item.

Collection SecurityIdentity contains the identity of a single caller. It is represented by interface ISecurityIdentityColl. Its properties are shown in Table 7.6.

Table 7.6   SecurityIdentity **Properties**

Property	Description
SID	The security identifier of the caller.
AccountName	The account name of the caller.
AuthenticationService	The authentication service used (NTLM, Kerberos, etc).
AuthenticationLevel	The authentication level used.
ImpersonationLevel	The impersonation level used.

When a client calls a method on the server object, the server object may in turn call a method on another server, which in turn may call another object, ad infinitum. COM+ maintains the list of callers in this chain of calls as part of a SecurityCallers collection. SecurityCallers is essentially a collection of SecurityIdentity objects. It is represented by the ISecurityCallersColl interface.

Collection `SecurityCallContext` is the one that we have already dealt with earlier. You just didn't know it. It is represented by the `ISecurityCallContext` interface (now it all becomes clear), and is the doorway to get to other collection objects. The properties supported by this collection are shown in Table 7.7.

Table 7.7   SecurityCallContext Properties

Identifier	Description	Type
NumCallers	Number of callers in the chain of calls.	Long
Callers	Identity of each caller in the chain of calls.	SecurityCallers
DirectCaller	The caller who is the immediate parent.	SecurityIdentity
OriginalCaller	The caller who originated the chain of calls.	SecurityIdentity
MinAuthenticationLevel	The least secure authentication level of all callers in the chain.	Long

Given the previous collection information, the function `GetOriginalCaller` referred to in the previous code snippet can be written as follows:

```
_bstr_t GetOriginalCaller(ISecurityCallContext* pSec)
{
  CComVariant vColl;
  pSec->get_Item(CComBSTR("OriginalCaller"), &vColl);

  CComPtr<IDispatch> spDisp = V_DISPATCH(&vColl);
  CComPtr<ISecurityIdentityColl> spIdentity;
  spDisp->QueryInterface(&spIdentity);

  CComVariant vAccountName;
  spIdentity->get_Item(CComBSTR("AccountName"), &vAccountName);
  return V_BSTR(&vAccountName);
}
```

Note the heavy dose of `VARIANT` and `IDispatch` type variables in the code. This is because all of the collection interfaces dealing with the security call context are geared for automation-compatible languages.

CLIENT-SIDE SECURITY PROGRAMMING

A client has to configure the underlying RPC run time to use one or more security packages and to set the default authentication level (and other security parameters) for the process. This is done by calling the `CoInitializeSecurity` function.

CoInitializeSecurity is perhaps the most important function that deals with COM security. Every process that uses COM (client or server) has to call CoInitializeSecurity. The function has to be called just once and before any interface is marshaled in or out of the process. If not called explicitly, COM will call the function automatically the first time a proxy (for the client) or a stub (for the server) is created.

Why didn't we deal with this function earlier when we were discussing server-side programming issues? Because this function cannot be called from a DLL-based component. Only EXE-based components (supported as non-configured components under COM+) are required to make this call and we haven't discussed EXE-based components in this book. For a configured COM+ component that is part of a server application, the COM+ surrogate (DllHost.exe) calls this function on startup.

The following is the prototype for the CoInitializeSecurity function:

```
HRESULT CoInitializeSecurity(
   [in] PSECURITY_DESCRIPTOR      pSecDesc,          // Server
   [in] LONG       cAuthSvc,                         // Server
   [in] SOLE_AUTHENTICATION_SERVICE *asAuthSvc,      // Server
   [in] void       *pReserved1,                      // NULL
   [in] DWORD      dwAuthnLevel,                      // Client/Server
   [in] DWORD      dwImpLevel,                        // Client
   [in] SOLE_AUTHENTICATION_LIST *pAuthList,          // Client
   [in] DWORD   dwCapabilities,                       // Client/Server
   [in] void       *pReserved3 );                     // NULL
```

CoInitializeSecurity has a fairly large number of parameters. However, some of these parameters are meaningful only if the process is running as a server. We will focus on the parameters that the client process can set. Parameters pSecDesc, cAuthSvc, and asAuthSvc, are pure server-side settings and will be set to NULL, -1, and NULL, respectively.

Parameter dwAuthnLevel is used to specify the authentication level (Table 7.1). Each higher level of authentication adds more security, but at the expense of decreased performance. A reasonable value to specify that lets COM pick the right authentication level using the security blanket negotiation is RPC_C_AUTHN_LEVEL_DEFAULT.

Parameter dwCapabilities is used to specify any extra authentication capabilities that the client wishes to use. As discussed earlier, authentication capabilities are defined by the EOAC_xxx constants. A combination of EOAC_xxx constants can be specified as the desired capabilities. EOAC_NONE is specified when no authentication capabilities are desired. We will look at some other useful capabilities as we go along.

Parameter `dwImpLevel` is used to specify the impersonation level (Table 7.2) and parameter `pAuthList` is used to specify the identity that should be used with each authentication service. Both these security parameters deserve detailed attention.

Impersonation Levels

The level of impersonation affects the following:

1. The ability of a server to access local resources, such as a local NTFS file.
2. The ability of a server to access network resources, such as an NTFS file present on a shared network.
3. The ability of a server to project the identity of the caller to another server on a remote machine.

In order to demonstrate the effect of various impersonation levels, we will conduct an experiment that involves chaining a call across various machines.

The experiment requires three computers, all running Windows 2000. In this experiment, the computers are `MYSVRA`, `MYSVRB`, and `MYSVRC`.

We also need three different user accounts for the experiment. In this experiment, the accounts are `usera`, `userb`, and `userc`.

Machine `MYSVRC` contains a local NTFS file, `LocalFileC.txt`, which is configured so that only `usera` can access it.

Machine MYSVRC also contains another file that is shared on the network, `\\MYSVRC\Data\NetFile.txt`. The file is also configured so that only `usera` can access it.

Machine `MYSVRB` contains a local NTFS file, `LocalFileB.txt`, which is configured so that only `usera` can access it.

We will develop three programs here: `ClientA`, `ServerB`, and `ServerC`.

`ServerC` is a COM+ configured component that runs on `MYSVRC` under the identity of `userc`. It implements a method `DoIt` that a) impersonates the caller, b) attempts to open `LocalFileC.txt` for reading, and c) returns the result of its attempt as an output parameter. The code snippet is as follows:

```
STDMETHODIMP CMyServerC::DoIt(BSTR *pbsRetVal)
{
  // Get the security interface pointer
  CComPtr<IServerSecurity> spSec;
  HRESULT hr =
    ::CoGetCallContext(__uuidof(IServerSecurity),
      (void**) &spSec);
  if (FAILED(hr)) {
    return Error(_T("Error getting call context"),
      __uuidof(IMyServerC), hr);
  }

  // Impersonate the client
  hr = spSec->ImpersonateClient();
  if (FAILED(hr)) {
    return Error(_T("Error impersonating client"),
      __uuidof(IMyServerC), hr);
  }

  // Check if you can open a local file
  CComBSTR bsOutput = "ServerC - Local file open: ";
  bsOutput += OpenFileForReadOnly(GetLocalFileName());

  *pbsRetVal = bsOutput.Detach();
  return S_OK;
}
```

ServerB is a COM+ configured component that runs on MYSVRB under the identity of userb. It implements a method, DoIt, that impersonates the caller and performs the following three operations:

1. Attempts to open the local file, LocalFileB.txt.
2. Attempts to open the network shared file, NetFile.txt.
3. Attempts to instantiate the ServerC component from machine MYSVRC and invoke method DoIt on the object.

ClientA is a client application that runs on MYSVRA under the identity of usera. After setting up various security parameters by calling CoInitializeSecurity, the client instantiates the ServerB component from machine MYSVRA and calls method DoIt. Essentially, we are setting up a chain of calls—ClientA from MYSVRA calls ServerB from MYSVRB which in turn calls ServerC from MYSVRC.

ClientA takes a command line parameter that dictates the impersonation level between ClientA and ServerB. The parameter maps to dwImp-

Level in the call to CoInitializeSecurity, as shown in the following code snippet:

```
HRESULT hr = ::CoInitializeSecurity(
  NULL,
  -1,
  NULL,
  NULL,
  RPC_C_AUTHN_LEVEL_DEFAULT,
  dwImpLevel,
  NULL,
  EOAC_NONE,
  NULL);
```

The impersonation level between ServerB and ServerC is set to RPC_C_AUTHN_LEVEL_IMPERSONATION. Being a configured component, ServerB obviously cannot call CoInitializeSecurity to do this. Fortunately, there is yet another way to specify the security blanket on a proxy—by calling the SetBlanket method on interface IClientSecurity. We will cover this interface in the next section.

Let's try various impersonation level settings between ClientA and ServerB and see the results.

Anonymous

As discussed earlier in the chapter, RPC_C_IMP_LEVEL_ANONYMOUS just gets promoted to RPC_C_IMP_LEVEL_IDENTIFY.

Identify

If impersonation level RPC_C_IMP_LEVEL_IDENTIFY is used, ServerB gets an error, ERROR_BAD_IMPERSONATION_LEVEL, when it tries to open either the local file or the network file. This is because, though the server was able to impersonate the client, the impersonation token does not contain any information about the client. This also results in access denial when ServerB tries to instantiate ServerC.

RPC_C_IMP_LEVEL_IDENTIFY allows the server to examine the access token of the caller and peek inside the token to get information such as the user identification, the groups the user belongs to, and so on. But it does not allow the object to open any secured objects, hence resulting in ERROR_BAD_IMPERSONATION_LEVEL.

Impersonate

If impersonation level RPC_C_IMP_LEVEL_IMPERSONATE is used, ServerB is able to open the local file, but gets an access denial message (E_ACCESSDENIED) when opening the network file. ServerB is able to instantiate ServerC. However, ServerC also gets E_ACCESSDENIED when opening the local file.

Let's see what this means.

RPC_C_IMP_LEVEL_IMPERSONATE allows a server to peek into the access token as well as to access the securable objects using the caller's credentials. However, the privilege extends only to one machine hop. As a result, ServerB could open the local resource. However, ServerB could not open the network resource, as the client credentials could not be forwarded to the third machine.

A similar problem exists when ServerB calls DoIt on ServerC. ServerC sees userb as the client and not usera. As only usera is allowed to access the local file on MYSVRC, ServerC object's attempt to access the file results in an access denial.

Delegation

If impersonation level RPC_C_IMP_LEVEL_DELEGATE is used, ServerB is able to open the local file as well as the network file. However, ServerC still gets an access denial trying to open the local file.

While the RPC_C_IMP_LEVEL_IMPERSONATE level impersonation restricts the client's credentials to be valid for just one machine hop, the RPC_C_IMP_LEVEL_DELEGATE level places no such restriction. The client's credentials can be passed across any number of machine hops.

This explains why ServerB could open the network file. However, it still doesn't explain why ServerC couldn't open the local file, even though ServerB was impersonating usera when it invoked the method on ServerC and ClientA had set delegate level impersonation.

When ServerB calls ServerC while impersonating ClientA (usera), the access token of ServerB (userb) is used even if ClientA has set delegate level impersonation. This means that ServerC sees the identity of the caller as userb—not usera.

This may seem contrary to what the delegation level impersonation was really supposed to do. However, this was deliberately set up this way for reasons of backward compatibility with the behavior of COM prior to Windows 2000, where delegation level impersonation was not available. So as not to break existing COM applications under Windows 2000, the existing semantics of impersonation were left unchanged.

So how could we achieve true delegation? This is done through cloaking, an idea introduced in COM+.

Before we look at cloaking, carefully make a note of the following statement:

In order for delegation to work, the following requirements have to be met:

1. As delegation level impersonation is supported only by Kerberos, the client, the server, and all downstream servers must be running Windows 2000 in a Windows 2000 domain.
2. The client account that will be delegated must not be marked "Account is sensitive and cannot be delegated." This property on the user can be manipulated from the "Active Directory Users and Computers" administrative tool.
3. The identity under which the server is running must be marked "Account is trusted for delegation."
4. The machine that runs the server must be marked "Trust computer for delegation." Once again, the same administrative tool mentioned earlier can be used for this purpose.

Note that the security APIs do not return a good description when delegation doesn't work. In most cases, the returned error is RPC_S_SEC_PKG_ERROR, indicating that a security-package-specific error has occurred.

If you are having problems getting delegation to work, and you think you have met all the requirements for delegation, just try rebooting all the involved machines. If this works, don't ask me why.

Cloaking

Cloaking does what the delegation level impersonation was supposed to do—make ServerC see the identity of caller as ClientA and not ServerB.

In order to use cloaking, the impersonation level between ClientA and ServerB should be at least RPC_C_IMP_LEVEL_IMPERSONATE, and the impersonation level between ServerB and ServerC should be RPC_C_IMP_LEVEL_DELEGATE. Note that ClientA need not use delegate level impersonation. However, without delegation level impersonation, the access to the network resource will be denied from ServerB.

Besides specifying delegation level impersonation, ServerB also needs to indicate that it intends to cloak the credentials of the impersonating thread. Specifying the cloaking flag in the authentication capabilities parameter of the security blanket does this.

Windows 2000 supports two types of cloaking—static (EOAC_STA-TIC_CLOAKING) and dynamic (EOAC_DYNAMIC_CLOAKING). With static cloaking, the client's credentials are determined during the first call on a proxy (or whenever IClientSecurity::SetBlanket is called). With dynamic cloaking, the client's credentials are determined each time a call is made on the proxy.

The following code fragment shows how ServerB can set the proxy on the ServerC object for dynamic cloaking:

```
STDMETHODIMP CMyServerB::DoIt(...)
{
  ...
  CComPtr<IClientSecurity> spClientSec;
  hr = spServerC->QueryInterface(&spClientSec);
  hr = spClientSec->SetBlanket(spServerC,
    RPC_C_AUTHN_DEFAULT,
    RPC_C_AUTHZ_DEFAULT,
    NULL,
    RPC_C_AUTHN_LEVEL_DEFAULT,
    RPC_C_IMP_LEVEL_DELEGATE,
    NULL,
    EOAC_DYNAMIC_CLOAKING);
  ...
  hr = spServerC->DoIt(&bsOutput);
}
```

With this code in place, when ClientA calls ServerB, ServerB can access the local as well as the network resource. When ServerB calls ServerC, ServerC sees the caller's identity as ClientA and can access the local file. The results of the experiment are summarized in Table 7.8.

Table 7.8   Results of Various Impersonation Levels

Level	Local resource from ServerB	Network resource from ServerB	Local resource from ServerC
Anonymous	Bad impersonation level	Bad impersonation level	Access denied instantiating ServerC
Identify	Bad impersonation level	Bad impersonation level	Access denied instantiating ServerC
Impersonate	OK	Access denied	Access denied
Delegate	OK	OK	Access denied
Cloaking	OK	OK	OK

Identity and Authentication Services

The seventh parameter to `CoInitializeSecurity`, `pAuthList`, is used to specify the identity that should be used with an authentication service. The structure that is pointed to by `pAuthInfo`, along with some other relevant C structures, is as follows:

```
typedef struct tagSOLE_AUTHENTICATION_LIST
{
  DWORD cAuthInfo;
  SOLE_AUTHENTICATION_INFO *aAuthInfo;
}SOLE_AUTHENTICATION_LIST;

typedef struct tagSOLE_AUTHENTICATION_INFO
{
  DWORD dwAuthnSvc;
  DWORD dwAuthzSvc;
  void *pAuthInfo;
}SOLE_AUTHENTICATION_INFO;

typedef struct _SEC_WINNT_AUTH_IDENTITY_W {
  unsigned short *User;
  unsigned long UserLength;
  unsigned short *Domain;
  unsigned long DomainLength;
  unsigned short *Password;
  unsigned long PasswordLength;
  unsigned long Flags;
} SEC_WINNT_AUTH_IDENTITY_W;

typedef struct _SEC_WINNT_AUTH_IDENTITY_EXW {
```

```
        unsigned long Version;
        unsigned long Length;
        unsigned short *User;
        unsigned long UserLength;
        unsigned short *Domain;
        unsigned long DomainLength;
        unsigned short *Password;
        unsigned long PasswordLength;
        unsigned long Flags;
        unsigned short * PackageList;
        unsigned long PackageListLength;
   } SEC_WINNT_AUTH_IDENTITY_EXW;
```

The SOLE_AUTHENTICATION_LIST structure contains a pointer to an array of SOLE_AUTHENTICATION_INFO structures. Each SOLE_AUTHENTI-CATION_INFO structure identifies an authentication service, the authorization service to be used with the authentication service, and the identity to be used with the authentication service. For NTLM and Kerberos packages, the identity is defined by the SEC_WINNT_AUTH_IDENTITY_W structure. For Snego, the identity is defined by the SEC_WINNT_AUTH_IDENTITY_EX_W structure.

When COM+ negotiates the default authentication service to be used for a proxy, it uses the information pointed to by pAuthInfo to obtain the identity that should be associated with the authentication service. If pAu-thInfo is NULL, COM+ uses the process identity to represent the client.

Parameter pAuthInfo is useful for a client that wants to use a different identity for making calls on the proxy. The following code snippet shows how a client can associate an identity for an authentication service. The code spec-ifies the same identity for NTLM and Kerberos services.

```
// Auth Identity structure
SEC_WINNT_AUTH_IDENTITY_W authidentity;
ZeroMemory( &authidentity, sizeof(authidentity) );

authidentity.User = L"pvguest";
authidentity.UserLength = wcslen( authidentity.User );
authidentity.Domain = L"pvhome";
authidentity.DomainLength = wcslen( authidentity.Domain );
authidentity.Password = L"mypassword";
authidentity.PasswordLength = wcslen( authidentity.Password );
authidentity.Flags = SEC_WINNT_AUTH_IDENTITY_UNICODE;

SOLE_AUTHENTICATION_INFO     authInfo[2];
ZeroMemory( authInfo, sizeof( authInfo ) );

// Kerberos Settings
```

```
authInfo[0].dwAuthnSvc = RPC_C_AUTHN_GSS_KERBEROS ;
authInfo[0].dwAuthzSvc = RPC_C_AUTHZ_NONE;
authInfo[0].pAuthInfo = &authidentity;

// NTLM Settings
authInfo[1].dwAuthnSvc = RPC_C_AUTHN_WINNT;
authInfo[1].dwAuthzSvc = RPC_C_AUTHZ_NONE;
authInfo[1].pAuthInfo = &authidentity;

SOLE_AUTHENTICATION_LIST    authList;

authList.cAuthInfo = 2;
authList.aAuthInfo = authInfo;

HRESULT hr = ::CoInitializeSecurity(
  NULL,                            // Security descriptor
  -1,                              // Count of entries in asAuthSvc
  NULL,                            // asAuthSvc array
  NULL,                            // Reserved for future use
  RPC_C_AUTHN_LEVEL_DEFAULT,.      // Authentication level
  RPC_C_IMP_LEVEL_IMPERSONATE,     // Impersonation level
  &authList,                       // Authentication Information
  EOAC_NONE,                       // Additional capabilities
  NULL                             // Reserved
  );
...
```

Note that the identity information set for an authentication service via CoInitializeSecurity is applicable only for proxies that the client obtains. It is not valid for activating the object that is done via CoCreateInstanceEx or its friends, CoGetClassObject, CoGetInstanceFromFile, etc. This distinction is very important. If a different identity needs to be used during activation, these functions accept an argument of the type COSERVERINFO. We used one of the member variables of this structure earlier to specify the name of the machine for remote object instantiate. Another variable of this structure, pAuthInfo, points to a structure of type COAUTHINFO that can be used to specify a different identity while activating an object. Using COAUTHINFO is left as an exercise for the readers. Hint: the usage is very similar to SOLE_AUTHENTICATION_INFO.

Also note that pAuthInfo can only be used under Windows 2000. It must be set to NULL on a Windows NT 4.0-based system.

Client Acting as a Server

So far we have tried setting parameters on `CoInitializeSecurity` that make sense for a client. However, there are cases when a client could act as a server. For such cases, it makes sense to specify server-side values for `CoInitializeSecurity`.

The most common case when a client is a server occurs when the client creates a sink object and hands it to the server. The intention is that the server will invoke methods on the sink object when it detects an interesting event.

To demonstrate the problem with such callbacks, let's develop a component that takes an interface pointer from the client and calls back on the interface. The following code fragment shows the interfaces involved and the server implementation of the interface:

```
// Interface definitions

interface ICallMe : IUnknown
{
  HRESULT Hello();
};

interface IMyServerX : IDispatch
{
  HRESULT Advise([in] ICallMe* pCallMe);
};

// MyServerX.cpp - Implementation

STDMETHODIMP CMyServerX::Advise(ICallMe *pCallMe)
{
  HRESULT hr = pCallMe->Hello();

  if (FAILED(hr)) {
    return Error(_T("Error invoking the sink"),
      __uuidof(IMyServerX), hr);
  }

  return S_OK;
}
```

Try to create a COM+ application to run under a specific user account. For my test case, it is `usera`. Add the component to this application.

Now let's write the client code that creates a sink object and calls `Advise` on the server object, passing the sink object as a parameter. The code snippet is as follows:

```
class CCallMe : public ICallMe, public CComObjectRoot
{
public:
  CCallMe() {}
  ~CCallMe() {}

BEGIN_COM_MAP(CCallMe)
  COM_INTERFACE_ENTRY(ICallMe)
END_COM_MAP()

  STDMETHODIMP Hello()
  {
    ::MessageBox(NULL, _T("Hello"), _T("Sink"), MB_OK);
    return S_OK;
  }
};

int WinMain(...)
{
  ::CoInitialize(NULL);

  CComPtr<CComObject<CCallMe> > spCallMe;
  HRESULT hr = CComObject<CCallMe>::CreateInstance(&spCallMe);
  _ASSERT (SUCCEEDED(hr));
  spCallMe->InternalAddRef();

  SERVERXLib::IMyServerXPtr spSvrX(
    __uuidof(SERVERXLib::MyServerX));
  spSvrX->Advise(
    reinterpret_cast<SERVERXLib::ICallMe*>
      (static_cast<ICallMe*>(spCallMe)));
}
```

Note that the client doesn't call CoInitializeSecurity explicitly. COM will automatically call it when generating the proxy for the IMyServerX interface.

Run the client application under an account other than the one specified for the server.

When the server tries to call Hello on the client's sink, it gets an E_ACCESSDENIED error. This is because, when COM calls CoInitializeSecurity, it sets up the default access for the client process to be accessed only by the client identity. Since the server is running under a different account, it cannot access the client's process, resulting in a failure.

The first parameter to CoInitializeSecurity, pSecDesc, is used to set up the default access permissions for the client process. If this parameter is specified as NULL, then COM sets up the access control so that any identity can access the client, as follows:

```
hr = ::CoInitializeSecurity(
   NULL,              // open access to everyone
   -1,
   NULL,
   NULL,
   RPC_C_AUTHN_LEVEL_DEFAULT,
   RPC_C_IMP_LEVEL_IDENTIFY,
   NULL,
   EOAC_NONE,
   NULL);
```

Though this solves the problem of the server calling back into the client, it opens up the client process to be accessed by anybody. This is not desirable.

Instead of specifying NULL for pSecDesc, we need to specify those users who can access the client. In our case this is just one user—the identity under which the server is running.

Parameter pSecDesc is a polymorphic pointer whose interpretation is based on the flag specified in dwCapabilities, the eighth parameter to CoInitializeSecurity.

If dwCapabilities specifies EOAC_NONE, then pSecDesc points to a Windows security descriptor. COM uses this security descriptor to set up the access permission on the client process.

If dwCapabilities specifies EOAC_APPID, pSecDesc points to a GUID of an AppID in the registry. In this case, COM obtains all the security settings from the registry.

Both of the above approaches tie COM to the underlying platform.

To specify the access control in a platform-independent way, COM defines a standard interface called IAccessControl. Using this interface, you can allow or deny access to specific users.

To use IAccessControl with CoInitializeSecurity, dwCapabilities should be specified as EOAC_ACCESS_CONTROL. In this case, COM expects pSecDesc to point to the IAccessControl interface pointer.

You don't have to implement this interface (although you can). COM provides a default implementation under a component named CLSID_DCOMAccessControl.

The following code fragment shows how to allow access to a user using the IAccessControl interface:

```
void InitializeSecurityWithAccessControl()
{
  CComPtr<IAccessControl> spAC;
  HRESULT hr = ::CoCreateInstance(CLSID_DCOMAccessControl, NULL,
    CLSCTX_INPROC_SERVER, IID_IAccessControl, (void**) &spAC);
  _ASSERT (SUCCEEDED(hr));

  ACTRL_ACCESSW access;
  ACTRL_PROPERTY_ENTRYW propEntry;
  access.cEntries = 1;
  access.pPropertyAccessList = &propEntry;

  ACTRL_ACCESS_ENTRY_LISTW entryList;
  propEntry.lpProperty = NULL;
  propEntry.pAccessEntryList = &entryList;
  propEntry.fListFlags = 0;

  ACTRL_ACCESS_ENTRYW entry;
  entryList.cEntries = 1;
  entryList.pAccessList = &entry;

  // Set up the ACE
  entry.Access = COM_RIGHTS_EXECUTE;
  entry.ProvSpecificAccess = 0;
  entry.Inheritance = NO_INHERITANCE;
  entry.lpInheritProperty = NULL;

  // allow access to "usera"
  entry.fAccessFlags = ACTRL_ACCESS_ALLOWED;
  entry.Trustee.TrusteeForm = TRUSTEE_IS_NAME;
  entry.Trustee.TrusteeType = TRUSTEE_IS_USER;
  entry.Trustee.ptstrName = L"PVHOME\\userb";
  entry.Trustee.pMultipleTrustee = NULL;
  entry.Trustee.MultipleTrusteeOperation = NO_MULTIPLE_TRUSTEE;

  hr = spAC->GrantAccessRights(&access);
  _ASSERT (SUCCEEDED(hr));

  hr = ::CoInitializeSecurity(
    static_cast<IAccessControl*>(spAC),
    -1,
    NULL,
    NULL,
    RPC_C_AUTHN_LEVEL_DEFAULT,
    RPC_C_IMP_LEVEL_IDENTIFY,
    NULL,
    EOAC_ACCESS_CONTROL,
    NULL);
  _ASSERT (SUCCEEDED(hr));
}
```

You may be wondering how you can `CoInitializeSecurity` after an object has been instantiated. `CoInitializeSecurity` can be called just once and COM would already have called it while instantiating the object.

Recall that `CoInitializeSecurity` is invoked only when the client first gets a proxy. The interface pointer returned from instantiating the access control object is a direct pointer and not a proxy. Hence, COM had no need to call `CoInitializeSecurity`.

Adjusting Security for a Proxy

`CoInitializeSecurity` sets up process-wide default values for the security settings. Any proxy that gets created within the client process inherits these values for setting up the security blanket.

Sometimes the client may need fine-grained security control on calls to particular interfaces. For example, the authentication might be set at a low level for the process, but calls to a particular interface may require a high level authentication, such as when a user is passing credit card information over the wire.

Similar to interface `IServerSecurity` that is available for servers, COM defines another interface, `IClientSecurity`, for clients. This interface is available on the proxy manager[5] for each remoted object that the client holds. A client can obtain the interface pointer by calling `QueryInterface` for `IID_IClientSecurity` on any interface of the remoted object.

 If `QueryInterface` for `IClientSecurity` fails, either the client has a direct pointer to the object or the object is remoted by some custom marshaler that does not support security.

Following is the IDL definition of interface `IClientSecurity`:

```
interface IClientSecurity : IUnknown
{
  // Obtain the current security blanket information
  HRESULT QueryBlanket (
    [in]  IUnknown   *pProxy,
    [out] DWORD      *pAuthnSvc,
    [out] DWORD      *pAuthzSvc,
```

---

[5] Recall from Chapter 5 that a proxy manager acts as the client-side entity for the remote object.

```
    [out] OLECHAR      **pServerPrincName,
    [out] DWORD        *pAuthnLevel,
    [out] DWORD        *pImpLevel,
    [out] void         **pAuthInfo,
    [out] DWORD        *pCapabilites );

// Modify the security blanket
HRESULT SetBlanket (
    [in]  IUnknown     *pProxy,
    [in]  DWORD        dwAuthnSvc,
    [in]  DWORD        dwAuthzSvc,
    [in]  OLECHAR      *pServerPrincName,
    [in]  DWORD        dwAuthnLevel,
    [in]  DWORD        dwImpLevel,
    [in]  void         *pAuthInfo,
    [in]  DWORD        dwCapabilities );

// Make a copy of the specified proxy
HRESULT CopyProxy (
    [in]  IUnknown     *pProxy,
    [out] IUnknown     **ppCopy );
}
```

Method `QueryBlanket` (and its equivalent helper API, `CoQueryProxy-Blanket`) is similar in functionality to `IServerSecurity::QueryBlanket`.

Method `SetBlanket` (and its equivalent helper API, `CoSetProxy-Blanket`) can be used to modify the current security settings for a specific interface proxy. We used this method earlier when we were discussing delegation. The following code snippet bumps up the authentication level to packet encryption. This is routinely done for secure credit card transactions.

```
hr = spClientSec->SetBlanket(pCreditCardServer,
    RPC_C_AUTHN_DEFAULT,
    RPC_C_AUTHZ_DEFAULT,
    NULL,
    RPC_C_AUTHN_LEVEL_PKT_PRIVACY,
    RPC_C_IMP_LEVEL_DEFAULT,
    NULL,
    EOAC_NONE);
```

The first parameter to the method is the proxy for the specific interface for which the security settings need to be changed.

Note that the new settings apply to any future caller of this particular interface within the same context. However, you can call `IClientSecurity::CopyProxy` (or its helper function, `CoCopyProxy`) to make a private copy of the interface proxy). `SetBlanket` can then be called on the copy, thereby ensuring that other callers are not affected.

SUMMARY

In this chapter, we looked at various security issues to be considered when using COM servers and COM clients. We learned the security basics of the Windows platform and looked at the security model provided by COM.

The COM security model provides many security settings that can be configured. Some security parameters are completely controlled by the client, some by the server, and the rest can be controlled either by the client or the server. COM+ negotiates the security blanket between the client and server.

The client dictates the impersonation level to be used during communication. We examined the implications of various levels of impersonation.

The security mechanism under COM can be subdivided into declarative security and programmatic security. Using declarative security, such as assigning user roles to an application, one can control access to a component without complex programming.

A finer control can be obtained by letting the server and the client programmatically define their individual security parameters.

Finally, we looked at programmatic aspects of security from the server's perspective as well as from the client's perspective.

REFERENCES

[Pin-98]   Jonathan Pinnock, *DCOM Application Development*, ISBN 1-861001-31-2, Wrox Press, 1998.

[Box-98]   Don Box, et al., *Effective COM*, ISBN 0-201-37968-6, Addison Wesley, 1998.

[Gri-97]   Richard Grimes, *Professional DCOM Programming*, ISBN 1-861000-60-X, Wrox Press, 1997.

[Edd-99]   Guy Eddon, "The COM+ Security Model Gets You Out of the Security Programming Business," *Microsoft Systems Journal*, November 1999.
           http://msdn.microsoft.com/library/periodic/period99/comsecurity.htm

[Cha-99]   David Chappell, "Exploring Kerberos, the Protocol for Distributed Security in Windows 2000," *Microsoft Systems Journal*, August 1999.
           http://msdn.microsoft.com/library/periodic/period99/Kerberos.htm

[Edd-98]   Guy Eddon and Henry Eddon, *Inside Distributed COM*, ISBN 1-57231-849-X, Microsoft Press, 1998.

[Bra-94]   Marshall Brain, *Win32 System Services*, ISBN 0-13-097825-6, Prentice Hall, 1994.

[Lev-99]   Marc Levy, "COM Internet Services," MSDN Library.
           http://msdn.microsoft.com/library/backgrnd/html/cis.htm

CHAPTER   8

Transactions

In an enterprise system, maintaining the
integrity of data across various applications and machines is critical. Regardless of the scope of the application, at least some aspects of transaction processing have to be implemented to guarantee the integrity of the data.
However, developing code to handle data integrity can be very challenging.
In this chapter, we will look at the issues involved and examine how the transaction support under COM+ helps simplify component development.

THE STOCK TRADER

We need an example to explore the transaction support under COM+. As I
have dabbled in trading stocks over the Internet, I would like to use a simple
stock trading system as an example. As for those lessons learned when trading stocks, I will leave that for another book.

Our brokerage firm, *MyBroker.com*, allows clients to trade stocks over
the Internet. In order to do so, a client has to maintain an account with the
firm.

Figure 8.1 identifies the requisite components to set up our stock trading system. The figure also illustrates the interaction between these components.

The trading system is based on a three-tier Windows DNA strategy.

The presentation layer (the first tier) is a Web-based user interface.

The business logic (the second tier) consists of three components:
`AccountMgmt.DLL`, `StockExchange.DLL`, and `TradeMgmt.DLL`.

The data for the clients and the stocks is stored in two different databases (the third tier): `AccountsDB` and `StocksDB`.

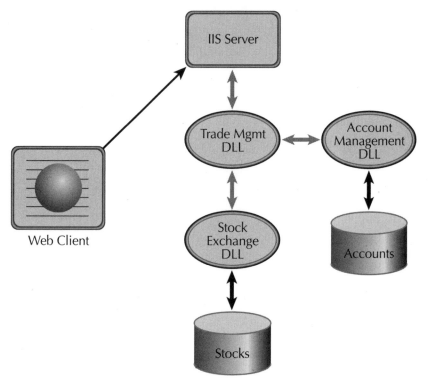

Figure 8.1   A sample stock trading system.

The account management component maintains the clients' accounts. The stock management component maintains the stocks' database. The trade management component lets the client buy a stock. It interacts with the other two components to update the respective databases.

The Database Layer

In this application, the Microsoft Data Engine (MSDE) will be the database server. It is a Microsoft SQL Server 7.0-compatible data storage server and is packaged with Microsoft Office 2000. Details of installing MSDE can be found in the MSDN article "Creating and Deploying Access Solutions with the Microsoft Data Engine" [Smi-99] by Scott Smith.

Using MSDE

MSDE comes with a command line program, `osql.exe`. We will use this program to create our databases. To use this program interactively, you can type:

```
osql.exe -U userid
```

where `userid` is the identification of the user allowed to access the database server. In our example, the `userid` is `sa` and the password field is empty.

Program `osql.exe` also lets you run SQL statements in a batch mode. Simply create a file containing the SQL statements and run the program specifying the filename as a parameter, as shown in the following example:

```
osql.exe -U sa -i MyQueryFile.sql
```

That's it as far as using MSDE goes. Now let's create our databases!

The Accounts Database

The `AccountsDB` database maintains account balances for our clients. It contains one table, `Accounts`, that defines two fields, `Client` (the client's name) and `Balance` (funds that can be used to purchase stocks). Table 8.1 shows the data stored in this table.

Table 8.1   `AccountsDB` **Database**

Client	Balance
Don	100000
Chris	90000
Richard	80000

To create this database, run the following SQL statements:

```
create database AccountsDB
go
use AccountsDB
create table Accounts ([Client] varchar (15) NOT NULL,
  [Balance] int NOT NULL)
create unique index Client on Accounts([Client])
insert into Accounts Values ('Don', '100000')
insert into Accounts Values ('Chris', '90000')
insert into Accounts Values ('Richard', '80000')
go
quit
```

The go SQL statement explicitly forces the execution of preceding SQL statements. For more information on SQL statements, consult the MSDE documentation.

The Stocks Database

The StocksDB database maintains information on the stocks that are currently traded on our fictitious stock exchange. It contains one table, Stocks, that defines three fields, Symbol (for stock symbols), Shares (number of outstanding shares for the stock that may be purchased at the market price), and MarketPrice (current market price for the stock). Table 8.2 shows the data stored in the Stocks table.

Table 8.2　　StocksDB **Database**

Symbol	Shares	MarketPrice
MSFT	50000	95
INTC	30000	75

To create this database, run the following SQL statements:

```
create database StocksDB
go
use StocksDB
create table Stocks ([Symbol] varchar (5) NOT NULL,
   [Shares] int NOT NULL,
   [MarketPrice] int NOT NULL)
create unique index [Symbol] on Stocks([Symbol])
insert into Stocks Values ('MSFT', '50000', 95)
insert into Stocks Values ('INTC', '30000', 75)
go
quit
```

Now let's take a look at the various components of the business logic.

The Business Logic

The Account Management Component

Component AccountMgmt.DLL is used to update the AccountsDB database. It has just one interface, IAccountMgr, that supports just one method, Debit. The interface is defined as follows:

```
interface IAccountMgr : IDispatch
{
  HRESULT Debit([in] BSTR bsClient, [in] long lAmount);
};
```

Method `Debit` decreases the account balance of the specified client by the amount specified. The implementation is shown in the following code fragment:

```
STDMETHODIMP CAccountMgr::Debit(BSTR bsClient, long
lAmount)
{
  try {
    ADOConnectionPtr spConn = OpenAccountsDB();
    long lCurrentBalance = GetBalance(spConn, bsClient);
    if (lCurrentBalance < lAmount) {
      return Error(_T("Not enough balance"),
        GUID_NULL, E_FAIL);
    }
    long lNewBalance = lCurrentBalance - lAmount;
    UpdateBalance(spConn, bsClient, lNewBalance);
  }
  catch(_com_error& e) {
    return Error(static_cast<LPCTSTR>(e.Description()),
      GUID_NULL, e.Error());
  }

  return S_OK;
}
```

The code snippet here uses Microsoft's Active Data Objects (ADO) to manipulate the database. ADO simplifies programming by isolating the details of underlying ODBC (Open Database Connectivity) drivers and/or native OLE DB drivers. In the simulation program, ADO uses a native OLE DB driver called SQLOEDB to access the MSDE database. Covering ADO is beyond the scope of this book. However, the code snippets that I will be presenting should illustrate the use of ADO interfaces clearly. More information on ADO can be found on the Microsoft platform SDK documentation. In particular, the SDK article, "Migrating from DAO to ADO using ADO with the Microsoft Jet Provider" [Hen-99] has a great introduction to ADO.

Method `Debit` calls `OpenAccountsDB` to open the `AccountsDB` database. It then calls `GetBalance` to obtain the balance for the specified client. Finally, it calls `UpdateBalance` to update the account balance for the client. The implementation of these methods is as follows:

```cpp
// File StdAfx.h
...
#import "c:\program files\common files\system\ado\msado15.dll"\
  rename ( "EOF", "adoEOF" )
typedef ADODB::_ConnectionPtr ADOConnectionPtr;
typedef ADODB::_RecordsetPtr ADORecordsetPtr;

#define CHECKHR(hr) \
  { if (FAILED(hr)) _com_issue_error(hr ); }

// File AccountMgr.cpp

ADOConnectionPtr CAccountMgr::OpenAccountsDB()
{
  ADOConnectionPtr spConn;
  HRESULT hr =
    spConn.CreateInstance(__uuidof(ADODB::Connection));
  CHECKHR(hr);

  // Use native OLE DB driver for MSDE when connecting to
  // to the database
  _bstr_t bsDSN = "provider=sqloledb;database=AccountsDB";
  _bstr_t bsUser = "sa";
  hr = spConn->Open (bsDSN, bsUser, (LPCTSTR) NULL, NULL);
  CHECKHR(hr);
  return spConn;
}

long CAccountMgr::GetBalance(ADOConnectionPtr spConn,
  BSTR bsClient)
{
  ADORecordsetPtr spRS;
  HRESULT hr = spRS.CreateInstance(__uuidof(ADODB::Recordset));
  CHECKHR(hr);

  // Construct a SQL query
  TCHAR buf[256];
  _stprintf(buf,
    _T("SELECT * FROM Accounts WHERE [client] = '%S'"),
      (LPCWSTR) bsClient);

  // Get the recordset
  _variant_t vConn = static_cast<IDispatch*>(spConn);
  hr = spRS->Open(buf, vConn, ADODB::adOpenKeyset,
    ADODB::adLockPessimistic, ADODB::adCmdText);
  CHECKHR(hr);

  return spRS->Fields->Item["Balance"]->Value;
}
```

```
void CAccountMgr::UpdateBalance(ADOConnectionPtr spConn,
  BSTR bsClient, long lBalance)
{
  // Construct a SQL statement to update the balance
  TCHAR buf[256];
  _stprintf(buf,
    _T("UPDATE Accounts SET Balance = %ld WHERE
      [client] = '%S'"), lBalance, (LPCWSTR) bsClient);

  // Execute the SQL statement
  _variant_t vRecordCount;
  spConn->Execute(buf, &vRecordCount,-1);
}
```

In the code above, if any ADO call fails, an exception of type `_com_error` is issued and further processing is stopped.

The Stock Exchange Component

This component supports one interface, `IStockMgr`. The interface is described as follows:

```
interface IStockMgr : IDispatch
{
  HRESULT BuyStock([in] BSTR bsSymbol, [in] long lShares,
    [out, retval] long* plValue);
};
```

Method `BuyStock` checks to see if the requested stock symbol and the requested number of shares are available in the `StocksDB` database. If a match is found, it reduces the number of available shares in the database and returns the total value of the trade, which is the product of the number of requested shares and the market price of the stock. The implementation for this method follows:

```
STDMETHODIMP CStockMgr::BuyStock(BSTR bsSymbol,
  long lRequestedShares, long *plValue)
{
  try {
    ADOConnectionPtr spConn = OpenStocksDB();

    long lAvailableShares, lMarketPrice;
    GetStockInfo(spConn, bsSymbol, lAvailableShares,
      lMarketPrice);
    if( lAvailableShares < lRequestedShares) {
      return Error(_T("Not enough shares"),
```

```
          GUID_NULL, E_FAIL);
   }
   // Reduce the available number of shares
   lAvailableShares -= lRequestedShares;
   UpdateAvailableShares(spConn, bsSymbol, lAvailableShares);
   *plValue = lRequestedShares * lMarketPrice;
   }
   catch(_com_error& e) {
     return Error(static_cast<LPCTSTR>( e.Description()),
       GUID_NULL, E_FAIL);
   }

   return S_OK;
}
```

The code here references two methods, `GetStockInfo` and `UpdateAvailableShares`. Their implementation is similar to those we saw earlier for the account management component. Consequently, the implementation is not shown here.

The Trade Management Component

Our final component of the business logic, the trade manager, is responsible for the overall management of buying stocks. It supports an interface, `ITradeMgr`. The interface is defined as follows:

```
interface ITradeMgr : IDispatch
{
   HRESULT BuyStocks([in] BSTR bsClient, [in] BSTR bsSymbol,
     [in] long lShares);
};
```

Interface method `BuyStocks` attempts to buy the specified number of shares for the specified stock on behalf of the specified client. To accomplish this, the trade manager interacts with the other two components of the business logic. The implementation for this method is as follows:

```
STDMETHODIMP CTradeMgr::BuyStocks(BSTR bsClient, BSTR bsSymbol,
   long lShares)
{
   try {
     //
     // First operation - Obtain the stocks.
     //
     IStockMgrPtr spStockMgr(__uuidof(StockMgr));
     long lAmount = spStockMgr->BuyStock(bsSymbol, lShares);
```

```
    //
    // Second operation - Debit the clien't account balance
    //
    IAccountMgrPtr spAccountMgr(__uuidof(AccountMgr));
    spAccountMgr->Debit(bsClient, lAmount);
  }catch(_com_error& e) {
    return Error(static_cast<LPCTSTR>( e.Description()),
      GUID_NULL, e.Error());
  }

  return S_OK;
}
```

The Simulation

Consider the case when one of the clients, say, Don, wants to buy 100 shares of MSFT. The following VbScript code shows the logic:

```
set TradeMgr = CreateObject("TradeMgmt.TradeMgr")
TradeMgr.BuyStocks "Don", "MSFT", 100
```

When this code is executed, 100 shares of MSFT are removed from the StocksDB database, and Don's account balance is debited by $9500 (recall that the market price of MSFT was $95).

To verify that the transaction succeeded, you can query the databases by running osql.exe. This is left as an exercise for you.

Now, consider another scenario. Let's say another client, Chris, wants to buy 1000 shares of MSFT. The following VBScript code shows the logic:

```
set TradeMgr = CreateObject("TradeMgmt.TradeMgr")
TradeMgr.BuyStocks "Chris", "MSFT", 1000
```

When this code is executed, 1000 shares of MSFT are removed from the StocksDB database. However, Chris' account balance will not get debited, as he does not have sufficient funds; he is short by $5000.

This transaction has created a problem for us. A thousand shares of MSFT have just disappeared from the exchange. At this rate, our stock exchange will pretty soon run into the ground!

An obvious solution is to modify the code so that the stocks are inserted back into the market in case of a failure. However, this solution is neither practical nor maintainable for transactions that involve many complex operations to perform. Moreover, it violates many important requirements for a transaction.

Let's examine the requirements for a transaction.

TRANSACTION THEORY

For our brokerage firm example, a "buy stock" transaction consists of the following two operations:

- Reduce the number of available shares for the specified stock in the `StocksDB` database.
- Debit the balance in the `AccountDB` database.

A transaction must be such that it entirely succeeds or entirely fails. This implies that all of the operations involved in the transaction must be updated successfully or nothing should be updated at all. This all-or-nothing proposition of a transaction is called *atomicity*.

A transaction must be *consistent*. Any individual operation within a transaction may leave the data in such a state that it violates the system's integrity. In our case, after the completion of the first operation, some shares have been taken out of the market. After the completion of the second operation, either the system should roll back to the original state (restore the shares that were taken out), or, upon success, go to a new state that still maintains the overall integrity of the system.

Now consider the case of concurrent transactions. Suppose that 100 shares of a stock X are available in the `StocksDB` database, and transaction A, consisting of two operations, is in progress. The first operation has added 50 shares of X into the `StocksDB` database. This change should be committed only if the second operation succeeds. However, before the second operation completes, another transaction, B, tries to obtain 125 shares of X from the database. Transaction B is able to use the uncommitted changes from transaction A; it actually sees 150 shares of X in the database. This is problematic. What happens if the second operation of transaction A fails and thus the first operation has to be rolled back? Transaction B has been infected with data that never really existed.

To avoid such problems, the system should *isolate* the uncommitted changes. Transaction B should only be able to see the data in the state before transaction A begins or in the state after transaction A completes, but not in some half-baked condition between the two states.

Finally, a transaction must be *durable*, that is, when a transaction is committed, the data sources involved must guarantee that the updates will persist, even if the computer crashes (or the power goes off) immediately after the commit. This requires specialized transaction logging that would allow the data source's restart procedure to complete any unfinished operation.

Atomicity, consistency, isolation, and durability; a transaction should support these properties. This is the ACID test for transactions.

 Most transactions are not reversible. However, some irreversible transactions can be undone by applying an equal but opposite transaction. An example of such a pair of operations is registering and unregistering a COM server. A transaction that can undo another transaction is referred to as a compensating transaction.

At this point, it is worth considering what implications this has on the underlying components. How on earth can you ensure that the changes in the system can be unwound if the transaction is aborted at some point? Even for our relatively simple example with just two operations, it is not a trivial task. Think about a transaction that involves many such operations.

Fortunately, COM+ provides the infrastructure to ease dealing with transactions.

Let's see it in action.

COM+ SUPPORT FOR TRANSACTIONS

At 25,000 feet, the support for transaction under COM+ is very straightforward. A transaction spans across many objects (that may access different databases). If an operation from any one object involved in the transaction fails, it indicates its failure status to COM+. The COM+ infrastructure can then roll back the changes to all the databases involved in the transaction.

A little clarification is in order. All the operations in a transaction need not always deal with databases, though a database operation is the most frequent use-case. Sending an e-mail or copying a file, for example, could also be considered as part of the transaction, and may require a rollback. Generally speaking, rollbacks are applied to any transactional resource, a database being just one such resource.

Two basic questions arise:

- How does the COM+ infrastructure know if an object will participate in a transaction?
- How does the object indicate, or *vote*, on the status of its operation?

Let's tackle the first question.

Configuring Transactions

COM+ defines an attribute on a component called the *transaction attribute*. By setting this attribute, a component tells COM+ to manage transactions on its behalf. When the component's object is activated, COM+ looks at the transaction attribute to determine the type of transaction protection it must provide in the object's context.

Why can't COM+ assume that a component will always participate in a transaction?

Forcing every object to participate in a transaction is not practical. The overhead of adding transaction protection to the context object is not acceptable for a component that has no interest in supporting a transaction.

The transaction attribute can be set from the Component Services snap-in. The property-page for setting transactional attributes is shown in Figure 8.2.

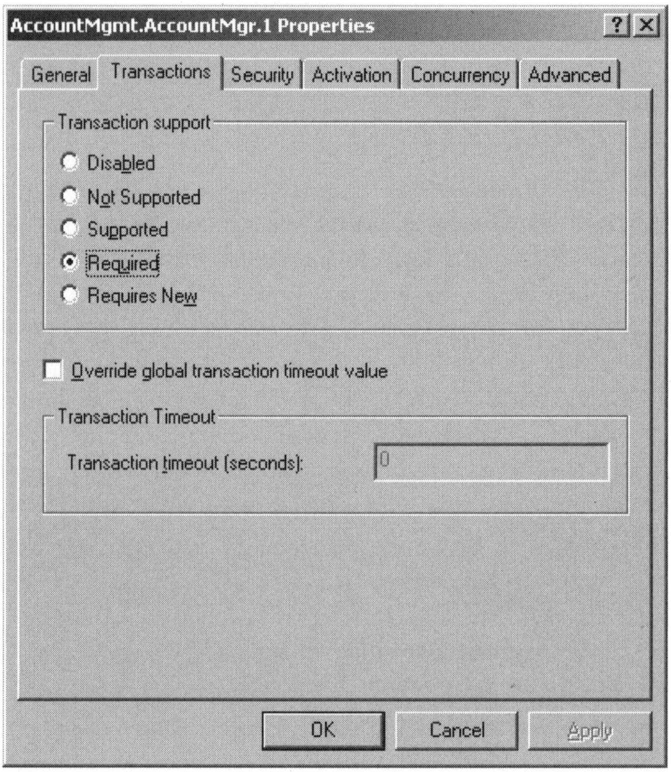

Figure 8.2 Transactional settings on a component.

The transaction attribute can be set to one of the following values:

- **Required:** This value implies that a component *must* have a transaction in order to do its work. If the component's object is activated within the context of an existing transaction, the transaction is propagated to the new object. If the activator's context has no transactional information, COM+ will create a brand new context containing transactional information and attach it to the object.

- **Required New:** Sometimes an object may wish to initiate a new transaction, regardless of the transactional status of its activator. When the *required-new* value is specified, COM+ will initiate a new transaction that is distinct from the activator's transaction. The outcome of the new transaction has no effect on the outcome of the activator's transaction.

- **Supported:** A component with this value set indicates that it does not care for the presence or absence of a transaction. If the activator is participating in a transaction, the object will propagate the transaction to any new object that it activates. The object itself may or may not participate in the transaction.

  This value is generally used when the component doesn't really need a transaction of its own but wants to be able to work with other components.

- **Not Supported:** The component has no interest in participating in a transaction, regardless of the transactional status of its activator. This guarantees that the component's object will neither vote in its activator's transaction nor begin a transaction of its own, nor will it propagate the caller's transaction to any object that it activates. This value should be chosen if you wish to *break* the continuity of an existing transaction.

  Not supported is the default value for all components.

- **Disabled:** If a component will never access a transactional resource, setting the transaction attribute to *disabled* eliminates any transaction-related overhead for the component. This attribute simulates the transaction behavior of a non-configured component.

The transaction attribute on a component can also be specified in the IDL file. The SDK defines the following constants. These constants are defined in the header file `<mtxattr.h>`.

- `TRANSACTION_REQUIRED`
- `TRANSACTION_REQUIRES_NEW`

- TRANSACTION_SUPPORTED

- TRANSACTION_NOT_SUPPORTED

The transaction attribute can be specified on the `coclass` entry in the IDL file, as shown here:

```
import "oaidl.idl";
import "ocidl.idl";
#include <mtxattr.h>
...
[
  uuid(0AC21FA4-DB2A-474F-A501-F9C9A062A63E),
  helpstring("AccountMgr Class"),
  TRANSACTION_REQUIRED
]
coclass AccountMgr
{
  [default] interface IAccountMgr;
};
```

When the component is installed, the Catalog Manager (see Chapter 5) automatically configures the component with the value specified in the IDL file. However, the administrator can override this value from the Component Service snap-in at any time.

Now, let's get the answer to the second question—how does an object cast its vote in a transaction?

Programmatic Voting

Once the components are set to participate in a transaction, each of the component's objects participating in the transaction has to indicate the outcome of its operation(s) individually.

Recall from Chapter 5 that, for a configured component, the state of the context object is available to the component's object via interface `IContextState`. This interface has a method on it called `SetMyTransactionVote`. Following is its prototype:

```
HRESULT SetMyTransactionVote(TransactionVote txVote);
```

Parameter `txVote` can be set to one of two possible values: `TxAbort` to indicate that an operation failed, and `TxCommit` to indicate that the operation succeeded.

Let's revise the account management code to use `SetMyTransac-tionVote`. The following code fragment shows the changes:

```
STDMETHODIMP CAccountMgr::Debit(BSTR bsClient, long lAmount)
{
  CComPtr<IContextState> spState;
  HRESULT hr = ::CoGetObjectContext(__uuidof(IContextState),
    (void**) &spState);
  if (FAILED(hr)) {
    return hr;
  }

  try {
    ADOConnectionPtr spConn = OpenAccountsDB();
    long lCurrentBalance = GetBalance(spConn, bsClient);
    if (lCurrentBalance < lAmount) {
      spState->SetMyTransactionVote(TxAbort);
      return Error(_T("Not enough balance"), GUID_NULL,
        E_FAIL);
    }
    long lNewBalance = lCurrentBalance - lAmount;
    UpdateBalance(spConn, bsClient, lNewBalance);
  }
  catch(_com_error& e) {
    spState->SetMyTransactionVote(TxAbort);
    return Error(static_cast<LPCTSTR>(e.Description()),
      GUID_NULL, e.Error());
  }

  spState->SetMyTransactionVote(TxCommit);
  return S_OK;
}
```

Similar changes need to be made to the stock manager and the trade manager components. The following code fragment shows the changes for the trade management component:

```
STDMETHODIMP CTradeMgr::BuyStocks(BSTR bsClient, BSTR bsSymbol,
  long lShares)
{
  CComPtr<IContextState> spState;
  HRESULT hr = ::CoGetObjectContext(__uuidof(IContextState),
    (void**) &spState);
  if (FAILED(hr)) {
    return hr;
  }
```

```
try {
  //
  // First operation - Obtain the stocks.
  //
  IStockMgrPtr spStockMgr(__uuidof(StockMgr));
  long lAmount = spStockMgr->BuyStock(bsSymbol, lShares);

  //
  // Second operation - Debit the clien't account balance
  //
  IAccountMgrPtr spAccountMgr(__uuidof(AccountMgr));
  spAccountMgr->Debit(bsClient, lAmount);
}catch(_com_error& e) {
  spState->SetMyTransactionVote(TxAbort);
  return Error(static_cast<LPCTSTR>(e.Description()),
    GUID_NULL, e.Error());
}

spState->SetMyTransactionVote(TxCommit);
return S_OK;
}
```

Let's run the simulation once again. Remember to set all the three components with the `Required` transactional attribute and to reset both the databases to the original values.

For your review, the `VBScript` code for the base client is shown below:

```
set TradeMgr = CreateObject("TradeMgmt.TradeMgr")
TradeMgr.BuyStocks "Chris", "MSFT", 1000
```

When the above code is executed, the transaction will fail, as Chris does not have enough funds to buy the stock. This result is the same as before. However, the difference will become apparent when you examine the `StocksDB` database. The number of shares for `MSFT` has not changed, unlike the earlier simulation where 1000 shares of `MSFT` just disappeared from the database.

COM+ provided automatic transaction support and rolled back the changes when the transaction failed.

This brings us to a new set of questions—how did COM+ know the type of resource a component uses? The simulation program never informed COM+ that it used two MSDE databases. What if the simulation used a normal file as one of the resources? Each type of resource involved in a transaction requires its own specialized rollback. Surely, it is not possible for the

COM+ infrastructure to have an intimate knowledge of rolling back changes for every possible resource type. How, then, can it still support transactions?

It's time to look at the architecture.

THE ARCHITECTURE

Resource Managers

COM+ is an infrastructure. As an infrastructure, it should handle any resource generically; and not know the details of any specific resource.

To access and modify the durable state of a resource in a generic fashion, COM+ relies on a software component called the *Resource Manager (RM)*.

A resource manager is a software component that has an intimate knowledge of a specific type of resource, such as a relational database. Under the influence of a transaction, the RM keeps track of the changes made to the resource. If the transaction aborts, the RM can roll back these changes on the resource and bring it back to the original state. A simple RM, for example, may *buffer* the changes made to the resource and persist the changes only if the transaction commits.

There are many commercially available RMs, including the ones for Microsoft SQL Server, Oracle, IBM DB2, Informix, and Sybase. The database server used in the simulation program, MSDE, also provides its own RM.

When a client instantiates an RM, the client gets a *proxy* to the RM. OLE DB drivers and ODBC drivers are examples of RM proxies. The RM proxy provides APIs to access the RM. Typically, the RM proxy provides COM interfaces, although it is not a requirement. ODBC drivers, for example, do not provide COM interfaces.

 An RM proxy is typically implemented as part of another software component called the *Resource Dispenser* (RD). Unlike a resource manager that manages the durable state of a resource, a resource dispenser manages the non-durable state of the resource, such as the number of connections to a resource. We will cover resource dispensers in Chapter 11 when we discuss scalability issues.

A transaction can involve many resource managers who may span multiple machines across the network. If some operation in a transaction fails, all the participating resource managers need to be informed so that the changes to the resources can be rolled back. This implies that some service should exist that can coordinate all the resource managers involved in the distributed

transaction. This service does exist and is called the Microsoft Distributed
Transaction Coordinator (MS-DTC).

The Distributed Transaction Coordinator

As the name implies, the Distributed Transaction Coordinator (DTC) coordinates a transaction that could potentially be distributed across the network.
More precisely, the DTC manages the resource managers. Based on the outcome of a transaction, it informs each of the participating resource managers
to either abort or commit the changes to their respective resources.

Each system that needs to use transactions must have the DTC installed.
If you install MS SQL Server or MSDE, the MS-DTC automatically gets
installed.

 The MS-DTC is a Windows NT service that can be started and stopped from
the service control panel or from the MS-DTC property page in the Component Services snap-in.

A non-transactional client (transactional clients let COM+ manage their
transactions) can obtain the DTC using the SDK API `DtcGetTransac-
tionManager` and explicitly request to begin a new transaction. The follow-
ing code snippet illustrates the process of using the DTC:

```
CComPtr<ITransactionDispenser> spTxDisp;
HRESULT hr = DtcGetTransactionManager(
    NULL,                                   // host name
    NULL,                                   // TM name
    __uuidof(ITransactionDispenser),        // interface
    0,                                      // reserved
    0,                                      // reserved
    0,                                      // reserved
    (void**) &spTxDisp);                    // [out] pointer

CComPtr<ITransaction> spTx;
hr = spTxDisp->BeginTransaction(
    NULL,                                   // outer component
    ISOLATIONLEVEL_ISOLATED,                // Isolation level
    ISOFLAG_RETAIN_DONTCARE,                // Isolation flag
    NULL,                                   // Options
    &spTx);                                 // [out] pointer
```

```
... // Enlist RMs and perform resource updates

if (bSuccess) {
  spTx->Commit(0, XACTTC_SYNC_PHASEONE, 0);
}else {
  spTx->Abort(NULL, 0, FALSE);
}
```

When the non-transactional client requests a new transaction, the DTC (more precisely, a part of the DTC called the *transaction manager*) dispenses the transaction as a pointer to interface `ITransaction`. The client can then enlist other appropriate RMs to participate in the transaction.

This COM+ mechanism of letting a non-transactional component handle a transaction manually is referred to as Bring Your Own Transaction (BYOT). An interesting use of BYOT is to manually create a transaction with an arbitrary, long timeout [Mar-00].

The DTC identifies each transaction uniquely as a C structure of type `XACTUOW`. A client can obtain this identification by calling `ITransaction::GetTransactionInfo`. As we will see later, COM+ reinterprets this structure as a GUID.

To commit a transaction, the client calls `ITransaction::Commit`. At this point, the DTC requests each of the enlisted RMs to commit its changes.

What if one of the RMs run into some internal problem and fails to commit?

Two-Phase Commit

To ensure that the all-or-nothing proposition is maintained for a transaction, the DTC mandates that each RM attempt the commitment in two phases, *prepare* and *commit*.

In the prepare phase, the RM should do everything it takes to ensure that the commit phase does not fail. It is up to the developer of the RM to define what "everything" means and how to make it happen. All possible internal problems that an RM can run into should be returned as an appropriate error in this phase.

If no problems are encountered during the prepare phase, the RM saves all of its state information in such a manner that failure to commit can no longer occur. It then returns from the prepare phase with a successful status indicating that it is ready to make the changes permanent.

In the commit phase, the RM applies the just-saved state information and makes the changes permanent. This phase should not fail, unless it runs into some catastrophe such as a power shutdown.

With the breakup of a transaction commitment into two phases, the interaction between the DTC and the RMs gets simplified. The following is the algorithm:

- The client requests the DTC to commit the transaction.
- The DTC sends a *prepare* request to each RM that has been enlisted in the transaction. Upon receiving this request, an RM prepares its internal state.
- If any RM returns a failure status during the *prepare* phase, the DTC informs the rest of the RMs to abort their changes.
- If all the RMs respond positively to the *prepare* request, the DTC requests each RM to commit its changes.

What if the RM runs into a catastrophic failure, such as a power shutdown, in the middle of the commitment phase?

It is the responsibility of the RM to persist its internal state after the *prepare* phase so that it will survive a system failure. Recall that this requirement comes from the *durability* property of the ACID test.

This brief introduction to the DTC and RM is enough for our current discussion. For more information, check out Richard Grimes' book, *Professional Visual C++ 6 MTS Programming* [Gri-99], that has one whole chapter dedicated to the DTC. Also, see Jonathan Pinnock's book, *Professional DCOM Application Development* [Pin-98], for an example of developing your own resource manager and resource dispenser.

Let's see how COM+ supports transactions automatically.

Automatic Transactions through COM+

A configured component indicates its interest in participating in a transaction by means of the transaction attribute.

When an object from such a component is activated, COM+ sets up the object's context to handle transactions.

COM+ automatically begins a transaction when it encounters either of the following conditions:

1. When a non-transactional client activates an object whose component has its transaction attribute set to either the `TRANSACTION_REQUIRED` or `TRANSACTION_REQUIRES_NEW` values.

2. When a transactional client calls an object whose component has its transaction attribute set to the TRANSACTION_REQUIRES_NEW value.

The object responsible for beginning a new transaction is referred to as the *root object* of that transaction. As we will see shortly, this root object has a special role in completing the transaction.

As a corollary, an object whose transaction attribute is set to TRANSAC-TION_REQUIRES_NEW will always be a root object.

When the root object is activated, COM+ transparently asks the DTC for a new transaction. The DTC returns an ITransaction pointer that COM+ stores in the object's context.

An object that subsequently gets activated within the boundary of this transaction, and is marked as either TRANSACTION_REQUIRED or TRANSAC-TION_SUPPORTED, will share the transaction.

A collection of one or more contexts that share a transaction is referred to as a *transaction stream.*

To ensure that all the contexts within a transaction stream share only one transaction at a time, COM+ mandates a component that requires a transaction should also require synchronization. Recall from Chapter 5 that COM+ sets up such a component to run under an *activity.*

More precisely, a transaction stream is completely contained inside an activity, but an activity can contain more than one transaction stream.

If an object is participating in a transaction, it can obtain its transaction ID from its context, as shown in the following code fragment:

```
CComPtr<IObjectContextInfo> spInfo;
HRESULT hr = CoGetObjectContext(__uuidof(IObjectContextInfo),
  (void**) &spInfo);
_ASSERT (SUCCEEDED(hr));

GUID tid;
hr = spInfo->GetTransactionId(&tid);
_ASSERT (SUCCEEDED(hr));
```

Note that COM+ returns the transaction ID as a GUID, and not as a XACTUOW structure.

When a transactional object accesses a transactional resource for the first time, the data access layer (such as ODBC and OLE DB) accesses the context's transaction automatically and enlists the corresponding RM with the DTC. In our simulation program, for example, when the account manager object opens the AccountsDB database using ADO, the underlying OLE DB driver (SQLOLEDB) enlists the MSDE resource manager with the DTC in the context of the current transaction. This *auto-enlistment* feature provided by the data access layer simplifies code development and is fundamental to the declarative programming model of COM+.

Each component participating in the transaction casts its vote by calling IContextState::SetMyTransactionVote, a method that we have already seen in action.

A transaction completes when the root object of the transaction is deactivated. At this point, COM+ checks to see if all the objects have individually given their consent to commit the transaction. Depending on the consensus, it either calls ITransaction::Commit or ITransaction::Abort on the current transaction.

The transactional objects themselves do not participate in the two-phase commit process; only the enlisted RMs do. In fact, the transactional objects do not even know about the commitment process, nor do they care.

A transaction also completes when it exceeds its timeout threshold. Transactions are generally designed to be short-lived, as locking a resource for an extended period of time can cause bottlenecks in the system. To ensure efficient performance, COM+ defines a global timeout period for transactions. The default is 60 seconds, but an administrator can change it to any suitable value. COM+ also provides a configuration setting to override the global timeout value for individual components.

If a transaction exceeds its timeout threshold, COM+ will deactivate all the participating objects and abort the transaction.

COM+ 1.0 (the current release) uses a "serializable" level of isolation for transactions. This level of isolation enforces highest level of locking on the underlying resource, thereby providing the highest degree of data integrity. In general, the higher the level of resource locking, the lower the scalability of the application. Under COM+ 1.x (the future release) you will be able to configure the isolation level on a per-component basis. The root object gets to dictate the isolation level for the transaction. Be aware though, that a lower level of isolation increases the chances of incorrect data.

Earlier, I said that, in order to commit a transaction, all the objects participating in the transaction need to cast a positive vote. An obvious improvement that can be made is that, instead of requiring *all* the participating objects to cast a positive vote, it is sufficient that *any one* participating object casts a negative vote. This in fact is the default behavior under COM+. The implication of this is that the developers of a transactional component need not call `SetMyTransactionVote(TxCommit)` on successful operations. They just need to indicate only the failure status (via `TxAbort`).

Lifetime of a Transaction

Consider the following base client `VBScript` code:

```
set TradeMgr = CreateObject("TradeMgmt.TradeMgr")
TradeMgr.BuyStocks "Don", "INTC", 100
TradeMgr.BuyStocks "Chris", "MSFT", 1000
TradeMgr = NULL
```

Recall that Chris does not have enough funds to buy 1000 shares of MSFT; Don, however, does have enough funds to cover 100 shares of INTC. However, if you execute the above code and check the values stored in the database, you will find that even Don was unable to buy the shares he wanted. What went wrong?

Recall that a transaction is considered complete only after the root object of the transaction gets deactivated. In the above lines of code, the root object gets deactivated after executing the two `BuyStocks` statements. As a result, both `BuyStocks` statements are considered to be part of the same transaction. When the second `BuyStocks` statement failed, all the changes, including the one from the first `BuyStocks` statement, were rolled back.

An obvious solution is to release the root object after the first call to `BuyStocks` and immediately recreate it before making the second call.

Though the proposed technique will work, releasing an object and recreating it each time is very inefficient.

Fortunately, COM+ offers a better solution.

COM+ provides a way to deactivate an object even if the base client has not released it. To make this possible, COM+ always returns a proxy pointer to the base client, instead of returning the actual reference to the object. This provides COM+ the flexibility to deactivate the actual object while keeping the proxy alive. When the base client makes a method call on the proxy, COM+ can transparently reactivate the object. This is referred to as *just-in-time* (JIT) activation.

JIT is covered in detail in Chapter 11 when we discuss scalability. The important point to note here is that COM+ enforces a component that requires a transaction to have JIT enabled.

COM+ will automatically enforce JIT Activation to TRUE and Synchronization as REQUIRED for any component marked as TRANSACTION_REQUIRED or TRANSACTION_REQUIRES_NEW.

An object that is JIT-enabled contains a bit in its context called the "*done*" bit or, more precisely, the *deactivate-on-return* bit. COM+ checks this bit after its return from each method call. If the bit is turned on, COM+ will deactivate the object. By default, COM+ turns this bit off before entering a method. However, one can change this behavior at the interface method level from the Component Services snap-in.

The *deactivate-on-return* bit can also be set programmatically by using the method SetDeactivateOnReturn available on the interface IContextState. The following is its prototype:

```
Interface IContextState : IUnknown
{
    ...
    HRESULT SetDeactivateOnReturn(VARIANT_BOOL bVal);
}
```

Using this method, method CTradeMgr::BuyStocks can be revised to deactivate the object on return, as shown in the following code fragment:

```
STDMETHODIMP CTradeMgr::BuyStocks(BSTR bsClient, BSTR bsSymbol,
  long lShares)
{
  CComPtr<IContextState> spState;
  HRESULT hr = ::CoGetObjectContext(__uuidof(IContextState),
    (void**) &spState);
  if (FAILED(hr)) {
    return hr;
  }
  hr = spState->SetDeactivateOnReturn(VARIANT_TRUE);
  _ASSERT (SUCCEEDED(hr));

  try {
    //
    // First operation - Obtain the stocks.
    //
    IStockMgrPtr spStockMgr(__uuidof(StockMgr));
    long lAmount = spStockMgr->BuyStock(bsSymbol, lShares);
```

```
  //
  // Second operation - Debit the clien't account balance
  //
  IAccountMgrPtr spAccountMgr(__uuidof(AccountMgr));
  spAccountMgr->Debit(bsClient, lAmount);
}catch(_com_error& e) {
  spState->SetMyTransactionVote(TxAbort);
  return Error(static_cast<LPCTSTR>(e.Description()),
    GUID_NULL, e.Error());
}

spState->SetMyTransactionVote(TxCommit);
return S_OK;
}
```

With this change in place, if you execute the base client VBScript code once again, you will see that this time Don's trade would go through and Chris' trade would fail, just as expected.

Manual Transactions

Allowing COM+ to automatically manage a transaction simplifies component development. However, there are times when the base client would like to control the outcome of a transaction.

To handle this, COM+ provides a component called the Transaction-Context class, represented by the PROGID TxCtx.TransactionObject.

The TransactionContext object supports interface ITransactionContext. Following is its definition, along with a short explanation for each interface method:

```
ITransactionContext : IDispatch
{
  HRESULT CreateInstance([in] BSTR pszProgId,
    [retval][out] VARIANT *pObject);      // instantiate an object
  HRESULT Commit();                        // commit a transaction
  HRESULT Abort();                         // abort a transaction
};
```

By calling the methods on the ITransactionContext interface, the base client can begin a transaction, compose the work of one or more COM+ components in the transaction, and explicitly commit or abort the transaction. This is illustrated in the following VBScript code snippet:

```
Dim txCtx
Set txCtx = CreateObject("TxCtx.TransactionContext")

Dim Accounts
set Accounts = txCtx.CreateInstance("AccountMgmt.AccountMgr")
Accounts.Debit "Don", 10

txCtx.Commit
msgbox "Done"
```

Note that an object that is activated by calling `ITransactionContext::CreateInstance` should belong to a COM+ configured component. Each activated object should cast its transaction vote using the context object. However, using the transaction context, the base client also can participate in the voting process.

Also notice the distinction between an object context and a transaction context. An object context relates to an individual object whereas a transaction context is related to the overall transaction.

COMPENSATING RESOURCE MANAGER

A resource manager has to pass the ACID test; it has to guarantee atomicity, consistency, isolation, and durability. Given the intricate footwork an RM has to perform, implementing an RM is not an easy task.

Let's look at the tasks of a typical RM.

- When a client accesses a transactional resource, the corresponding RM should support enlistment with the DTC. The RM may also make a temporary copy of the resource and lock access to the actual resource (so that no other client can use it).
- When the primary client attempts to modify the resource, the RM has to *record* the change and apply the change to the copy (not the actual resource).
- If the DTC asks the RM to *prepare*, the RM has to play back the recorded sequence, and create an internal state for the commit phase. Alternatively, an RM may delay the playback to the commit phase, if it is confident that the updates will not fail.
- If the DTC asks the RM to *commit*, the RM may use the prepared internal state to commit the changes or play back the recorded sequence and apply the changes to the resource.
- If the DTC asks the RM to *abort*, the RM may just discard the prepared internal state (or the recorded sequence).

Given that a large portion of functionality is common from one RM to another, a reasonable question to ask is if there is a way to share this functionality. This would certainly simplify developing an RM.

It turns out that COM+ designers had already thought of this possibility. COM+ provides a framework to develop RMs. An RM developed using this framework is referred to as a Compensating Resource Manager (CRM).

The developer of a CRM has to write two cooperating components called the CRM worker and the CRM compensator.

The CRM worker exposes necessary COM objects to the clients. When the client requests that the resource be modified, the worker simply records the change (using CRM's service).

The CRM compensator reads the recorded changes (supplied by the CRM service) and either commits or aborts the changes.

Note that there is no direct communication between the CRM worker and the CRM compensator. The only data that has to be passed from the worker to the compensator is the sequence of changes applied on the resource.

To facilitate storing the sequence of changes, COM+ provides a component called the *CRM clerk*. The CRM worker instantiates the CRM clerk and starts recording the changes with the clerk. When the transaction closes, COM+ launches the CRM compensator and calls prepare, commit, or abort in whatever combination that is appropriate, and plays back the sequence of records to the compensator.

The CRM clerk supports an interface, `ICrmLogControl`. The following is its prototype:

```
ICrmLogControl : public IUnknown
{
  [propget] HRESULT TransactionUOW([retval][out] BSTR *pVal);
  HRESULT RegisterCompensator(
    [in] LPCWSTR pwszProgId,
    [in] LPCWSTR pwszDesc,
    [in] LONG lCrmRegFlags);
  HRESULT STDMETHODCALLTYPE WriteLogRecordVariants(
    [in] VARIANT *pLogRecord);
  HRESULT ForceLog();
  HRESULT ForgetLogRecord();
  HRESULT ForceTransactionToAbort();
  HRESULT WriteLogRecord(
    [size_is][in] BLOB rgBlob[],
    [in] ULONG cBlob);
};
```

Method `RegisterCompensator` is used to associate a CRM worker with a specific CRM compensator. It is the responsibility of the CRM worker to call this method.

Parameter `pwszProgId` is the `PROGID` of the CRM compensator that should be associated with the CRM worker. Parameter `pwszDesc` describes the CRM compensator. A transaction-monitoring program can use this description string for display purposes. Parameter `lCrmRegFlags` specifies the possible phases (prepare, commit, or abort) that can be passed to the CRM compensator. For example, if the compensator does not do anything specific to abort a transaction, then `CRMREGFLAG_ABORTPHASE` need not be specified as a possible phase.

Method `WriteLogRecord` can be used to record a change that is being made to the resource. The data is recorded in a form called BLOB (Binary Large Object). A BLOB is a structure that can carry any opaque data as a pointer. The structure of the BLOB is defined as follows:

```
struct BLOB{
  ULONG cbSize;                         // the size of the data
  [size_is(cbSize)] BYTE* pBlobData;    //the actual data
};
```

The CRM worker can record a resource change by passing one or more BLOBS to the method `WriteLogRecord`.

Each call to `WriteLogRecord` results in a single record stored with the CRM clerk. When the transaction completes, the CRM clerk instantiates the CRM compensator and plays back the records in the same sequence as they were originally received.

Associating more than one BLOB with a single record is just a convenience provided to the CRM worker. The CRM clerk internally pastes all the BLOBS together as one big BLOB.

Method `ForceTransactionToAbort` can be used to abort a transaction.

Let's turn our attention to the CRM compensator.

A CRM compensator has to support an interface, `ICrmCompensator`. The following is its prototype:

```
ICrmCompensator : public IUnknown
{
  HRESULT SetLogControl( [in] ICrmLogControl *pLogControl);

  // Prepare phase
  HRESULT BeginPrepare( void);
  HRESULT PrepareRecord( [in] CrmLogRecordRead crmLogRec,
    [retval][out] BOOL *pfForget);
```

```
  HRESULT EndPrepare( [retval][out] BOOL *pfOkToPrepare);

  // Commit phase
  HRESULT BeginCommit( [in] BOOL fRecovery);
  HRESULT CommitRecord( [in] CrmLogRecordRead crmLogRec,
    [retval][out] BOOL *pfForget);
  HRESULT EndCommit( void);
  // Abort phase
  HRESULT BeginAbort( [in] BOOL fRecovery);
  HRESULT AbortRecord( [in] CrmLogRecordRead crmLogRec,
    [retval][out] BOOL *pfForget);
  HRESULT EndAbort( void);
};
```

Data type `CrmLogRecordRead` is a C structure that contains a BLOB (that was previously recorded using `WriteLogRecord`) and some other fields that might be useful for debugging.

The compensator should implement code for all three phases, at least to satisfy the compiler. The DTC enters a phase by calling the `BeginXXX` method on that phase, followed by one or more calls to `RecordXXX`, and completes the phase by calling the `EndXXX` method.

Once a record has been digested in any phase, if the CRM compensator feels that the record serves no purpose to some other phase that it may enter later, it can inform the CRM clerk to lose the record by setting `pfForget` flag to TRUE.

With this brief background, let's build a CRM.

Our CRM will use a text file as a resource. To verify its functionality, we will modify the account manager component from the previous simulation program to use a text file, `W:/DB/Accounts.txt`, as a transactional resource (replacing the MSDE database).

The CRM worker component will support interface `IMyFileDB`, as defined here:

```
interface IMyFileDB : IDispatch
{
  HRESULT Open([in] BSTR bsFilePath);
  HRESULT GetBalance([in] BSTR bsClient,
    [out, retval] long* plBalance);
  HRESULT UpdateBalance([in] BSTR bsClient,
    [in] long lNewBalance);
};
```

With this component in place, the `CAccountMgr::Debit` logic should be modified to use the file-based resource. The revised implementation is shown below:

```
STDMETHODIMP CAccountMgr::Debit(BSTR bsClient, long lAmount)
{
  CComPtr<IContextState> spState;
  HRESULT hr = ::CoGetObjectContext(__uuidof(IContextState),
    (void**) &spState);
  if (FAILED(hr)) {
    return hr;
  }

  try {
    IMyFileDBPtr spConn(__uuidof(MyFileDB));
    spConn->Open("w:/DB/Accounts.txt");
    long lCurrentBalance = spConn->GetBalance(bsClient);
    if (lCurrentBalance < lAmount) {
      spState->SetMyTransactionVote(TxAbort);
      return Error(_T("Not enough balance"), GUID_NULL,
        E_FAIL);
    }
    long lNewBalance = lCurrentBalance - lAmount;
    spConn->UpdateBalance(bsClient, lNewBalance);
  }
  catch(_com_error& e) {
    spState->SetMyTransactionVote(TxAbort);
    return Error(static_cast<LPCTSTR>(e.Description()),
      GUID_NULL, e.Error());
  }

  spState->SetMyTransactionVote(TxCommit);
  return S_OK;
}
```

When `IMyFileDB::Open` is invoked, the CRM worker should first instantiate the CRM clerk and register the associated CRM compensator. The code snippet is shown below:

```
HRESULT CMyFileDB::InitCRM()
{
  if (ISNOTNULL(m_spCrmLC)) {
    m_spCrmLC = NULL;
  }

  HRESULT hr = ::CoCreateInstance(
    __uuidof(CRMClerk),
    NULL,
    CLSCTX_INPROC_SERVER,
    __uuidof(ICrmLogControl),
    (void**) &m_spCrmLC);
```

```
            if (FAILED(hr)) {
              return hr;
            }

            // Register the compensator.
            // Try 5 times if a recovery is in progress
            for(int i=0; i<5; i++) {
              hr = m_spCrmLC->RegisterCompensator(
                L"TextFileDB.MyFileDBCompensator",
                L"My file db compensator",
                CRMREGFLAG_ALLPHASES);

              if (SUCCEEDED(hr)) {
                return S_OK;
              }

              // deal with recovery in progress
              if (XACT_E_RECOVERYINPROGRESS == hr) {
                Sleep(1000); // sleep for a second
                continue; // and try again
              }
            }

          m_spCrmLC = NULL;
          return hr;
        }
```

Note that it is possible for the CRM worker to receive an XACT_E_RECOV-ERYINPROGRESS error during the call to RegisterCompensator. If this happens, the CRM worker should call the method a few more times until it succeeds.

The data file for our CRM contains clients and their respective balances. The CRM worker loads the file into memory as an STL map. Loading all the data into memory is not always efficient. However, it works for our demonstration.

```
typedef std::map<CComBSTR, long> MYACCOUNTDB;

class CMyFileDB :
  ...
{
  ...

private:
  CComPtr<ICrmLogControl> m_spCrmLC;
  MYACCOUNTDB m_AccountDB;
};
```

I have encapsulated serializing the MYACCOUNTDB data type to a file in class CMyFile and will not discuss it further. The code can be found on the CD.

There are only two commands that the CRM worker needs to record: the command to open a file and the command to update an account. As the command to obtain the balance does not really change the resource, there is no real need to record it.

To facilitate converting the command information into a BLOB, let's define some relevant data structures:

```
enum DBACTIONTYPE {dbOpen = 0x10, dbUpdate = 0x20};

#pragma warning(disable : 4200)      // do not warn on
                                     // zero-sized arrays

#pragma pack(1)                      // Pack the following
                                     // structures tightly

struct DBACTION {
  DBACTIONTYPE actionType;
};

struct DBACTIONOPEN : public DBACTION
{
  DBACTIONOPEN()
  {
    actionType = dbOpen;
  }
  WCHAR pszFileName[0];
};

struct DBACTIONUPDATE : public DBACTION
{
  DBACTIONUPDATE()
  {
    actionType = dbUpdate;
  }
  long lNewBalance;
  WCHAR pszClient[0];
};

#pragma pack()                       // back to default packing
#pragma warning(default : 4200)      // back to default warning
```

Note that packing the data on the byte boundary is important for reinterpreting a BLOB to its original structure.

Also note that I am defining a zero-sized array for a variable-sized string. I am just taking advantage of the fact that data is stored contiguously in a BLOB.

With these structures in place, the `CMyFile::Open` method can be implemented as follows:

```
STDMETHODIMP CMyFileDB::Open(BSTR bsFilePath)
{
  HRESULT hr = InitCRM();
  if (FAILED(hr)) {
    return hr;
  }

  // Open the file
  USES_CONVERSION;
  LPCTSTR pszFile = W2T(bsFilePath);
  CMyFile file;
  hr = file.Open(pszFile, CMyFile::READ);
  if (FAILED(hr)) {
    m_spCrmLC->ForceTransactionToAbort();
    return hr;
  }

  // Log info with CRM that the file is being opened
  DBACTIONOPEN openAction;

  BLOB blobArray[2];
  blobArray[0].pBlobData = (BYTE*) &openAction;
  blobArray[0].cbSize = sizeof(DBACTIONOPEN);
  blobArray[1].pBlobData = (BYTE*) bsFilePath;
  blobArray[1].cbSize = ::SysStringByteLen(bsFilePath) +
    sizeof(OLECHAR); // account for the end of string
  hr = m_spCrmLC->WriteLogRecord(blobArray, 2);
  if (FAILED(hr)) {
    m_spCrmLC->ForceTransactionToAbort();
    return hr;
  }

  // Now load file into memory
  hr = file.Load(m_AccountDB);
  if (FAILED(hr)) {
    m_spCrmLC->ForceTransactionToAbort();
    return hr;
  }

  return S_OK;
}
```

Method `IMyFileDB::UpdateBalance` records its operations similarly. The code is not shown here.

Now let's build the CRM compensator component.

The CRM component that we are building need not take any specific action in the *prepare* or *abort* phase. Consequently, we will focus on just the *commit* phase. Specifically, we will look at implementing two `ICrmCompensator` methods—`CommitRecord` and `EndCommit`.

Method `CommitRecord` decodes the BLOB and, depending on the action type, either loads the file into memory or updates the in-memory copy with the new balances from the clients, as follows:

```
STDMETHODIMP CMyFileDBCompensator::CommitRecord(
    /* [in] */ CrmLogRecordRead crmLogRec,
    /* [retval][out] */ BOOL __RPC_FAR *pfForget)
{
  *pfForget = FALSE; // don't drop the record
  BLOB& blob = crmLogRec.blobUserData;
  DBACTION* pAction =
    reinterpret_cast<DBACTION*>(blob.pBlobData);
  if (dbOpen == pAction->actionType) {
    DBACTIONOPEN* pActionOpen =
      reinterpret_cast<DBACTIONOPEN*>(pAction);
    m_bsFilePath = pActionOpen->pszFileName;

    // load the contents of the file
    USES_CONVERSION;
    CMyFile file;
    HRESULT hr = file.Open(W2T(m_bsFilePath), CMyFile::READ);
    if (FAILED(hr)) {
      return hr;
    }
    hr = file.Load(m_AccountDB);
    if (FAILED(hr)) {
      return hr;
    }
    return S_OK;
  }

  if (dbUpdate == pAction->actionType) {
    DBACTIONUPDATE* pActionUpdate =
      reinterpret_cast<DBACTIONUPDATE*>(pAction);
    long lNewBalance = pActionUpdate->lNewBalance;
    LPWSTR pwszClient = pActionUpdate->pszClient;
    MYACCOUNTDB::iterator i = m_AccountDB.find(pwszClient);
```

```
if (i == m_AccountDB.end()) {
  return E_INVALIDARG;
}
(*i).second = lNewBalance;

return S_OK;
}

return S_OK;
}
```

Method `EndCommit` saves the in-memory copy back into the file, as shown here:

```
STDMETHODIMP CMyFileDBCompensator::EndCommit(void)
{
  // Save the information back to file
  USES_CONVERSION;
  CMyFile file;
  HRESULT hr = file.Open(W2T(m_bsFilePath), CMyFile::WRITE);
  if (FAILED(hr)) {
    return hr;
  }
  file.Save(m_AccountDB);
  return S_OK;
}
```

Congratulations! You have just finished building your first CRM.

The CRM components can be installed as a server application.[1] It is recommended that both the CRM worker and the CRM compensator for a specific CRM be installed in the same application.

For CRM components it is important to turn the "Enable Compensating Resource Managers" option on (from the Component Services snap-in). Otherwise, a call to `RegisterCompensator` will result in a "catastrophic failure" error.

The CRM worker should be marked with the transaction setting as `REQUIRED` (which will automatically force `JIT Activation=TRUE` and `Synchronization= REQUIRED`). The CRM compensator, however, should be marked with the transaction as disabled, the synchronization as disabled, and the JIT turned off.

---

[1] It can also be installed as a library application. Check the online documentation for more details.

SUMMARY

In this chapter, we first looked at the issues involved while updating multiple transactional resources.

To ensure system integrity, a transaction has to support four properties: atomicity, consistency, isolation, and durability. Collectively, these properties are referred to as the ACID properties.

A resource manager (RM) is a software component that manages the durable state of a specific type of transactional resource, such as a relational database.

A distributed transaction coordinator (DTC) coordinates a transaction across multiple machines over the network. Each RM involved in a transaction is enlisted with the DTC. When the transaction completes, the DTC informs the participating RMs to either commit the changes made to their respective resources or to abort the changes. A transaction is committed using a two-phase protocol.

COM+ simplifies developing components by automatically managing a transaction. A COM+ component can indicate its interest in transactions by a configurable attribute. When such an object is activated, COM+ sets its context to deal with transactions. A participating object has to individually indicate to COM+ if its operations succeeded or failed. If any participating object indicates a failure condition, COM+ aborts the transaction. If all the participating objects vote positively, COM+ commits the transaction.

If a component is marked as requiring a transaction, COM+ automatically enforces that the component is marked as `JIT Activation=TRUE` and `Synchronization=Required`. By forcing JIT activation, a component can achieve transactional correctness without sacrificing efficiency.

Finally, we looked at the infrastructure provided by COM+ to develop a compensating resource manager.

REFERENCES

[Smi-99]   Scott Smith, "Creating and Deploying Access Solutions with the Microsoft
             Data Engine," Microsoft Development Network Online, Microsoft Corp., Jan-
             uary 1999. *http://msdn.microsoft.com/library/techart/msdedeploy.htm*
[Hen-99]   Alyssa Henry, "Migrating from DAO to ADO Using ADO with the
             Microsoft Jet Provider," Microsoft Platform SDK, Microsoft Corp., March
             1999. *http://msdn.microsoft.com/library/techart/daotoadoupdate.htm*
[Mar-00]   Davide Marcato, "Create and Customize Transactions," *Visual C++ Devel-
             opers Journal*, January 2000.

[Gri-99]   Richard Grimes, *Professional Visual C++ 6 MTS Programming*, ISBN 1-861002-3-94, Wrox Press, 1999.

[Pin-98]   Jonathan Pinnock, *Professional DCOM Application Development*, ISBN 1-861001-31-2, Wrox Press, 1998.

Message Queuing

$\mathbf{S}$o far, we have looked at how the COM/COM+ architecture helps us to build distributed and non-distributed applications. Under COM, remote method calls are based on RPC, which is a synchronous, connection-oriented communication mechanism. Any method call that is made gets blocked until a result is returned.

While a synchronous mode of operation fits the bill for many applications (and is certainly simple to use), there are cases where communicating asynchronously is more appropriate.

Microsoft Message Queue Server (MSMQ) provides an infrastructure for developing distributed components that can communicate with each other asynchronously via messages.

In this chapter, we examine the MSMQ architecture and see how highly scalable applications can be developed using MSMQ COM components. Then we examine Queued Components, a COM+ service built on top of MSMQ that simplifies application development by hiding all the details of MSMQ programming.

Those of you who are somewhat familiar with the MSMQ architecture can skip the first two sections and go straight to the section on MSMQ COM components.

MESSAGE-BASED QUEUING

The idea behind message-based queuing is very simple. As shown in Figure 9.1, a queue manager maintains a number of queues and provides the ability to create or delete queues (1). A queue stores messages addressed to it (2). An application builds a message and sends it to a specific queue (3). Some other

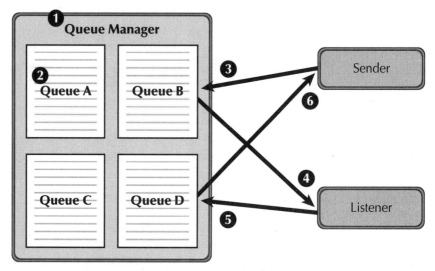

Figure 9.1   Basic message-based queuing.

part of the application (or some other application) can then read the message and remove it from the queue (4). If needed, this reader can respond by sending another type of message to some queue (5) that the original sender (or somebody else) can read (6).

The queue manager, the sender, and the receiver may all be on different machines.

As the messages flow through a separate process (the queue manager), the receiver need not be online when the messages are sent. Likewise, when the messages are being received, the sender need not be online.

What kind of data can be passed in the message?

A message is a flexible way for two applications to exchange information. The contents of the message are not fixed; a sender can send any kind of data. However, in order for the receiving application to interpret the data, the sender and the receiver must agree on the format of the message.

The Need for Queuing

Why do we need message queuing?

Consider the case when component A is communicating with another component, B, that is installed on a remote machine. Based on some user action, A sends some data to B via some interface method.

If the remote machine is unreachable (for example, if the network is down) or if the remote machine has been shut down, the interface method call will fail. To address such situations, some applications prefer storing the data locally and sending it to the remote machine whenever the machine is up and online. For such applications, it is acceptable if the data is not transferred immediately, as long as it is done "soon enough."

A separate queue manager can be used to provide this asynchronous mode of operation. Component A would then send the data to the queue manager and let the queue manager worry about storing the data and deal with any network connectivity issues.

Using a separate queue manager also addresses issues related to performance and scalability. When a client makes an interface method call, the call may take considerable time to execute, even if the server resides on the local machine. Meanwhile, the caller is blocked. As a result, other users trying to access the caller lose responsiveness (and patience). Recall the frustration you went through when the NASDAQ was down by more than 100 points and you were desperately trying to sell the stocks you owned but your brokerage system was just not responding.

Message queuing doesn't just solve the problem of a server not being online; the clients can be offline and still do some work. For example, a salesman who is on the road can enter a sales order on his laptop that is not connected to the corporate network at that time. He can later connect to the server to process the data generated during the offline operation.

Consequently, if you wish to develop an enterprise application that is scalable, responsive, and requires that all the participants need not run at the same time, you will need to use some form of message queuing.

Why Use MSMQ?

One can certainly write code to handle asynchronous communication to take care of cases when the remote machine is not reachable, perhaps by storing the data in a local database and then pushing it to the remote machine when it comes back online. However, wouldn't it be better if someone else provides this infrastructure so that you can focus on your business needs? MSMQ provides this infrastructure.

MSMQ, however, goes far beyond queuing messages. It provides a broad range of features for message-oriented applications:

1. The MSMQ architecture provides a unifying way to organize computers across a large enterprise. It groups machines in physical proximity and offers a cost-based message routing between the groups, resulting in highly scalable networking.

2. MSMQ offers exceptional security features. It is completely integrated with the Windows 2000 security environment and permits access control to be enforced on all the operations. Message senders can be authenticated to the receivers. Furthermore, messages can be encrypted for transmission across the network.

3. MSMQ provides auditing on all the operational activities.

4. For important messages, MSMQ provides guaranteed delivery.

5. MSMQ provides built-in transaction support and is completely integrated with the COM+ transaction service.

6. The architecture enables connectors to be built. A connector makes it possible to communicate with foreign (non-Windows) systems such as IBM's MQSeries and other message queuing products.

7. The data transport mechanism is very efficient. As a matter of fact, the performance difference between MSMQ and RPC is insignificant.

8. And most importantly—it provides easy-to-use COM components.[1]

MSMQ OVERVIEW

The whole MSMQ network is referred to as an enterprise. Figure 9.2 shows the logical view of an enterprise.

An enterprise might be comprised of every computer in an organization, or just those computers that wish to participate in message queuing.

Normally, an organization would have just one enterprise, although it is possible to have multiple enterprises and pass messages between them.

An enterprise is further subdivided into *sites*. A *site* consists of machines that generally have fast and reliable links between them. Often, physically close machines (such as machines within a building) are grouped together as a site. Machines within a site are connected by a LAN rather than a WAN.

A site is connected to another site by one or more links. Each link has an associated *cost* that MSMQ can use to efficiently route messages between the sites.

---

[1] MSMQ also provides a rich set of C language APIs. Our focus is on the COM components, however.

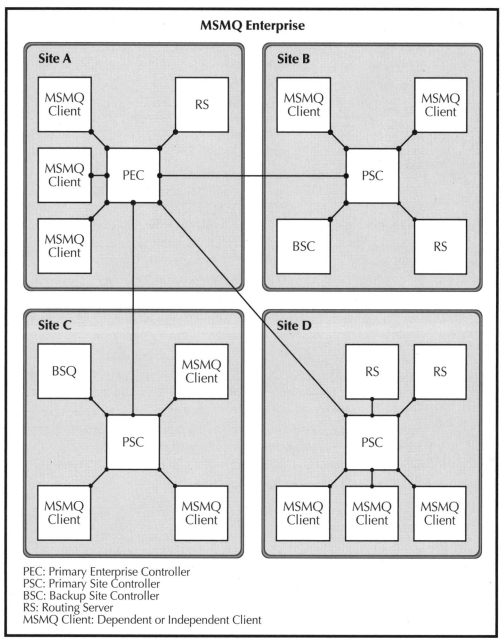

Figure 9.2 MSMQ enterprise.

An enterprise can also be logically subdivided by *connected networks* (not shown in the figure). A *connected network* defines a set of machines that communicate directly by using the same protocol (IP or IPX for example). A connected network may mirror a site, but it doesn't have to. It may span more than one site.

All the machines within an MSMQ enterprise are classified as MSMQ servers or MSMQ clients.

MSMQ Servers

An enterprise is built as a hierarchical topography of sites. One computer forms the root of this hierarchy and is designated as the *Primary Enterprise Controller* (PEC). The PEC is an MSMQ server that stores, among other things, the details of all the queue locations within an enterprise and the costs of the site links. It uses Active Directory to store this information.

Within each site, one server is designated as the *Primary Site Controller* (PSC). The PSC maintains a local copy (read-only) of PEC's database.

A site may also contain one or more *Backup Site Controllers* (BSC). When a PSC fails, the BSC temporarily fills in for the server.

A PEC is also a PSC for the site in which it is located.

An MSMQ server can also be set up as a *Connector Server*. A connector server is a bridge between MSMQ and non-Microsoft queuing systems.

Some MSMQ servers can be designated as *Routing Servers* (RS). The routing servers are responsible for passing messages through the enterprise. The PECs, PSCs, and BSCs are all de facto routing servers.

An MSMQ server can be installed only on a Windows 2000 Server or a Windows 2000 Advanced Server machine.

MSMQ Clients

MSMQ client machines are either *Dependent* or *Independent*.

A dependent client requires a reachable network connection to an MSMQ server. All the MSMQ operations are actually carried out on the server on the client's behalf.

An independent client maintains its own queues. Thus, messages can be created (and queued) even when it is disconnected from the network. Laptops and notebook computers are good candidates for being independent clients.

Queue Types

A message queue is a repository for messages. It resides on one machine only, but can be read by any machine in the enterprise, as long as the reader has read-access to the queue.

There can be many different queues on a single machine. These queues can be seen and administered through the Computer Management snap-in provided with Windows 2000. Figure 9.3 shows a snapshot of MSMQ queues present on my machine.

Queues can be divided into two groups: application queues and system queues. Application queues are created by applications. System queues are created by MSMQ.

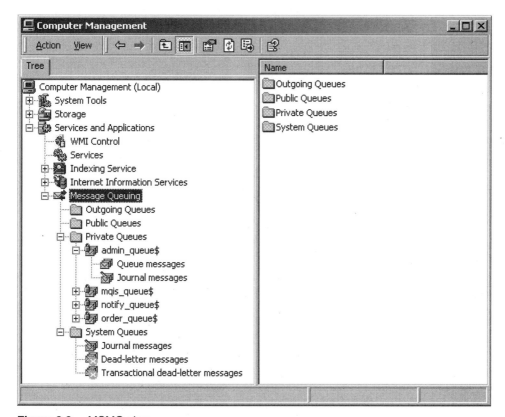

Figure 9.3   MSMQ view.

Application Queues

Application queues are created by applications. Once created, applications can send messages to and receive messages from the queue.

There are three types of application queues—message, response, and administration.

A message queue is a queue where messages are normally sent to and read by applications.

A response queue is a message queue that is used to store the return messages from the reader, primarily directed towards the sender.

Administration queues are specialized queues to hold ACK or NACK messages.

When created, an application queue can be designated as a public queue or a private queue.

A public queue is registered in the Active Directory. The properties of a public queue are replicated throughout the enterprise; any application can use MSMQ lookup APIs to locate them.

A private queue is registered on the local machine and typically cannot be seen by other applications. An application that creates a private queue must somehow distribute the location of the queue to the receiving applications.

As private queues do not use the directory services, they are faster to create, have no latency, and no replication. As creating the queue does not require the directory service to be available, the private queues are useful for offline operations.

System Queues

System queues are created by MSMQ. Only MSMQ can send or receive messages on system queues.

There are two types of system queues—journal queues and dead-letter queues.

A journal queue is automatically created each time an application queue is created. A journal queue can be used to keep track of messages sent or retrieved from its corresponding application queue. However, an application has to explicitly request journaling capability. To save a copy of a message sent from the computer, *source journaling* needs to be enabled. This is done by specifying a property when a message is being sent. If a copy of a message that is being retrieved from a queue needs to be saved, *target journaling* needs to be enabled. This is done by setting the journaling level property of the queue, either during creation time or later.

Dead-letter queues are used for storing messages that cannot be delivered. A message specifies a time limit for it to reach the queue, the default being a value LONG_LIVED. A typical value for LONG_LIVED is 90 days, but this can be adjusted by a system administrator. If a message cannot be delivered within the specified time, it is moved to the dead-letter queue.

MSMQ maintains two dead-letter queues on each MSMQ server or independent client—one for transactional messages and one for non-transactional messages.

Besides system and dead-letter queues, MSMQ also creates a third type of queue called the *outgoing queue*. These queues are used internally for routing purposes and cannot be manipulated by an application.

Enough with the overview! I am itching to write some code (and you must be too). There are some excellent references at the end of this chapter to get a better understanding of MSMQ architecture.

There is just one more thing that deserves some attention from a programming perspective: how can you identify a queue uniquely?

Queue Naming

A queue is uniquely identified by a name. Two types of names are used: a pathname and a format name.

The pathname of a queue is similar to a file name. Table 9.1 shows some examples of a pathname.

Table 9.1   Examples of a Queue Pathname

Description	Pathname
A public queue MyPubQueue on machine MyPC	MyPC\MyPubQueue
A public queue MyPubQueue on the local machine	.\MyPubQueue
A private queue MyPrivQueue on machine MyPC	MyPC\Private$\MyPrivQueue
A private queue MyPrivQueue on the local machine	.\Private$\MyPrivQueue

A pathname is represented as a string of UNICODE characters.

 The maximum length of a queue pathname is 124. Do not exceed this limit.

A format name also uniquely identifies a queue. While the pathname is used primarily to create a queue, the format name is used for most other operations on the queue, including sending and receiving messages.

When a queue is created, MSMQ generates the format name for the queue. The following VBScript code snippet creates a queue and displays its format name:

```
set qi = CreateObject ("MSMQ.MSMQQueueInfo")

' Set Queue Information
qi.PathName = ".\PRIVATE$\TestQueue"
qi.Label = "Test Queue"

' Create the queue
qi.Create

' Display the format name for the newly created queue
msgbox qi.FormatName
```

The output of the program is shown in Figure 9.4.

MSMQ defines many kinds of format names.

A *public* format name is used for public queues. When a public queue is created, MSMQ generates a queue identifier that is a GUID. This identifier can be viewed by bringing up the properties dialog box for a public queue through the Computer Management snap-in.

A public format name has the following syntax:

```
PUBLIC=QueueGUID
```

A private format name identifies a private queue. Its syntax is:

```
PRIVATE=MachineGUID\QueueNumber
```

Here, `MachineGUID` is the GUID of the machine where the private queue resides and the `QueueNumber` is a hexadecimal number generated to identify the private queue.

Figure 9.4   An example of a queue's format name.

A *direct* format name is useful to send or retrieve messages directly from a queue in one step (no routers involved), or to open a queue that is not in the current enterprise. Some examples of the direct format names are:

```
DIRECT=OS:MyPC\MyPubQueue
DIRECT=OS:MyPC\Private$\MyPrivQueue
DIRECT=TCP:15.65.87.252\MyPubQueue
```

Now let's get on with the programming. We will pick some more information as we go along.

MSMQ COM COMPONENTS

MSMQ provides ten COM components that offer the same functionality as MSMQ C language APIs, such as support for queue lookup, queue management, message management, queue administration, and transactions. Table 9.2 lists the components along with their functionality.

Table 9.2   MSMQ COM Components

Component	Functionality
MSMQApplication	Helps obtain a machine's identifier.
MSMQCoordinatedTransactionDispenser	Helps participate in a transaction.
MSMQEvent	Event handler for messages arriving at one or more queues.
MSMQMessage	Allows various properties to be set on a message and to send the message.
MSMQQuery	Allows querying the directory service for existing public queues.
MSMQQueue	Represents an open instance of an MSMQ queue. Helps traverse the messages in the open queue.
MSMQQueueInfo	Helps queue management for example, creating or opening a queue and changing a queue's properties.
MSMQQueueInfos	Represents a set of queues, typically obtained via the MSMQQuery component.
MSMQTransaction	Represents a transaction object. Provides methods for committing or terminating the transaction.
MSMQTransactionDispenser	Helps create a new MSMQ internal transaction object.

All MSMQ components support `IDispatch`-based interfaces. This enables them to be used not just from C/C++ programming languages, but also from Visual Basic, ActiveX Scripting environments (such as IE and IIS/ASP), and Java applets.

If you are using Visual C++ for developing MSMQ-based applications, you can use the *import* feature provided by the compiler as shown below:

```
#import "mqoa.dll" no_namespace
```

This will enable you to develop code in an easy-to-use syntax similar to that of Visual Basic.

Import `mqoa.dll` in your Visual C++ source code for developing MSMQ applications.

Now let's build our knowledge of the MSMQ COM components by starting with a simple example.

Sending and Receiving Messages

The following code snippet shows how to send a text string as a message:

```
#define MY_QUEUE_PATHNAME "ROS84157LAP\\MyPubQueue"

void SendMessage()
{
    // Step 1: Set properties on queue-information object
    IMSMQQueueInfoPtr spQInfo("MSMQ.MSMQQueueInfo");
    spQInfo->PathName = MY_QUEUE_PATHNAME;

    // Step 2: Open the queue for send operation
    IMSMQQueuePtr spQSend =
      spQInfo->Open(MQ_SEND_ACCESS, MQ_DENY_NONE);

    // Step 3: Set message-information properties
    IMSMQMessagePtr spQMsg("MSMQ.MSMQMessage");
    spQMsg->Label = "Test Message";
    spQMsg->Body = "This is my test message";

    // Step 4: Send the message on the queue
    spQMsg->Send(spQSend);
```

```
// Step 5: Close the queue
spQSend->Close();

::MessageBox(NULL, _T("Message Sent"),
    _T("Test Send Message"), MB_OK);
}
```

The first step is to create an MSMQQueueInfo object and set various properties on it.

A queue has over a dozen properties: creation and modification times, pathname, label, instance properties, and more. The SDK contains more information on each of these properties. The above code uses just one property, PathName, to identify the pathname of the queue.

The second step is to open the queue. The first parameter specifies how an application accesses the queue. We use MQ_SEND_ACCESS to inform MSMQ that the queue needs to be opened for sending messages. The second parameter specifies who can access the queue. For sending messages, the only valid option is MQ_DENY_NONE, which indicates that the queue is available to everyone.

If the queue gets opened successfully, it returns a pointer to interface IMSMQQueue.

The third step is to create an MSMQMessage object and set various properties on it.

A message has almost 50 properties that provides a great deal of control over how a message is sent and handled en route, how it should be encrypted, the identity of the queue to respond to, the priority of the message, and many other useful features.

The body of the message is one such property (and the most important one). Its type is a variant, thus handling a wide variety of data types.

A message can also be assigned a label, which is just a string that describes the message.

The fourth step is to send the message on the queue and the fifth step is to close the queue.

This is as simple as it gets to send a message.

Astute readers may be wondering how is it possible to open the queue without specifying the format name. It turns out that for a public queue, the MSMQ components automatically do the translation from the pathname to the format name. In order to do so, however, the client machine should be able to access the directory service, that is, it has to be online.

If the format name is available before the queue is opened, then the independent client machine need not be online. To verify this, step one of our previous code can be modified to obtain the format name before opening the queue, as follows:

```
void SendMessage()
{
    // Step 1: Set properties on queue-information object
    IMSMQQueueInfoPtr spQInfo("MSMQ.MSMQQueueInfo");
    spQInfo->PathName = MY_QUEUE_PATHNAME;
    spQInfo->Refresh();
    ::MessageBox(NULL, spQInfo->FormatName, _T("Format Name"),
      MB_OK);
    . . .
}
```

Once the message box is displayed with the format name, one can unplug the network cable. The message will still go through, that is as far as the sender program is concerned. If you check the outgoing queues (from the Computer Services snap-in) of the local machine, you will notice that the message is sitting in the outgoing queue. Once the network cable is plugged back in, the local queue manager will forward the message to the destination queue.

The receiving program code is as simple as the sending code:

```
void ReceiveMessage()
{
    // Step 1: Set properties on queue-information object
    IMSMQQueueInfoPtr spQInfo("MSMQ.MSMQQueueInfo");
    spQInfo->PathName = MY_QUEUE_PATHNAME;

    // Step 2: Open the queue for receive operation
    IMSMQQueuePtr spQRec =
      spQInfo->Open(MQ_RECEIVE_ACCESS, MQ_DENY_NONE);

    // Step 3: Attempt to receive a message
    // (with one second timeout)
    _variant_t vtReceiveTimeout = 1000L;
    IMSMQMessagePtr spRMsg = spQRec->Receive(&vtMissing,
      vtMissing, &vtMissing, &vtReceiveTimeout);

    // Step 4: Retrieve the message body and label
    if (NULL != spRMsg) {
      _bstr_t bsBody = spRMsg->Body;
      _bstr_t bsLabel = spRMsg->Label;
      ::MessageBox(NULL, bsBody, bsLabel, MB_OK);
    }else {
```

```
        ::MessageBox(NULL, _T("No messages found"),
            _T("Test Receive Message"), MB_OK);
    }

    // Step 5: Close the queue
    spQRec->Close();
}
```

Step one is similar to that of the sending program.

Step two specifies opening the queue for receiving messages by setting the first parameter to MQ_RECEIVE_ACCESS. The second parameter (the sharing mode) can be set as before to MQ_DENY_NONE. In this case, other listener applications may contend to retrieve messages from the queue. To exclusively retrieve the messages from the queue, the sharing mode can be set to MQ_DENY_RECEIVE_SHARE.

The third step is to receive the message. If the message is not already available in the queue, method Receive waits for a specific timeout interval to check if a message arrives on the queue and could be retrieved. If the timeout interval expires, the method call returns with a NULL value for the message.

The fourth parameter to the Receive call controls the timeout interval. The code in the last example shows how to set a timeout value of 1000 milliseconds. If you do not want to wait at all, you can use a timeout value of 0. A value of –1 indicates that you want to wait indefinitely. This is also the default value if a parameter is not specified.[2]

Step four displays the message and step five closes the queue.

The above example code receives messages synchronously. The Receive method call is blocked until a message arrives on the queue or a timeout occurs. While this style of coding allows you to process messages as they arrive, it also holds the calling thread hostage. An alternative technique is to use the MSMQ events mechanism. As messages arrive on the queue, MSMQ raises a notification. The application can then respond to the notification and retrieve the message. This style of asynchronous programming is discussed in the next chapter.

Guaranteed Delivery

By default, messages are designated as express messages. An express message is stored in memory until it can be delivered. Since express messages are

---

[2] Any parameter that is marked as optional in the IDL file can be specified as vtMissing under Visual C++-native COM support.

not written to disk, they offer extremely high-speed communications. However, if the machine shuts down unexpectedly, an express message is lost.

A message can be marked as recoverable. Recoverable messages are stored in a backup file at each intermediate queue until delivered to the destination queue. Thus, such messages are not lost if the machine or the queue manager crashes. However, you gain this failure protection at the expense of communication speed.

To set a message as recoverable, the `Delivery` property on the message should be specified as `MQ_MSG_DELIVERY_RECOVERABLE`. Obviously, this has to be done before the message is sent. The following code snippet illustrates the logic:

```
// Step 3: Set message-information properties
IMSMQMessagePtr spQMsg("MSMQ.MSMQMessage");
spQMsg->Label = "Test Message";
spQMsg->Body = "This is my test message";
spQMsg->Delivery = MQMSG_DELIVERY_RECOVERABLE;
```

Responding to a Message

When a client application makes a method call on a remote object, it is often desirable that it gets back some return value from the remote object. This is not a problem when DCOM/RPC is used. A method call gets blocked until the remote method is executed, and the requested values are returned as output parameters to the method call. However, when MSMQ is used, the input data is sent as a message to a queue but no output data can be obtained immediately because of the asynchronous nature of the communication.

MSMQ's solution is to ask the server to send the response back as another message.

Which queue should the response message be sent to?

When sending a message, the client application has to supply the response queue information as one of the properties, `ResponseQueue-Info`, of the message.

The following code snippet is a modified version of the earlier example. Here, the client is interested in getting the product of two numbers. The numbers are packed as one string.

```
// Step 3: Set response queue information
IMSMQQueueInfoPtr spResponseQInfo("MSMQ.MSMQQueueInfo");
spResponseQInfo->PathName = MY_RESPONSE_QUEUE_PATHNAME;
```

```
// Step 4: Set message-information properties
IMSMQMessagePtr spQMsg("MSMQ.MSMQMessage");
spQMsg->Label = "Need product of two numbers";
spQMsg->Body = "2 5";
spQMsg->Delivery = MQMSG_DELIVERY_RECOVERABLE;
spQMsg->ResponseQueueInfo = spResponseQInfo;
```

The response queue for the example had been created as a private queue.

```
#define MY_RESPONSE_QUEUE_PATHNAME ".\\Private$\\MyResponseQueue"
```

A private queue is a perfect candidate for receiving response messages; there is no need for lookup in the directory service, thereby saving processing cycles, networking bandwidth, and disk space.

Sending Objects in the Message Body

In the previous example, we had to pass two parameters into the message body. This was accomplished by packing the parameters as one string. The listener application had to parse the string to obtain the parameters.

Though packing parameters as one string and passing the string as a message is not that inconvenient programmatically, MSMQ offers a better solution: it lets you store a COM object inside the message body. The object can hold any number of parameters as needed.

Not all objects can be stored in the message body. MSMQ requires that an object support one of the two standard interfaces that are needed for persistence—IPersistStream or IPersistStorage. MSMQ can then serialize such an object into and out of a message body.

To illustrate storing objects in the message body, we will modify our earlier program. As XML is becoming very popular as a format for exchanging data, we will store an XML object in the message body. Fortunately, the XML parser that comes standard on Windows 2000, Microsoft.XMLDOM, supports the IPersistStream interface. We can use this knowledge to our benefit and pack our parameters into XML.

For the demonstration, I will load the XML tree from a file. The file format and the implementation for loading the file is shown here:

```
// File MyInput.xml
<Root>
  <First>2</First>
  <Second>5</Second>
</Root>

// Function to create XML document
MSXML::IXMLDOMDocumentPtr CreateXMLDOcument()
{
  MSXML::IXMLDOMDocumentPtr spDoc(__uuidof(MSXML::DOMDocument));
  spDoc->load("MyInput.xml");
  return spDoc;
}
```

When the message body is fetched in the listener application, MSMQ creates a new instance of the XML object and initializes the object (by calling the Load method of IPersistStream). The application can read this XML tree and compute the product of the two numbers. The implementation is shown in the following code:

```
int ComputeProduct(MSXML::IXMLDOMDocumentPtr spDoc)
{
  MSXML::IXMLDOMElementPtr spRoot = spDoc->firstChild;

  MSXML::IXMLDOMElementPtr spFirstChild =
    spRoot->selectSingleNode("First");
  long nVal1 = spFirstChild->nodeTypedValue;

  MSXML::IXMLDOMElementPtr spSecondChild =
    spRoot->selectSingleNode("Second");
  long nVal2 = spSecondChild->nodeTypedValue;

  return nVal1 * nVal2;
}
```

The following code snippet shows the relevant code for the sender and the listener applications:

```
// Sender
 ...
// Step 4: Set message-information properties
IMSMQMessagePtr spQMsg("MSMQ.MSMQMessage");
spQMsg->Label = "Need product of two numbers";
spQMsg->Body = _variant_t(static_cast<IUnknown*>(CreateXMLDOcument()));
spQMsg->Delivery = MQMSG_DELIVERY_RECOVERABLE;
spQMsg->ResponseQueueInfo = spResponseQInfo;
 ...
```

```
// Listener

// Step 4: Process the message body
int nProduct = ComputeProduct(spRMsg->Body);
...
```

The current implementation of the XML parser that ships with Windows 2000 has a bug that causes MSMQ to fail when it tries to recreate the XML document from the message body. Microsoft is investigating this problem.

As you can see, passing persistable objects is quite easy. One thing to keep in mind though: as a new instance of the class is created on the listener's machine, the DLL server that implements the class should also be registered on this machine.

For an example of passing an ADO recordset into the message body, see Ted Pattison's article, "Using Visual Basic to Integrate MSMQ into Your Distributed Applications" [Pat-99]. The article also gives an excellent introduction to using VB with MSMQ.

Transactions

Earlier in the section, we talked about the possibility of losing "express" messages. The suggested workaround is to use a "guaranteed" message by setting the Delivery property of the message to MQMSG_DELIVERY_RECOVERABLE. This ensures that the message will be delivered to the queue, at the expense of performance, however.

Even if a message is marked as recoverable, there is one more potential problem: the message could be delivered to the destination queue more than once. This could happen, for example, if the queue manager on the sender machine does not receive an acknowledgement from the queue manager on the receiving machine within a specified time. Assuming that the message is lost, the queue manager resends the message. Consequently, the listener application would process the same request multiple times.

If processing the same message multiple times is not desirable, there is yet another level of reliability that you can add—use a *transactional* queue.

A transactional queue guarantees two things:

1. Messages are not lost or duplicated, and

2. Messages inside a single transaction get delivered in the order they were sent.

If this is all that you need, and if you don't have to coordinate the transaction with any other type of resource manager (such as an SQL Server database), MSMQ offers its own internal mechanism for handling a transaction.

 The transactional attribute has to be set on the queue at the time of creation. It cannot be changed later.

MSMQ is also capable of participating in an external transaction coordinated by the DTC (DTC is covered in Chapter 8). For example, you can write a transaction that receives a request message, modifies an SQL Server database, and sends a response message. As all the three operations are part of a single transaction, the DTC enforces the ACID rules to all three operations.

The internal transaction mechanism does not use the DTC. Instead, it uses a more efficient protocol tuned for transactional messaging. Consequently, internal transactions are faster than externally coordinated transactions.

Internal Transaction

Let's extend the listener code in the earlier example to receive a request message and send two response messages, all being part of one internal transaction. The following is the revised code snippet:

```
// Step 3: Start the transaction
IMSMQTransactionDispenserPtr spTD("MSMQ.MSMQTransactionDispenser");
IMSMQTransactionPtr spTransaction = spTD->BeginTransaction();
_variant_t vtTransaction =
  static_cast<IDispatch*>(spTransaction);

// Step 4: Attempt to receive a message (with one second timeout)
_variant_t vtReceiveTimeout = 1000L;
IMSMQMessagePtr spRMsg = spQRec->Receive(&vtTransaction,
  &vtMissing, &vtMissing, &vtReceiveTimeout);

if (NULL == spRMsg) {
  ::MessageBox(NULL, _T("No messages found"),
    _T("Test Receive Message"), MB_OK);
  return;
}
```

```
// Step 5: Process the message body
int nProduct = ComputeProduct(spRMsg->Body);

// Step 6: Prepare two response messages
IMSMQMessagePtr spResponseMsg1("MSMQ.MSMQMessage");
spResponseMsg1->Label = "Returned value 1";
spResponseMsg1->Body = (long) nProduct;
spResponseMsg1->CorrelationId = spRMsg->Id;

IMSMQMessagePtr spResponseMsg2("MSMQ.MSMQMessage");
spResponseMsg2->Label = "Returned value 2";
spResponseMsg2->Body = (long) nProduct;
spResponseMsg2->CorrelationId = spRMsg->Id;

// Step 7: Open the response queue
IMSMQQueuePtr spResponseQ =
  spRMsg->ResponseQueueInfo->Open(MQ_SEND_ACCESS, MQ_DENY_NONE);

// Step 8: Send the responses
spResponseMsg1->Send(spResponseQ, &vtTransaction);
spResponseMsg2->Send(spResponseQ, &vtTransaction);

// Step 9: Commit the transaction
spTransaction->Commit();
```

To start an internal transaction, you must create a new `MSMQTransactionDispenser` object and invoke its `BeginTransaction` method. A call to `BeginTransaction` returns an `MSMQTransaction` object. You can pass a reference to this `MSMQTransaction` object in your message's `Send` or `Receive` operations. The transaction is completed when the `Commit` method is called on the `MSMQTransaction` object.

MSMQ requires that the pointer to the `IMSMQTransaction` be passed as a VARIANT to an interface method that needs it as a parameter. This VARIANT must be explicitly set to the `VT_DISPATCH` type (not `VT_UNKNOWN`). In the above code snippet, if `spTransaction` is cast to `IUnknown*` instead of `IDispatch*`, as shown below, MSMQ will fail with a "parameter-type-mismatch" error.

```
_variant_t vtTransaction =
  static_cast<IUnknown*>(spTransaction);
```

If all that is needed is to send just one message as part of an internal transaction, MSMQ provides a shortcut. You can pass `MQ_SINGLE_MESSAGE` when you call `Send`, as shown here:

```
_variant_t vtTransaction = (long) MQ_SINGLE_MESSAGE;
spQMsg->Send(spQSend, &vtTransaction);
```

 Here's one thing to keep in mind while using internal transactions: in order to obtain a higher level of concurrency, MSMQ runs at a lower isolation level than those of other resource managers such as SQL server. This may result in some oddities. For example, let's say two transactions are being run by two different listener applications. If transaction A receives the message from the queue, transaction B will see the queue as empty. If transaction A aborts later, the message will be written back to the queue. The queue was really never empty. Transaction B saw the queue as empty because it read the queue in an uncommitted state.

External Transactions

MSMQ provides a component for creating DTC-based transactions called the `MSMQCoordinatedTransactionDispenser`. Similar to the `MSQM-TransactionDispenser` component that we saw earlier, this component exposes a single method, `BeginTransaction`, which returns a transaction object. In fact, in most cases, these two components can be interchanged.

The coordinated dispenser lets you enlist other resource managers, such as SQL Server, into a transaction. Consequently, updating a database and sending a response message, for example, can be handled as one transaction. If any of the operations fail, the whole transaction fails.

Though we can use the `MSMQCoordinatedTransactionDispenser` component for creating an external transaction, let's take the benefit of COM+ services instead and simplify our code.

Recall the stock trader example that we used in the previous chapter. Once shares of a stock are bought on a client's behalf, the trade-management component requests the account-management component (synchronously) to debit the client's account by a certain amount.

It is possible that the account-management component may reside on a different machine. If there is a network outage and the machine is not reachable, the whole transaction would fail and the shares just bought would have to be returned.

Using MSMQ would be perfect for such a situation. Instead of making a DCOM method call, the trade-management component would send a message to a queue. The account-management component would listen on this queue. If a new message becomes available, it will carry out the following actions:

1. Retrieve the message from the queue.
2. Update the database, if sufficient funds are available in the account.
3. Send a response message back to the sender.

If any of these three actions fail, the transaction should be aborted. The database should be restored back to its initial state and the message should go back into the queue where it came from.

To demonstrate MSMQ external transaction support, I will create a COM component that supports an interface method called Listen. The following code snippet shows the implementation of this method:

```
STDMETHODIMP CMyListener::Listen()
{
  // Get the context state
  CComPtr<IContextState> spState;
  HRESULT hr = ::CoGetObjectContext(__uuidof(IContextState),
    (void**) &spState);
  if (FAILED(hr)) {
    return hr;
  }

  // Listen/retrive a message
  try {
    hr = ListenEx();
    if (FAILED(hr)) {
      spState->SetMyTransactionVote(TxAbort);
      return hr;
    }
  }catch(_com_error& e) {
    spState->SetMyTransactionVote(TxAbort);
    return Error((LPWSTR) e.Description(),
      __uuidof(IMyListener), e.Error());
  }

  // Commit the transaction
  spState->SetMyTransactionVote(TxCommit);
  return S_OK;
}

HRESULT CMyListener::ListenEx()
{
  // Step 1: Set properties on queue-information object
  IMSMQQueueInfoPtr spQInfo(__uuidof(MSMQQueueInfo));
  spQInfo->FormatName = MY_TRANS_QUEUE_PATHNAME;
```

```
// Step 2: Open the queue for receive operation
IMSMQQueuePtr spQRec = spQInfo->Open(MQ_RECEIVE_ACCESS,
  MQ_DENY_NONE);

// Step 3: Attempt to receive a message within one second
_variant_t vtTransaction = (long) MQ_MTS_TRANSACTION;
_variant_t vtReceiveTimeout = 1000L;
IMSMQMessagePtr spRMsg =
  spQRec->Receive(&vtTransaction, &vtMissing,
    &vtMissing, &vtReceiveTimeout);

if (NULL == spRMsg) {
  return Error(OLESTR("No messages found"),
    __uuidof(IMyListener), E_FAIL);
}

// Step 4: Process the message body
_bstr_t bsClient;
long lAmount;
ParseXMLInput(spRMsg->Body, bsClient, lAmount);

// Step 6: Open and update the database
ADOConnectionPtr spConn = OpenAccountsDB();
long lCurrentBalance = GetBalance(spConn, bsClient);
if (lCurrentBalance < lAmount) {
  return Error(_T("Not enough balance"),
    __uuidof(IMyListener), E_FAIL);
}
long lNewBalance = lCurrentBalance - lAmount;
UpdateBalance(spConn, bsClient, lNewBalance);

// Step 7: Prepare a response message
IMSMQMessagePtr spResponseMsg(__uuidof(MSMQMessage));
spResponseMsg->Label = "Updated the database";
spResponseMsg->Body = VARIANT_TRUE;
spResponseMsg->CorrelationId = spRMsg->Id;

// Step 8: Open the response queue
IMSMQQueuePtr spResponseQ =
  spRMsg->ResponseQueueInfo->Open(MQ_SEND_ACCESS,
    MQ_DENY_NONE);

// Step 8: Send the response
spResponseMsg->Send(spResponseQ, &vtTransaction);

return S_OK;
}
```

A significant portion of the code came from our example in the previous chapter; the rest came from our previous receive-message example.

The code is rather straightforward. The main method, `Listen`, either commits or aborts the transaction based on the outcome of method `ListenEx`. Method `ListenEx` receives the message, updates the database, and sends a response message back.

The only part that is somewhat different is that the transaction-type parameter passed to `Send` and `Receive` is of type `MQ_MTS_TRANSACTION`. This is just to inform these methods that they are being called as part of an external transaction.

It should be noted that a message that is sent as part of a transaction is not transmitted while the transaction is active. If the transaction aborts, the message has to be recalled as part of the rollback process. However, a message being transmitted is like an arrow leaving the bow; there is no way to recall it. Therefore, COM+ will not send the message until the transaction commits successfully.

After sending a message as part of a transaction, do not wait for a response message within the transaction. You will not get the response message while the transaction is active.

At this point, we should be reasonably comfortable with MSMQ's programming model.

Though MSMQ COM components offer a rich set of features, one has to be careful with some nasty details during implementation. Moreover, programming with MSMQ (or any other queuing architecture) requires a different frame of mind than what we are generally used to. Wouldn't it be nice if someone or something could hide the nasty details of MSMQ programming from you, but still let you enjoy the benefits of MSMQ?

The folks at Microsoft COM+ design team made this magic happen by providing a service called Queued Components (QC).

QUEUED COMPONENTS

A queued component looks and feels like any other COM component that you develop. A client application makes method calls on a queued object much like any other COM object, except that the infrastructure can queue the method calls.

Developing queued components is just as easy. You just write a COM component in the way you are used to, with whatever tools you like (ATL,

VB, etc.). There are some relatively minor restrictions on the interface method, such as it cannot have [out] parameters. Next, install the component as a COM+ application, marking its interfaces as queued via the Component Services snap-in. This is all you have to do. COM+ will take care of listening for incoming MSMQ messages from clients and calling your component's methods when they arrive.

Before we get into the architectural details, let's see the queued components in action.

A Simple Phone Book Example

Let's create a simple phone book application. The application stores phone numbers of your friends in an MSDE database. Let's name the database as PhonebookDB. This database contains a table, Friends, that has three columns—LastName, FirstName, and PhoneNumber. A friend is identified by his last name and first name.

The following SQL statements can be used to create the database (see Chapter 8 on how to execute these statements):

```
create database PhoneBookDB
go
use PhoneBookDB
create table Friends (
      [LastName] varchar (15) NOT NULL,
      [FirstName] varchar (15) NOT NULL,
      [PhoneNumber] varchar (15) NOT NULL)
create unique index MyFriend on Friends([LastName], [FirstName])
go
quit
```

Let's develop a component that a client can use to enter the phone number. The following is the VBScript use case:

```
Set phoneEntry = CreateObject("PhoneBook.MyPhoneEntry")
phoneEntry.FirstName = "Pradeep"
phoneEntry.LastName = "Tapadiya"
phoneEntry.PhoneNumber = "(222) 333-4444"
phoneEntry.Update
MsgBox "Added a new person to the hit-list"
```

Using the ATL wizard, I generated the component code and added the requisite logic. The code can be found on the CD. The following code snippet is relevant to our discussion:

```
STDMETHODIMP CMyPhoneEntry::put_FirstName(BSTR newVal)
{
  m_bsFirstName = newVal;
  return S_OK;
}

STDMETHODIMP CMyPhoneEntry::put_LastName(BSTR newVal)
{
  m_bsLastName = newVal;
  return S_OK;
}
STDMETHODIMP CMyPhoneEntry::put_PhoneNumber(BSTR newVal)
{
  m_bsPhoneNumber = newVal;
  return S_OK;
}

STDMETHODIMP CMyPhoneEntry::Update()
{
  try {
    ADOConnectionPtr spConn = OpenPhoneBookDB();
    InsertEntry(spConn, m_bsLastName, m_bsFirstName,
      m_bsPhoneNumber);
  }catch(_com_error& e) {
    return Error((LPCWSTR) e.Description(),
      __uuidof(IMyPhoneEntry), E_FAIL);
  }

  return S_OK;
}
```

This code is very simple. Observe that we do not have a single line of code that deals with MSMQ programming.

Let's see how we can configure this component to take advantage of MSMQ.

1. Using the Component Services snap-in, create a new COM+ *server* application. I will call it "My Phonebook Application."
2. From the Queuing tab, mark the application as "*Queued*" and "*Listen,*" as shown in Figure 9.5.
3. Add the PhoneBook component to this application.
4. Mark the interface IMyPhoneEntry of this component as "*Queued,*" as shown in Figure 9.6.

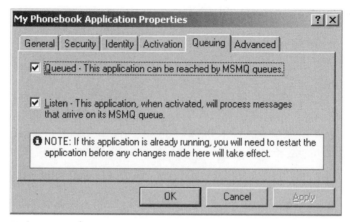

Figure 9.5   Queuing options.

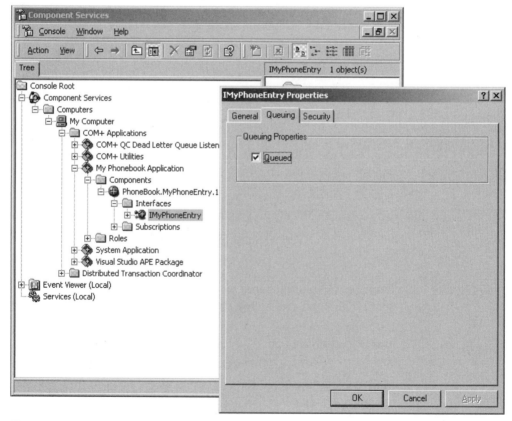

Figure 9.6   Configuring an interface for queuing.

Only *server* applications can avail COM+ queuing services.

When the application is marked as Queued, COM+ creates message queues for the use of any queued components that may be added to the application. One public queue and six private queues are created. A snapshot of the queues created for "My Phonebook Application" is shown in Figure 9.7. When the queue is also marked as Listen, it tells COM+ that, when the application is activated, it should activate a listener service to receive incoming calls on the public queue.

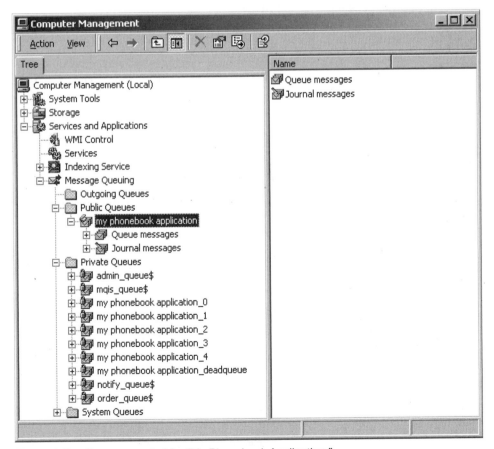

Figure 9.7   Queues created for "My Phonebook Application."

When an interface is marked as `Queued`, COM+ expects to receive messages for that interface.

For our demonstration, I will run the client script from a machine other than the one that has the queued component installed.

Typically, a `VBScript` client code activates an object using `CreateObject` (`CoCreateInstance` in C++). For a queued component, however, the activation is slightly different. It uses a VB function `GetObject` (`CoGetObject` in C++). This function takes a textual string and obtains the specified object.[3] The format of the text string for obtaining a queued component is as follows:

```
"queue:ComputerName=MachineName/new:ProgId"
```

If the component is running on the local machine, the `ComputerName` field can be omitted, as shown here:

```
"queue:/new:ProgId"
```

For our experiment, PVDEV is the machine where the component will be executed. PVTEST is the machine where the client script will be executed. Note that, in order to use queued component, the application has to be installed on both machines.

The following is our revised client script:

```
Set phoneEntry = _

GetObject("queue:ComputerName=PVDEV/new:PhoneBook.MyPhon
eEntry")
phoneEntry.FirstName = "Pradeep"
phoneEntry.LastName = "Tapadiya"
phoneEntry.PhoneNumber = "(222) 333-4444"
phoneEntry.Update
MsgBox "Added a new person to the hit-list"
```

Before we run our test, let's check the `PhonebookDB` database (using `osql.exe`). The database should currently have no records.

---

[3] `CoGetObject` converts the passed string into a moniker and then binds to the object identified by the moniker. See MSDN documentation for monikers.

```
1> use PhonebookDB
2> go
1> select * from Friends
2> go
 LastName          FirstName         PhoneNumber
 --------------    --------------    --------------

(0 rows affected)
1>
```

Now I will unplug the network cable for the PVDEV machine and execute the script.

The script executed just fine, even though PVDEV was not reachable.

If you check the outgoing queues on PVTEST, you will notice that there is a message sitting under a queue named "PVDEV\My Phonebook Application."

Let's plug the network cable back in.

Shortly after you check the public queue, "My Phonebook Application" on PVDEV, you will see that a message is sitting in the queue. The message has moved from the outgoing queue of PVTEST to the public queue of PVDEV.

On PVDEV, from the Component Services snap-in, right-click on "My Phonebook Application" and select the start menu item.

Soon the message from the public queue will disappear.

Let's check the database.

```
1> select * from Friends
2> go
 LastName          FirstName         PhoneNumber
 --------------    --------------    --------------
 Tapadiya          Pradeep           (222) 333-4444

(1 row affected)
1>
```

Voila!

We managed to work with a queued component even when the server machine was not available, and without touching the MSMQ API.

Let's see how this magic happened!

Queued Component Architecture

Recall from Chapter 5 that under classic DCOM, when a client activates a remote object, the client gets connected to a proxy. When a method call is made on the proxy, the data is marshaled and sent over the RPC channel to the stub where the data gets unmarshaled and passed to the actual object's method. The whole operation is synchronous and is depicted in Figure 9.8.

With a queued component, the communication between the client and the server is handled with MSMQ instead, as shown in Figure 9.9.

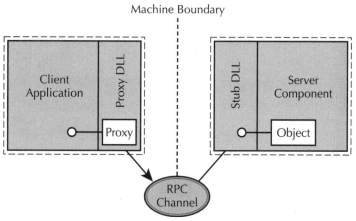

Figure 9.8   Classic DCOM using RPC.

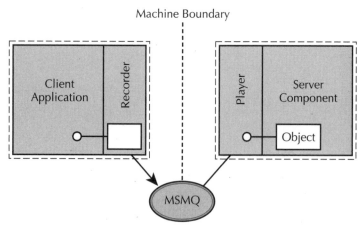

Figure 9.9   Queued component using MSMQ.

When a client activates a queued object, the client is not connected to the actual object but to a queued component recorder. The recorder examines the server component's type library to obtain the type of interfaces supported by the object, the methods and properties each interface contains, and the parameters for each method. The recorder then exposes the interfaces of the actual object to the client. The client makes method calls in the usual manner, but they get recorded on the client side. When the client deactivates the object, the recorder packages all the method calls made, along with the call parameters, into one MSMQ message, and sends it to the application-specific public queue on the destination machine.

COM+ provides a utility component called `QC.ListenerHelper`. When the server application is launched,[4] COM+ activates the `QC.ListenerHelper` object. This object listens to the public queue specific to the application, retrieves the message, and passes it to the queued component player. The player invokes the actual server component and makes the same method calls in the order they were recorded.

If the destination machine is not reachable, the message gets stored in the outgoing queue of the local machine and is forwarded whenever the connection becomes available. As MSMQ uses a transacted protocol for store-and-forward messages, the messages will not be lost.

Note that QC abstracts the details of MSMQ programming; neither the client developer nor the component developer deals with MSMQ directly.

The higher level of abstraction provided by QC has several advantages:

1. There is no need to learn the MSMQ programming model.
2. Developing a queued component is no different than developing a typical COM component.
3. The component can be used either synchronously (via `CoCreateInstance`, for example) or asynchronously (using `CoGetObject`).

Note that the recorder flushes its call buffer only when the object is deactivated. There is no way to forcibly flush the call buffer without deactivating the object. However, by using a queued component, the client is saying that it doesn't really care exactly when the call gets processed. Consequently, flushing the buffer is not a concern for QC developers.

---

[4] A server application can be launched either from the Component Services snap-in or programmatically through the Catalog Manager interfaces.

Designing queued components has one restriction: any interface that needs to be queued should be unidirectional, that is, it cannot have any method with [out] or [in, out] parameters. Bidirectional interfaces can only be used with synchronous COM applications, as the method calls get blocked until a result is returned. The asynchronous nature of QC makes it impossible to wait for a result; you do not know when the server will receive (and respond to) your request.

How can we get a response back from the server?

Getting a Response

An obvious solution is to get the response back asynchronously as well. Essentially, the server becomes the client.

To accomplish this, the server object has to get enough information so that it can construct the display name that identifies the object to be created. Recall that a queued component is created using the following syntax:

```
"queue:ComputerName=MachineName/new:ProgId"
```

All that is needed then is the name of the client's machine and the PROGID of the component interested in receiving the response (as with MSMQ, the component receiving the response need not be the same as the component originating the response).

One way to specify this information is for the client to provide its local machine name and the PROGID as parameters to some method calls on the original QC interface. This gives the server the ability to construct the display name and activate the object using CoGetObject.

To demonstrate this, let's extend our earlier example. We will add two new methods to the original interface.[5] The first method, Response, is the response the client expects to receive. It passes a string as a parameter describing the result of the update operation. The implementation is shown in the following code:

```
STDMETHODIMP CMyPhoneEntry::Response(BSTR bsDesc)
{
  USES_CONVERSION;
  ::MessageBox(NULL, W2T(bsDesc), _T("PhoneBook"),
MB_OK);

  return S_OK;
}
```

[5] The author believes that an interface is immutable only after it leaves his lab.

Note that I am displaying a message box within a method call. As I am running the application as the interactive user, the message box window would pop up in the interactive window station so that I could see it. In general, it is not a good idea to mix user-interface code with non-user-interface code.

The second method, `UpdateWithResponse`, is a replacement for our original `Update` method. It takes a machine name as a parameter. The PROGID is hard-coded for the demonstration. The implementation of `UpdateWithResponse` is shown in the following code:

```
STDMETHODIMP CMyPhoneEntry::UpdateWithResponse(
  BSTR bsClientMachine)
{
  CComBSTR bsDesc;
  try {
    ADOConnectionPtr spConn = OpenPhoneBookDB();
    InsertEntry(spConn, m_bsLastName, m_bsFirstName,
      m_bsPhoneNumber);
    bsDesc = "Added entry: ";
  }catch(_com_error& e) {
    bsDesc = static_cast<LPCWSTR>(e.Description());
  }

  bsDesc += m_bsFirstName;
  bsDesc += " ";
  bsDesc += m_bsLastName;

  // Construct display name to identify the object
  CComBSTR bsDisplayName = "queue:ComputerName=";
  bsDisplayName += bsClientMachine;
  bsDisplayName += "/new:PhoneBook.MyPhoneEntry";

  CComPtr<IMyPhoneEntry> spPhoneEntry;
  HRESULT hr = ::CoGetObject(bsDisplayName, NULL,
    __uuidof(IMyPhoneEntry), (void**) &spPhoneEntry);
  if (FAILED(hr)) {
    return hr;
  }
  spPhoneEntry->Response(bsDesc);
  return S_OK;
}
```

After updating the database, the server object constructs the string describing the result of the operation, constructs the display name to identify the object, activates the object, and invokes the `Response` method on it.

This code should also give you an idea of how to activate a queued component from C++.

The original `VBScript` client code has to be slightly modified to use the newly added method.

```
Set phoneEntry = _
GetObject("queue:ComputerName=PVDEV/new:PhoneBook.MyPhoneEntry")
phoneEntry.FirstName = "Pradeep"
phoneEntry.LastName = "Tapadiya"
phoneEntry.PhoneNumber = "(222) 333-4444"
phoneEntry.UpdateWithResponse "PVTEST"
```

The client machine in my experiment is PVTEST. When this script was executed from PVTEST, a message box popped up on the screen after a few seconds that said the database could not be updated because a record with the index (`FirstName+LastName`) already exists. This error message is what was expected. Our earlier experiment had already added the specific record to the database.

Transaction Support

The transaction support that is available in the underlying MSMQ mechanism is also available to QC.

Between the client and the recorder

The recorder takes the same attributes as the client. If the client creates a queued component within the context of an existing transaction, the transaction is propagated to the recorder. When the recorder is deactivated, it hands over the message to MSMQ in the context of the transaction. MSMQ buffers the message pending the outcome of the transaction. If the transaction commits, MSMQ transmits the message to the recipient. If the transaction aborts, MSMQ discards the message; the server never gets the recorded COM calls.

On the server side

QC uses the transactions on the server side as well. If the component is marked as transactional, the QC Listener helper on the server side becomes the root of the transaction. If a server-side operation aborts for some reason, the message that triggered it is put back on the queue for a later retry.

There is a problem associated with putting the message back into the queue for a later retry, however; some messages may cause a transaction to abort repeatedly. If such a message is put back into the queue, the next time the component dequeues the message the transaction will abort and the message will go back to the queue. Other messages in the queue would never get retrieved. One bad message may just hang up the whole application. This is unacceptable.

In order to solve this problem, QC moves the message to a different queue so that it doesn't block other messages. Now you know why COM+ created six private queues when the application was marked as `Queued`. An aborted message moves to queue 0 and moves upwards as future retries continue to fail. Higher numbers indicate longer time intervals between the retries. After five attempts (that brings the message to queue 4), the message is moved to the private queue called the `DeadQueue`, from which it will not be retried.

Once in a while, the system administrators should check the dead queue, fix the cause of failures, and move the message back to a lower queue. Alternatively, you can write some administrative code to periodically check this queue and take action.

Using Non-Transactional Queues

Transactional messages in general are slow. You get robustness at the cost of performance.

When an application is marked as queued, the default behavior of COM+ is to create the application-specific queues as transactional. Recall that the transactional attribute on a queue cannot be changed once the queue is created.

If you know that the components you have do not require transactions, there is a way to make the queues non-transactional. Before installing the application, manually create the queues (as non-transactional). Just remember to use the correct queue names. Install the application after creating the queues. As the queues already exist, COM+ will just reuse them. All of the QC's internal operations will then use the non-transactional queues and execute somewhat faster.

SUMMARY

The first part of the chapter provided an overview of MSMQ.

MSMQ facilitates asynchronous communication between two software programs by way of messages. A message can contain any data, including persistable objects. The sender and the receiver have to agree on the format.

An MSMQ enterprise is built as a hierarchical topography of sites. An MSMQ server can be installed in a number of ways including a Primary Enterprise Controller, a Primary Site Controller, a Connecter server, a Routing server, etc.

An MSMQ client could be installed to be dependent or independent.

An MSMQ message can be sent as *express* or *guaranteed*. An MSMQ message can also participate in a transaction internally, as well as one coordinated externally.

In the first part of the chapter, we also observed how to develop scalable applications using MSMQ components.

In the second part of the chapter, we looked at Queued Components (QC), a service provided by COM+ that uses the MSMQ infrastructure for asynchronous communication but hides the details of MSMQ programming from the developers. We looked at the QC architecture and examined ways to respond to messages, and participate in transactions.

For more information on MSMQ and QC, I have included some references. The MSDN library is also a good reference source (and the documentation keeps on getting better).

REFERENCES

[Pin-98]   Jonathan Pinnock, *Professional DCOM Application Development*, ISBN 1-861001-31-2, Wrox Press, 1998.

[Pat-99]   Ted Pattison, "Using Visual Basic to Integrate MSMQ into Your Distributed Applications," *Microsoft Systems Journal*, vol. 14, no. 5, May 1999. *http://msdn.microsoft.com/library/periodic/period99/msmq.htm*

[Dic-98]   Alan Dickman, *Designing Applications with MSMQ—Message Queuing for Developers,* ISBN 0-201-32581-0, Addison Wesley, August 1998.

[Cha-98]   David Chappell, "Microsoft Message Queue Is a Fast, Efficient Choice for Your Distributed Applications," *Microsoft Systems Journal*, vol. 13, no. 7, July 1998. *http://msdn.microsoft.com/library/periodic/period98/messagequeue.htm*

[Buk-98]   Mike Bukovec and Dick Dievendroff, "Use MSMQ and MTS to Simplify the Building of Transactional Applications," *Microsoft Systems Journal*, vol. 13, no. 7, July 1998. *http://msdn.microsoft.com/library/periodic/period98/mtsmsmq.htm*

[Pla-99]   David Platt, "Building a Store-and-Forward Mechanism with Windows 2000 Queued Components," *Microsoft Systems Journal*, vol. 14, no. 6, June 1999. *http://msdn.microsoft.com/library/periodic/period99/queued.htm*

[Blu-98]   William Blum, "Using Microsoft Message Queue Server," *Windows Developer's Journal*, vol. 9, no. 11, November 1998.

Events

One of the key challenges in distributed computing is to provide a mechanism that enables interested parties to receive notification regarding changes to data. In this chapter, we will look at the infrastructure provided by COM+ to set up clients to receive notifications.

INTRODUCTION

Notifying interested parties of changes to data is a very common requirement under distributed computing. A stock ticker program needs to notify clients with a change in stock price; a computer monitoring program needs to inform the administrators of the status of the system; a virus detection program needs to warn the computer user if a virus is detected; a medical monitoring program needs to page a doctor if a patient requires immediate attention, and so on.

Instead of referring to the interested parties as clients, we will use a different terminology. We will call them subscribers; programs that are interested in receiving information. Likewise, programs that provide such information will be referred to as publishers. As we will see shortly, when a publisher notifies a subscriber of a change in some data, the traditional role of a COM client and a COM server reverses temporarily; the COM client becomes a COM server and the COM server becomes a COM client. Using the terms publishers and subscribers will keep us sane.

So the publisher detects the changes the subscriber is interested in, but how does the subscriber find out from the publisher when a change takes place? The simplest approach is for the subscriber to poll the publisher every so often, similar to you refreshing a web page periodically to get the latest stock quotes. Under COM terminology, the subscriber would obtain an interface from the publisher object and periodically call a method on that interface to see if any changes had taken place. The following code illustrates this approach:

```
while(true) {
  bool bMarketClosed = spStockWatcher->IsMarketClosed();
  if (bMarketClosed) {
    break; // time for dinner.
  }
  currentQuote = spStockWatcher->GetQuote("MSFT");
  ...
}
```

Such polling interaction between a subscriber and a publisher is depicted in Figure 10.1.

While this strategy is simple to implement, it is a terrible idea for several reasons:

- **Inefficient resource utilization:** If the data doesn't change that often, the subscriber wastes an enormous amount of CPU cycles asking for the same data and the publisher wastes enormous time replying with the same answer. Even worse is wasting network bandwidth when the publisher resides on a remote machine—possibly on the other side of the country.
- **Time lag between the occurrence of the event and the receiving of data:** Polling involves some inevitable amount of latency between the time the change occurs and the time the subscriber gets around to polling for it. This latency is non-deterministic—it varies from one occurrence to another.

A better approach would be for the publisher to initiate the notification process when it detects the data has changed. Instead of you refreshing the stock quote web page periodically, let the changed data come to you.

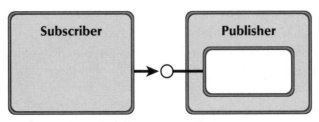

Figure 10.1   Subscriber polls for data.

Under COM terminology, a publisher-initiated notification process is referred to as *firing* an event.

COM offers various degrees of support to implement firing and receiving an event. You choose a technique depending upon your needs.

We need a simple example to demonstrate these techniques. Our example will be a component that provides updated stock prices to interested applications.[1]

Let's start dissecting these techniques!

TIGHTLY COUPLED EVENTS (TCEs)

Under this technique, the subscriber knows exactly which publisher to request notification from. During run time, the subscriber enlists itself with the publisher to receive events, and un-enlists itself when it is no longer interested in receiving the events.

In order for this technique to work, the publisher and the subscriber need to agree upon a predefined interface to be used for communication. The subscriber provides the publisher with an object that implements this interface, and the publisher calls a method on it when something interesting happens.

This bidirectional communication between the publisher and the subscriber is illustrated in Figure 10.2.

The agreed-upon predefined interface is referred to as the *source* or the *outgoing* interface and the object the subscriber provides to the publisher is called the *sink* object.

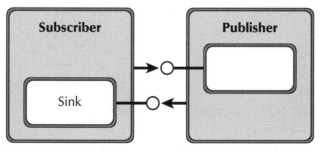

Figure 10.2   Interaction in a tightly coupled event system.

---

[1] Almost all of the examples ever published on COM/COM+ events seem to deal with changes in stock prices. This leads me to believe that developers seem to understand the movement in stock prices better than any other changes.

For our example, we will define a *source* interface, `IStockPriceUp-date`, that can be used to inform a subscriber if the price of a stock has changed. The following is the definition of this interface:

```
interface IStockPriceUpdate : IUnknown
{
  HRESULT NewQuote([in] BSTR bsSymbol, [in] double dPrice);
};
```

Each time the price of a stock changes, the publisher is expected to call the `NewQuote` method on this interface, passing in as arguments the symbol of the stock and its current price.

Now let's look at a commonly used technique for implementing a tightly coupled event system called the *connection point*.

Connection Points

The *connection point* technique is also referred to as the connectible object technique, and is used in many Microsoft COM-based technologies. In particular, ActiveX controls, ActiveX scripting engines, and VB class modules use the connectible object technique to fire events.

To understand the connection point technique, the following analogy would be helpful.

You are a stock trader who just bought a pager and are interested in receiving stock quotes on the pager. There are many brokerage firms that would provide their clients with stock quotes. However, not all of them provide paging service. Some of them use e-mail as the means to inform their clients. Some others probably provide both services. It is now up to you to ensure that the brokerage firm you choose provides the paging service. This is how your conversation with the broker would go:

You: Do you have any service to inform the clients of a stock price change?

Broker: Yes.

You: Is paging a service that you provide?

Broker: Yes.

You: OK. Here is my pager number. Put me on the list and give me a tracking number that I can use later in case I wish to cancel the paging service.

This is pretty much how connection points work under COM. A subscriber asks the publisher if it supports the connection point mechanism by querying for a standard COM interface `IConnectionPointContainer`, as shown here:

```
CComPtr<IConnectionPointContainer> spCPC;
hr = spMyBroker->QueryInterface(
   __uuidof(IConnectionPointContainer), (void**) &spCPC);
```

Interface IConnectionPointContainer supports a method, FindConnectionPoint, that can be used to check if the object supports the connection point of a specific interface type. On success, FindConnectionPoint returns a pointer to another standard interface IConnectionPoint, as shown here:

```
CComPtr<IConnectionPoint> spCP;
hr = spCPC->FindConnectionPoint(
   __uuidof(IStockPriceUpdate), &spCP);
```

At this point, the subscriber is ready to create a sink object. The following code fragment shows an implementation of the outgoing interface IStockPriceUpdate:

```
class CMySink :
  public IStockPriceUpdate,
  public CComObjectRoot
{
public:

BEGIN_COM_MAP(CMySink)
  COM_INTERFACE_ENTRY(IStockPriceUpdate)
END_COM_MAP()

  STDMETHODIMP NewQuote(BSTR bsSymbol, double dPrice)
  {
    ...
  }
};
```

Interface IConnectionPoint supports a method, Advise, that can be used to enlist a sink object. On success, Advise returns a cookie (the tracking number), as shown here:

```
CComPtr<CComObject<CMySink> > spSink;
hr = CComObject<CMySink>::CreateInstance(&spSink);
spSink->InternalAddRef();
DWORD dwCookie;
hr = spCP->Advise(spSink, &dwCookie);
```

The subscriber is now ready to receive the data. Whenever the price of a stock changes, the publisher can call the NewQuote method for all the enlisted objects.

If the subscriber is no longer interested in receiving the data, it can call Unadvise method on the IConnectionPoint interface, passing the cookie (the tracking number) as a parameter, as shown here:

```
hr = spCP->Unadvise(dwCookie);
```

The pointers to IConnectionPointContainer and IConnection-Point can be released after Advise has been called. They can be recreated whenever needed.

If you observe the subscriber code, it should be obvious that the connection point is not an efficient mechanism. It takes as many as five round trips to enlist and un-enlist the sink object.[2] It should be noted that a connection point is not the only way to establish a bi-directional communication. All that is needed is for the subscriber to hand out a sink object to the publisher. Whenever possible, one should look for a simpler mechanism for the subscriber to hand out the sink object to the publisher.

The implementation of the publisher code requires a little more work. Obviously, the publisher should support the IConnectionPointContainer interface. It should also implement a mechanism to manage a list of sink objects, and should provide the logic to detect the change in data and to fire the events. Fortunately, ATL wizard makes it easy to generate the mundane connection point code. The detection of data change is specific to each component and has to be implemented by the developer. The broker example implementation generates some fake data and fires an event every five seconds apart. The source can be found on the CD.

Beware of ATL-generated connection point code. It is not thread-safe. It works fine for an apartment-threaded publisher. For a non-STA object or if the events need to be fired from a worker thread, you not only have to provide the thread-safe logic but also the code to marshal the sink interface to the worker thread. Using GIT (see Chapter 6) would be a good way to achieve both thread-safety as well as marshaling.

---

[2] The subscriber's code shows only four round trips. The fifth round trip comes from the publisher. The publisher receives the sink object as IUnknown reference from the Advise method. Therefore, the publisher ends up calling QueryInterface on the sink object to receive the typed event interface.

The outgoing interface that was defined for our example is suitable for typed languages. Untyped languages such as VBScript can work only with dispatch interfaces. If the interface is defined as *dual*, it should work from an ActiveX Script supported environment, such as Microsoft Internet Explorer (IE). However, marking a sink interface as *dual* is a problem for the publisher. Should the publisher fire events on the custom interface or on the dispatch interface? This issue is discussed at length in "Effective COM" [Box-98].

Under no clear guidelines, a typical implementation ends up using the IDispatch::Invoke mechanism. Therefore, a *dual* interface as an outgoing interface doesn't serve any real purpose. A pure dispatch interface (dispinterface) is more preferable as an outgoing interface.

For those interested, I have included on the CD a modified version of the sample that uses a dispinterface-based outgoing interface.

Receiving Messages with MSMQ Events

Recall from Chapter 9 that the listener sample received messages synchronously. The Receive method on the IMSMQQueue interface is a blocking call. It doesn't return until it receives a message or a timeout occurs. While this style of coding allows you to process messages as they arrive, it also holds the calling thread hostage.

To support receiving messages asynchronously, MSMQ supports connection points. It defines the following outgoing interface:

```
dispinterface _DMSMQEventEvents {
properties:
methods:
   [id(0)] void Arrived([in] IDispatch* Queue, [in] long Cursor);
   [id(1)] void ArrivedError([in] IDispatch* Queue,
     [in] long ErrorCode, [in] long Cursor);
};
```

Some programming environments such as VB and ActiveX script engines are capable of creating a sink object based on the definition of the *source* interface. The interface should be present in the publisher's type library.

A type library defines many interfaces. How would one know which of the interfaces is the *source* interface?

To address this problem, IDL supports an attribute called *source* that can be set on an interface. For instance, MSMQ defines a publisher class, MSMQEvent, to describe outgoing asynchronous events. The class definition is shown here:

```
[uuid(D7D6E07A-DCCD-11D0-AA4B-0060970DEBAE)]
coclass MSMQEvent {
  interface IMSMQEvent;

  ...
  [default, source] dispinterface _DMSMQEventEvents;
};
```

Let's see how we can implement an MSMQ event subscriber.

Though we can use C++ language to develop the code, let's use VBScript for a change. After all, dispinterface is meant for late-bound languages such as this.

Since the version of IE that ships with Windows 2000 supports VBScript, we will develop and host a web page in IE. To have some fun, we will develop a DHTML-based web page instead of the more traditional HTML web page. For those not familiar with DHTML, here is a little background. When a portion of a web page needs updating, an HTML-based web page requires the whole page to be refreshed. DHTML is an extension of HTML. Under DHTML, only a section of the web page can be updated, thus reducing the flicker on the screen. *Why is it fun to use DHTML?* You would know if you are a programmer.

To activate an object within IE, an HTML tag called OBJECT needs to be used, as shown here:

```
<OBJECT VIEWASTEXT ID=MyRequestEvent
  CLASSID="clsid:D7D6E07A-DCCD-11D0-AA4B-0060970DEBAE">
</OBJECT>
```

The CLSID of the component is specified within the OBJECT scope. In the above code, the CLSID is that of the MSMQ event class described earlier.

When IE parses this tag, it activates the MSMQ object. This object is referred to by the name MyRequestEvent anywhere in the HTML document.

Based on the type library, IE also recognizes that the object supports firing events. IE then parses the rest of the document to see if either the MyRequestEvent_Arrived or MyRequestEvent_ArrivedError subroutines have been defined (recall that Arrived and ArrivedError are the two methods available on the *source* interface). If any of the methods are found, IE creates a sink and sets up the connection point. When the publisher invokes a method on the source interface, IE is capable of receiving the event and invoking the appropriate VBScript subroutine.

The main body of the DHTML page is shown here:

```
<BODY>
  <H2>Receive MSMQ messages</H2>
  <INPUT TYPE="button" VALUE="Start"
ID=MyStartButton><BR/><BR/>
  <DIV ID=MyDisplayLine></DIV>
</BODY>
```

For those unfamiliar with DHTML, the following VBScript line of code would update just the section identified as `MyDisplayLine`.

```
MyDisplayLine.innerText = "Hello World"
```

The DHTML body above sets the browser environment that, when the user clicks the "Start" button, a user-defined VBScript function, `MyStart-Button_OnClick`, will be called. Our implementation of this method will enable receiving MSMQ messages, as follows:

```
Sub MyStartButton_onclick
  MyStartButton.disabled = true 'Start can be clicked just once
  set MyQueueInfo = CreateObject("MSMQ.MSMQQueueInfo")
  MyQueueInfo.PathName = ".\MyPubQueue"
  Set MyRequestQueue = MyQueueInfo.Open(1, 0)
  MyRequestQueue.EnableNotification MyRequestEvent
  MyDisplayLine.innerText = "Waiting for messages..."
End Sub
```

The logic of opening an MSMQ queue is similar to the one we saw in Chapter 9.

After opening the queue, we call the `EnableNotification` method on the `IMSMQQueue` interface (as opposed to the `Receive` method we called in the earlier samples). As the name indicates, `EnableNotification` turns on asynchronous messaging. The method takes the sink object as a parameter.

All that is left is to implement the logic to receive and process the message:

```
Sub MyRequestEvent_Arrived(ByVal queue, ByVal Cursor)
  Dim MyMsg
  Set MyMsg = queue.Receive(0)
  if Not (MyMsg is Nothing) then
    MyDisplayLine.innerText = MyMsg.Body
  end if
  queue.EnableNotification MyRequestEvent
End Sub
```

When the message arrives, we use our familiar `Receive` method to retrieve the message. Note that the timeout value we specify is zero milliseconds. Since we were notified that a message has arrived, the message will most likely be there in the queue and therefore we don't really need to wait. However, there is a distinct possibility that someone else has received the message. Therefore, we explicitly check to see if the message is not NULL before updating the display.

Also note that the above code calls `EnableNotification` every time an `Arrived` event is received. This is required because MSMQ sets up a notification only for the next message when `EnableNotification` is called. To continue receiving ongoing notifications, you must keep calling `EnableNotification` each time you process the `Arrived` event.

Also note that once `EnableNotification` is set, MSMQ raises events for messages already present in the queue as well as newly arrived messages.

Loosely Coupled Events (LCEs)

While the TCE techniques are quite useful, they have some drawbacks in certain scenarios:

- The lifetime of the publisher and the subscriber is tightly coupled. The subscriber has to be running and connected to the publisher to receive the events. This is not usually a problem for subscribers such as ActiveX controls, which has no reason to receive events outside the lifetime of their containers. However, in an enterprise system, forcing the subscriber to run at all times doesn't scale well.

- The TCE techniques were developed without regard to distributed environments. A technique such as connection points is not very efficient in terms of the number of round trips required to establish and break down the connection. More importantly, there is no support in place to guarantee a persistent connection, as the only binding between the entities is the exchanged interface pointer.

- Under TCE, there is no mechanism in place to filter events. For instance, in the earlier stock price events example, a subscriber ends up getting the price changes for all the stocks even though the subscriber is interested in watching only a selected list of stocks.

One way to address these problems is to bind the two entities at a higher level of abstraction than the interface pointer. Using this higher level binding information, the publisher can connect to the subscriber at the time the event is fired. The lifetime of the publisher and the subscriber are no longer tightly coupled. If the subscriber is not running at the time of firing the event, the mechanism will automatically start the subscriber. Likewise, a subscriber can still subscribe to an event even if there is no publisher running. Such a system is referred to as a *loosely coupled event* (LCE) system.

A simple way to implement an LCE system is to have the publisher maintain an external database of subscriber CLSIDs. The publisher also documents the mechanism by which a subscriber can add its CLSID to the database. When it is time to fire an event, the publisher goes through each CLSID in the database, instantiates an object of the class, and calls a method on that object. The database schema can easily be extended to let the subscriber define their filtering criteria.

This design approach has two snags:

- Each publisher will need to develop and maintain the code to manage the subscription database.
- As each publisher defines its own subscription process, there is no standard process to subscribe to an event and/or define the filters on the event.

COM+ defines a standard mechanism to publish and subscribe an LCE event that overcomes both of the above-mentioned problems. This mechanism is called COM+ *Events*.

COM+ Events Architecture

The COM+ Events architecture provides built-in logic for managing and maintaining subscription database. In addition, it defines a standard format for the publisher to advertise information on the events it can fire and for the subscriber to locate and subscribe to the event.

The COM+ Events architecture is shown in Figure 10.3. Under this architecture, the publisher and the subscriber are decoupled by means of an intermediary object called the *event class*. An event class is a COM+ component that contains the interfaces and methods used by a publisher to fire events. An *event* is defined as a single call to one of the interface methods from the event class. A subscriber implements the interfaces and the methods of the event class it wants to receive events from while the publisher calls a specific interface method to fire an event.

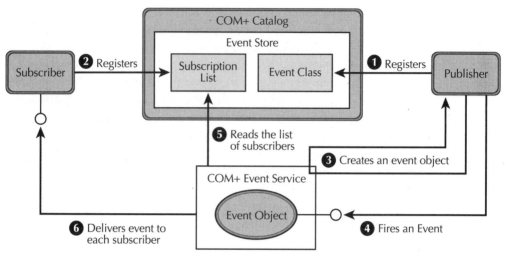

Figure 10.3   COM+ Events architecture.

Event classes are stored in the COM+ catalog, typically placed there by the publishers. The part of the catalog that stores event information is referred to as the *event store*.

Matching and connecting publishers and subscribers is done by a COM+ service called the COM+ Event service.

To indicate its desire to receive events, the subscriber registers a subscription with the COM+ event service. A subscription is a data structure that provides the event service with information about the subscriber so that it can connect to the subscriber to deliver an event. Among other things, it specifies the event class and the specific interface or method within the event class the subscriber wants to receive calls from.

Subscriptions can be registered either by the subscribers themselves or by some administrative programs. When registered, the subscription information is stored in the COM+ catalog.

A subscription comes in two flavors: persistent and transient. Persistent subscriptions survive a system restart. They exist independently of the lifetime of the subscriber object. A transient subscription requests that event calls be made to a specific running instance of a subscriber. Even though a transient subscription is stored in the COM+ catalog, the subscription does not survive a system shutdown.

When a publisher wants to fire an event, it creates an object of the desired event class (using `CoCreateInstance` in C++ or `CreateObject` in VB). This object, known as the *event object*, is synthesized by the event service. It contains the event service's implementation of the requested interface. The publisher then calls the event method it wants to fire an event on. When the method is invoked, the synthesized implementation of the method looks in the COM+ catalog and obtains a list of all the subscribers that have registered subscriptions to that interface method. It then instantiates the subscriber and calls the specified event method. The instantiation logic could create either the subscriber object directly or use monikers or queued components, as we will see later.

From the publisher's perspective, firing an event is as simple as calling the appropriate method on the event class. It is the responsibility of the event service to deliver the event to the subscribers. For a persistent subscription, the event service creates the subscriber object, invokes the appropriate method on the subscriber object, and releases the object. For a transient subscription, the subscriber object already exists, eliminating the need to create and destroy objects on each event call.

As there could be more than one subscriber to a specific event, the event service places some restrictions on the interface method that receives the event—the method cannot have any output parameters. It can only return an HRESULT to indicate success or failure. Not only does this simplify the publisher's logic, it also makes it possible to queue an event if a subscriber is not running when an event is fired, as we will see later.

Queued or non-queued, firing an event is always synchronous with respect to the event object. When a publisher fires an event, all the non-queued subscriptions are called immediately and the queued subscriptions are recorded for later playback. When the event call returns from all the subscribers, the event service consolidates the return codes (HRESULTs) from each subscriber and returns one aggregated HRESULT value to the publisher. Table 10.1 lists some possible return codes to the publisher.

Table 10.1　Event Method Return Codes

Return Code	Description
S_OK	All of the subscribers were successfully invoked.
EVENT_S_SOME_SUBSCRIBERS_FAILED	Some subscribers could not be invoked or some subscribers returned a failed HRESULT code.
EVENT_E_ALL_SUBSCRIBERS_FAILED	None of the subscribers could be invoked.
EVENT_E_NOSUBSCRIBERS	There are no subscribers for the fired event.

If one or more subscribers fail, there is currently no simple way to identify the subscribers or the reason for failure. This, in general, is not a problem as an LCE publisher rarely cares about subscribers' identities. If the publisher does need to get this information, it would have to implement a publisher filter, as we will see later.

The event service does not currently provide any mechanism for specifying the order in which the subscribers receive an event. The default protocol is to deliver the event to one subscriber at a time. However, this default behavior can be changed by instructing the event service to fire an event in parallel, that is, to deliver an event to multiple subscribers concurrently.[3] This reduces the average delivery time of event notifications.

By default, the in-process activation of subscribers is prohibited for security reasons. However, this behavior can be changed by setting an option on the event class.

With this background, let's now look at the implementation specifics of the publisher and the subscriber.

A Simple Event Example

We will continue with the theme of monitoring changes in stock prices. Following is the interface definition for the event class:

```
interface IMyStockPriceEvent : IDispatch
{
  HRESULT NewQuote([in] BSTR bsSymbol, [in] double dValue);
};
```

The publisher application will simulate stock price changes by calling the `NewQuote` method. The subscriber application will pop up a message box each time it receives an event.

Registering an Event Class

An event class is a COM+ configured component that requires the following:

1. A GUID to represent the event class. This GUID is referred to as `EventCLSID`. The `EventCLSID` is specified as the CLSID of the component.
2. A readable unique identifier, called `EventClassName`, for the event class. The `EventClassName` is specified as the PROGID of the component.

---

[3] Currently, there is no multicasting mechanism for event delivery. The event service just uses a thread pool to reach multiple subscribers concurrently.

3. A type library. In order to synthesize the event object and provide marshaling logic for the event class interfaces, the event service requires that the interfaces contained in the event class be provided in a type library.

4. An optional publication attribute called the `PublisherID`. A subscriber can choose to use `PublisherID` instead of `EventCLSID` to identify an event class.

When defining an event class interface, you have to use automation-compliant method parameters. Do not use MIDL attributes such as `size_is` and `length_is`; they do not work with type library marshaling.

Being a COM+ configurable component, the event class requires a self-registering DLL that exports `DllRegisterServer` (to register the component) and `DllUnregisterServer` (to unregister the component).

The easiest way to create an event class is to use the ATL COM AppWizard to generate a dummy component. The `coclass` section in the IDL file should indicate the desired interfaces the event class intends to support. This is illustrated in the following IDL code fragment. It is taken from the ATL AppWizard generated project that I created to define our stock price event class.

```
library STOCKPRICELib
{
    ...
    coclass MyStockPriceEvent
    {
        [default] interface IMyStockPriceEvent;
    };
}
```

Note that the internal structure of the ATL COM AppWizard requires us to provide the implementation of the interface methods. However, the methods on this component are never called by the event service (the service provides its own implementation of the event class). Therefore, the method implementation can just be a stub that simply returns `S_OK`.

To register the event class, first create a new COM+ application using the Component Services snap-in. Add a new component to this application. This brings up the component-install dialog box shown in Figure 10.4.

Click on the "Install new event class" button. Enter the path to the event class component. This brings you to the dialog box shown in Figure 10.5.

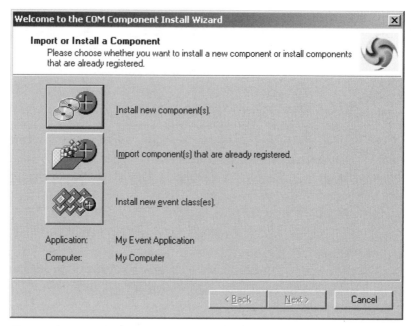

Figure 10.4   Installing an event class component.

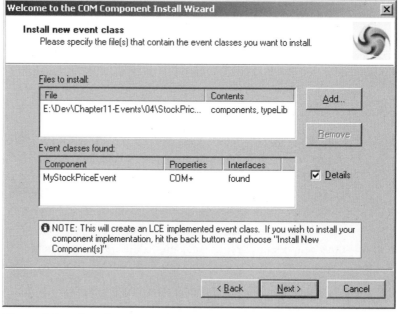

Figure 10.5   Installing event class files.

Click Next followed by Finish.

You have just finished adding an event class to the COM+ catalog!

 An event class could also be installed using the COMAdmin administrative object. COMAdmin objects are covered in Chapter 12. You can find a VBScript program on the CD to install the event class using the COMAdmin object. For those interested, you have to call the InstallEventClass method on the ICOMAdminCatalog interface, which is what the Component Services snap-in does internally.

When viewed from the Component Services snap-in, the event class component doesn't look any different from a typical component. The only difference is that the Advanced tab of the component's property sheet contains a few more entries, as shown in Figure 10.6. For our example, I have defined the identification of a publisher as "My Stock Price Publisher." However, defining this field is not mandatory.

We are done registering the event class. Now let's see how we can implement a subscriber.

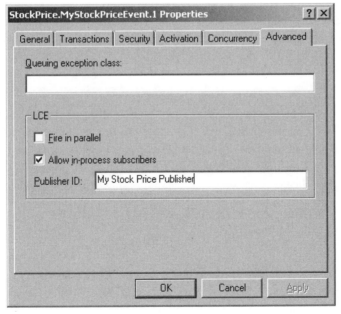

Figure 10.6   Event class properties.

Subscribing for an Event

For our demonstration, we will look at creating a persistent subscription. Transient subscriptions will be covered later.

A persistent subscriber is a regular COM+ configured component. As such, it can be developed using the ATL AppWizard. The important thing to keep in mind is that the component must support the event interface(s) on which it is interested in receiving events as shown in the following C++ class definition:

```
class CMyStockEventSubscriber :
  public IDispatchImpl<IMyStockPriceEvent,
    &IID_IMyStockPriceEvent, &LIBID_STOCKPRICELib>,
    . . .
{
  . . .
// IMyStockPriceEvent
public:
  STDMETHOD(NewQuote)(BSTR bsSymbol, double dValue);
};
```

Do not forget to refer to the event interface within the `coclass` section of the IDL file for the subscriber. Otherwise, the event interface will not be available for subscription.

Always refer to the interested event interfaces in the subscriber's IDL file.

Implementing an event interface is all it takes to create a subscriber. This is as simple as it gets. Compare this to the connection point implementation that required a boatload of code to set up the connection.

Our demonstration example will just bring up a message box when an event gets delivered via `NewQuote` method as shown in the following code snippet:

```
STDMETHODIMP CMyStockEventSubscriber::NewQuote(BSTR bsSymbol,
  double dValue)
{
  TCHAR buf[100];
  _stprintf(buf, _T("%S %lf"), bsSymbol, dValue);
  ::MessageBox(NULL, buf, _T("Stock Price"), MB_OK);

  return S_OK;
}
```

Now, compile and link the subscriber code.

Next, we need to add the subscriber to the COM+ catalog. For that, we first need to install the subscriber as a regular COM+ configured component. We will create a new application from the Component Services snap-in and add the component in the usual manner to this application.

Note that the subscriber need not be added to a separate application. You can add the subscriber to the same application as that of the event class component, if desired.

Once a component is added, you will notice that each component shown in the Component Services snap-in contains two folders—one is our all-too-familiar interfaces folder, and the second one is a Subscriptions folder. This is shown in Figure 10.7.

Select "Add New Subscription" from the context menu of the subscription folder. This brings up a subscription wizard that lists all the interfaces that the component claims to support (from the `coclass` section of the IDL file). This is shown in Figure 10.8.

You can subscribe to a single method or to all the methods on an interface. If you want to receive events on more than one method, but not every method, you have to add a separate subscription for each desired method.

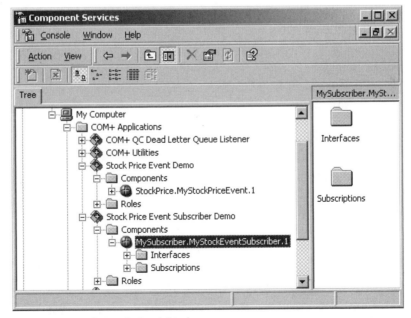

Figure 10.7   Subscription folder.

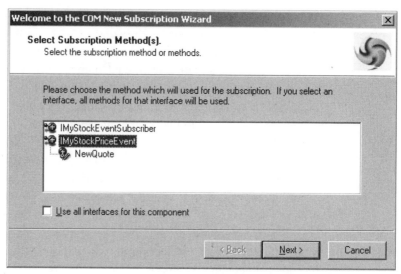

Figure 10.8   Available interfaces for subscription.

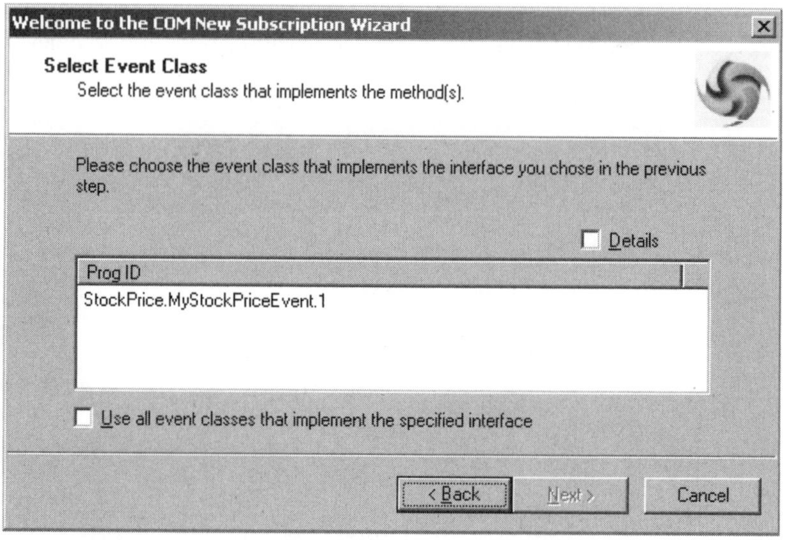

Figure 10.9   Event class choices for subscription.

Once you choose an interface or a specific method on the interface and click on the "Next" button, the subscription wizard searches through the COM+ catalog for registered event classes that support the specified interface and offers you a choice to subscribe, as shown in Figure 10.9.

You can select a specific event class (recall that an event class is typically tied to a publisher). Alternatively, if you don't care for a specific event class, you can select all the event classes that implement the specified interface.

Selecting an event class brings up the next dialog box that requires you to specify a name for the subscription, as shown in Figure 10.10.

A subscription may be enabled or disabled. If disabled, a subscription does not receive any event notification. For our demonstration, we select the option to enable the subscription from the subscription wizard dialog box. Alternatively, we could have done this later from the property sheet for the subscription.

Click the "Next" button followed by the "Finish" button. At this point, the wizard adds the subscription information to the subscription list in the catalog.

Similar to the event class installation, a subscription can also be installed programmatically using the COMAdmin objects. You can find a VBScript file on the CD that demonstrates this.

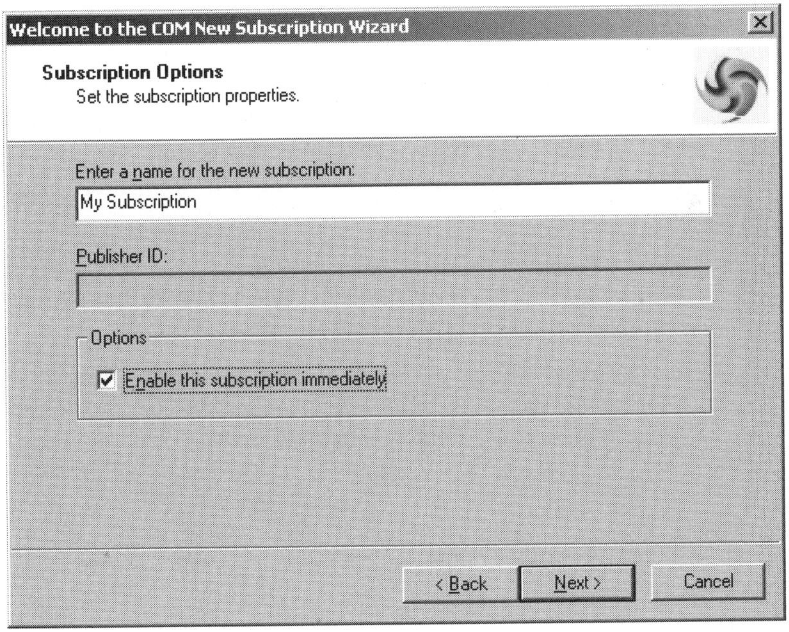

Figure 10.10   Subscription properties.

Firing an Event

A publisher need not be a COM component. It can be any application that is interested in firing an event. When the publisher wants to fire an event, it simply creates an object of the event class and calls the appropriate method on it. The following `VBScript` code fragment shows how to fire our stock price change event:

```
Set stockPriceEvent=CreateObject("StockPrice.MyStockPriceEvent")
stockPriceEvent.NewQuote "MSFT", 100.0
msgbox "Done"
```

Firing an event is as simple as this. There's no need to maintain and manage a list of subscribers; COM+ does the work.

Transient Subscriptions

We know that a persistent subscriber can exist independently of the lifetime of the publisher. If the subscriber is not running at the time the event is fired, the COM+ event service forces it to start. Essentially, the service manages the lifetime of the subscriber.

There are cases, however, where the lifetime of a subscriber object is controlled externally. For example, the lifetime of an ActiveX control is tied to the lifetime of its container. If the container application quits, the ActiveX control object dies. Such a subscriber would only care about getting updates during its externally controlled lifetime. This is where transient subscriptions come into play.

A transient subscription requests that the event calls be delivered to a specific existing subscriber object. Transient subscriptions do not survive system shutdown, although they are stored in the catalog.

Developing the subscriber for transient subscription is similar to that of a persistent subscription in that the subscriber has to support the interested event interface. The implementation follows:

```
class CMyTransientEvent : public IMyStockPriceEvent
{
public:
    ...
// IMyStockPriceEvent
public:
    STDMETHOD(NewQuote)(BSTR bsSymbol, double dValue);
};
```

```
// Create the object
CComPtr<CComObject<CMyTransientEvent> > spEvent;
HRESULT hr =
CComObject<CMyTransientEvent>::CreateInstance(&spEvent);
_ASSERT(SUCCEEDED(hr));
spEvent->InternalAddRef();
```

The Component Services snap-in doesn't have any provision to set up a transient subscription. One has to use the COMAdmin objects to do so.

The first step is to obtain the list of transient subscriptions from the catalog as shown here:

```
COMAdmin::ICOMAdminCatalogPtr spCat(

    __uuidof(COMAdmin::COMAdminCatalog));
COMAdmin::ICatalogCollectionPtr spColl =
    spCat->GetCollection("TransientSubscriptions");
```

The second step is to add the transient subscription to the TransientSubscriptions collection object, represented by the ICatalogCollection interface.

Adding a transient subscription requires the following items:

1. A user-defined name for the transient subscription.
2. The IID of the interface it wishes to receive events on.
3. An interface pointer to the subscriber object.
4. Optionally, the EventCLSID or the PublisherID of the publisher's event class.

The following code fragment shows how to add a transient subscription:

```
IDispatchPtr spDisp = spColl->Add();
COMAdmin::ICatalogObjectPtr spCatObject = spDisp;
spCatObject->Value["Name"] = bsSubscriptionName;
spCatObject->Value["InterfaceID"] =
  "{A9E6D819-1891-462D-B32C-ED4AFD61B08B}";
// spCatObject->Value["EventCLSID"] =
//   "{1F6F353D-5738-4C05-9DA1-A64E19370A0E}";      // optional
// spCatObject->Value["PublisherID"] =
//   "My Stock Price Publisher";                    // optional
spCatObject->Value["SubscriberInterface"] =
  static_cast<IUnknown*>(spEvent);
spColl->SaveChanges();
```

Notice the call to the `SaveChanges` method. Without this call, no changes are saved in the catalog.

The object is now set to receive events!

To stop receiving events, the transient subscription has to be programmatically removed from the catalog, as shown here. The code is included on the CD.

```
spColl = spCat->GetCollection("TransientSubscriptions");
spColl->Populate();
long lIndex = GetIndexInCollection(spColl, bsSubscriptionName);
spColl->Remove(lIndex);
spColl->SaveChanges();
```

In a persistent subscription, a subscriber object is repeatedly constructed and destructed each time an event is fired. In a transient subscription, however, the subscriber object is constructed just once. This makes a transient subscription more efficient than a persistent subscription.

Events and Queued Components

LCE in COM+ greatly simplifies publisher coding. To fire an event, the publisher just creates a single event class object and calls an appropriate method on it. Keeping track of the subscribers and delivering events to the subscribers is left to the COM+ event service.

There are two problems with this mechanism:

1. Consider the case where the event class is installed on a remote machine. If the network is down, the publisher will not be able to create an event object, and therefore cannot fire any events. However, some subscribers may be interested in receiving the events when the network eventually comes back up.

2. In an enterprise system, there could be many subscribers spread across many machines. When an event is fired, there is a possibility that either a subscriber is not running or a subscriber could not be reached because the network is down.

In both these cases, the problem stems from the fact that the normal event firing or event delivery mechanism uses synchronous DCOM, and synchronous DCOM calls fail if the remote object cannot be reached.

If you haven't skipped Chapter 9, you know that the solution lies in using Queued Components.

Fortunately, COM+ events were designed to work closely with Queued Components.

The first problem can be easily solved by making the event class itself a Queued Component. You do this by marking the event class' application as "queued" and "listen," as well as marking the event interface as "queued" (see Chapter 9).

Of course, in order to connect to the Queued Component's recorder, the publisher needs to instantiate the object using the queue moniker syntax. The following code fragment illustrates the technique:

```
Set stockPriceEvent = GetObject( _
  "queue:ComputerName=PVDEV/new:StockPrice.MyStockPriceEvent")
stockPriceEvent.NewQuote "MSFT", 100.0
stockPriceEvent = NULL
msgbox "Done"
```

The second problem can also be solved similarly. In order to queue the publisher's event and replay it to the subscriber later, the specific subscription should be marked as queued. This can be done from the "Options" tab on the property sheet of the subscription, as shown in Figure 10.11.

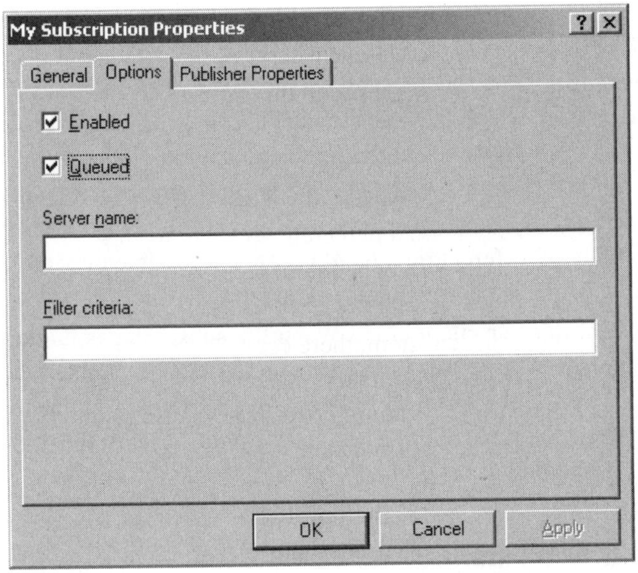

Figure 10.11   Marking a subscription as queued.

Once the subscriber is marked as queued, the event object will create a queued connection to the subscriber. However, to create a queued connection, marking just the subscription as queued is not enough. You need to mark the subscriber's application as "queued" and "listen" and the event interface as "queued." For our demonstration sample, interface `IMyStockPriceEvent` should be marked as queued.

In summary, to queue a COM+ event to a subscriber:

- the application the subscriber belongs to should be marked as "queued" and "listen"
- the event interface on the subscriber should be marked as "queued"
- the subscription itself should be marked as queued

Note that firing an event is always synchronous with respect to the event object. When an event method returns, calls to all Queued Component subscribers have already been recorded. If it is a persistent subscriber, the message will be enqueued for transmission (recall from Chapter 9 that a recorded message is not enqueued until the object is released). For a transient subscriber, as the object is released only after its subscription is removed, a message is not enqueued while the subscription is active.

There is an order of delivery implication to consider when using Queued Components. Within the lifetime of a single subscriber object, all the event calls are recorded as one message. Therefore, all calls will be replayed in the order in which they were made. However, if the publisher fires on more than one event object from the same application, the order cannot be guaranteed. This is because the COM+ QC listener service uses multiple threads to receive MSMQ messages. Essentially, anything in the OS can affect the scheduling of different threads. It is entirely possible that the second message may get dequeued before the first message.

A similar problem exists when the subscriber is marked as a Queued Component. Multiple event notifications will be queued as multiple messages. The COM+ listener service may pick the second message before the first one. If the subscriber is dependent on the order of the event notifications, queuing should not be used.

Events and Filtering

So far we have learned that it is reasonably easy to set up an LCE-based application under COM+. A publisher fires an event and the subscriber receives it.

There are situations, however, when a subscriber might not care for all the events that a publisher fires. For example, most investors are probably interested in a handful of stocks, and would only want the price changes for these stocks.

A subscriber can certainly write code to filter out uninteresting stocks. However, it would be nice if this task could be handled administratively. Some reasons for this follow:

- Less code for the subscriber to write and maintain.
- A subscriber object is created and destroyed each time an event is fired. Also, the event, even if it is an uninteresting one, gets delivered to the subscriber, taking up unnecessary CPU time as well as network bandwidth.

Likewise, there are times when a publisher wants to selectively pass an event to the subscriber. Some examples of such cases are:

- The subscriber may not be licensed to receive the events.
- The subscriber may indicate to the publisher some other event filtering criteria.

The COM+ event service offers a simple subscriber-side filtering of events and a not-so-simple publisher-side filtering of events. Let's take a look.

Subscriber Parameter Filtering

The COM+ event service provides a simple mechanism to define filters on event method parameters. The type of filtering used is on a per-method per-subscription basis. The filter can be specified from the Options tab on the property sheet of the subscription, as shown in Figure 10.12.

The filter criteria string supports relational operators (=, ==, !, !=, ~, ~=, <>), nested parentheses, and logical keywords AND, OR, or NOT.

Filtering criteria can also be specified programmatically using COMAdmin objects. For those interested, it is the FilterCriteria property on the subscription collection.

When an event is fired, the event service checks the filtering criteria for each subscription and delivers the event only if the filter matches the current event values.

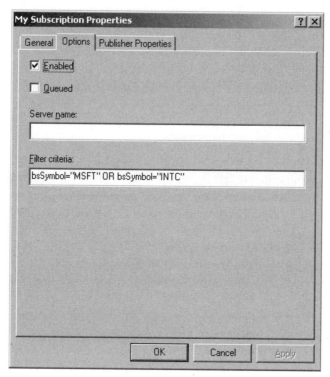

Figure 10.12   Filtering criteria for a subscription.

Beware of entering a syntactically incorrect filter. The Component Services snap-in does not complain about it. However, the event system logs an error entry into the Windows event log. Be sure to check the event log while testing your filters.

Publisher Filtering

Filtering can also be done at the publisher level instead of the event service level. Not only is this more efficient, but it also provides the following advantages to the publisher:

- The publisher can control the order of firing the events. Perhaps some subscribers might have paid extra for priority notification.
- The publisher can check the returns status from each individual subscriber.

- The publisher can check if the subscriber is licensed to receive event notifications.

The publisher can exercise fine-grained control over the event firing process by adding the necessary logic in the publisher code itself. However, when used this way, the filter behavior cannot be changed without rebuilding the entire publisher program. Moreover, it won't help you control a publisher for which you have no source code.

Fortunately, the COM+ event system provides a mechanism by which a publisher filter can be defined as a separate COM+ configured component. When installing an event class, you can specify which publisher filter to use by setting the event class' `PublisherFIlterCLSID` property in the COM+ catalog. Unfortunately, the Component Services snap-in doesn't let you specify the filter component; you need to write your own administrative program to do this. You can find an example on the CD.

This filter class needs to support a COM+ provided standard interface, `IMultiInterfacePublisherFilter`.[4] Table 10.2 lists its methods.

Table 10.2 `IMultiInterfacePublisherFIlter` **Methods**

Method	Description
Initialize	Called by the event system when the event object is first created.
PrepareToFire	Called by the event system when an event needs to be fired.

Besides supporting `IMultiInterfacePublisherFilter`, the filter class should also support the event interfaces supported by the event class, as illustrated in the following code-fragment:

```
class CMyFilterImpl :
  public IMultiInterfacePublisherFilter,
  public IMyStockPriceEvent,
  . . .
{
  . . .
// IMyStockPriceEvent
  STDMETHOD(NewQuote)(BSTR bsSymbol, double dValue);

// IMultiInterfacePublisherFilter methods
  STDMETHOD(Initialize)(IMultiInterfaceEventControl *pMIEC);
```

---

[4] This interface replaces an earlier interface, `IPublisherFilter`. The latter interface still exists but its use is deprecated.

```
STDMETHOD(PrepareToFire)(REFIID riid, BSTR methodname,
   IFiringControl* pFC);

private:
  CComPtr<IEventObjectCollection> m_spColl;
  CComPtr<IFiringControl> m_spFC;
};
```

When the publisher creates the event object, the event system reads the CLSID of the filter specified for the event class and creates an object of the filter class. If the filter object cannot be created, the creation of the event object fails.

After creating the filter object, the event system calls the IMultiInterfacePublisherFilter::Initialize method, passing in a pointer to IMultiInterfaceEventControl. This interface supports a method, GetSubscriptions, that returns a subscription list for a given interface and a given method. The filter should hold on to this collection, as shown here:

```
STDMETHODIMP CMyFilterImpl::Initialize(
IMultiInterfaceEventControl *pMIEC)
{
  _ASSERT (ISNULL(m_spColl));

  int nErr = 0;
  HRESULT hr = pMIEC->GetSubscriptions(
    __uuidof(IMyStockPriceEvent),
    g_bsMETHODNAME,
    0,
    &nErr,
    &m_spColl);
  return hr;
}
```

Note that our example event class has just one interface with just one method, making us cache just one collection. In general, you may have to cache many collections. For a more complex example, check the Event-Monitor sample program on the platform SDK.

When the publisher calls a method on the event interface, the event system calls the filter's IMultiInterfacePublisherFilter::PrepareToFire method. The first two parameters identify the event interface and the event method. The last parameter is a pointer to the IFiringControl interface. This interface has a method, FireSubscription, that we need to use later for delivering events to the subscribers.

```
STDMETHODIMP CMyFilterImpl::PrepareToFire(REFIID riid,
  BSTR methodname, IFiringControl* pFC)
{
  if (NULL == pFC)
    return E_INVALIDARG;

  _ASSERT (__uuidof(IMyStockPriceEvent) == riid);
  _ASSERT (!wcsicmp(methodname, g_bsMETHODNAME));

  m_spFC = pFC;

  return S_OK;
}
```

The event system now invokes the event method on the filter object. At this point, the filter object can choose to filter event notification to some subscribers and can control the order of firing events.

For our sample, we will check to see if a subscriber is licensed to receive the events.

The event system supports a notion of specifying arbitrary name/value pairs to a subscription. These pairs are referred to as the publisher properties and can be added to a subscription from its property sheet, as shown in Figure 10.13.

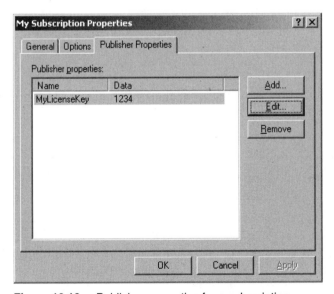

Figure 10.13   Publisher properties for a subscription.

For our sample program, the filter expects each subscription to have a property called "`MyLicenseKey`." The magic value for the license is 1234. The following code shows the license-check logic.

```
STDMETHODIMP CMyFilterImpl::NewQuote(/*[in]*/ BSTR bsSymbol,
  /*[in]*/ double dValue)
{
  _ASSERT (ISNOTNULL(m_spFC));
  _ASSERT (ISNOTNULL(m_spColl));

  CComPtr<IEnumEventObject> spEnum;
  HRESULT hr = m_spColl->get_NewEnum(&spEnum);
  RETURNIFFAILED(hr);

  ULONG nRet = 0;
  CComPtr<IUnknown> spUnk;
  while(S_OK == (hr = spEnum->Next(1, &spUnk, &nRet))) {
    CComPtr<IEventSubscription> spSub;
    hr = spUnk->QueryInterface(&spSub);
    RETURNIFFAILED(hr);
    spUnk = NULL;

    CComVariant v;
    hr = spSub->GetPublisherProperty(CComBSTR("MyLicenseKey"),
      &v);
    if (FAILED(hr)) {
      continue; // not a valid subscriber
    }

    if (wcscmp(V_BSTR(&v), L"1234")) {
      continue; // not a valid subscriber
    }

    hr = m_spFC->FireSubscription(spSub);
  }

  return hr;
}
```

In the above code, when the event method is invoked, the filter object goes through each subscription looking for the license key property. If the value for this property matches the magic value, the filter object tells the event system to deliver the event to the specific subscriber, using the `Fire-Subscription` method. This method invokes all the event system's standard delivery mechanism, including the parameter filtering described earlier.

SUMMARY

An event is a notification of a change in some interesting data. The publisher fires an event, and one or more subscribers receive the event.

Event system implementation can be broadly categorized as tightly coupled events (TCEs) or loosely coupled events (LCEs).

Under TCE, the publisher and the subscriber have a direct connection to each other. The lifetimes of the publisher and the subscriber are tightly coupled. A connection point is a commonly used technique for TCEs.

Another example of TCE implementation is MSMQ. When a message listener enables notification on a specific MSMQ queue, MSMQ fires an event when a message arrives in the queue.

Under LCE, the publisher and the subscriber do not have a direct connection to each other. COM+ events is a mechanism based on LCE. Under COM+ events, the publisher and the subscriber are decoupled by an event class.

COM+ events can have persistent subscribers or transient subscribers. Persistent subscribers can survive a system shutdown while the transient subscribers cannot.

COM+ events support queuing the method call, from the publisher to the event class as well as from the event class to the subscribers.

COM+ events also support filtering of data, both at the publisher's side as well as the subscriber's side.

REFERENCES

[Box-98]   Don Box *et al.*, *Effective COM*, Addison Wesley Longman, Inc., ISBN 0-201-37968-6, December 1998.

[Pla-99]   David Platt, "The COM+ Event Service Eases the Pain of Publishing and Subscribing to Data," *Microsoft Systems Journal*, vol. 14, no. 9, September 1999. *http://msdn.microsoft.com/library/periodic/period99/com+event.htm*

[Arm-99]   Tom Armstrong, "COM+ Events," *Visual C++ Developers Journal*, vol. 2, no. 3, July/August 1999.

[Pro-2000] Jeff Prosise, "A Hands-On Look at COM+ Events," *Visual C++ Developers Journal*, vol. 3, no. 1, January/February 2000.

CHAPTER 11

Scalability

$\mathbf{A}$n enterprise system must be designed to handle hundreds of clients concurrently. Furthermore, each client request should be serviced in a reasonable amount of time. Rather than designing the software to maximize performance, thereby reducing the amount of time to service a single request, the developers have to focus on maximizing throughput—the number of requests that can be serviced in a given amount of time.

COM+ provides many services that make it relatively easy to develop such scalable applications. In the previous chapters we looked at some of them, such as queuing and events, which directly or indirectly help in developing scalable applications. In this chapter, we shall examine several other COM+ mechanisms that help developers write sophisticated, highly scalable applications.

INTRODUCTION

Scalability is defined as the measure of an application's resistance to performance degradations when it services multiple concurrent requests. A perfectly scalable application would provide constant performance regardless of the number of concurrent users. However, such an application exists only in theory, as it requires infinite resources. In the real world, it is very common for two applications to contend for a shared resource such as memory, database access, or CPU time. In this case, one application has to wait until the other is finished using the resource, resulting in degraded performance.

There are several ways to resolve this problem, including the following:

- Increase the supply of available resources (more processors, memory, database handles, etc.)
- Design the application so that each request uses shared resources as efficiently as possible.

For the greatest degree of scalability, the developers may end up doing both.

While the first method requires a hardware or software upgrade to the system, the second method can be achieved programmatically.

Let's look at some COM+ services that help us achieve the second option.

RESOURCE DISPENSERS

Consider the following scenario:

Assume that a component is set to open a connection to an SQL server database during activation. Let's say the component is being used over and over again, very quickly. Each time the component is used, a connection to the database is created. This is very inefficient; making a connection to a database can be very time consuming.

A better strategy would be to keep the connection alive and reuse it for the next invocation.

This is what a *resource dispenser* (RD) does.

A resource dispenser is a software component that manages the non-durable state of a resource, such as the connection to a database.

Do not confuse the resource manager with the resource dispenser, although both often work hand in hand:

- An RM manages the durable state of the resource, such as the changes to a relational database. An RD manages the non-durable state of the resource, such as the connection to the database.
- An RM is almost always implemented as an `out-of-process` server. An RD is always within the same process as that of the client.

Recall from Chapter 8 that, when a client connects to a resource manager, it gets a proxy to the resource manager (RM proxy). The RM proxy provides interfaces or APIs so that the client can talk to the resource manager.

An RM proxy is typically implemented as part of the Resource Dispenser.

Some commonly used examples of RDs are ODBC driver managers and OLE DB providers. Pooling offered by ODBC driver managers is called *connection pooling*. Pooling offered by OLE DB providers is called *resource pooling*.

An application can make its database connection by using an ODBC database driver either natively or by using ADO. The following code snippet uses ADO with ODBC to open a connection to an SQL server database AccountsDB.

```
Set aConn = CreateObject("ADODB.Connection")
aConn.Open "DSN=LocalServer;database=AccountsDB;UID=sa;PWD=;"
```

When a client makes a database connection using ODBC, the ODBC driver manager keeps the connection in a pool and returns a copy to the client. When the client releases the connection, the ODBC driver manager does not drop the connection. Instead, it waits for a certain amount of time to see if the connection can be reused. When the next connection to the database is made, if the data source and the user information match the one in the pool, the request is satisfied from the connection in the pool. If there is no match, then a new connection is made to the database.

If the connection in the pool could not be used within the timeout period, the ODBC driver manager drops the connection.

To take advantage of ODBC connection pooling, the underlying ODBC driver must be thread-safe. Fortunately, the latest versions of the most popular ODBC drivers (SQL Server, Oracle, Access, etc.) are all thread-safe.

ODBC connection pooling can be enabled (or disabled) programmatically (as well as by other means such as manipulating the Windows registry). See the MSDN article, "Pooling in the Microsoft Data Access Components," [Ahl-99] for details. For a COM+ application, connection pooling is automatically enabled. You do not have to explicitly enable it.

An application can also use OLE DB to create a data source object, either by invoking the data provider directly or by using ADO. The following code snippet uses ADO to create an OLE DB data source object to an SQL Server database AccountsDB:

```
Set aConn = CreateObject("ADODB.Connection")
aConn.Open "Provider=SQLOLEDB;database=AccountsDB;UID=sa;PWD=;"
```

When the application creates an OLE DB data source object, the OLE DB services create a proxy data source object in the application's process. When the application attempts to create another data source object, the proxy tries to reuse the existing initialized data source to the database, if possible.

When the application releases the data source object, it is returned to the pool.

Notice the difference between ODBC connection pooling and OLE DB resource pooling. The former pools the ODBC connections to the database. The latter pools the OLE DB data source objects.

OLE DB resource pooling can be configured programmatically. The MSDN article, "Pooling in the Microsoft Data Access Components," [Ahl-99] provides an in-depth coverage on this topic.

JUST-IN-TIME (JIT) ACTIVATION

In an enterprise system, a user-driven client application often creates an object, makes a method call, and holds on to the object to use it later. The time between calls can vary from seconds to minutes or even hours. Meanwhile, on the server side, the object continues to stay alive, tying up resources. Imagine the resource-sharing problem that would arise if a hundred or more clients locked access to the resources that they weren't even using.

Just-in-time (JIT) activation is a mechanism provided by COM+ to manage the lifetime of an object more efficiently. The idea is very simple— the actual object is activated just prior to the first call made on it and is deactivated immediately after finishing its work.

Here's how it works.

When the client creates an object that is marked for JIT activation, COM+ activates the actual object and returns a proxy to the client, as shown in Figure 11.1.

Once the object is created, the client makes method calls on it as usual. When the object is finished doing its work, COM+ deactivates the actual object. However, the proxy, the stub, and the ORPC channel connecting them are all still in place. The client continues to hold the reference to the object via its proxy, unaware that the underlying object has been deactivated. This is illustrated in Figure 11.2.

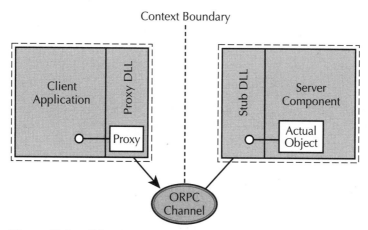

Figure 11.1   JIT activation: Client gets a proxy.

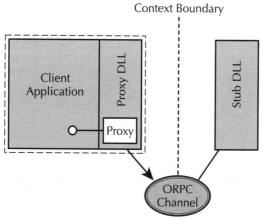

Figure 11.2   JIT activation: The actual object has been deactivated.

When a client makes a call on the proxy, the proxy informs the stub. At this point, COM+ activates a new instance of the object, as shown in Figure 11.3.

A component is marked for JIT activation from the Component Services snap-in, as shown in Figure 11.4.

Context Boundary

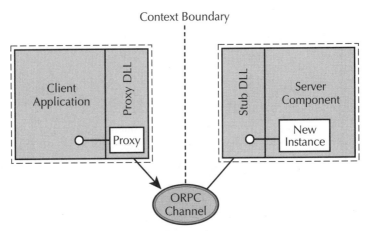

Figure 11.3   JIT activation of a new instance.

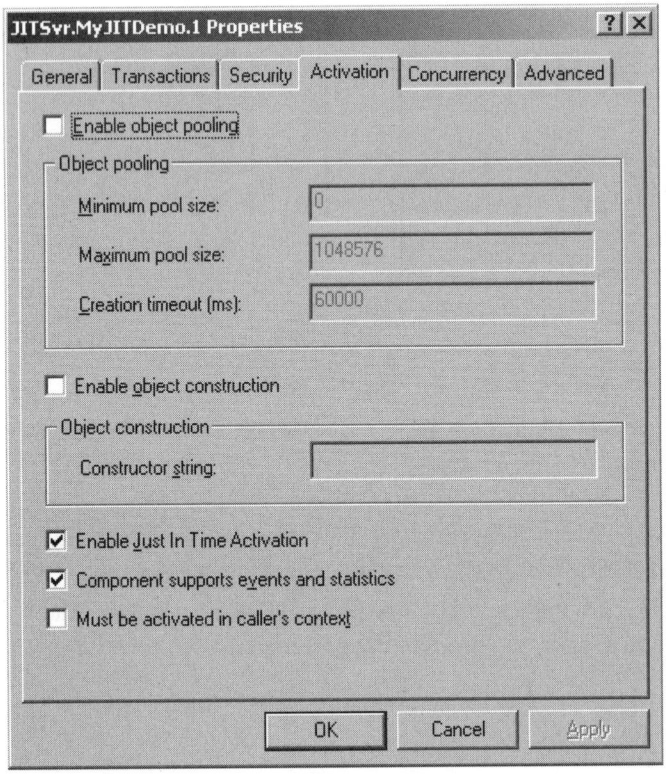

Figure 11.4   Enabling a component for JIT activation.

Now comes the million dollar question—how does COM+ know that it is safe to deactivate the object?

COM+ could perhaps wait for a predefined timeout period to check if the client makes any call. If no call comes in within this timeout period, then COM+ can deactivate the object. However, such a timeout-based deactivation mechanism may result in an unexpected behavior.

Consider, for example, a component that supports obtaining salary information for an employee. It implements the following interface:

```
interface IMyJITDemo : IDispatch
{
  HRESULT SetEmployee([in] BSTR bsEmployeeName);
  HRESULT GetSalary([out, retval] long* pVal);
};
```

The idea is that the client first calls SetEmployee to specify the employee name, and then calls GetSalary to obtain the salary of the employee. Let's say the client doesn't call GetSalary within the timeout period. As a result, COM+ deactivates the object. Later, when GetSalary call comes in, a new instance is activated. However, the new instance has no idea who the employee is for which GetSalary is being called. In the best case, the call will return a failure condition. In the worst case, it will return an invalid value.

The real problem is that when the original object was being deactivated, it was in a state—a state that contained the name of the employee. When the object got deactivated, this state got lost.

In order for JIT to work, the object should be deactivated when it is "stateless," that is, it either contains no data, or contains data that is not important and may be discarded.

But the stub doesn't have the foggiest idea about the statelessness or the statefulness of an object. As far as it is concerned, the object is nothing but an implementation of a bunch of interfaces.

Unlike the stub, however, the object does know what state it is in. If only it can inform the stub that it is done with the work it is supposed to do. Then the stub can go ahead and deactivate the object.

In our example case, it is not okay to deactivate the object after calling SetEmployee, but it is perfectly fine to deactivate the object after the client calls the GetSalary method.

An object that is JIT-enabled contains a bit in its context called the "done" bit or, more precisely, the *deactivate-on-return* bit. COM+ checks this bit after its return from each method call. If the bit is turned on, COM+ will deactivate the object. By default, COM+ turns this bit off before entering a method. However, one can change this behavior at the interface method level from the Component Services snap-in.

The *deactivate-on-return* bit can also be set programmatically by using the method `SetDeactivateOnReturn` available on the interface `IContextState`. The following is its prototype:

```
Interface IContextState : IUnknown
{
    ...
    HRESULT SetDeactivateOnReturn(VARIANT_BOOL bVal);
}
```

Parameter `bVal` informs COM+ whether or not the object should be deactivated.

`SetDeactivateOnReturn` requires `VARIANT_BOOL` (and not `BOOL`) as the parameter type. Do not use `TRUE` or `FALSE` as the parameter. Use `VARIANT_TRUE` or `VARIANT_FALSE` instead.

Method `CMyJITDemo::SetSalary` can now be implemented as follows:

```
STDMETHODIMP CMyJITDemo::GetSalary(long *pVal)
{
  CComPtr<IContextState> spState;
  HRESULT hr = ::CoGetObjectContext(__uuidof(IContextState),
    (void**) &spState);
  hr = spState->SetDeactivateOnReturn(VARIANT_TRUE);
  ...
  return S_OK;
}
```

Note that the implementation of `SetEmployee` need not explicitly set the deactivate-on-return bit to `VARIANT_FALSE`. This is because, by default, COM+ automatically sets this bit to `VARIANT_FALSE` before calling a method.

When JIT activation is enabled on a component, COM+ enforces the `Synchronization` attribute to be set to `Required`. The reason for this is simple. If two clients were simultaneously calling a JIT-activated component, and a method call from one of them causes the object to be deactivated on return, the other method call would be left accessing invalid memory location or other such resources. This problem can be avoided by ensuring that only one method call gets serviced at a time, which is exactly what Synchro-nization=Required does (see Chapter 6).

Although JIT activation results in reclaiming the resource taken up by the object, it is often less than what you think. Even though the COM object that finished its work is deactivated, the channel and the stub still stay in place. Only when the object consumes considerably more memory than these infrastructural items does JIT activation provide some benefit. However, keep in mind that repeated activation/deactivation of the object results in some performance degradation. Before enabling JIT activation, you should consider if the benefit of saving resources outweighs performance degradation. JIT activation is more beneficial when deactivating an object recovers a scarce, expensive resource, such as a database connection.

The real benefit of JIT is that it enforces transactional correctness. Recall from Chapter 8 that a transaction is completed only after the root object of the transaction is deactivated. Forcing the client to release the root object and re-create it for each transaction not only requires some programming effort on the part of the client, but it is also inefficient, as the proxy, the stub, and the channel are torn down every time. Marking the root-object transactional component as JIT-activated and setting the deactivate-on-return bit within an appropriate method implementation deactivates the root object. Not only does this enforce transaction completion, it also leaves the setup (the proxy, the stub, and the ORPC channel) intact. In fact, JIT activation is so crucial for transactional correctness that, if a component is marked to participate in a transaction, COM+ enforces that the component gets enabled for JIT activation.

If JIT activation is enabled on a component, it implies that its objects are created and destroyed frequently. The primary intention of destroying an object is to force the object to release its resources. If somehow we can force the object to release its resources without actually destroying the object, we could reuse the object without having to create it, thus saving some CPU cycles. This is what *object pooling*, a COM+ provided mechanism and our next topic of discussion, tries to achieve. By pooling JIT-activated objects, you can greatly speed up object reactivation for the client.

OBJECT POOLING

The concept of object pooling is simple. Using the Component Services snap-in, the administrator marks a component as *pooled*. The relevant property page for the component is shown earlier in Figure 11.4. When the COM+ application containing the component is first activated, COM+ creates a bunch of objects (the exact number is specified as the minimum pool size) and holds them in a pool. When a client creates an object, by calling `CoCre-ateInstance`, for example, COM+ first checks the pool to see if the object of the specified type is available. If so, COM+ activates the object from the pool instead of creating a new one. If the object is not available, COM+ will create a new one, up to the maximum specified size of the pool. When the object is released, either through a direct client request or as a result of the JIT deactivate-on-return bit set, the object goes back to the pool for reuse.

If all the objects up to the maximum specified limit are already in use when a new object creation request comes in, COM+ waits for a specified timeout interval (configurable through the Component Services snap-in) to see if any of the used objects become available for reuse. If not, the object creation fails with the error, `CO_E_ACTIVATIONFAILED_TIMEOUT`.

Note that so far in this chapter, and at many places in the earlier chapters, we deliberately chose the words object *activation* and *deactivation*, as opposed to object *creation* and *destruction*. The semantic difference between the two should now become clear. When an object is *activated*, it either gets *created* or *fetched* from a pool of existing objects. When an object is *deactivated*, it either gets *destroyed* or *placed back* in the pool.

When an object is being deactivated, it needs a way to know this so that it can release its resources. Likewise, an object needs to know when it is being activated so that it can initialize its state. To accomplish this, COM defines a standard interface, `IObjectControl`. The following is its definition:

```
IObjectControl : IUnknown
{
  HRESULT Activate();
  void Deactivate();
  BOOL CanBePooled();
};
```

Any `coclass` whose objects are interested in receiving activation and deactivation notifications should support `IObjectControl`.

Implementing `IObjectControl` is not mandatory for object pooling. Implement it only if you wish to receive activation and deactivation notifications.

When an object is being activated, COM+ queries the object for the `IObjectControl` interface and calls its `Activate` method before handing the object over to the client. This gives the object a chance to do any necessary initialization.

When an `Activate` call comes in, you can obtain a reference to the object's context object and store it as a member variable. This way, you don't have to acquire the context object each time you want to use it.

The `Activate` method can also be used to obtain the security credentials of the caller (see Chapter 7) and either allow or deny access to the caller.

When the object is being deactivated, COM+ calls the `Deactivate` method. This is the object's chance to perform whatever cleanup is necessary, such as releasing any held resources, before it is destroyed or recycled.

If you are holding the context object as a member variable, do not forget to release it when `Deactivate` is called.

Immediately after calling `Deactivate`, COM+ calls the `CanBePooled` method on the object to check if the object is willing to be pooled for reuse. If the object returns `FALSE`, COM+ destroys the object. Otherwise, COM+ places (or may place) the object back into the pool.

Note that returning `TRUE` from `CanBePooled` does not guarantee that the object will be recycled; it only gives COM+ the permission to recycle it. Returning `FALSE`, however, guarantees that the object will be destroyed.

Requirements for Poolable Objects

With object pooling, a specific instance of a poolable object can be used by multiple clients. In order to work properly with multiple clients, poolable objects have to meet certain requirements.

Stateless

To maintain security, consistency, as well as isolation, poolable objects must not hold any "client-specific" state from one client to another. Otherwise, for example, a resource opened with the security token of one client may inadvertently get used with another client. Therefore, a per-client state should be managed using `IContextControl`, performing client-specific context initialization with `Activate`, and cleaning up any client state with `Deactivate`.

No Thread Affinity

It is possible that a poolable object gets created on one thread (at startup time) but gets activated on another thread (when it is taken from the pool and connected to the client). Therefore, the object should be designed so that it doesn't care which thread it receives calls on. This means the object must live in either an MTA or neutral apartment, which implies the component cannot be marked with `ThreadingModel=Apartment`.[1] In addition, poolable objects should not use thread local storage (TLS), nor should they aggregate the FTM (see Chapter 5).

Aggregatable

When COM+ activates a pooled object, it aggregates the actual object to manage its lifetime. Therefore, the object implementation should support aggregation. This is not such a terrible problem as the code generated by the ATL wizard supports aggregation by default.

Transactional Components

Poolable objects that participate in transactions must turn off the automatic enlistment of managed resources (Chapter 8). The transactional resources must be enlisted manually. Otherwise, if an object holds managed resources between clients, there will be no way for the resource manager to automatically enlist in a transaction when the object is activated in a given context.

Note that this is not an issue if the managed resource gets loaded when `Activate` is called. However, for performance optimization, many components load the managed resource during the construction phase of the object. Such components should add the logic to disable automatic enlistment of the managed resource during the construction phase and enable it each time `Activate` is called.

The steps for automatic or manual enlistment of a managed resource are very specific to the resource manager of the resource in question. You should consult the documentation for your resource manager. See the MSDN article, "COM+ Technical Series: Object Pooling," [MSDN-00] for a code example on manually enlisting an ODBC resource.

---

[1] Though `ThreadingModel=both` is supported, the "Apartment" part of the threading model never gets used. The objects are always created from an MTA thread.

COM+ treats transactional objects in a special way when they are pooled. Generally, when a client requests a pooled object, COM+ may fetch any object from the available pool. However, for transactional objects, COM+ uses a different algorithm. It scans the pool for an available object that is already associated with the current transaction. If an object with the transaction affinity is found, it is returned to the client; otherwise, an object from the general pool is returned. When the object with the transaction affinity is used, the object must have already enlisted its resources. Therefore, before enlisting a resource, you should first check for transaction affinity and enlist the resource only if the object was fetched from the general pool.

ASYNCHRONOUS METHOD CALLS

Under the conventional COM+ model, when a client application calls a method on an object, the client thread blocks until the method executes and returns. Making such a synchronous call is by far the most popular technique to the clients. However, there are times when a client application would want to do some other work while the call is in progress, rather than waiting for the call to complete.

One way to accomplish this is for the client to spawn a worker thread to make the method call. The primary thread is now free to do some other work while the worker thread blocks until the method call returns.

Though this technique will certainly work, it is better if the underlying infrastructure provides this type of service. This reduces the thread management code for the client, especially if the client intends to make many concurrent calls. Moreover, the infrastructure can optimize the low-level calls to make it more performance-efficient.

The RPC layer under Windows 2000 includes support for asynchronous calls. COM+ leverages this feature to support asynchronous call processing at the interface method level. The architecture is such that both the client and the server can independently deal with asynchronous method calls:

- The client code can be developed to make asynchronous method calls without requiring the server to implement any special code. The COM+ MIDL compiler can generate proxies and stubs that do all the dirty work.
- The server code can process calls asynchronously without requiring any special action on the part of the client. As a matter of fact, the server can process a method call in an asynchronous fashion even if the client makes a synchronous method call. Once again, the MIDL-generated proxies and stubs do all the magic.

To explore COM+ support for asynchronous calls, we will develop a very simple server component. The component returns the sum of two numbers. Following is the interface definition used for the demonstration:

```
interface IMySum : IUnknown
{
  HRESULT GetSum([in] long lVal1, [in] long lVal2,
    [out, retval] long* plSum);
};
```

The implementation of such an interface method is shown below. It is quite straightforward. To ensure that the method call execution takes some time, I have deliberately added a five-second sleep in the code:

```
STDMETHODIMP CMySum::GetSum(long lVal1, long lVal2, long *plSum)
{
  ::Sleep(5 * 1000); // sleep for 5 seconds
  *plSum = lVal1 + lVal2;
  return S_OK;
}
```

In order for MIDL to generate proxy/stub code that deals with asynchronous method calls, the interface definition needs to be marked with an attribute named [async_uuid], as shown here:

```
[
  ...
  uuid(1189F283-7248-43C7-988B-57397D67BAB5),
  async_uuid(E58D142E-0199-4178-B93A-9F1919DE42D3),
]
interface IMySum : IUnknown
{
  HRESULT GetSum([in] long lVal1, [in] long lVal2,
    [out, retval] long* plSum);
};
```

When MIDL sees the async_uuid attribute, it generates the proxy/stub code for two versions of the interface IMySum.

1. A synchronous version of the interface, named IMySum, with interface ID taken from the uuid interface attribute. This is the normal MIDL processing that we are accustomed to.

2. An asynchronous version of the interface, named AsyncIMySum, with interface ID taken from the async_uuid interface attribute.

The `AsyncIMySum` interface contains two methods for each method found in the `IMySum` interface. A "`Begin_`" and "`Finish_`" token, as shown below, prefixes each method:

```
interface AsyncIMySum
{
  HRESULT Begin_GetSum([in] long lVal1, [in] long lVal2);
  HRESULT Finish_GetSum( [out, retval] long* plSum);
};
```

You can easily guess that a client would call the "`Begin_`" version of the method to start an asynchronous method call, and the "`Finish_`" version to obtain the outcome of the method call.

The `coclass` implements the `IMySum` interface as usual. Typically, it does not implement the asynchronous version of the interface. Instead, COM+ implements the `AsyncIMySum` interface and makes it available to the client.

Note that only the `[in]` parameters of the original method appear in the `Begin_GetSum` method and only the `[out]` parameters of the original method appear in the `Finish_GetSum` method. Had the original method contained any `[in, out]` parameter, it would appear as an `[in]` parameter in the "`Begin_`" version, and as an `[out]` parameter in the "`Finish_`" version.

Before we go further, there are a few general limitations concerning asynchronous support in COM+ you should be aware of:

1. COM+ doesn't support asynchronous calls from configured components. As a workaround, you can make an asynchronous call to a non-configured component and have that component call the configured component.

2. Asynchronous interfaces can only be derived from asynchronous interfaces. This rules out deriving interfaces from `dispinterface` or `IDispatch`. Interface `IUnknown`, as you might have guessed, is marked to support asynchronous calls, making it possible to define custom asynchronous interfaces.

3. As asynchronous call support is implemented by the proxy/stub code, type library marshaling cannot be used. The proxy/stub DLL has to be built and registered.

4. As the asynchronous magic happens because of the proxy/stub logic, a client cannot use a direct interface pointer to the object. A simple way to ensure that the client gets a proxy is to make the component an out-of-process server.

5. As the proxy/stub code is meant to execute only on Windows 2000 or later versions of the OS, the code compilation requires that a macro, `_WIN32_WINNT`, be defined as at least 0x0500 (for NT 5.0).

If you are using ATL to develop the server, be sure to pass `FALSE` as a parameter to the `_Module.RegisterServer` call. This will ensure that the type library does not get registered. Also, you need to edit the ATL wizard-generated proxy stub `makefile` and redefine the `_WIN32_WINNT` macro to `0x0500`.

Let's look at how a client can make asynchronous calls.

Asynchronous Clients

First, we need to understand the client-side architecture of asynchronous calls.

As mentioned earlier in the section, the server object typically implements the synchronous version of the interface and COM+ implements the asynchronous version. More precisely, a separate object, known as a *call object*, implements the asynchronous version of the interface. A client can get hold of the call object through the proxy manager.

Recall from Chapter 5 that when a client activates an object from a context that is incompatible with that of the object's configuration, a proxy manager gets loaded in the client's context. The proxy manager acts as the client-side identity of the object.

Figure 11.5 illustrates the interfaces exposed by the proxy manager for our sample application.

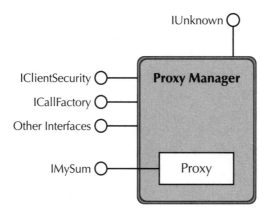

Figure 11.5
Interfaces exposed by the proxy manager.

Besides exposing the interfaces supported by the actual object, the proxy manager also exposes some other interfaces. One such interface that we saw earlier in Chapter 7 is `IClientSecurity`. Another interface that the proxy manager implements, and the one that is of interest to us, is `ICall-Factory`. Following is its definition:

```
interface ICallFactory : IUnknown
{
   HRESULT CreateCall(
      [in] REFIID riid,
      [in] IUnknown *pCtrlUnk,
      [in] REFIID riid2,
      [out, iid_is(riid2)]IUnknown **ppv );
}
```

Method `CreateCall` lets the client create a call object.

Parameter `riid` lets you specify the identifier of the asynchronous interface you are interested in. An object may support more than one asynchronous interface. By specifying the asynchronous interface identifier, the call factory can create a call object appropriate for the specific asynchronous interface.

Parameter `pCtrlUnk`, if not `NULL`, is used for aggregating the call object. We will see its use later.

Besides supporting the asynchronous interface, a call object supports two more interfaces, `ISynchronize` and `ICancelMethodCalls`, as illustrated in Figure 11.6. Parameter `riid2` specifies the identifier of the interface you wish to obtain on the call object.

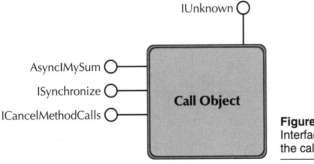

Figure 11.6
Interfaces exposed by the call object.

Given this client-side architecture, the procedure for executing an asynchronous method call to GetSum can be summed up as follows:

1. Create the object that implements IMySum, using CoCreateInstance, for example.
2. Query the obtained proxy manager for the ICallFactory interface.
3. Call ICallFactory::CreateCall to create a call object that supports the AsyncIMySum interface.
4. Call AsyncIMySum::Begin_GetSum on the call object to initiate an asynchronous call.
5. Later, call AsyncIMySum::Fetch_GetSum on the call object to retrieve the call's output parameters.

The following code fragment demonstrates this procedure. As usual, error checking has been omitted for clarity.

```
void SimpleAsyncExecution()
{
  // Step 1: Create the instance
  CComPtr<IUnknown> spUnk;
  HRESULT hr = ::CoCreateInstance(__uuidof(MySum), NULL,
    CLSCTX_SERVER, __uuidof(IMySum), (void**) &spUnk);

  // Step 2: Get the call factory
  CComPtr<ICallFactory> spCallFactory;
  hr = spUnk->QueryInterface(&spCallFactory);
  spUnk = NULL; // not needed anymore

  // Step 3: Get the async interface
  CComPtr<AsyncIMySum> spMySum;
  hr = spCallFactory->CreateCall(__uuidof(AsyncIMySum),
    NULL,
    __uuidof(AsyncIMySum),
    (IUnknown**) &spMySum);
  spCallFactory = NULL; // not needed anymore

  // Step 4: Initiate the call
  hr = spMySum->Begin_GetSum(10, 20);

  // Step 5: Get the value
  long lSum;
  hr = spMySum->Finish_GetSum(&lSum);
  cout << "Sum is: " << lSum << endl;

  // Step 6: Clean up
  spMySum = NULL;
}
```

Note that the call to `Begin_GetSum` returns immediately, giving the caller a chance to do some other processing before calling `Finish_GetSum`.

A couple of things to keep in mind while using the call object:

1. It is important to pair every call to the `Begin` method with a call to the corresponding `Finish` method. COM+ allocates memory to hold the call's output parameters when `Begin` is called. If `Finish` isn't called, this memory (and some other resources) is not freed until the call object is released.

2. A call object supports only one outgoing call at a time. A client cannot call the `Begin` method a second time without calling the `Finish` method first. This is not really a problem. To execute multiple calls concurrently, the caller just has to create multiple call objects.

Under the hood, when `Begin` is called, the ORPC channel executes an asynchronous RPC call and provides the RPC subsystem with the address of a callback function. The `Begin` method then returns, freeing the caller's thread. When the asynchronous RPC call completes, it invokes the callback function. The callback function in turn signals the call object that the call has returned.

If `Finish` is called after the asynchronous RPC call is completed, the method returns immediately (with the call's output parameters). If the asynchronous RPC call is not completed when `Finish` is called, `Finish` will block until the call completes.

Checking Call Status

To prevent `Finish` from blocking, a client can check to see if the RPC call has completed. It can do so by calling `ISynchronize::Wait` on the call object. A return value of `RPC_S_CALLPENDING` indicates that the call has not been completed (and hence a call to `Finish` at the moment would block). The following code snippet demonstrates how to check for call completion:

```
// Step 5: Check for call completion every one second
CComPtr<ISynchronize> spSync;
hr = spMySum->QueryInterface(&spSync);
_ASSERT (SUCCEEDED(hr));
for(;;) {
  Sleep(1 * 1000);
  hr = spSync->Wait(0, 0);
```

```
      if (RPC_S_CALLPENDING != hr) {
        // finished call completion. Get the value.
        break;
      }
      cout << "Call is pending" << endl;
    }
```

Call Completion Notification

Polling from time to time is one way to check for call completion. COM also provides another way wherein the client can be notified asynchronously when the call completes. This is accomplished by a little trick.

When the asynchronous RPC call completes, COM notifies the call object by querying it for the ISynchronize interface and calling the Signal method on it. If the caller provides a call object of its own that supports ISynchronize and aggregates the system-supplied call object, then querying the call object for the ISynchronize returns a pointer to the caller-provided call object. The Signal method will then be called on this object instead of the system-supplied call object. The following ATL-based code shows an implementation of such a call object:

```
class CMyCallNotify :
  public ISynchronize,
  public CComObjectRootEx<CComMultiThreadModel>
{
public:
  CMyCallNotify() {}
  HRESULT Init(ICallFactory* pCallFactory);
  ~CMyCallNotify() {}

DECLARE_GET_CONTROLLING_UNKNOWN ()

BEGIN_COM_MAP(CMyCallNotify)
  COM_INTERFACE_ENTRY(ISynchronize)
  COM_INTERFACE_ENTRY_AGGREGATE_BLIND (m_spUnkInner.p)
END_COM_MAP()

// ISynchronize
public:
  STDMETHOD(Wait)(ULONG dwFlags, ULONG dwMilliseconds);
  STDMETHOD(Signal)();
  STDMETHOD(Reset)();

private:
  CComPtr<ISynchronize> m_spSyncInner;
  CComPtr<IUnknown> m_spUnkInner;
};
```

```
HRESULT CMyCallNotify::Init(ICallFactory* pCallFactory)
{
  // Step 1: Create a call object.
  HRESULT hr = pCallFactory->CreateCall(__uuidof(AsyncIMySum),
    GetControllingUnknown(),
    IID_IUnknown, &m_spUnkInner);
  if (FAILED (hr))
    return hr;

  // Cache a pointer to the aggregated object's
  // ISynchronize interface.
  hr = m_spUnkInner->QueryInterface(__uuidof(ISynchronize),
    (void**) &m_spSyncInner);
  if (FAILED (hr)) {
    m_spUnkInner = NULL;
    return hr;
  }

  return hr;
}

STDMETHODIMP CMyCallNotify::Wait(ULONG dwFlags,
  ULONG dwMilliseconds)
{
  // Forward the call to the inner object
  return m_spSyncInner->Wait(dwFlags, dwMilliseconds);
}

STDMETHODIMP CMyCallNotify::Signal()
{
  // Forward the call to the inner object
  HRESULT hr = m_spSyncInner->Signal();

  // Notify the user
  cout << "Call finished." << endl;
  cout << "Press enter to fetch the sum" << endl;

  return hr;
}

STDMETHODIMP CMyCallNotify::Reset()
{
  // Forward the call to the inner object
  return m_spSyncInner->Reset();
}
```

Note that the outer call object only implements ISynchronize methods. If queried for any interface other than ISynchronize, the outer call object blindly delegates the call to the inner object.

Also note that, for proper functioning, it is important to delegate all the ISynchronize calls to the inner object. In particular, if Signal is not forwarded, a call to Finish_GetSum will block indefinitely.

Call Cancellation

Once a call is initiated, a client has no control over how long the call takes to finish. In some cases, the client may wish to cancel the call if it hasn't returned after a specified period of time. The call object supports another interface, ICancelMethodCalls, to do exactly this. The following code snippet shows its usage:

```
// Cancel the call if the call takes more than a second
CComPtr<ICancelMethodCalls> spCancel;
hr = spMySum->QueryInterface(&spCancel);
_ASSERT (SUCCEEDED(hr));
spCancel->Cancel(1);

// Get the value
long lSum;
hr = spMySum->Finish_GetSum(&lSum);
```

The parameter to ICancelMethodCalls::Cancel specifies the number of seconds Cancel should wait before canceling the call in progress. A value of 0 implies that the call in progress should be canceled right away.

Note that, for proper cleanup, a client should still call Finish after calling cancel. Of course, Finish will fail with an RPC_E_CALL_CANCELED error message. The client should just ignore the output parameters in this case.

When a client cancels a call in progress, the Finish method returns immediately with a RPC_E_CALL_CANCELED message. However, the server is not aware about the client-side cancelation and will continue to execute the method thereby wasting CPU time.

The server could be designed to detect cancelation. Recall from Chapter 7 that a server can obtain its call context by calling CoGetCallContext. This call context supports interface ICancelMethodCalls, which the server can use to check periodically if a call has been cancelled. The following code demonstrates this procedure:

```
STDMETHODIMP CMySum::GetSum(long lVal1, long lVal2, long *plSum)
{
  CComPtr<ICancelMethodCalls> spCancel;
  HRESULT hr = ::CoGetCallContext(__uuidof(ICancelMethodCalls),
    (void**) & spCancel);

  for(int i=0; i<5;i++) {
    ::Sleep(1 * 1000);
    hr = spCancel->TestCancel();
    if (RPC_E_CALL_CANCELED == hr) {
      return RPC_E_CALL_CANCELED;
    }
  }
  *plSum = lVal1 + lVal2;

  return S_OK;
}
```

Asynchronous Servers

With a conventional COM server, when a call enters the server process, the calling thread gets blocked until the call finishes its execution and returns.

If the call is expected to take a significant amount of time to execute, one can employ some clever techniques in the server code to free up the calling thread in a short time. For example, the server can spawn a thread and dispatch the method call to the thread, thus freeing up the calling thread immediately.

COM+, however, offers a formal architecture for developing asynchronous COM servers. An asynchronous server written the COM+ way processes the incoming call in two stages, `Begin` and `Finish`, much like the asynchronous method calls the clients made in the earlier section. If the client makes asynchronous method calls, the stub maps them to the server implementation of the method calls. In case the client makes a synchronous method call, the stub calls the `Begin` and `Finish` methods on the client's behalf.

In order to develop an asynchronous COM server, the following requirements have to be met:

1. The `coclass` has to implement the `ICallFactory` interface.
2. When the stub calls the `ICallFactory::CreateCall` method, the `coclass` implementation should respond by creating a server-side call object and returning it to the stub.

3. The `coclass` need not implement the synchronous version of the interface. Even if it does, the stub never invokes the synchronous interface methods.

Following are the requirements for the server-side call object:

1. The call object must be an aggregatable object. When the stub creates your call object, it aggregates the call object with a system-supplied call object whose `IUnknown` is provided in the second parameter to `CreateCall`.
2. The server-side call object should implement the asynchronous version of the interface.
3. The server-side call object should also implement the `ISynchronize` interface.
4. The call object should ensure that only one call can be processed at a time. The `Begin` method should reject a second call by returning `RPC_S_CALLPENDING` if it is called while the call object is already processing another method call.
5. If `Finish` is called without calling the corresponding `Begin` method first, `Finish` should reject the call by returning `RPC_E_CALL_COMPLETE`.
6. If the processing of the call fails, the failure status should be returned as HRESULT when `Finish` is invoked.

Implementing the `coclass` is relatively straightforward. The following code snippet shows the implementation for a class that supports `IMySum2`. This interface is equivalent in functionality to `IMySum` that we used earlier.

```
class CMySum2 :
  public IMySum2,
  public ICallFactory,
  ...
{
  ...

BEGIN_COM_MAP(CMySum2)
  COM_INTERFACE_ENTRY(IMySum2)
  COM_INTERFACE_ENTRY(ICallFactory)
END_COM_MAP()

// IMySum2
public:
  STDMETHOD(GetSum)( long lVal1, long lVal2, long* plSum);
```

```
// ICallFactory
  STDMETHOD(CreateCall)(REFIID riid1, IUnknown* pUnk,
    REFIID riid2, IUnknown** ppv);
};

STDMETHODIMP CMySum2::CreateCall(REFIID riid1, IUnknown* pUnk,
  REFIID riid2, IUnknown** ppv)
{
  *ppv = NULL;

  // Step 1: Ensure that input parameters are valid
  if (__uuidof(AsyncIMySum2) != riid1) {
    return E_INVALIDARG;
  }
  if (NULL != pUnk && IID_IUnknown != riid2) {
    return E_INVALIDARG;
  }

  // Step 2: Create call object and aggregrate it with pUnk
  CComPtr<CComPolyObject<CMyAsyncSumCallObject> > spCallObject;
  HRESULT hr =
    CComPolyObject<CMyAsyncSumCallObject>::CreateInstance(
      pUnk, &spCallObject);
  _ASSERT (SUCCEEDED(hr));
  spCallObject->InternalAddRef();

  // Step 3: Return the requested interface
  return spCallObject->QueryInterface(riid2, (void**) ppv);
}
```

Implementing a call object requires implementing the `ISynchronize` and `AsyncIMySum` interfaces.

Instead of implementing your own `ISynchronize` interface, you can use one from the system-supplied object whose CLSID is `CLSID_Manual-ResetObject`. All you need to do is to aggregate the system-supplied object with your call object and delegate `QueryInterface` requests for `ISynchronize` to the aggregatee. In ATL, this can be done in one step by using the `COM_INTERFACE_ENTRY_AUTOAGGREGATE` macro. The class definition for our call object is shown here:

```
class CMyAsyncSumCallObject :
   public AsyncIMySum2,
   public CComObjectRoot
{
public:
   CMyAsyncSumCallObject();
```

```
    HRESULT FinalConstruct();
    ~CMyAsyncSumCallObject();

DECLARE_GET_CONTROLLING_UNKNOWN ()

BEGIN_COM_MAP(CMyAsyncSumCallObject)
    COM_INTERFACE_ENTRY(AsyncIMySum2)
    COM_INTERFACE_ENTRY_AUTOAGGREGATE(IID_ISynchronize,
        m_spUnkInner.p, CLSID_ManualResetEvent)
END_COM_MAP()

// AsyncIMySum2
public:
    STDMETHOD(Begin_GetSum)(/*[in]*/ long lVal1,
        /*[in]*/ long lVal2);
    STDMETHOD(Finish_GetSum)(/*[out, retval]*/ long* plSum);

    CComPtr<IUnknown> m_spUnkInner;

private:
    friend class CMyThread;
    CMyThread m_Thread;
    long m_lVal1;
    long m_lVal2;
    long m_lSum;

    typedef CCPLWinSharedResource<bool> SAFEBOOL;
    SAFEBOOL m_bCallInProgress;
};
```

It should be noted that the system-supplied call object also implements the ISynchronize object. Your ISynchronize interface is used only if your call object is not aggregated by the stub. This only happens if your call object resides in the same apartment as the thread that calls ICallFactory::CreateCall.

In the above class definition, member variable m_bCallInProgress is used to make certain that only one Begin call is serviced at a time by the call object. As the Begin and Finish methods can be accessed from multiple threads, this variable needs to be thread-safe, which is what the CCPLWinSharedResource template does (see Chapter 6 for its usage).

A typical implementation of a call object spawns a thread in response to an incoming Begin call and delegates the processing to the thread. When the thread finishes processing, it needs to notify the call object by calling the ISynchronize::Signal method. My implementation of the call object uses a thread class, CMyThread, to accomplish this. The implementation of its main thread procedure is shown here:

```
void CMyThread::Proc()
{
   _ASSERT (NULL != m_pCallObject);

   // Step 1
   // For the simulation, sleep for five seconds
   // before computing the sum.
   ::Sleep(5 * 1000);
   m_pCallObject->m_lSum =
     m_pCallObject->m_lVal1 + m_pCallObject->m_lVal2;

   // Step 2
   // Signal the call object that the sum has been computed
   CComPtr<ISynchronize> spSync;
   HRESULT hr =
     m_pCallObject->QueryInterface(__uuidof(ISynchronize),
        (void**) &spSync);
   _ASSERT (SUCCEEDED(hr));
   spSync->Signal();
}
```

When the finished state is signaled, the stub calls `Finish_GetSum` on the call object to obtain the output parameters. Following is the implementation of the `Finish_GetSum` method:

```
STDMETHODIMP CMyAsyncSumCallObject::Finish_GetSum(
   /*[out, retval]*/ long* plSum)
{
   *plSum = 0; // initialize

   // Ensure that begin has been called
   SAFEBOOL::GUARD guard(m_bCallInProgress);
   bool& bCallInProgress = guard;
   if (false == bCallInProgress) {
     // "Finish" called before "Begin"
     return RPC_E_CALL_COMPLETE;
   }

   // wait till the thread signals the completion
   CComPtr<ISynchronize> spSync;
   HRESULT hr = this->QueryInterface(__uuidof(ISynchronize),
      (void**) &spSync);
   _ASSERT (SUCCEEDED(hr));
   spSync->Wait(0, INFINITE);
   spSync = NULL;

   *plSum = m_lSum;
   bCallInProgress = false;
   return S_OK;
}
```

Note that `Finish_GetSum` calls the `ISynchronize::Wait` method. This will ensure that `Finish` will not return bogus results if it is called before the spawned thread finishes its processing.

Why can't you just wait for the thread handle to close instead? Well, there is a problem doing so. When the spawned thread calls `ISynchronize::Signal`, the stub uses the same thread to call `Finish_GetSum`. `Finish_GetSum` would then be waiting for the current thread handle to close, resulting in a deadlock.

Canceling a Synchronous Call

Whether or not you use the asynchronous call mechanism in your application, there is one COM+ feature that deserves special attention. Under Windows 2000, it is possible to cancel a synchronous blocking call! Here's how it works.

Obviously, a thread that is waiting for the blocking call to return cannot cancel itself. However, another thread can cancel the call on the calling thread's behalf. First, the thread obtains the `ICancelMethodCalls` interface by calling a Win32 API, `CoGetCancelObject`. Then it calls `ICancelMethodCalls::Cancel`. The implementation is shown below:

```
void CMyCancelThread::Proc()
{
  CComPtr<ICancelMethodCalls> spCancelMethodCalls;
  HRESULT hr = ::CoGetCancelObject(m_dwThreadId,
    __uuidof(ICancelMethodCalls),
    (void**) &spCancelMethodCalls);
  spCancelMethodCalls->Cancel(0);
}
```

Note that the ability to cancel synchronous calls is disabled by default. Each thread that requires the ability to cancel a method call that it makes (from some other thread) must enable call cancellation by calling the `CoEnableCallCancellation` API. The thread can later disable call cancellation by calling the `CoDisableCallCancellation` API. However, be aware that enabling call cancellation results in serious performance degradation.

COM+ PIPES

The standard marshaling technique under COM was originally designed to hide the details of the RPC mechanism as much as possible. When the client calls a method, the `[in]` parameters are transferred to the server, and the `[out]` parameters are returned at the end of the call. In general, the amount of data that is passed over the network via method parameters is not much; the performance of data transfer is not that big an issue. However, if a large amount of data needs to be transferred, the standard transferring mechanism is not adequate. Pipes were introduced in COM+ to facilitate bulk data transfer within a method call.

A COM+ pipe is an ordered sequence of elements of the same type. It supports two methods, Push and Pull. As should be obvious, Push is used to send data to the server and Pull is used to fetch data from the server. The SDK defines a template-like interface definition for the pipe, shown as follows:

```
interface IPipe##name : IUnknown
{
  HRESULT Pull(
    [out, size_is(cRequest), length_is(*pcReturned)]type *buf,
    [in] ULONG cRequest,
    [out] ULONG *pcReturned     );

  HRESULT Push(
    [in, size_is(cSent)] type *buf,
    [in] ULONG cSent );
}
```

Based on this template, COM+ defines three pipe interfaces: IPipeByte (to transfer BYTE data type), IPipeLong (to transfer LONG data type), and IPipeDouble (to transfer DOUBLE data type).

An IPipeXXX interface can be used as any regular interface—the server can implement the interface and the client can query for the interface.

The following code snippet shows an implementation of the IPipe-Long::Push method:

```
STDMETHODIMP CMyPipeSvr::Push(LONG *buf, ULONG cSent)
{
  ::MessageBox(NULL, _T("Received data"), _T("Server"), MB_OK);
  for (ULONG i=0; i<cSent; i++) {
    // do something with buf[i]
  }
  return S_OK;;
}
```

The corresponding client-side implementation that calls the IPipe-Long::Push method is shown below. It generates sequential numbers and passes it to the server.

```
void sub()
{
  // Instantiate the object
  IUnknownPtr spUnk(__uuidof(MyPipeSvr));

  // Obtain the IPipeLong interface
  IPipeLongPtr spPipe = spUnk;

  // Push data to the pipe
  const int BUFSIZE = 100000;
  LONG buf[BUFSIZE];
  for (long i=0; i<BUFSIZE; i++) {
    buf[i] = i;
  }

  HRESULT hr = spPipe->Push(buf, BUFSIZE);
  if (FAILED(hr)) {
    _com_issue_error(hr);
  }
  ::MessageBox(NULL, _T("Sent data"), _T("Client"), MB_OK);
}
```

Looking at the server and the client code, IPipeXXX doesn't look any different from other interfaces. So what's so special about these interfaces? The answer lies in the COM+ implementation of the proxy stub for IPipeXXX interfaces. For each pipe interface, COM+ provides a corresponding asynchronous version. The proxy/stub code for the pipe interfaces performs read-ahead and write-behind buffer management using asynchronous versions of the pipe interfaces. When Push is called from the client, the proxy pushes the data into the ORPC channel and returns immediately. This transparently improves the performance of large data transfer within the application.

SUMMARY

In this chapter, we looked at various features that COM+ provides to help develop scalable enterprise systems. These features include:

- ODBC connection pooling and OLE DB resource pooling
- JIT activations
- Object pooling
- Asynchronous method calls
- COM+ pipes

There were more scalability features that were initially planned to be released with Windows 2000 but were ultimately dropped. Two such features were Component Load Balancing (CLB) and In-Memory Database (IMDB).

CLB will be included with a new product from Microsoft named App-Center Server. With this technology, the client requests the AppCenter Server machine to activate an object. The COM+ Service Control Manager (SCM) on the AppCenter Server has been modified to handle the request locally or forward it to one of the specified set of machines based on dynamic input collected and analyzed by the load-balancing service. See Tim Ewald's article in *Microsoft Systems Journal* [Ewa-00] for more details.

With IMDB, a database can be completely loaded into memory. As the data is now accessed from the memory instead of a very slow (comparatively) hard disk, the throughput increases significantly. IMDB is very useful for those applications where reads vastly outnumber writes. See David Platt's book [Pla-99] for more details. The current status of IMDB can be found at the Microsoft website [MSDN-01].

A future release of COM+ (COM+ 1.x) will provide more services that will improve the scalability of a COM+ application. You will be able to configure the isolation level of a transaction (see Chapter 8) on a per-component basis. The release will also provide a mechanism to automatically and gracefully shutdown and restart a server process whose performance has degraded over time (for example, because of memory leaks). This feature is referred to as *process recycling*.

REFERENCES

[Ahl-99]   Leland Ahlbeck and Don Willits, "Pooling in the Microsoft Data Access Components," MSDN Library, May 1999. *http://msdn.microsoft.com/library/techart/pooling2.htm*

[Zim-99]   Steve Zimmerman, "Scalability, State, and MTS," *Microsoft Internet Developer*, vol. 4, no. 3, March 1999. *http://msdn.microsoft.com/library/periodic/period99/extreme0399.htm*

[MSDN-00] "COM+ Technical Series: Object Pooling," MSDN Library, August 1999. *http://msdn.microsoft.com/library/techart/complusobjpool.htm*

[Pro-00]   Jeff Prosise, "Asynchronous Method Calls Eliminate the Wait for COM Clients and Servers Alike," *MSDN Magazine*, vol. 15, no. 4, April 2000. *http://msdn.microsoft.com/library/periodic/period00/async.htm*

[Edd-99]   Guy Eddon and Henry Eddon, *Inside COM+ Base Services*, ISBN 0-7356-0728-1, Microsoft Press, 1999.

[Sab-99]   Brian Sabino, "Non-Blocking Method Calls," MSDN Library, Microsoft Corporation, August 1999. *http://msdn.microsoft.com/library/techart/nbmc.htm*

[Ewa-00]   Timothy Ewalds, "Use AppCenter Server or COM and MTS for Load Bal-
            ancing Your Component Servers," *Microsoft Systems Journal*, vol. 15, no. 1,
            January 2000. *http://msdn.microsoft.com/library/periodic/period00/load-
            bal.htm*

[MSDN-01]   "What Happened to IMDB?" MSDN Library, Microsoft Corporation, Sep-
            tember 1999. *http://msdn.microsoft.com/library/techart/whatimdb.htm*

Administration

$\mathbf{I}$n the previous chapters, we examined the COM+ programming model and learned how to create COM+ applications that can avail various services provided by COM+. We also observed that the configured settings on a component are stored in the COM+ catalog. On several occasions, we used the Component Services snap-in tool to specify these settings.

To help you install and configure components programmatically, COM+ provides a set of automation objects that expose all of the functionality of the Component Services snap-in. Using these automation objects, you can develop, for example, batch mode installation programs or scripts to perform routine administrative tasks.

In this chapter, we will examine the administration object model of COM+ and see how we can automate some routine tasks.

OVERVIEW

COM+ stores all the information about an application in a persistent storage called the COM+ catalog (henceforth, simply the catalog).

The catalog uses two different stores:

- the Windows registry (HKEY_CLASSES_ROOT)
- the COM+ registration database (called RegDB)

When a component is installed in the catalog, the classic COM aspects of registration, such as the PROGID of the class and the complete path to the component DLL, are stored under the Windows registry. The Windows registry is also used to store the type library and proxy/stub information. All other configuration attributes are stored in the RegDB database. This *split-registration* makes it easy to migrate existing components (components based on classic COM) into the catalog without having to rebuild the component.

The catalog stores the configuration attribute at the application level, the component level, the interface level, as well as the interface method level. These configuration settings help an application specify and use various COM+ services such as transactions, synchronization, security, object pooling, JIT activation, component queuing, and COM+ events.

To access the catalog, COM+ provides an administrative component called the Catalog Manager. The Catalog Manager exposes a set of automation objects collectively referred to as the COMAdmin objects. Using these COMAdmin objects, you can read and write information that is stored in the catalog and perform tasks such as:

- install and configure COM+ applications
- manage installed COM+ applications
- manage and configure COM+ services
- export existing COM+ applications for deployment to other machines
- remotely administer component services on a different machine

The COMAdmin objects can be used to develop either lightweight scripts or general-purpose administration tools. For example, you can:

- write scripts to perform routine administrative tasks
- develop tools to administer and monitor component services
- create installation programs for your COM+ applications

In fact, the Component Services snap-in itself is just a convenient graphical front-end that is based on the COMAdmin objects.

On each Windows 2000 machine there is a COM+ catalog server running as a component in the system application. The catalog server controls access to the catalog data stored on the local machine. The catalog server essentially is a query engine that allows data to be read from and written to the catalog on that machine.

In order to access the catalog on a machine, a session has to be opened with the catalog server on that machine. As we will see shortly, one of the COMAdmin objects lets us do just this.

Let's look at the COMAdmin objects in detail.

COM+ ADMINISTRATION OBJECT MODEL

The COMAdmin objects offer a simple object model for accessing the catalog.

- The data stored in the catalog is treated as a hierarchy of collections. Collections serve as a container of homogeneous items. For instance, a COM+ application contains a collection of components; each component contains a collection of interfaces; each interface contains a collection of methods, and so on.
- Each item in a collection exposes a set of properties that is consistent across the collection. For instance, every item in the "Applications" collection will expose a "Name" property, an "AppId" property, and so forth. Depending on how the properties are accessed, some properties are read-only while others can be read or written to.

Table 12.1 lists some of the collection types that are currently exposed through the COMAdmin object model.

Table 12.1   COMAdmin Collections

Collection	Description
Applications	List of all COM+ applications installed on the local machine
Components	List of all components in an application
DCOMProtocols	List of all the protocols used by DCOM
ErrorInfo	Extended error information when a method on any COMAdmin object fails
InprocServers	List of all the in-process COM servers registered with the system
InterfacesForComponent	List of all the interfaces exposed by a component
LocalComputer	List of computer-level settings information
MethodsForInterface	List of all the methods on an interface
PropertyInfo	List of all the properties that a specified collection supports
RelatedCollectionInfo	List of other collections related to the collection from which this method is called
Roles	List of roles for an application
UsersInRole	List of users in a role

The hierarchy of collection objects is shown in Figure 12.1.

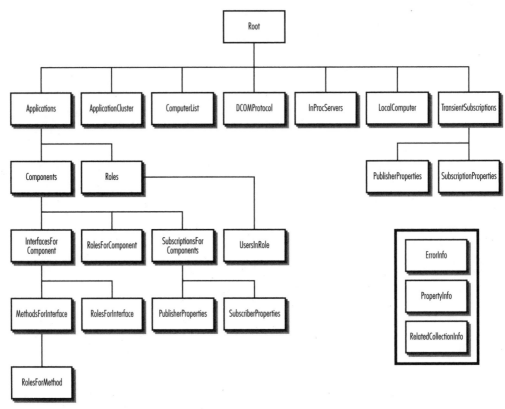

Figure 12.1   Hierarchy of COM+ administrative collections. Adapted from [Pla-99].

Note that three collections are missing from the hierarchical representation: `ErrorInfo`, `RelatedCollectionInfo`, and `PropertyInfo`. This is because these three collections have special meaning and can be obtained from any other collection.

The `ErrorInfo` collection provides extended error information in case of failure while using `COMAdmin` methods to read or write to the catalog.

The `PropertyInfo` collection provides information about the properties that a specified collection supports.

The `RelatedCollectionInfo` collection provides information about other collections related to the collection from which it is called.

We will see the programming usage of these three collections later in the chapter.

In order to access the catalog, the collections in the catalog, the items in the collections, and the properties on these items, the COMAdmin library provides three (and only three) generic objects: COMAdminCatalog, COMAdminCatalogCollection, and COMAdminCatalogObject. Each object implements a dual interface, making it convenient to be used from early bound development tools as well as late bound development tools such as VB, VBScript, JScript, etc.

COMAdminCatalog Object

The COMAdminCatalog object is used to represent the catalog itself. It is the fundamental object that is used for any programmatic administration. It supports an interface, ICOMAdminCatalog, that provides methods to implement a variety of administrative tasks. Some of these tasks are listed below:

- Connect to a catalog server, on either the local or the remote machine.
- Retrieve various collections from the catalog.
- Install, export, start, shutdown, and obtain information regarding COM+ applications.
- Install or import single COM+ components, that is, components that are not part of any COM+ applications.
- Start and stop COM+ services.

Table 12.2 describes some selected methods from ICOMAdminCatalog interface.

Table 12.2   Selected Methods From Interface ICOMAdminCatalog

Method	Description
Administrative Methods	
Connect	Opens a session with the catalog server on the specified machine
GetCollection	Retrieves the specified collection
GetCollectionByQuery	Retrieves any collection anywhere in the hierarchy
Component Methods	
ImportComponent	Places an already registered component into the catalog
InstallComponent	Installs a new component into the catalog
GetMultipleComponentsInfo	Retrieves information about one or more components

Table 12.2   Selected Methods From Interface `ICOMAdminCatalog` (cont.)

Method	Description
Application Methods	
ShutdownApplication	Shuts down a running server application
ExportApplication	Produces a self-contained installation file (.MSI) for installing the application onto other machines
InstallApplication	Reads an MSI file and installs the application
Services Methods	
StartRouter	Starts the load-balancing router service (if installed)
StopRouter	Stops the load-balancing router service (if installed)
StartIMDB	Starts the in-memory database service (if installed)
StopIMDB	Stops the in-memory database service (if installed)
ServiceCheck	Checks the status of a COM related service
Events Method	
InstallEventClass	Installs an event class into an application
GetEventClassesForIID	Gets a list of event classes matching the specified interface
Backup Methods	
BackupREGDB	Backup RegDB into a file
RestoreREGDB	Restore RegDB from a file

COMAdminCatalog can be instantiated using the PROGID "COMAdmin.COMAdminCatalog," as shown in the following VBScript code fragment:

```
Set Catalog = CreateObject("COMAdmin.COMAdminCatalog")
```

When COMAdminCatalog is instantiated, it opens a session with the local catalog server. To open a session to a remote catalog server, the Connect method on the object can be called, as illustrated in the following VBScript code fragment:

```
Catalog.Connect("myremotemachinename")
```

We will cover some other methods later in the chapter.

`COMAdminCatalogCollection` Object

`COMAdminCatalogCollection` is a generic object used to represent any collection. It supports an interface, `ICatalogCollection`, that enables you to:

- enumerate through the items contained within the collection
- add or remove items to or from the collection
- save or discard any pending changes made to the collection or to the items it contains
- retrieve a related collection from the catalog

Table 12.3 describes some selected methods from the `ICatalogCollection` interface.

Table 12.3   Selected Methods From the `ICatalogCollection` Interface

Method	Description
Populate the collection	
Populate	Reads in current data from the catalog for all objects in the collection
PopulateByKey	Reads in data only for the specified objects
PopulateByQuery	Reads in data for the objects matching the query. Not implemented in the current release
Information Retrieval	
Count	Obtains the number of items in the collection
Item	Obtains an item given its index from the collection
_NewEnum	Obtains an enumerator for the collection
Item Manipulation	
Add	Adds a new element to the collection
Remove	Removes a specified element from the collection
SaveChanges	Saves any changes made to the collection or its objects
Related Collection	
GetCollection	Gets a collection related to this collection's specific object

A collection can be obtained in two ways:

1. By calling `GetCollection` on the `COMAdminCatalog` object.
2. By calling `GetCollection` on the `COMAdminCatalogCollection` object.

Actually, `GetCollection` just sets up the returned list to be filled. The list is not filled until `Populate` (or its variants) is called, in which case the list gets filled up with the current items from the catalog. The usage is illustrated in the following lines of code:

```
set Applications = Catalog.GetCollection("Applications")
Applications.Populate
```

`Populate` can be called as many times as desired. Each call just synchronizes the list with the latest data from the catalog. Note that it is possible that some other application would have changed the collection that you are holding.

When a collection is retrieved, the data is actually stored in a transient cache. If an item is added, removed, or modified in the collection, the transient cache gets modified, not the actual catalog. To commit the changes to the catalog, you should call `SaveChanges`. After calling `SaveChanges` you would need to reload the collection list (by calling `Populate`), as shown in the following code fragment:

```
' Add a new appliction
Dim newApplication
Set newApplication = applications.Add
... ' Set various properties on newApplication

' Commit new application and reload the list
applications.SaveChanges
applications.Populate
```

It is possible that multiple programs may be working on the catalog simultaneously. While you are working on your transient copy of the data, someone else may have modified the catalog, either programmatically or through the Component Services snap-in. If there is any contention when the changes are being saved, the general rule is that the last writer wins, that is, the data stored in the catalog is the one that came from the last one to save it.

COMAdminCatalogObject Object

COMAdminCatalogObject is a generic object that can be used to represent any item contained in a collection. It exposes an interface, ICatalogObject, that can be used to:

- obtain information about an item (in the collection) and its properties
- modify the properties of the item

Table 12.4 shows some properties available on the ICatalogObject interface.

Table 12.4 Selected Properties From the ICatalogObject Interface

Method	Description
Name	Gets the name of the item
Key	Gets the unique ID of the item
Value	Gets or sets a named property on the item

Each item in a collection has a name and a unique key. The key serves as the primary identifier for the item. In some cases it is a GUID, such as the CLSID for a component; in some cases it is the name of the item itself.

Each item in a collection contains properties that apply to that type of item. For example, every item in the *applications* collection represents an *application* object. Each application object has properties such as *activation*. (This property indicates if the application is a library application or a server application.)

Each property of a specific collection is uniquely identified by a name. The *Value* property on the ICatalogObject interface is used to obtain or save a specific named property exposed by an item.

The following VBScript code fragment lists each application installed on the local system. For each application, the code displays the application's key and whether the application is a library application or a server application.

```
' Instantiate a COMAdminCatalog object
Set Catalog = CreateObject("ComAdmin.COMAdminCatalog")

' Get the "Applications" collection and populate it
set Applications = Catalog.GetCollection("Applications")
Applications.Populate
```

```
' Display the name of each application
for each AppObject in Applications
  DispString = AppObject.Name & " " & AppObject.Key
  if AppObject.Value("Activation") = 0 then
    DispString = DispString & " - INPROC"
  else
    DispString = DispString & " - LOCAL"
  end if
  wscript.Echo DispString
next
```

Some collections may expose the name and key of an item as properties as well. For example, the key of an application object can also be obtained as `AppObject.Value("ID")`. If you add a new object and save it with the key property of an existing object, you will overwrite the existing object.

Beware of setting the "key" property on an item. In most cases, it is better to let the catalog generate the key for you.

If a property is modified, the change is not committed until `SaveChanges` is called on the collection.

All the COMAdmin classes are served by one DLL—ComAdmin.DLL. It can be found in the system32\COM subdirectory.

PROGRAMMING CONSIDERATIONS

Now that we understand the administrative object model and various types of collections available in the catalog, we are almost ready to automate some common administration tasks. Before we do that, however, there are a few other programming issues we need to examine.

Error Handling

As with all COM interface methods, COMAdmin objects return error codes in the form of HRESULTs. For the benefit of C++ programmers, these error codes are defined in `<winerror.h>` as "COMADMIN_E_XXX" error messages. For VBScript programmers, error codes can be accessed through the familiar `err` object.

When you use methods such as `Populate` and `SaveChanges` on `COMAdminCatalogCollection`, you could be reading or writing data for every item in the collection. Complicated errors can occur and they can be difficult to diagnose based on a single numeric error code. To address this problem, `COMAdmin` objects provide extended error information through a special collection called the `ErrorInfo` collection.

The `ErrorInfo` collection can be obtained in one of the following two ways:

1. By calling `GetCollection` on the `COMAdminCatalog` object with `ErrorInfo` as the name of the collection.
2. By calling `GetCollection` on the `COMAdminCatalogCollection` object with `ErrorInfo` as the name of the collection, leaving the second parameter blank.

When a `COMAdmin` object method fails, you must fetch and `Populate` the `ErrorInfo` collection immediately (before calling any other method on the object). Otherwise, the `ErrorInfo` collection gets reset and you will lose the extended error information.

Each `ErrorInfo` object in the collection has two important properties—`Name` and `ErrorCode`. The first property indicates the name of the object or file that had an error, and the second property contains the error code for the object or file.

The following VBScript code fragment shows how to retrieve and display the extended error information:

```
on error resume next
' do some operation that may fail
if err <> 0 then
   Dim errorInfo
   set errorInfo = catalog.GetCollection("ErrorInfo")
   errorInfo.Populate
   Dim item
   for each item in errorInfo
     msgbox item.Name & " " & hex(item.Value("ErrorCode"))
   next
end if
```

Administrative Tasks and Transactions

Sometimes, it is desirable to perform all the administrative operations within a single transaction so that the configuration changes are committed or aborted as one atomic operation. Some of the benefits of doing this are:

- Consistency of data—The administrative operations performed within a transaction are committed or aborted as a whole.
- Consistent deployment across multiple machines—If a COM+ application is deployed across multiple machines, it is guaranteed that all servers are left with an identical configuration.
- Performance—When you perform multiple operations within a transaction, all writes to RegDB are performed at once. Writing to RegDB is a relatively expensive operation. If you are making many writes to RegDB (by calling SaveChanges, for example), you will get better performance.

The good news is that the registration database (RegDB) is a transacted resource manager, that is, it can be enlisted with the DTC (see Chapter 8).

The bad news is that many other resources involved in normal administrative tasks, such as the Windows registry, the file system, and the Windows Installer (MSI), are not transactional. In case of an error, any changes made to these resources will not be rolled back. For example, if there is an error installing a COM+ application from an MSI file, the application will not appear in the catalog, but some files that were copied to the hard disk may still be left there, in which case one has to manually delete them.

Changes to the normal administration programming model

To ensure proper data consistency, RegDB forces certain blocking and isolation behavior that you should be aware of.

When any COMAdmin method is called within a transaction that causes a write to the catalog, the catalog server puts a writer lock on the catalog, that is, any other writer trying to modify the catalog gets blocked until the current transaction gets committed or aborted. Only those writers that are part of the current transaction are allowed to enter the lock.

The readers are not blocked. However, the data that the *external* readers see will not reflect any interim changes made within the transaction until the transaction commits. Only those readers participating in the current transaction can see the interim data states.

To achieve this isolation behavior, `RegDB` effectively provides a data cache for the transaction to use. This impacts the behavior of the `SaveChanges` method.

Normally, a call to `SaveChanges` writes all the changes back to the catalog. Within a transaction, however, `SaveChanges` returns immediately, whether or not all changes have been transitionally committed to `RegDB`. This is particularly a problem for the `StartApplication` method call subsequent to a `SaveChanges` method call. There is no guarantee that `StartApplication` will use fresh data.

Within a transaction, it is a good idea to introduce a "sleep" for a few seconds between `SaveChanges` and `StartApplication` calls.

Now that we understand the transactional behavior of `RegDB` and the caveats thereof, let's see how we can perform administrative tasks within a transaction.

Participating in a Transaction

Using the transaction context object would probably be the simplest way to perform administrative operations within a transaction. Recall from Chapter 8 that a non-transactional client can use a transaction context object to create a single transaction.

The following VBScript code fragment illustrates the use of a transaction context object:

```
' Create the transaction context
Dim txCtx
Set txCtx = CreateObject("TxCtx.TransactionContext")

' Create the catalog object within the transaction
Dim catalog
Set catalog = txctx.CreateInstance("COMAdmin.COMAdminCatalog")
...
if err <> 0 then
  txCtx.Abort
else
  txCtx.Commit
end if
```

SOME COMMON ADMINISTRATIVE TASKS

In this section, we will develop some simple `VBScript`-based programs to automate some common administrative tasks. To keep the code simple, I will assume that our administrative tasks will not fail; consequently, the error checking code is not written. The code is included on the CD. You may wish to add error checking yourself.

Uninstalling an Application

We will remove an application by its name.

An application belongs to the `Applications` collection. Let's obtain this collection first, as shown below:

```
' Create the catalog object
Dim catalog
Set catalog = CreateObject("COMAdmin.COMAdminCatalog")

' Get the applications collection
Dim applications
Set applications = catalog.GetCollection("Applications")
applications.Populate
```

Now, removing an application is as easy as iterating through the `Applications` collection, searching the application by its name, and removing the application once found.

```
' Remove an application identified by applicationName
Dim i, numPackages, bChanged
bChanged = False
numPackages = applications.Count
For i = numPackages - 1 To 0 Step -1
   If applications.Item(i).Value("Name") = applicationName Then
      applications.Remove (i)
      bChanged = True
   End If
Next
```

As the name of an application is not unique, the code above attempts to remove all the applications that match the name.

Notice that we are iterating through the collection in a backward order. This is because when an item is removed from the collection, the `COMAdmin` library reindexes the items with higher indices downward to fill the removed item's place. Iterating backwards through the indices is the simplest way to reach each item exactly once.

Also notice the use of the boolean variable `bChanged`. Recall that the changes are not persisted back into the catalog until a `SaveChange` is called. Variable `bChanged` just offers us a little optimization in that we can commit the changes only if the named application was removed. The code fragment is shown below:

```
' Commit our deletions
If (bChanged = true) Then
   applications.SaveChanges
End If.
```

When an application gets removed, all of the components that belong to the application get unregistered. In addition, if an application was installed from an MSI file, the installation files will get deleted.

Installing an Application

Now let's develop a script to do the following operations:

* Install a library application named "My Test Application"
* Add a user role called "Managers" to the application
* Add a component with synchronization set to required, transaction set to required, and just-in-time activation enabled

Before installing an application, it is always a good idea to check if the application might already exist in the catalog. If it does, we need to remove such entries. Our earlier code to remove an application can be used here once again (which is why I dealt with uninstalling an application first).

The next step, as you have already guessed, is to fetch the `applications` collection and add the new application to the collection.

```
' Add the new appliction
Dim newApplication
Set newApplication = applications.Add
newApplication.Value("Name") = applicationName
newApplication.Value("Activation") = 0 ' Inproc=0, Local=1
applications.SaveChanges
```

The possible choices for `activation` property are `COMAdminActivationInproc` and `COMAdminActivationLocal`. These enumeration constants, along with enumeration constants for many other properties such as synchronization, transaction, authentication, etc., are all defined in

ComAdmin.idl and can be used directly in a C++ program. VBScript programmers, however, have to be content with using numeric values.

Once the application has been added to the catalog, performing any task on the application, such as adding components underneath it, requires us to obtain the key for the application. Do not forget to call Populate first on the just-saved collection. The code is shown here:

```
applications.Populate
' Get the application key
dim appKey
numPackages = applications.Count
For i = 0 To (numPackages - 1)
   If applications.Item(i).Value("Name") = applicationName Then
      appKey = applications.Item(i).Key
   End If
Next
```

To add a user-role to the application, we just get the related collection called roles for the application (identified by its key).

```
' Add a role called "Managers"
Dim roles
Set roles = applications.GetCollection("Roles", appKey)
roles.populate

Dim newRole
Set newRole = roles.Add
newRole.Value("Name") = "Managers"
roles.SaveChanges
```

To install a component, the COMAdminCatalog object has a method, InstallComponent. The method takes four parameters. The first two parameters are the application key and pathname of the DLL containing the component. The third parameter specifies an external type library file. If there is no external type library, an empty string can be passed. The fourth parameter specifies the proxy/stub DLL for the component, if there is one. Otherwise, an empty string can be passed. The code is shown here:

```
' Install a component
catalog.InstallComponent appKey, _
   "F: \MTAServer\Debug\MTAServer.dll" , "", ""
```

The first parameter to `InstallComponent` can either be the application key or the name of the application.

In order to set any configuration on the just-added component, the `components` collection for the application has to be accessed, and the component has to be identified. For administrative tasks, a component is typically identified by its `ProgID`, as shown in the following code snippet:

```
Dim components
Set components = applications.GetCollection("Components", appKey)
components.Populate

dim numComponents
numComponents = components.Count
for i = numComponents-1 to 0 step -1
  if components.Item(i).Value("ProgID") =    "MTAServer.MyTest.1" _
  then
    components.Item(i).Value("Synchronization") = 3
    components.Item(i).Value("Transaction") = 3
    components.Item(i).Value("JustInTimeActivation") = true
  end if
next
components.SaveChanges
```

The numeric values for synchronization and transaction settings can be obtained from `ComAdmin.idl` or from the SDK help documentation.

We are done installing an application.

This example provides the salient features of the `COMAdmin` programming model. Though these are just three object types they provide significant functionality and are easy to use.

Deploying an Application

Deploying an application that is installed on one machine to another machine requires the following three steps:

1. Create an installation package for the application
2. Copy the installation package to a network share directory that is accessible from the remote machine

3. Connect to the remote machine's catalog server and install the application from the installation package

To create an installation package, the `COMAdmin` library provides a method, `ExportApplication`, on the `COMAdminCatalog` object. When this method is called, COM+ generates Windows Installer (MSI) compatible installation image, which is a single file containing all the necessary pieces to install the application on another machine. This includes:

- The application's set of classes, components, and attributes at the application, component, interface, and interface method levels.
- All the DLLs and type libraries that describe the interfaces implemented by the application's classes.

In addition to the `.msi` file, `ExportApplication` creates a cabinet (CAB) file. This file, in effect, wraps the `.msi` file, allowing the users to download the application from a web browser such as Microsoft Internet Explorer.

In the following sample code, I create a MSI file, `MyApp.MSI`, from the application that I had installed earlier in the section:

```
Dim applicationName
applicationName = "My Test Application"

' Create the catalog object
Dim catalog
Set catalog = CreateObject("COMAdmin.COMAdminCatalog")

' Export the app to a file
catalog.ExportApplication applicationName,
".\MyApp.MSI", 0
```

`ExportApplication` requires three parameters—the application identifier (either the name or the key), the output file name, and a `long` value to specify some option flags. The option flags can be obtained from the SDK documentation. In the above code, I used a 0 value to indicate that I wish to export user-role information without exporting the actual list of users assigned to each role.

The second step of deployment is to copy the just-generated MSI file to a network share that is accessible to the remote machine.

The third step is to connect to the remote machine, using the `Connect` method, and install the application using the `InstallApplication` method. Both these methods are available on the COMAdminCatalog object. In the code snippet below, I install the application from the MyApp.msi file that is present on my local network share, \\PVDEV\MyNetShare, to a remote machine called PVDC.

```
' Connect to the remote catalog server
Dim catalog
Set catalog = CreateObject("COMAdmin.COMAdminCatalog")
catalog.Connect "PVDC"

' Install the app from the file
catalog.InstallApplication "\\PVDEV\MyNetShare\MyApp.MSI"
```

When a COM+ application is installed from an MSI file, the Windows Installer extracts the necessary files into the \Program Files\COMPlus Applications\{AppKey} directory, where AppKey is a GUID unique to the application. The installer also adds an entry in the Add/Remove Programs control panel.

FUTURE ENHANCEMENTS

The future release of COM+ (COM+ 1.x) will add many services that will increase the overall scalability, availability, and manageability of COM+ 1.0 applications. Some of these features follow:

- The ability to gracefully shutdown and restart a server process whose performance has degraded over time (for example, because of memory leaks).
- The ability to run a COM+ 1.x application as a service.
- Ability to disallow servers to be loaded or components to be created under low memory conditions. This feature is referred to as the memory gates. For example, a process-creation memory gate can be defined as "do not create a process if 80% of the virtual memory on the system is already being used. Similarly, an object-creation memory gate can be specified such that an object is not created under low-memory conditions. In this case, the client receives E_OUTOFMEMORY when it tries to create an object.
- A COM+ server application can be paused. Any future activation returns E_APP_PAUSED error code. A paused application can be resumed later to allow future activations.

- A COM+ application (library or server) can be disabled. This feature is similar to pausing an application except that this attribute survives system reboots. A disabled application can be enabled anytime later to allow future activations.

- Ability to allow an administrator to dump the entire state of a process without terminating it. This eases the troubleshooting process for a COM+ application.

- The ability to alias a single component with multiple CLSIDs. Each of the aliased component can be configured individually.

- The ability to mark a component as private. A private component can only be seen and activated from other components within the same application.

- The ability to allow multiple configurations of a single application on a machine.

The COMAdmin SDK will provide the necessary APIs to support these features.

SUMMARY

This chapter concerns the administration of COM+ applications and services. The COM+ catalog, organized as a hierarchy of collections, uses the Windows registry and an auxiliary database called RegDB to persist attributes concerning applications. While the PROGID of a class, path to the component DLL, type library, and proxy/stub information are stored in the Windows registry, COM+ configuration attributes are stored in RegDB. Typical RegDB data includes settings for the use of transactions, synchronization, security, object pooling, JIT activation, queuing, and COM+ events.

The catalog server on each Windows 2000 machine acts as a query engine that allows data to be read and written to the catalog.

The administration object model defines three COMAdmin objects. These COMAdmin objects are used to read and write information that is stored in the catalog. Furthermore, the admin objects are also used to manage COM+ applications and services, including the installation of applications on the local machine and the deployment of applications to remote machines.

The COMAdminCatalog object is used to represent the catalog itself. It is the fundamental object that is used for any programmatic administration. It supports the ICOMAdminCatalog interface, which provides methods to implement a variety of administrative tasks.

The COMAdminCatalogCollection is a generic object used to represent any collection. It supports an interface, ICatalogCollection, which enables one to: enumerate through collections, add and remove items from a collection, and retrieve related information from a collection.

The COMAdminCatalogObject is a generic object that can be used to represent any item contained in a collection. It exposes an interface, ICatalogObject, that can be used to obtain and/or modify information about an item (in the collection) and its properties.

Error handling issues that arise from attempts to modify the catalog must be considered when using the COMAdmin objects. The programming model provides the ErrorInfo collection to obtain extended error information in case of failure.

Administrative operations may be performed within a transaction so that the configuration changes are committed or aborted as one atomic operation.

The future release of COM+ (COM+ 1.x) will add many services that will increase the overall scalability, availability, and manageability of COM+ applications.

REFERENCES

[Pla-99]   David Platt, *Understanding COM+*, Microsoft Press, ISBN 0735606668, 1999.
[MS-00]   "Overview of the COMAdmin Objects," Microsoft Platform SDK.
          http://msdn.microsoft.com/library/psdk/cossdk/pgcreatingapplications_auto matingadmin_64fn.htm

Index

Company does not warrant that the SOFTWARE will meet your requirements or that the operation of the SOFTWARE will be uninterrupted or error-free. The Company warrants that the media on which the SOFTWARE is delivered shall be free from defects in materials and workmanship under normal use for a period of thirty (30) days from the date of your purchase. Your only remedy and the Company's only obligation under these limited warranties is, at the Company's option, return of the warranted item for a refund of any amounts paid by you or replacement of the item. Any replacement of SOFTWARE or media under the warranties shall not extend the original warranty period. The limited warranty set forth above shall not apply to any SOFTWARE which the Company determines in good faith has been subject to misuse, neglect, improper installation, repair, alteration, or damage by you. EXCEPT FOR THE EXPRESSED WARRANTIES SET FORTH ABOVE, THE COMPANY DISCLAIMS ALL WARRANTIES, EXPRESS OR IMPLIED, INCLUDING WITHOUT LIMITATION, THE IMPLIED WARRANTIES OF MERCHANTABILITY AND FITNESS FOR A PARTICULAR PURPOSE. EXCEPT FOR THE EXPRESS WARRANTY SET FORTH ABOVE, THE COMPANY DOES NOT WARRANT, GUARANTEE, OR MAKE ANY REPRESENTATION REGARDING THE USE OR THE RESULTS OF THE USE OF THE SOFTWARE IN TERMS OF ITS CORRECTNESS, ACCURACY, RELIABILITY, CURRENTNESS, OR OTHERWISE.

IN NO EVENT, SHALL THE COMPANY OR ITS EMPLOYEES, AGENTS, SUPPLIERS, OR CONTRACTORS BE LIABLE FOR ANY INCIDENTAL, INDIRECT, SPECIAL, OR CONSEQUENTIAL DAMAGES ARISING OUT OF OR IN CONNECTION WITH THE LICENSE GRANTED UNDER THIS AGREEMENT, OR FOR LOSS OF USE, LOSS OF DATA, LOSS OF INCOME OR PROFIT, OR OTHER LOSSES, SUSTAINED AS A RESULT OF INJURY TO ANY PERSON, OR LOSS OF OR DAMAGE TO PROPERTY, OR CLAIMS OF THIRD PARTIES, EVEN IF THE COMPANY OR AN AUTHORIZED REPRESENTATIVE OF THE COMPANY HAS BEEN ADVISED OF THE POSSIBILITY OF SUCH DAMAGES. IN NO EVENT SHALL LIABILITY OF THE COMPANY FOR DAMAGES WITH RESPECT TO THE SOFTWARE EXCEED THE AMOUNTS ACTUALLY PAID BY YOU, IF ANY, FOR THE SOFTWARE.

SOME JURISDICTIONS DO NOT ALLOW THE LIMITATION OF IMPLIED WARRANTIES OR LIABILITY FOR INCIDENTAL, INDIRECT, SPECIAL, OR CONSEQUENTIAL DAMAGES, SO THE ABOVE LIMITATIONS MAY NOT ALWAYS APPLY. THE WARRANTIES IN THIS AGREEMENT GIVE YOU SPECIFIC LEGAL RIGHTS AND YOU MAY ALSO HAVE OTHER RIGHTS WHICH VARY IN ACCORDANCE WITH LOCAL LAW.

ACKNOWLEDGMENT

YOU ACKNOWLEDGE THAT YOU HAVE READ THIS AGREEMENT, UNDERSTAND IT, AND AGREE TO BE BOUND BY ITS TERMS AND CONDITIONS. YOU ALSO AGREE THAT THIS AGREEMENT IS THE COMPLETE AND EXCLUSIVE STATEMENT OF THE AGREEMENT BETWEEN YOU AND THE COMPANY AND SUPERSEDES ALL PROPOSALS OR PRIOR AGREEMENTS, ORAL, OR WRITTEN, AND ANY OTHER COMMUNICATIONS BETWEEN YOU AND THE COMPANY OR ANY REPRESENTATIVE OF THE COMPANY RELATING TO THE SUBJECT MATTER OF THIS AGREEMENT.

Should you have any questions concerning this Agreement or if you wish to contact the Company for any reason, please contact in writing at the address below.

Robin Short
Prentice Hall PTR
One Lake Street
Upper Saddle River, New Jersey 07458

About the CD-ROM

The CD-ROM included with *COM+ Programming: A Practical Guide Using Visual C++ and ATL* contains the following:

I. CONTENTS OF THE CD

This CD contains all the sample programs that were referred to in the book. All the programs have been organized by chapters. Each subfolder within a chapter folder contains one sample application. Subfolders with numeric names indicate a progression from one sample to the next.

Each subfolder also contains a ReadMe.txt file describing the intent of the sample application.

The CD also contains some useful C++ classes that I refer to as the COM+ Programming Library (CPL). The CPL files can be found in the `DevInclude` directory.

II. SYSTEM REQUIREMENTS

- Visual C++ 6.0 Service Pack 3
- Platform SDK (at least January 2000 edition)
- Windows 2000 System

License Agreement

Use of the software accompanying *COM+ Programming: A Practical Guide Using Visual C++ and ATL* is subject to the terms of the License Agreement and Limited Warranty, found on the previous two pages.

Technical Support

Prentice Hall does not offer technical support for any of the programs on the CD-ROM. However, if the CD-ROM is damaged, you may obtain a replacement copy by sending an email that describes the problem to: disc_exchange@prenhall.com.